CASS LIBRARY OF VICTORIAN TIMES

No. 10

General Editor: Anne Humpherys
Herbert H. Lehman College, New York

VOICES OF THE POOR

VOICES OF THE POOR

Selections from the *Morning Chronicle*
'Labour and the Poor' (1849-1850)

BY

HENRY MAYHEW

Edited, and with an introduction by

ANNE   HUMPHERYS
Herbert H. Lehman College, New York

FRANK CASS & CO. LTD.
1971

Published by

FRANK CASS AND COMPANY LIMITED

67 Great Russell Street, London WC1B 3BT

Mayhew's Letters first published
in the *Morning Chronicle*   1849–1850
New edition   1971

ISBN 0 7146 2929 4

PUBLISHER'S NOTE

This book contains selections from those of Henry Mayhew's letters to the *Morning Chronicle* which did not subsequently appear in his four-volume survey, *London Labour and the London Poor* (reprinted Frank Cass, London, 1967). Published here in book form for the first time, they constitute a fifth volume to that monumental work.

Printed in Great Britain by
Clarke, Doble & Brendon Ltd.
Plymouth

Contents

List of Illustrations

A *Note on the Illustrations:* Mayhew's *Morning Chronicle* letters were not illustrated, but to stress the unity of this text with the illustrated four-volume *London Labour and the London Poor* (reprinted Frank Cass, London, 1967), several contemporary engravings are included here. Some of the illustrations, however, date from a later period than the interviews Mayhew conducted. The early working men's illustrated journals and papers were more concerned to educate their readers about life outside their workshops than to create a sense of pride in themselves as workers. Thus, though one can find pictures of Chinamen, there are very few pictures of London cobblers. The illustrated series on craftsmen begun in 1855 by the *British Workman and Friend of the Sons of Toil* was one of the first of its kind. The illustrations themselves were sometimes of craftsmen at an earlier period, so I have felt justified in including some of these handsome engravings here. All are reproduced by courtesy of the Trustees of the British Museum.

Introduction

In a March 1850 issue of *Punch*, William Makepeace Thackeray remarked about the letters (or articles) on 'Labour and the Poor', written by Henry Mayhew for the *Morning Chronicle*:

> What a confession it is that we have almost all of us been obliged to make! A clever and earnest-minded writer gets a commission from the *Morning Chronicle* newspaper, and reports upon the state of our poor in London; he goes amongst labouring people and poor of all kinds—and brings back what? A picture of human life so wonderful, so awful, so piteous and pathetic, so exciting and terrible, that readers of romances own they never read anything like to it; and that the griefs, struggles, strange adventures here depicted exceed anything that any of us could imagine. . . . But of such wondrous and complicated misery as this you confess you had no idea? No. How should you?—you and I—we are of the upper classes; we have had hitherto no community with the poor . . . until . . . some clear-sighted, energetic man like the writer of the *Chronicle* travels into the poor man's country for us, and comes back with his tale of terror and wonder.[1]

Though this was high praise indeed from the author of *Vanity Fair*, Thackeray was not indulging in journalistic exaggeration in his enthusiasm for these articles which were to be the forerunners and partly the basis for Mayhew's *London Labour and the London Poor*. He repeated the praise the following year in a letter to Lady Stanley: "Have you got London Labour and the London Poor—for yourself only—It's better and more romantic than any romance including the forthcoming one of Yours dear lady Stanley most truly. . . ."[2]

Thackeray was not alone in his enthusiastic response to the "wondrous and complicated misery" revealed by Mayhew's contributions to the *Chronicle's* survey of conditions among the lower classes. Charles Kingsley and the Christian Socialists were evidently moved to press for sanitation reform because of Mayhew's revelations about Jacob's Island, a notorious slum in south London.[3] Kingsley also pasted together excerpts from Mayhew's accounts of East-End sweatshops in 'Cheap Clothes and Nasty', and incorporated some of Mayhew's material into the novel *Alton Locke*.[4] After Mayhew's exposé of the condition of sweated seamstresses, the upper-class philanthropists Sidney Herbert and Lord Shaftesbury founded the 'Female Emigration Society', a charitable organization whose purpose was to help poor women of unimpeachable character to emigrate.[5] As a further tribute to his work, hundreds of pounds for the relief of the poor poured into the *Chronicle* offices from ordinary Londoners, engaged by the dignity and enraged by the destitution described by Mayhew.

The strength of the response of Mayhew's readers is somewhat surprising for 1849. The miserable condition of many of the poor in England was not unknown to the *Chronicle* readers; the newspaper's investigation appeared in the wake of more than a decade of grim exposés of what Carlyle had labelled in 1840 the "Condition-of-England-Question". Frederick Engels's documentation in his *Condition of the Working Class in England in 1844* bears eloquent testimony to the large number of Englishmen who publicized the miserable condition of the industrial poor in the late 1830s and early 1840s. Doctors, clergymen, and interested citizens issued pamphlets and books based on their own investigations and experiences.[6] In the widely-read Select Committee Reports of government investigations into working conditions, or the 'Blue Books' as they were popularly known from the colour of their covers, the government itself laid bare unbelievable exploitation and misery among women and child labourers in factories (1832), in mines (1842), and in potteries (1843). *The Sanitary Condition of the Labouring Population of Great Britain*, an official report to the Poor Law Commissioners by their secretary Edwin Chadwick, had been one of the best sellers of 1842. Even the 'light reading' of the 1840s fed the seemingly insatiable hunger for social comment about the poor, as is demonstrated by the popularity of the novels of social protest by Disraeli (*Coningsby*, 1844; *Sybil*, 1845; *Tancred*, 1847), Kingsley (*Yeast*, 1848), and Mrs. Gaskell (*Mary Barton*, 1848), not to mention those of Dickens, particularly *Oliver Twist* in 1839 and *The Chimes* in 1844.

The wealth of material available tended to be as confusing as it was enlightening, however. No clear picture of overall economic conditions emerged. Some local situations, such as that of the handloom weavers, were worse than others; wages in some trades, such as parts of the building trades, were more depressed than others.[7] Nearly all private and public investigations of conditions of the lower classes before 1849, moreover, concerned only those workers outside London. The actual state of the poor in the metropolis was further obscured by the difficulty of collecting information from the different parishes in the city. The situation in London, where crafts were dominant and heavy industry virtually non-existent, was only vaguely similar to that in Manchester or in Leeds.

As a result of this confused picture, Mayhew states in his initial letters that he will try to uncover the facts about working conditions in London and not to make any generalizations about the causes of low wages or the cure for poverty. "My vocation is to collect facts and register opinions," he says in Letter II. By "facts", then, Mayhew also meant the opinions of the poor as to the causes of and cures for their situation. The early letters, however, mirroring an early Victorian assumption,[8] seem to equate "facts" with statistics. Yet the statistical results of Mayhew's interviews are the least valuable part of his work. For the most part he used figures already available in McCulloch's *A Statistical Account of the British Empire*, or Porter's *Progress of the Nation* or government and other sources. (His statistics on how many sweated labourers there were in each trade he investigated were largely original, as were his calculations of hourly wages. His statistics on the street trades in *London Labour* were wholly original.)

The value of Mayhew's interviews is really a by-product of his original intentions and grew out of his desire to "register opinions". The early interviews, in keeping with the desire for numerical information, are short and limited: What kind of work do you do? How much are you paid? To what do you attribute your low wages? and then on to the next man. But as the series develops, Mayhew's questions become more detailed, and the questions about the causes of low wages lead to more rambling conversations and extensive probing on how the worker can live on such a wage. Consequently, the interviews become much more interesting and valuable as human documents which give a picture of the lower classes unequalled in its "wondrous complexity", to paraphrase Thackeray.

But before investigating the nature of these interviews more closely, one needs some information about the interviewer himself, the one constant in the hundreds of varied reports which Mayhew wrote. Though little biographical information about Mayhew appears to have survived, an outline of his early career can be pieced together.[9] He was born in 1812, the fourth son of a well-to-do London solicitor. His father was a stern Victorian parent who required his seven sons, even when middle-aged men, to address him as "Sir" and to remain standing until he gave them permission to sit. While living at home, if any son returned home after midnight, he would find the house locked. His father would toss a shilling from an upper window, telling the offender to "go and get yourself a bed somewhere else". At 21 years of age, each son in turn was given an allowance of £1 a week.[10]

Joshua Mayhew was also determined that each of his seven sons should emulate his own idea of a respectable life, namely an education at a good public school, a turn on the continent, and then a stable life and profitable career as a solicitor in his father's firm. Only one son actually acceded to his father's plan, and Henry rebelled against it almost from the beginning. He ran away from Westminster School rather than receive what he considered an unjust flogging. Having tried unsuccessfully to convince his father to let him become an experimental chemist, Henry failed dismally as his father's legal apprentice. Tradition has it that he forgot at one point to file some crucial papers with the result that he and the entire family were interrupted at dinner by a bailiff who had come to arrest Mayhew senior. Away from home, Henry spent his time in the 1830s conducting chemical experiments (nearly blowing up his brother's house at one point) and writing for some of the little journals of humour and political comment which flourished at that period. He maintained his disparate interests in 'natural philosophy', as the study of physical science was then referred to, and the Bohemian existence of a Fleet Street hack writer late into the 1840s.

His biggest success in these years before the *Chronicle* series was the launching of *Punch* in 1842. Unfortunately for Mayhew, his connection with *Punch* was short-lived. Though he had shared the editorship of the magazine with Mark Lemon in the beginning, when the ownership was transferred to the firm of Bradbury and Evans, Mayhew, an erratic editor at best, was eased out of the top position in favour of Lemon. Subsequently Mayhew tried a number of times to publish popular treatises (for instance, *What to Teach and How to Teach It*, 1842), and experimented with various journalistic ventures. None of his schemes caught fire, however, and one, his connection with the railroad newspaper *The Iron Times*, led to his bankruptcy in 1847 and serious quarrels with both his father and father-in-law, Douglas Jerrold. He also tried, with his brother Augustus, writing novels in the currently popular mode mildly satirizing the middle classes (*The Greatest Plague in Life*, 1847; *Whom to Marry and How to Get Married*, 1848, and others). Although these novels were financially successful, Mayhew appears to have found little in the writing of novels to stimulate his energies. Henry Vizetelly later said that Henry had all the ideas but Augustus had to do all the writing, Henry being too lazy to follow his ideas through to completion.[11]

Henry Mayhew as Knowell in Charles Dickens's amateur production of *Every Man in his Humour*

By 1849, Mayhew was at the end of seven years of disappointment and failure.

Then, in September of 1849, the *Morning Chronicle*, the major competitor to *The Times*, sent Mayhew to Jacob's Island in Bermondsey to bring back an eyewitness account of the slum where the most recent outbreak of cholera had occurred. The *Morning Chronicle* at this time had a large audience and good resources. It was the spokesman for the Peelites and the Free Traders and had a tradition of concern about social conditions. (Earlier the paper had printed the first of the *Sketches by Boz*.) The assignment to Henry Mayhew probably grew out of the intermittent reports which he had done for the *Illustrated London News*. But this particular assignment gave Mayhew the challenge he needed, the challenge which was to result in his monumental work on the poor.

He was first concerned about how to report what he saw in Jacob's Island. His tendency from the beginning was to be as objective as he could, to avoid emotional rhetoric and instead to describe what he saw as accurately and precisely as he would the results of a chemical experiment. But he also wanted his report to move his readers' consciences. The way in which he reconciled these aims was to be the pattern for all the subsequent reports. He combined his eye for physical detail and his sensitivity to language and wrote in a coolly factual style which is almost like the language of the physical sciences in its preciseness, accuracy, and lack of emotional bias. Yet the description is profoundly moving.

After this visit to Jacob's Island, Mayhew and the editors of the *Chronicle* met the next challenge. In a later prospectus to *London Labour* (to be seen in the British Museum), Mayhew claimed that he had suggested the 'Labour and the Poor' investigation to the *Chronicle* proprietors as early as August 1849, which would imply that the visit to Bermondsey was also Mayhew's idea. But whether the idea for the series came from the proprietors of the newspaper, as has always been assumed, or whether it did in fact originate with Mayhew, it was in full operation by October 1849. The scope of the project and its purpose were discussed by the editors in a leader on October 18, 1849: "It is proposed to give a full and detailed description of the moral, intellectual, material, and physical condition of the industrial poor throughout England". There were special correspondents to report on the industrial towns and others to report on the rural districts.[12] Mayhew himself became the "Metropolitan Correspondent", his beat, the vast complexities of London itself.

In the course of the next year, Mayhew proceeded to write some eighty letters, in the beginning at the rate of two or three a week. Aided by statisticians, assistants, and a generous expense account, he toured the poorer districts of London and spoke with hundreds of members of London's lower classes. His survey, however, is not complete. The 1851 census listed sixteen general groups of occupations of which only one, "persons engaged in providing dress", was covered by Mayhew with any thoroughness. Many of the skilled crafts, such as clock-making, jewelry-making, carriage-making and related crafts, he did not approach at all. Several times in the course of the year's work, he interrupted his survey of the skilled workers with letters on dock workers, street hucksters and entertainers, tramps and vagrants, sailors in the merchant marines, the transit system, and even a few letters on the Ragged Schools. He also promised material which never appeared, such as a survey of prison labour for which he periodically mentioned collecting statistics.

Mayhew's reports soon fell into a pattern. He began each survey of the weaving, tailoring, toy-making, and cabinet-making trades with a general description of how the trade was organized, and a statistical analysis of the number of men involved, the number of coats or cabinets or dolls produced, etc. After this general picture, Mayhew reproduced the data on which the generalizations rested, namely the increasingly detailed and always fascinating personal interviews with individual members of the trade. These interviews soon absorb nearly all the space in his letters as well as all his readers' attention.

Mayhew's approach to his task of interviewing was unusual for the mid-nineteenth century. In February 1850, he described the aims of his survey, then five months old:

> The labour question was to be investigated without reference to any particular prejudice, theory, party, or policy, and it was with his spirit that I set out upon my mission. I made up my mind to deal with human nature as a natural philosopher or a chemist deals with any material object; and, as a man who had devoted some little of his time to physical and metaphysical science, I must say I did most heartily rejoice that it should have been left to me to apply the laws of the inductive philosophy for the first time, I believe, in the world to the abstract questions of political economy.[13]

Thus, Mayhew apparently envisaged himself as imposing on his social investigation the rigour of the empirical methods in the physical sciences as he understood them.

This effort to imitate the techniques he had learned when studying chemistry had an important effect on his methods of interviewing and his reports of his results. For example, in his reports, he scrupulously details for his reader all his methods both as investigator and as reporter. He discusses how he finds his informants, what the situation of the interview is, and by Letter X, he has worked out a set of questions generally along this line: What do you do? How much do you earn for this? Are you paid by the piece or by the week? Are your wages better or worse than before the repeal of the Corn Laws? To what do you attribute your low wages? How do you manage to live on these wages? Sometimes a short biography of the informant follows, given in his own words. Several weeks into the series, Mayhew began to convoke large meetings of workers both to corroborate information he received and to increase the number of people who could contribute to his survey.

Mayhew reproduces faithfully the data he collected in these interviews, including the most seemingly irrelevant remarks. Such details have both scientific and literary advantages. For example, in Letter VII (see pages 56–7 of this text), a woman he interviews is periodically interrupted by another woman opening the door. Mayhew's informant owes the second woman a shilling. He faithfully describes each of these interruptions and, as a result, the interview strikes us as both authentic and dramatic. In the same way, in an interview with a French maker of papier-maché toys, Mayhew convinces us of his scientific integrity by reporting all his informant's remarks, one of which shows some suspicion about the interviewer's motivations and consequently humanises the interviewee: "I make forty dozen domestic animals a week. Why do you come here to ask? Lately my trade has been bad" (Letter XXXVIII, p. 170 in this text). In this way the sheer number of apparently irrelevant or repetitious details contributes to the reliability and scientific validity of the work.

In addition, Mayhew made a considerable effort to achieve some sort of 'scientific' objectivity in his approach to and his treatment of his subject. This presented him with the biggest difficulties. He tried to achieve it through his use of a precise style, but despite his attempt to be a "mere collector of facts", Mayhew may have unconsciously distorted what he saw. Even the most well-intentioned social investigator may unintentionally predetermine or distort his interviews, particularly when delving into the lives of a body of people as alien in experience and values as the lower classes are from himself.

Mayhew might well have fallen prey to middle-class distortions, for he shared many of the middle-class attitudes which hampered other nineteenth-century social investigators from the popularizer Charles Knight to the first professional sociologist of the poor, Charles Booth. Mayhew accepted, apparently unquestioningly, the then current view of prostitution as the crime of putting a woman's charms to vile uses owing to an inability to feel shame, a woman's virtue.[14] He also accepted for the most part the idea of the lower classes as 'dangerous' and he used the conventional and condescending distinction between the 'deserving' and the 'undeserving' poor. Any of the attitudes implied by these ideas might have affected the objectivity of Mayhew's interviews.

But his work is consistently ambivalent about all his middle-class assumptions. Frequently he makes a judgment which is contradicted elsewhere. In *London Labour*, for example, he states that the costermongers, in their "ignorance and vice" are "breeding a social pestilence in the very heart of the land" (*London Labour and the London Poor*, I, 100). Yet in the pages preceding this judgment, Mayhew has implicitly contradicted this judgment by his interviews which recreate the energetic, inventive, vital lives of the costers with both sympathy and delight. He is obsequious almost to the point of fawning in an interview with a distressed gentlewoman supporting herself by needlework.[15] Yet the contrasting attitude which he expresses elsewhere, that distressed gentlefolk are seldom the most deserving of the poor,[16] is evident in his report. The gentlewoman whines and complains despite the fact that she has more outside help than most of the other seamstresses. By reporting the whole interview Mayhew unconsciously undercuts his conscious deference.

The reasons for the ambivalence which complicates Mayhew's response to the poor and protects him from middle-class bias in his reports lie partly in the character of the man himself. In addition to his scientific leanings, he had another side to him, a Bohemian temperament always at odds with middle-class respectability. This aspect of his character made him irresponsible with money and always in debt; he consistently failed to finish a single joint project and failed in personal obligations in other ways. He was unable to do sustained work for the most part, was restless and lazy. "Though his mind was brilliant and inventive, his will was untutored"; he was, Spielman remarked, of "an essentially indolent nature".[17] Vizetelly said that he "was a man of multifarious schemes and singularly original ideas, but torpid energy; nimble of speech, but nerveless in action. . . ."[18] Perhaps as a result of this tension between his middle-class assumptions and his Bohemian temperament, between the influence of and his unconscious rejection of the prevalent values stridently endorsed by the "respectable" classes, Mayhew was able to identify with the lower classes, not only with down-and-out workers but also with tramps and vagrants and the foot-loose, colourfully irresponsible street folk. Mayhew may have sublimated an unconscious rejection of the narrowness of his own middle-class background into a consuming curiosity about the most trivial details of the life of the lower classes. Moreover, his peculiar position as social investigator—neither alms-giver nor slummer—enabled him to satisfy this curiosity without condescension on the one hand or a loss of his own social status on the other.

This "subjective" response to his informants, far from destroying the objectivity of his work, actually enhances it by enabling him to break down the barriers between himself and his subjects. His interviews with the poor suffer less from middle-class bias than those of any other investigator of the century, including those of Charles Booth and his associates. In addition, the very real respect for the lower classes implied by his curiosity untinged by condescension loosened the tongues of his informants. Impressed by his interest in them, his subjects poured more information about their lives into his receptive ear than anyone else in the century was able to collect by any means. The pathetic candour with which the needlewomen forced by poverty into prostitution tell their stories to Mayhew, for example (see Letters VIII and XV, pp. 84–100 in this text), testifies to their confidence in their interviewer's respect.

Nor did he betray this trust. He protected the anonymity of his subjects, yet never dehumanized them. Despite an almost monotonous similarity in the grim stories of the needlewomen prostitutes, Mayhew was consistently able to project the details in every interview which made each woman unique: one woman lived with a tinman; on a winter night another walked the streets homeless until the legs of her baby froze to her side.

As discussed earlier, Mayhew's initial justification for the number and thoroughness of such details was his desire to give all the raw data and let the reader draw his own conclusions, or at least check the validity of Mayhew's. But another and equally important justification for the details was the very way in which they make his subjects come alive for the reader, who thus has a more direct experience of the hideous slums and the lives of the poor as individuals.

Furthermore, though presented at length, the interviews are not simulated recordings made in the days before the tape recorder, as were the interviews by the government Select Committees. In a sense, Mayhew shapes his reports much as the twentieth-century social anthropologist Oscar Lewis shapes his interviews with the Mexican and Puerto Rican poor. In spite of the important role which the interviewer naturally plays, Mayhew, like Lewis, removed himself from the text of his report by removing the questions he asked, though they are easily deducible and usually incorporated in the respondents' answers. The interviews are thus dramatically immediate for the reader. There is none of the judicial form of question and answer so often found in the Blue Books. Instead of faceless men and women giving the facts of their lives, there emerge a series of "autobiographies" in which the experience and the thoughts of each individual worker and the special meaning of his life as he sees it are recreated in the uninterrupted flow of his own words. With the interviewer a shadowy figure in the background, the seemingly disparate details coalesce into portraits as vividly individualized as characters in a novel by Dickens.

Bishopsgate in London's East End, by Gustave Doré

These interviews are the basis of Mayhew's importance as social historian, his precocity as a sociologist, and his brilliance as an elucidator of what Oscar Lewis calls "the culture of poverty". Mayhew elicited from men and women not just the facts but the totality of the individual worker's personality. He did this by asking direct questions, by calling upon the subject for an association of ideas (as when he asks a blind boot-lace seller for his feelings about an interview with a crippled nutmeg-grinder seller [*London Labour and the London Poor*, I, 407]), and by a sympathetic identification. When the hundreds of individual stories are put together, one has a "history of the people from the lips of the people themselves", as he claimed in his preface to *London Labour*. Mayhew filled the role of Matthew Arnold's ideal critic for his audience: he made them see things as they really were.

Mayhew's readers responded to his reports with generous but unexpected outrage because they did indeed learn something new from Mayhew—namely, that the poor were human beings disturbingly similar to their 'betters' in their thoughts, responses, and aspirations. What Thackeray found more astonishing than romances in Mayhew's articles was the individual humanity of the poor themselves, an explanation he himself touched upon when he described the misery Mayhew revealed not only as "wondrous" but also as "complicated". No nineteenth-century social investigator before Mayhew and few after him succeeded in creating the particularized reality of the lower classes so profoundly.

A few words about the publication history of Mayhew's work on the poor is in order here. The publication of his investigations is complicated, and is made more so by the general availability today of only a part of his work, *London Labour and the London Poor*. Between October 1849 and December 1850, Mayhew wrote for the *Morning Chronicle* some eighty articles on the London poor, covering skilled artisans in several trades, dock workers, street hucksters and entertainers, transit workers and various other subjects. In October of 1850 Mayhew had officially left his position as Metropolitan Correspondent, ostensibly because of an old antagonism with the editors of the *Morning Chronicle* over their censoring material, firstly sentiments against Free Trade and then negative remarks about a big advertiser. His letters, however, continued to appear for a number of weeks.[19]

Sometime in December 1850, he started on his own a weekly publication, *London Labour and the London Poor*, dealing in the beginning with interviews with street sellers but intended to cover eventually all occupations in London. A suit in Chancery over minor financial matters, however, interrupted the publication of *London Labour* in 1852. The first two volumes of this 1851–1852 publication are identical with those of the 1861–1862 four-volume edition of *London Labour and the London Poor*, reprinted by Frank Cass in 1967. Volume III of *London Labour* was begun but not published in 1856 when Mayhew also made an abortive attempt to resume his work with *The Great World of London*, published as *The Criminal Prisons of London* in 1862 (reprinted Frank Cass, London, 1968). Mayhew himself wrote only the first thirty-seven pages of Volume IV of *London Labour*. Though there were two editions of *London Labour* in the 1860s, Mayhew faded into obscurity after 1862 and died in 1887 an essentially forgotten and nearly penniless man.

The following book contains a selection of interviews from Mayhew's letters to the *Morning Chronicle* in 1849–1850. It represents over two-thirds of the material Mayhew did not reprint in his later work. My principle of selection was simply to include the best of the full-length interviews not in print since 1849–1850. Because I thought it important that individual interviews should not be shortened, the interviews which appear in this text are complete except for a few which are minus charts or income tallies. But even though a number of interesting and expanded interviews have been eliminated altogether, I have tried to keep the general scope of each survey intact so that the reader can see the breadth as well as the depth of Mayhew's accomplishment. All material which Mayhew later reprinted in *London Labour* has been omitted. To enable the reader to see at a glance the series as a whole, I have appended a chart giving the number, date, and subject of each letter, as well as an indication of whether or not it was reprinted in *London Labour*.

Ellipses in the text indicate where entire interviews have been omitted or material left out of a given interview. No ellipses are used, however, to indicate omission of Mayhew's summaries of former or future letters or the general statistics which usually appeared at the beginning or end of a letter. I have kept the chronological order of the original letters except in several cases where I sacrificed chronology for the sake of coherency. The first selection from each letter is headed by the letter number and date.

I have kept the original punctuation and spelling for the most part, with one major exception: I have systematically paragraphed the entire work since in the letters as they appeared in the *Morning Chronicle*, there was little paragraphing inside a given interview. Material in brackets and italics is either my editorial insertion or the substitution of a singular for a plural reference where the second interview has been eliminated.

My own editorial insertions, however, have been kept to a bare minimum. Mayhew was precise and articulate about what he saw, and he leaves little to explain. Except for a handful of explanatory notes, Mayhew's interviews with the working-class poor of London at mid-century are presented to today's readers as they were to those over a hundred years ago with full confidence in their undiminished ability to move, to inform, to amuse, to enrage, and to astonish those who read them.

A.H.

Herbert H. Lehman College, New York, 1970

NOTES

1 *Punch*, March 9, 1850, p. 93.
2 *Letters*, ed. Gordon N. Ray (Cambridge, Mass., 1945) II, p. 817.
3 See Frederick Maurice, *Life of Frederick Denison Maurice* (London, 1884), pp. 13 and 35.
4 In *Alton Locke*, see chapter XXXV, 'The Lowest Deep' as well as references throughout to kidnapped Irishman in sweaters' dens.
5 See articles on the society, its formation, and purpose, in the *Morning Chronicle*, December 4, 1849, p. 6, and December 5, 1849, p. 6.
6 In the translation of Engels's *Condition* . . . by W. O. Henderson and W. H. Chaloner (London, 1958), the translators append a list of 24 books and pamphlets cited by Engels in addition to many newspapers which he used. Among those works cited are such titles as *The Moral and Physical Condition of the Working Classes Employed in the Cotton Manufacture in Manchester* by J. P. Kay-Shuttleworth (1832; reprinted Frank Cass, London, 1970); *Observations on the Management of the Poor in Scotland and its Effects on*

the Health of the Great Towns by William Pultenay Alison (1840); Stubborn Facts from the Factories by a Manchester Operative by James Leach (1844); and On the Present Condition of the Labouring Poor in Manchester by R. Parkinson (1841).

7 The argument about how hungry the Hungry Forties really were continues even today. See J. H. Clapham, *An Economic History of Modern Britain*, 2 vols. (Cambridge, I, 2nd ed., 1930; II, 1952), and J. L. and Barbara Hammond, *The Age of the Chartists* (London, 1930) for representative and opposing discussions of economic conditions in England during the 1840s. It appears that at the time of the *Chronicle* investigation, thanks to the repeal of the Corn Laws in 1846, bread prices all over the country were lower than they had been for years, and conditions in lower-class housing and working conditions were also very slowly improving, difficult though it was to see the improvement in local situations.

8 See Harald Westegaard, *Contributions to the History of Statistics* (London, 1932).

9 The most nearly complete biography of Henry Mayhew is found in John L. Bradley, 'Introduction', *Selections from London Labour and the London Poor* (London, 1965), pp. vii–xl. See also E. P. Thompson, 'Political Education of Henry Mayhew', *Victorian Studies* XI (September, 1967), pp. 41–62.

10 The anecdotes given here have been taken either from memoirs by contemporaries of Mayhew or from an unpublished biography of the Brothers Mayhew by the late Mrs. L. M. Coumbe, a descendant of Alfred Mayhew. I am grateful to Patrick Mayhew for permission to use this manuscript.

11 Henry Vizetelly, *Glances Back Through Seventy Years* (London, 1893), I, p. 408.

12 For a discussion of the other correspondents and the text of their reports, see *Provincial Labour and the Provincial Poor of the Mid Nineteenth-Century England. The Condition and Prospects of the Labouring Classes in England and Wales, 1849–1852*, edited by J. Ginswick (Frank Cass, London, 1971).

13 From a letter to the editors of the *Morning Chronicle*, February 5, 1850. Quoted in 'Report of the Speech of Henry Mayhew, (London, 1850), p. 6. During this period the terms 'science' and 'philosophy' were used interchangeably.

14 See his remarks about prostitutes in *The Criminal Prisons of London* (1862; reprinted Frank Cass, London, 1968), p. 455

15 See the *Morning Chronicle*, Letter IX, November 23, 1849, and pages 71–5 of this text.

16 In 'Answers to Correspondents' on the cover of part 29 of *London Labour* (June 28, 1851), Mayhew says "Two years' close association with what are called the 'lowest classes' has proved the justice of [my assertion]; for it has been invariably found . . . that 'those who have seen better days' constituted the worst class of the poor".

17 M. H. Spielman, *The History of Punch* (New York, 1895), pp. 268–269.

18 Vizetelly, *op. cit.*

19 There is some doubt about the authorship of Letters LXXV–LXXXII, though I believe Mayhew wrote some of them. (For example, he uses part of the last letter in *London Labour*.) The problem of collaboration generally in Mayhew's work is a difficult one. He had help in some of his research, and his brother Augustus is known to have written a few parts of *London Labour*. The bulk of the *Chronicle* interviews, however, were undoubtedly written by Henry Mayhew.

I
LONDON

JACOB'S ISLAND

From *Morning Chronicle*, September 24th, 1849

[The following description of Jacob's Island—a section of south London already made notorious by Oliver Twist*—was the prelude to the 'Labour and the Poor' series in the* Morning Chronicle. *Tradition has it that this visit to the cholera districts of Bermondsey so shocked Mayhew that as a result he and the editors of the* Chronicle *decided on the project of investigating the conditions of poor throughout England.]*

The striking peculiarity of Jacob's Island consists in the wooden galleries and sleeping-rooms at the back of the houses which overhang the dark ditch that stagnates beside them. The houses are built upon piles, so that the place has positively the look of a Flemish street, flanking a sewer instead of a canal; while the little rickety bridges that span the huge gutters and connect court with court, give it the appearance of the Venice of drains, where channels before and behind the houses do duty for the ocean. Across some parts of the stream, rooms have been built, so that house adjoins house; and here, with the very stench of death rising through the boards, human beings sleep night after night, until the last sleep of all comes upon them, years before its time. Scarce a house but yellow linen is hanging to dry over the balustrade of staves, or else run out on a long oar, where the sulphur-coloured clothes hang over the waters, and you are almost wonderstruck to see their form and colour unreflected in the putrid ditch below.

At the back of nearly every house that boasts a square foot or two of outlet— and the majority have none at all—are pigsties. In front waddle ducks, while cocks and hens scratch at the cinder-heaps. Indeed, the creatures that fatten on offal are the only living things that seem to flourish here.

The water of the huge ditch in front of the houses is covered with a scum almost like a cobweb, and prismatic with grease. In it float large masses of green rotting weed, and against the posts of the bridges are swollen carcases of dead animals, almost bursting with the gases of putrefaction. Along the banks are heaps of indescribable filth, the phosphoretted smell from which tells of the rotting fish, while the oyster-shells are like pieces of slate from their coating of mud and dirt. In some parts the fluid is almost as red as blood, from the colouring matter that pours into it from the reeking leather-dressers close by.

On entering the precincts of the pest island, the air has literally the smell of a graveyard, and a feeling of nausea and heaviness comes over any one unaccustomed to imbibe such an atmosphere. It is not only the nose, but the stomach, that tells how heavily the breeze is loaded with sulphuretted hydrogen; and as soon as you cross one of the crazy rotting bridges spanning the reeking ditch, you know, as surely as if you had chemically tested it, by the black colour of what was once the white-lead paint upon the door-posts and window-sills, that the atmosphere is thickly charged with this deadly gas. A silver spoon, of which I caught sight in one of the least wretched dwellings, was positively chocolate-coloured by the action of the sulphur on the metal.

In answer to my questions, one of the inmates of these pest-houses told me she was never well. Indeed, the signs of the deadly influence of the place were painted in the earthy complexion of the poor woman. "Neither I nor my children know what health is," said she. "But what is one to do? We must live where our bread is. I've tried to let the house, and put a bill up, but cannot get any one to take it."

A medical gentleman, who had kindly undertaken to pilot me through the island, led me to narrow close courts, where the sun never shone, and the air seemed almost as stagnant and putrid as the ditch we had left. The blanched cheeks of the people that came out to stare at us, were white as vegetables grown in the dark; and as we stopped to look down the alley, my informant told me that the place teemed with children, and that if a horn was blown, they would swarm like bees at the sound of a gong. The houses were mostly inhabited by "corn-runners," coal porters, and "long-shore-men," getting a precarious living— earning sometimes many shillings a day, and then for weeks doing nothing.

At one house, a child sat nursing a dying half-comatose baby on a door-step. The skin of its little arms, instead of being plumped out with health, was loose and shrivelled, like an old crone's, having a flabby monkey-like appearance more than the character of the human cuticle.

I was stopped by my companion in front of a house "to let." The building was as narrow and as unlike a human habitation as the wooden houses in a child's box of toys. "In this house," said my guide, "when the scarlet fever was raging in the neighbourhood, the barber who was living here suffered fearfully from it; and no sooner did the man get well of this, than he was seized with typhus, and scarcely had he recovered from the first attack, than he was struck down a second time with the same terrible disease. Since then, he has lost his child with cholera, and at this moment his wife is in the workhouse suffering from the same affliction. The only wonder is that they are not all dead, for as the man sat at his meals in his small shop, if he put his hand against the wall behind him, it would be covered with the soil of his neighbour's privy, sopping through the wall."

As I passed along the reeking banks of the sewer, the sun shone upon a narrow slip of water. In the bright light it appeared the colour of strong green tea, and positively looked as solid as black marble in the shadow,—indeed, it was more like watery mud than muddy water; and YET I WAS ASSURED THIS WAS THE ONLY WATER THE WRETCHED INHABITANTS HAD TO DRINK.

As I gazed in horror at it, I saw drains and sewers emptying their filthy contents into it; I SAW A WHOLE TIER OF DOORLESS PRIVIES IN THE OPEN ROAD, COMMON TO MEN AND WOMEN, BUILT OVER IT; I heard bucket after bucket of filth splash into it; and the limbs of the vagrant boys bathing in it seemed, by pure force of contrast, white as Parian marble.

And yet, as I stood doubting the fearful statement, I beheld a little child, from one of the galleries opposite, lower a tin can with a rope, to fill a large bucket that stood beside her. In each of the balconies that hung over the stream the self-same tub was to be seen. In this the inhabitants put the mucky liquid to stand, so that they may, after it has rested for a day or two, skim the fluid from the solid particles of filth, pollution, and disease which have sunk below.

As the little thing dangled her tin cup as gently as possible into the stream, a bucket of night-soil was poured down from the next gallery.

In this wretched place I was taken to a house where an infant lay dead of the cholera. I asked if they *really did* drink the water?

The answer was, "They were obliged to drink the ditch, unless they could beg or thieve a pailfull of pure water." "But have you spoken to your landlord about having it laid on for you?" "Yes, sir; and he says he'll do it, and do it—but we know him better than to believe him."

"Why, sir," cried another woman, who had shot out from an adjoining room, "he won't even give us a little whitewash, though we tell him we'll willingly do the work ourselves: and look here, sir," she added, "all the tiles have fallen off, and the rain pours in wholesale."

In a place called Joiner's-court, with four wooden houses in it, there had been as many as five cases of cholera. In front, the poor souls, as if knowing by an instinct that plants were given to purify the atmosphere, had pulled up the paving stones before their dwellings, and planted a few stocks here and there in the rich black mould beneath. Here, I was taken up into a room where the window was within four feet of a high wall, at the foot of which, until very recently, ran the open common sewer. The room was so dark, that it was several minutes before I could perceive anything within it, and there was a smell of must and dry rot that told of damp and imperfect ventilation, while the unnatural size of the pupils of the wretched woman's eyes showed how much too long she had dwelt in this gloomy place.

Here, as usual, I heard stories that made the blood curdle, of the cruelty of those from whom they rented the sties called dwellings. They had begged for pure water to be laid on, and the rain to be excluded; and the answer for eighteen years had been, that the lease was just out.

"They knows it's handy for a man's work," said one and all, "and that's the reason why they imposes on a body."

This, indeed, seems to be the great evil. Out of these wretches' health, comfort, and even lives, small capitalists reap a petty independence; and until the poor are rescued from the fangs of such mercenaries, there is but little hope either for their physical or moral welfare.

LOW LODGING-HOUSES

From Letter IV, October 30th, 1849

[Low lodging-houses were hotels of a sort where a bed or a part of one or perhaps only a part of the floor was rented for as low as twopence a night. No questions were asked of prospective "guests" and there was usually an indiscriminate mixing of the sexes in the same room, sometimes in the same bed.]

A few days ago I made an attempt to fathom the secrets of one of the low lodging-houses in the neighbourhood *[of the docks]*; and though I had proof demonstrative that the endeavour was attended with considerable personal risk, still I was determined to compass my end, so as to be able to give the public some idea of the misery and crime that infested that part of the town.

Entrusting myself to an experienced guide, I was led to one of the most frequented and cheapest lodging-houses in the neighbourhood. It was a large outhouse, about the size of a small barn, and about as rudely put together. The walls were unplastered, and the tiles above barely served to cover it in. In the wet weather we were told it leaked like a sieve. Around the room ran a long dirty table, at which sat some score of ragged, greasy wretches. The others were huddled round the fire. Some were toasting herrings, others drying ends of cigars for tobacco, and others boiling potatoes in coffee-pots. I soon communicated to them the object of my visit; and having inquired how many of them out of those then present worked at the docks, I found them ready to answer any questions in a more courteous manner than I had expected. There were 29 people in the shed, and about a fourth were occasional dock labourers.

"I worked at the docks half a day this afternoon," said one, "and all yesterday, and half a day on Monday—three days last week, and never above two or three days in the week these last nine weeks." This one appeared to have been about the most successful of the number; and when I asked the rest what they did when they were wholly unemployed, the answer was, they were forced to walk the streets all night, and starve. "There are plenty of us" said another, "who have to walk the streets of a night, though 'the bunks' (beds) are only two-pence here, and there's no other crib so cheap anywhere near." I asked those who spoke of having walked the streets all night till daylight what they had done for food? "I've been two days," cried one, "without taste or sup;" and one in the corner, with his head down, and his chin resting on his chest, cried, "I've been three days without food— haven't had a bit in the world." "Ah! it's plaguy hard times in the winter time with us, that it is," said a youth who could not have been more than seventeen.

"Average it all the year round," cried a tall fellow in a canvas-smock, "I've worked eleven years in the dock as an extra, and it don't give more than 5s. in the week. Why, we're very very often three or four weeks and earn nothing in the winter time." "But you must get something," I said. "Yes, we goes about jobbing, doing things down at Billingsgate. We gets a twopenny and a threehalfpenny job very often. If we don't get that, we have to go without anything for lodging, and walk and starve." "I'll have to do that to-night, sir," cried the man at the corner of the room, who still sat with his chin on his chest—"I'll have to walk the streets all night." "Yes," said a second, "and there's another besides him that'll be obligated to walk the streets. The Refuge isn't open yet." I asked them what they usually had to eat. One had had "taters and herrings and a pound of bread." Another "a pound of bread and a farthing's worth of coffee." "I've had two or three hard crusts," cried the man again who sat alone at the end of the room. "That's about the living we all has," I was told. "When we go without food all day," they said, "it's generally the depth of winter, wet weather, or something like that. We give those that want a bit of ours, whatever it may be. We gather all round for him if we can."

I asked them how much money they had got. "I've got 4d.," cried one. "I've got 1s. 3d.," cried another. "I've got just enough for my bed." "I've got three-half-pence." "I've got 1d." "I haven't one half-penny," said the man at the end of the room. "No more have I," cried a second. "There's another one here hasn't got one," exclaimed a third. "Ah, if you was to come in here to-morrow night, you'd find half of us had not got any—full half."

At this moment a boy, about thirteen years of age, in rags and tatters, with his hands full of halfpence, entered the room. There was a cunning about his expression that half told his calling. "What's he been at?" said our guide; "spouting a fogle, think you?" At this there was a loud laugh all through the company. "He's been on the monkey, sir." I requested an explanation, and was informed that he had been begging. The boy had retired to the further corner of the apartment, and was busy changing his clothes. "Do you see, sir," said one of the company, "he's going to call at the same houses over again—he's changing his dress ready for it." "I'll lend you my cap, Jim," said a lad to the young but experienced mendicant.

I asked them whether they all usually slept there of a night. "Bless you," was the answer, "I've known many here six months without sleeping in a bed." One of the youths saw me writing, and cried as he laughed, "Ah, they'll make a good play of this here, and have it out at the Standard." "I've been for the whole winter round," said a beardless young man, "and never slept in a bed at a stretch. I laid for three solid months on Billingsgate stones. Some here lives by begging, but I don't; there's two in the place now." The boy who had entered with the half-pence here approached me, and, looking up impudently in my face, cried, "I lives by cadging, master, and that's the plain truth. I gets sometimes 4d.; had two six-penny jobs to-day, carrying gentlemen's parcels." I wished to know something more definite about their living. I asked one what he was boiling; he told me that it was a farthing's worth of coffee, and that was his supper. "There's a shop round here makes farthings' worths of everything," said they. "A farthing's worth of sugar, a farthing's worth of coffee, butter, and 'bacca. A halfpenny worth of bread—a farthing's worth of that ain't no good."

I then inquired as to the state of their clothing. "I've got a clean shirt to put on to-morrow morning, and that's the first I've had these eight months," cried the first.

St. Giles in 1849

"I've got no shirt at all," said another. "I've none," said a third; "and that there down there ain't got none, I know;" he spoke of the same man at the far end of the room.

Next I sought to find out how many among the number had been confined in prison. "I've been in quod, sir, I have," cried one. "I've been in, too," shouted a second. And finding the answers to come too quickly for me to take down, I requested those who had been inmates of a gaol to hold up their hands. They did so, and I counted eighteen out of the twenty-nine who were my companions. "Ah, there's quite that," said the best-looking man of the party; "if the whole twenty-nine of us was down, it would not be too much, I'm sure." The young beggar-boy here advanced again to me, and with a knowing wink, cried, "I can't tell how many times I've been in—oh! it's above counting. I'm sure it's above a dozen times."

I wished to see the size of the farthing's worth of coffee and sugar that they had spoken of as constituting their meals, and I spoke to the gentleman who had brought me to the place as to the possibility of getting a sample of the quantity. He directed me to give one of the boys a shilling, saying the lad would fetch what I wanted. Seeing that I hesitated doing as he requested, he took one from his purse, and giving it to a lad of the name of Dan, whose physiognomy was not of the most prepossessing description, he told him to go for what I wished. The boy quitted the room, and I must confess I never expected to see him enter it again.

I now asked the lodgers the reason why they preferred theft to work. "We don't" was the answer; "it's precious hard work having to walk the street, I can tell you; but we can't get nothing to do." "Look at me," cried one standing up. The man was literally a mass of rags and filth. His tattered clothes and shirt were black and shiny as a sailor's dreadnought with grease and dirt. "Look at me; who'd give me a day's work in the state I am? Why, the best job I've had I only got 3d. by, and I don't make above 2s. 6d. a week honestly at the outside. We couldn't live on what we get, and yet we can live on a precious little here. Get a meal for five farthings. A farthing's worth of coffee, a farthing's worth of sugar, and half a pound of bread, three farthings. We can have a slap-up dinner for twopence; a common one for a penny." "Oh, yes! a regular roarer for twopence," cried the beggar boy. "Three halfpenny worth of pudding, and a halfpenny worth of gravy." "Or else we can have," said another, "2½lb. of taturs—that's a penny—and ¼lb. fourpenny bacon—that's another penny. That's what we calls a fust-rate dinner. Very often we're forced to put up with a penn'orth of taturs and a halfpenny herring—that's a three-halfpenny dinner. There's a chap here was forced to do to-day with a ha'p'orth of taturs. He's been out ever since, and perhaps won't come in at all to-night. He'll walk the streets and starve."

At this point the boy came back with the farthing's worth of coffee and sugar, and to my utter astonishment produced the 11½d. of change. He was without shirt to his back or shoe to his foot; and when I asked him whether he had ever been in prison, he told me he had been "quodded" three times for vagrancy, and once on suspicion of highway robbery! I expressed my surprise at the honesty of the young thief. "Why, there's not a chap among them that wouldn't have done the same thing," said my companion, who knew their characters well; "they would all have done the same, except that one smoking there," pointing to an ill-looking lad in a Scotch cap. "When you gave me the shilling," cried Dan, "he followed me out into the yard, and told me to hook it."

I whispered with my companion as to whether it were possible to take the poor shoeless boy, who had resisted this double temptation, from the wretched and demoralizing associations of the place, and make an honest man of him. "No," was his answer; "he is hopeless. This is the chivalry of these people. Make friends of them, and they will scarcely ever deceive you. They may be trusted with pounds by those whom they know, but as for industry or getting an honest living, it's out of the question. I have known a few in my time that have been reclaimed, but they are the exceptions, and certainly not the rule."

Their habits could not be attributed to ignorance, for I found that 18 out of 29 could read and write; nor could their propensities be said to be due to the influence of early associations, for on inquiring as to their parentage, one told me that his father kept about forty or fifty horses. "My father was a schoolmaster," said a second; "And mine a dyer," said a third. "My father was a hatter," cried a fourth. Observing that the individuals were mostly youths, I wished to know how many were under 21; and, on inquiry, I found that 15 out of the 29 were below that age—9 were under 19, 5 under 17, and 3 under 15. . . .

[B]efore my departure I went to inspect the "bunks", as the beds are called, for which they are charged 2d. per night. The dormitory was at first appearance exactly similar to a small dissenting chapel, the divisions between the beds standing up like the partitions between the pews. On inspection, however, I found they were much closer, the partitions being only 22 inches apart. So close, indeed, were the bunks together, that 120 of them were stowed into a place about double the size of a four-stall stable. At the bottom of each of these was spread a leather, and as I walked round the place I saw many shirtless men stretched there like corpses, in a bed as narrow as a coffin, with another leather to cover. The stench of the room was overpowering, and I hurried from the place, indeed a wiser and a *sadder* man.

RAGGED SCHOOLS

From Letter XLIV, March 25th, 1850

[On March 19, 1850, Mayhew launched an investigation into the Ragged Schools, charity institutions which were to teach children of the poor to read and write at no cost to their parents. Mayhew's conclusions were not favourable to the schools, and his criticisms resulted in an acrimonious exchange between himself and the Secretary of the Ragged School Union. The following excerpts are a few of the interviews Mayhew reproduced in his letters to substantiate his reservations about the effects of the Ragged Schools.]

A superintendent of police who had lately retired, and who had "served" principally, for many years, in the Westminster district, gave me the following account:

"I have known this district for upwards of twenty years, and remember the Ragged Schools starting. Nothing worse under the sun could exist than Westminster when I first knew it in 1829. A competent authority convinced me that it was worse than St. Giles's, when St. Giles's was at its worst. And when St. Giles's was rookeried out afterwards, Westminster got worse, although I reckoned it 'worst' long before—as bad as could be. But hundreds came from St. Giles's. They must go somewhere. The low lodging-houses here were crammed from cellar to garret. I can't describe the places in decent language. Crimes went on there that are not fit to be mentioned—nothing could be compared to the crime but the dirt. Male and female lay promiscuously. Such places are the great facilities of crime; they give *such* facilities. The lodging-houses are the policeman's great hindrance. He needn't look for criminals there—they're hidden. The lodging-house beats Scotland-yard.

"There is a large class, too, of 'general dealers' who buy anything brought to them; the key of his mother's door, stolen by a child next door to the general dealer—he buys that for a halfpenny, and says, 'There's a clever boy.' I have seen decent children in those places, and went and expostulated with the man, who laughed at me, as the law was then on his side. At the time when New Oxford-street was building, the streets in Westminster swarmed with vicious boys and girls, driven from their St. Giles's haunts, and added to the Westminster vice. I knew one ———, living near the police-station, who regularly lived on his three daughters' prostitution; he and his wife did. The girls dursn't go home empty handed. There are lots of such in Westminster, I can tell you. Such men may have been bad mechanics, or lazy fellows, who would do anything rather than work. The general dealers, who buy door-keys or anything, are what you may call loose traders; the trading class that won't work is far the worst. They take to buying and selling, and sit idle, with their hands in their pockets. A shocking class, sir; they ought all to be registered. A working man is a king to such fellows. They carry on in a cellar, or anywhere, and boast that they are respectable tradesmen, and pay their rents regularly—many of them do. All lodging-houses should be licensed like beer-shops; no doubt at all about it. They are brothels some; some thieves' houses; all bad, where *anybody* can be admitted. Many that keep lodging-houses are general dealers too, such as I've told you of, and so they pull both ways. Most children, not bred thieves by their parents, begin stealing at home, and go to the general dealer; they may hear of him from boys in the street who look out for decent children.

"When the Ragged Schools were started, the streets did seem to me rather thinned. But they want supervision. If bad poor children meet together, and go away together, they are sure to go to some mischief or some robbery. Without complete supervision, Ragged Schools are of no good effect—nothing adequate to the good meant. The intent is good, merciful, and kind; and I believe they have done good. I believe that I could have given instances of their having done good, but I can't recollect one now, with any particulars. No doubt there is a great risk run at these Ragged Schools; bad boys, in a cluster, will always corrupt good boys. Worse still with girls. A decent girl *must* be corrupted among bad girls. Bad women and bad girls corrupt more of their own sex than men do; that's quite obvious. . . . I never knew a girl, a scholar in a Ragged School, in the streets afterwards; but they're young when they're at the school, and would grow out of my knowledge. Many houses have been pulled down in Westminster, and that has swept away many a curse of a house—to carry a curse somewhere else, perhaps—and has made the streets less crammed with vicious boys and girls; besides that they go to the Ragged Schools, many of them, and are then out of sight.

"The beer-shops are a great evil. The streets are better now; but they are too bad still. At one time, before the police began, a man could hardly go into the Almonry, or some of the streets off Orchard-street, without being robbed, or perhaps stripped; aye, even in the day-light. A man could hardly get through with a good hat, or a woman with a decent bonnet. If either was tipsy, it was all up with them. A complaint about it was laughed at, and a man was told he had no business there. At night the people there went prowling all over.

"I can't charge my memory with any particular boy or girl at the Ragged Schools going wrong afterwards, but no doubt there are such. My opinion altogether is this: with a proper supervision, and a prudential training, Ragged Schools do good; without it, they are dangerous. The nation loses far more in stolen property than would provide honest means of living for all the young thieves in London. There's far more property stolen than you hear of. Some won't prosecute; some compromise. I'll tell you how to help Ragged Schools better than money. Register general dealers: the young thief begins there. Just look at Orchard-street, and license the low lodging-houses, with the police to inspect them, or else our Ragged Schools haven't much chance. The clergymen may labour, and the Rector of St. John's is indefatigable in doing good, but general dealers and low lodging-houses are too much for them. Children mixed up together must turn out either thieves or prostitutes, whether they've been at a Ragged School or not; they have no other chance; they can't meet and mix one with another, anywhere, without supervision, but the bad will corrupt the good. I've known numbers of thieves, grown-up fellows, go out in the morning, smoking at the corners of the courts or at some doors here in Westminster, and they talk of their doings, and what they will do—and children going to a Ragged School, perhaps, to hear something good, will stop and listen to these fellows, and know they live well, and can drink and be idle—and so they may go to the Ragged School to say to others what a fine life a thief's was.

"Mere reading and writing is a harm to a vicious child. It makes him steal more boldly, because with more judgment, for he sees prices marked. Without moral training it's a harm. The smartest thieves I have met with, and those having the longest run, could all read and write, and some could defend themselves at trial without a lawyer, just by having studied the newspapers. The nation is paying the penalty now for so long neglecting the care of the youth of London.". . .

In the course of my inquiries I heard that several boys who had been in the Ragged Schools, had subsequently been in prison, and that some were there now. I therefore called upon Lieut. Tracy, the governor of the Tothill-fields prison, to inquire into this subject. He expressed an opinion—cursorily given he said—that Ragged Schools were not adapted to the reformation of the juvenile criminals of London who resorted there; inasmuch as the great evil to be guarded against, to arrest the progress of criminality, was the *congregating* of criminals. Evil always resulted, and must result, from that; and criminal offenders met in Ragged Schools, and congregated afterwards.

He summoned one of his principal officers who was familiar with the habits and character of juvenile offenders, and the latter expressed an opinion—unequivocally—that the boys in prison from Ragged Schools were generally worse than boys who had not been so educated. He had known above a dozen boys in that prison who had been in Ragged Schools within a recent period. He attributed great evil to vicious boys associating together, under any circumstances, at the Ragged Schools, or elsewhere. The schoolmistress of the prison stated that the girls who had been in Ragged Schools, and afterwards in prison, were neither better nor worse than other girls in prison.

Through the courtesy of Lieut. Tracy, I am enabled to give two statements from children then in prison. The first was an intelligent-looking boy (who had an impediment in his speech), and declared his anxiety to speak nothing but the truth—the governor and officer being convinced that his statement might be relied on. He said:

"I am 12, and have been three times in prison once for stealing cigars, once for a piece of calico, and once for some pigs' feet. I have been twice whipped. I was twelve months at the Exeter-buildings Ragged School, Knightsbridge. I learned reading, writing, and Church of England there. I was brought up there to the Church of England. I know I was, because I went to church with the schoolmaster. I know it was a church. A church is bigger than a chapel, and has a steeple. I learned sums, too, and the commandments, and the catechism. I can't read well. [He was tried on an act of Parliament as to his ability to read. It began "whereas the laws now existing." "Whereas" he could not make out anyhow, and "the laws now" he called "the lays no." He was unable to read any word of two syllables.] At the Ragged School, there were forty or fifty boys. We went at nine, left at twelve, and went back at two. Between twelve and two I was out with the other

c

boys, and we often made up parties to go a thieving. We thieved all sorts of things. We taught one another thieving. We liked to teach very young boys best; they're pluckiest, and the police don't know them at first. I knew good boys at the Ragged School—good when they went there—and we taught them to thieve. If we could get a good boy at the Ragged School we taught him to thieve, for he's safe some time from the police, and we share with him. At the Ragged School I was taught that I must keep my hands from picking and stealing, but I thought it fun to steal. The schoolmaster didn't know I ever stole.

"God is a spirit in heaven, and is everywhere. If I do wrong I shall go and be burnt in fire. It frightens me to think of it sometimes. I was first taught and tempted to steal by a boy I met at the Ragged School. He said 'Come along, and I'll show you how to get money.' I stole some cigars, and the other boy, a little boy, kept watch. I was nailed the first time. I shouldn't have been a thief but for the Ragged Schools, I'm sure I shouldn't."

The other boy, a healthy-looking child, said:

"I am ten, and have been twice in prison, and once whipped. I was in prison for 'a fork' and 'some lead.' I sold them in rag-shops. I was three months in Pye-street Ragged School, Westminster. I was a month at the St. Margaret's National School (Westminster). At the Ragged School I learned reading, writing, tailoring, shoe-making, and cleaning the place. [He then read a verse in the Bible imperfectly, and by spelling the words, but quite as well as could be expected]. There were forty or fifty boys at the Ragged School; half of them were thieves, and we used to go thieving in gangs of six. When we were away from school we went thieving. We taught any new boy how to thieve, making parties to do it. We would teach any good boy to thieve. I know four or five good boys at the Ragged Schools taught to thieve by me and others. We got them to join us, as we got afraid ourselves, and the police don't so soon 'spect new boys. Thieving is wrong. Some boys where I lived taught me to thieve. They did not go to a Ragged School, that I know of.". . .

From a good-looking and well-spoken girl I had the following statement. I called to see her father, who was absent, and the girl gave me the information I required:

"I learned all I know," she said, "(and I can read any chapter in the Bible), at the Ragged School close by here. But for it I mightn't have known how to read or write. I hope it's a good place but I'm sure I don't know, I've met such bad girls there. I've known them bring songs and notes that they'd written at night, to give to the boys when they met them out of school. I don't know what sort the songs were, or what was in the notes. I never saw either, as it was a secret among them. The schoolmistress knew nothing about it. I don't think I ever heard the girls say anything bad in school; but often when I've left at night I've seen the girls waiting for the boys, or the boys for the girls as happened. I don't know how many, but a knot of them, and they used to go away together. I don't know where they went, whether thieving or what; but if I've been behind the other girls a minute or so in leaving school, I've had to go through a little knot of them, and might stop a minute or two perhaps, and I've heard them swear and curse, and use bad words, such as no modest girl ever would use. I've never done anything a modest girl mightn't, though I've been tempted [she blushed].

"Nine at night is such a late hour to stay at school, that the scholars get tired and long for a change. There's too much of it. I always went straight home, and the bad girls never troubled or teased me. If I hadn't gone straight home I should have been beaten by my father. My brother went to the same Ragged School, and I'm afraid it did him harm. He has ran away every now and then, and has always come back ragged and poorly—far worse than when he left home. I don't know what made him run away, unless he was tempted to do it by boys he met at the Ragged School; but I can't speak as to that. I don't know whether he went thieving or not. He never says anything about it when he comes back, let him be punished anyhow. He is a worse boy now than when he went to the school first. I don't know if he has any young girl he runs away with when he's absent. He's about fifteen or more, perhaps. I don't know exactly how old we are.

"The boys and girls I've seen go away together after we left the Ragged Schools were too young to be honest sweethearts and to think of marrying. If they would only listen to the schoolmistress they would know what it was to do wrong; but some of them don't, for in going home of a night I've heard them boast of having been wicked with men and boys; but I can't tell you more about that—I can't, indeed. My brother is playing in the street there—shall I call him in?" I requested her to do so; but on being desired to come in the youth disappeared.

"My father," the girl continued, "is a tinman, but he seldom has work; my mother sweeps a crossing, and has the cleaning of two and sometimes three gentlemen's houses. My father and mother are kind to me. When I'm not washing or cleaning here, as you've found me now, I go out hawking, chiefly with tins. We are often badly off—often wanting a meal. I can't say how much we earn in a week. I've told you nothing at all, indeed, sir, but what I know, or have seen, or heard myself."

From Letter XLV, March 29th, 1850

An experienced officer, who attended at a Ragged School in Lambeth, gave me the result of his observation on the subject. The superintendent of the district, to whom I had been directed by the Commissioners, referred me to two officers as best qualified to give me information. I subjoin the statement of the first I saw:

"At the —— street Ragged School (Lambeth), none live in the house, but the attendance in the winter averages about 400 boys and girls every Sunday evening. The gentlemen who manage the Ragged School do everything they can to instruct and encourage the children in well-doing; they make them presents of Testaments and Bibles" (I find by the Reports that they are sold), "and give them occasional tea parties. In fact, everything is done to improve them in the school. The patience of the teachers is surprising. The boys and girls are separated in school; there are more boys than girls—perhaps 300 boys to 100 girls. The girls are better behaved than the boys; they are the children of very poor people in the neighbourhood, such as the daughters of people selling fruit in the street, and such like. Some few years ago I had some inquiries to make on the subject, and found several children of street-beggars there.

"I have not recognized a girl in this part on the town whom I knew at the school. Most of those that have grown into women since I knew them at the school sell things in the streets; they are very audacious, but I can't say that they are prostitutes. I have, however, seen bigger boys, not of the school, but street vagabonds whom I knew to be of bad character, waiting about the school until it broke up, and then go away with the bigger girls. These girls when in the street are indecent in their language, and immodest in their behaviour; quite different from what they appear in the school. The boys, as I have said, are worse than the girls. When gathered in the street, previously to being let into the school, their conduct is very bad. Some of them smoke short pipes which they pocket when let into school. While waiting on the Sunday evening, they sing, and caper, and some stand on their heads and clap their feet together, and fight frequently and swear, and make all manner of noises. As soon as they get into school they pull long faces. I have often heard them, when hymns were sung, sing something along with it quite different to a hymn. I have seen them too, when a gentleman has been addressing them on religious topics, wink one to another, and put their tongues in their cheeks.

"The school has been opened perhaps nine years. The police have been obliged to be in attendance since within three months of the opening, and I often turn a dozen boys out of the school in a night for misbehaviour. These boys, in my opinion, have different objects in going to the Ragged School. Some few go really with the intention of learning. The great proportion go for warmth, or a change, or for shelter, or for a lark. I know it from their behaviour, for I can tell the boys who wish to learn from the others, by their conduct to the teacher. The worst class of boys always laugh and make faces at the teacher the moment his back is turned, and sometimes even before his face. I have seen many boys at the school whom I have known in custody for felony, and others whom I have seen in prison. On leaving school their behaviour is very disorderly; you can hear them half a mile off; they never seem to have benefited by the excellent things they may have heard; in fact, for bad and obscene language, cursing, swearing, and noise of every kind, they are worse in coming out than going in. When school is over they throw off all restraint. I can only judge by their conduct, and from that it does not appear to me that they pay the least attention to the good and religious advice given to them by their excellent teachers. I have often known the Rev. Mr. —— visit the school, and take great pains to impress upon the children the evil of their ways, but from their conduct after his lessons, after they get outside the door, and from their filthy and bad language, I fear no good effect has been produced.

"The boys generally go to the school in small parties, who know each other— four, five, or six; and if one won't go in the others won't; and when they leave, they go away together. After that they are beyond my observation. In the school I think the boys do behave rather better than they once did, but no better in the street. There is as much street gambling as ever. The boys are very bad in this neighbourhood. The boy-thieves are generally intelligent in all their wicked ways; clever, artful, and deceitful to the last degree; they would impose upon any one; they are capable of making people believe they are quite good innocent boys, and laugh at them just after. I've seen some of the most hardened shed tears, and protest they had never done anything wrong; and so naturally that it would impose upon any person unacquainted with their deep tricks.". . .

The Ragged School to which I principally directed my attention is situated in

John Pounds, the founder of the Ragged Schools

one of the worst quarters of Westminster. The street—in which it is the best and cleanest house—and all the circumjacent streets, with their many courts and alleys, and what are well described as "blind passages"—is mainly occupied by the destitute and the criminal. Low lodging-houses abound. "Lodgings for Travellers," at "3d." (and sometimes 2d.) "a night," are the predominating signs. The shattered and ill-patched windows of very many houses—where sheets of brown paper occupy the place of glass—and the open and unpainted doors, allow even a cursory observer to notice much filth and laziness in the rooms within. In some houses each room has its family, and sometimes almost every upper window has its yellow patched or ragged linen hanging out to dry on something like a small bowsprit rigged out of the window.

Young thieves, with greasy side-curls, and unoccupied costermongers are lounging at the corners of the streets—some few smoking—some tossing in the open road, with an eager crowd of lads gathered round them—some gambling at pitch and toss, in a dirty corner or bye place—others leaning against a post or a wall, seemingly as much asleep as awake—and all appearing to strive to while away the time as best they can. Empty costermongers' carts stand by the edge of the kerb-stone, and capless women, with fuzzy hair, eyes bloodshot with drink or want of sleep, and with dirty shawls over their shoulders, either loll out of the windows or sit on the door step. An oppressive odour seems always to pervade the atmosphere—and cocks and hens scratch at the heaps of filth in the street. The people look generally unhealthy.

Here and there, as you emerge from the low and filthy streets, there rises in startling contrast, some towering gin-palace, the squalor of its noisy customers being again in full contrast with its glittering decorations and glare of light. The house that now forms the Ragged School (I learn from Mr. Walker's account) was once a public-house, in which thieving, or rather one of its branches, that of pocket-picking, was taught as a science, a pair of trowsers supplying the means of tuition. A master-thief illustrated and explained the adroitest modes of picking pockets to perhaps half a hundred keen pupils. A mock Old Bailey trial frequently followed, and the lads who evinced most skill either in practising on the trowsers (which were hung from the ceiling), or in defending themselves from any Old Bailey charge, were encouraged with drink and skittles. Very near to this spot stood another public-house—a resort of Dick Turpin and of others whose names modern literature has made more familiar to that criminal neighbourhood, and far more popular than did tradition or any other previous cause. Turpin's resort is now an Institute for Working Men.

The number of boys employed in tailoring, when I visited the school, at the time of industrial training, was 26. Of these 3 were fourteen years old, 1 was thirteen, 8 were twelve, 6 were eleven, 2 were ten, 4 were nine, 1 was eight, 1 was six. There were also 22 boys engaged in shoe-making, whose ages were in the same proportion as those who were tailoring. All these boys, as far as I ascertained, expressed their sense of the kindness with which they were treated, and of the pains taken to do them good. Of these boys, I learned from their own admissions, that six had been (collectively) thirteen times in prison. As they detailed their experience in prison, the other boys, who declared that they had never been in prison, laughed and grinned admiringly. One boy said to a gentleman who accompanied me, "Master, what do you think that boy was in prison for?" "I can't tell," was the answer. "He stole a pig," whispered the urchin, laughing and smiling approvingly as he whispered.

The Master Tailor, who was the only officer in attendance when I called, did not know, he said, of any boy having been transported; nor could he at first remember any boy having been imprisoned from that school. At last he suddenly recollected that two boys were in prison at that time from the Ragged School (the two I had seen at Tothill-fields); even this fact, however, he could not remember, until reminded of it by my inquiry whether Ragged Schools were not intended, if possible, to bring about the reformation of thieves. Neither did he know of any boys of the Ragged School who had been in prison within the last twelve months, but the school-boys present (one especially) numbered up eight very rapidly. When a boy disappears, he added, the Ragged School managers do not inquire after him, as they have not time to go to the police-office. They keep no records of the imprisonment of their scholars.

The Master Tailor had been there about three years. He had belonged to a society in connexion with the honourable trade about ten years ago. Within three years ten boys had been apprenticed to tailors. A premium of £10 used to be given—now it is £5. Small masters generally get the apprentices. The articles made by the boys, I was informed, were given to the scholars as rewards for good conduct. I found out afterwards, by inquiry among the boys, that a small price was charged for them. I was furnished with an account of the number of shoes, jackets, &c., made by the boys in the course of last year, and upon investigation I found that "forty-eight boys in school had received nineteen jackets, thirty-four pairs of trowsers, and twenty-eight pairs of shoes;" four of the lads, however, were without shoes, and five wore women's or girls' boots, and often odd boots.

A boy in school told me he had known the school boys go thieving after school hours. Another lad knew boys, but not school boys, go thieving in small gangs. Another boy remembered the school being robbed; the police came, but no charge was made. He had heard that the thieves about the street corners had got hold of some of the boys. A policeman searched the boys. Four of the boys I saw in the school had fathers only living (one of whom was in prison); eleven had only mothers (but two of the fathers of these children were not dead, for one was transported and one was in a workhouse); and one had neither father nor mother living. The others had both parents alive.

In order that I might have the best and most trustworthy information as to the quality of the work and the probable consequences of the instruction of the boys of a Ragged School (with industrial training superadded to the usual reading, writing, and arithmetic), I took with me two well-informed, experienced, and unprejudiced men—a tailor and a shoemaker—on whose judgment and fairness, from my inquiries among the trade, and from my recent investigations, I knew I could rely. I give their statements—the first being that of the tailor. He said:

"I have noticed the work of the Ragged School boys, whom I have seen making or repairing their clothes, and I have formed the following opinion. The boys have attained just that degree of proficiency in their tailoring which would make them available for the slopworker or the sweater—more particularly for the slopworker, as the work of the sweater must be of a better character. They are proficient enough to do their work regularly, but not well; the sewing is thin but regular; by thin, I mean too small a number of stitches in a given space; but the stitches, as I have said, are regular and in good form. Indeed the work of some of the poor little fellows rather surprised me, as it is not very easy to sew fustian and cord, such as their jackets and trowsers are made of.

"I consider that the teacher of the children has exercised due pains and skill. I think that boys so circumstanced, whatever may be the immediate advantage, are likely to prove a very serious injury to the working men in my trade—I mean, of course, the honourable trade. It is not possible that these boys can remain long in their present state, so that some other place must be found for them, or they must resort to thieving. I see no alternative for the poor fellows. If, indeed, they are apprenticed, it will most likely be to small masters, or sweaters, for sweaters are often small masters—that is, they are able to do a small quantity of work on their own account, underselling the very masters who employ them. They may not be so apprenticed now, but this is what it must come to. To small masters or sweaters the premium is generally the grand object; they care nothing what becomes of the boy, as our police reports too frequently prove. The boy, if not thus apprenticed, may possibly resort to the slop-market, and there he can never rise into the means of earning a fair remuneration, for his abilities are not sufficient to elevate him. He may, and *will*, drag better workmen down to his level, but he cannot rise; and so he may marry—as reckless people will—and his children may be reared in a poverty that will tempt them to crime far more promptly than any institute (however well intended) can check them.

"I see no other career for such a boy, and no other likely result. If he is to be sent abroad, where is the use of teaching him the trade of a tailor? Let him go to any of the colonies, he will find that the slop-seller—maintained by such labour as schools like these create—is there before him. There is not a market they do not supply. One of these poor lads, when he has had two or three years' instruction (according to his quickness) at a school such as that we have visited to-day, is able to earn a trifle from a slop-worker, and he grows up a slop workman, and adds to the poverty, and perhaps the crime, of the country, as a consequence of the very system adopted to make him a good member of society. It is impossible he can become a first-rate workman, unless he be altogether an exception to the general rule; and so he adds to the already overstocked, little-skilled, or unskilled labour-market which is producing such sad consequences to the superior artisans, and to the best masters in England.

"I have very carefully watched this matter in all its bearings for more than sixteen years—Government contracts, police clothing, prison and workhouse labour, philanthropic and industrial schools; and this last and worst phase of all—Ragged Schools. The conclusion forced upon me is, that there is no hope for bettering the condition of any trade in which these things exist, or upon which they are brought to bear, whilst such practices are persevered in. Such practices produce starvation wages, on which men cannot live. Some parish authorities are so convinced of this that workhouse labour has been abandoned. I am afraid that many excellent persons who encourage such institutions as the Ragged Schools look only at the surface. Ragged School tailors must ultimately lower tailors' wages, and so increase the very evil they are intended to destroy."

The Shoemaker's statement I now give, which is as follows:

"I found, on counting heads, while at the school, that twenty-one boys were at work there; but I was told by several of these boys that there were others who were not at present in the shop. The number absent were some nine or ten. Mr. ———, the master, was not there at the time, so I had no means of testing the variety of ability displayed. One, the eldest of the number, had a rather more conspicuous seat than the rest; his age was sixteen, and he had the name given to him of monitor, by way of distinction.

"Here I may state that the boys were somewhat grotesquely grouped in three separate classes. The first, or youngest class, were six in number, and were seated round a low square table, garnished with a few much-worn knives, a pair of very narrow-nibbed pincers, and an edged tin plate, covered with small bits of rounded wax. This, the initiative class were generally employed in what is called 'stabbing' bits of leather, this being a mere exercise of the awl. The scrap of leather is held in the instrument called the 'clams,' which are two long bowed staves, the mouth or upper part tightly nipping whatever substance may be placed between them, and thus enabling the operator to have complete command over whatever material he may be engaged upon. None of these boys had any knowledge of, or had received any instruction in the sort of work named 'blind stabbing'—a very beautiful and most essential process—indeed, one which cannot be done without when the boy is intended to be the 'boot-closer;' and a process, too, which only can be effectually learned in early life, when the sense of touch is most delicate, and the fingers the most expert.

"The second class were the cobblers; and these I found numbered seven, and they appeared to take much more delight in making the hammer sound, in beating the leather on the 'lapstone' than in putting in stitches. Some were sewing patches on the upper leathers, or drawing together rents; but the greater part, as I have said, kept striking away on the stone; while two or three were nailing pieces on the heels, which, as I observed, they found to be very weak, in consequence of the severe battering which the bit of bull-hide had received.

"The third class—with the 'monitor,' in the absence of the 'master baker,' presiding in a somewhat dignified manner over his fellow-boys of younger years and less size—were the 'new' shoemakers. The 'monitor' himself had just finished the sewing round or the 'stitching' of a shoe which would fit a lad of about fourteen years of age. He said that his own age was sixteen, and that he had been at the shoe-making for upwards of a year; that he could sew a shoe round, of the sort I have mentioned, in an hour, which is about half the time a man would take to accomplish a similar piece of inferior work, although the perfect 'stitching' of a light boot or shoe will often require from two to three hours. Two other of these boys of the third class gave me likewise their work to examine; this, although very coarse in quality, as might be expected, seemed to be drawn together firmly—the workers, as I perceived, appearing always to make the best use of the 'hand-leather,' in accordance, no doubt, with their instructions. As this, though a means, is how-ever no security for solidity, it often happens that the mere fact of the shoemaker labouring at his work is only doing so in vain; for if there is not the proper foundation laid in the getting up of a shoe, as of a house, in the nice and close fitting and adjustment of the materials before hand, no mere thickness of thread or strength of pull will avail in securing a truly serviceable article.

"The generality of these boys had very bad shoes, and the rest no shoes at all. On inquiring how this happened, the information was given that the right to have shoes came by purchase; ninepence per pair being the price charged to every boy or girl to whom shoes are given. 'And these trowsers' said one of the little shoe-makers, 'cost me also ninepence;' while another told me that he also paid the same sum for his jacket. 'And if you have not this money,' I asked, 'you neither get shoes, nor trowsers, nor jackets?' 'No,' was the general and immediate reply. 'My mother,' one said, 'is to give me the ninepence on Saturday, and then I shall have these shoes to go out in on Sunday.' And the poor boy had here, indeed, a great blessing in prospect, for he was actually barefoot.

" 'Do you want an apprentice, sir,' now inquired the 'monitor,' perceiving that I was examining somewhat closely the pair of shoes which had just been handed to me, and imagining, as I suppose, that I was in quest of a boy, from the manner of my inspection. I gave him to understand that I was not seeking an apprentice, but only came there for general information. The work which I examined, though very inferior indeed, was still, considering all things, as well got up as might be expected, the boys being employed only at short intervals; the early part of the day, from nine in the morning till the hour of dinner, being set apart for school-ing purposes; and the afternoon, from two till five, for learning shoemaking, five days in the week. Boys so taught, however, are never to be supposed capable of earning a livelihood through the extent of their capacity, but can only be made so far useful as to become the apprentice of the slop home-worker, or garret-master—a class of people who are always on the look-out for cheap labour and an 'apprentice fee;' the latter to enable them to buy 'stuff,' or the material for their low-priced goods. With such people the helpless position of the apprentice allows every chance of their compelling the greatest possible amount of exertion from the lads."

II
UNSKILLED WORKERS

LUMPERS

From Letter XXIV, January 8th, 1850

[In the early letters, Mayhew divided his survey into skilled and un-skilled workers, but his main interest was always in the skilled artisans. His few letters on unskilled workers were limited to dock labourers; these letters were reprinted in volume III of London Labour, *with the exception of the following interviews from Letter XXIV.]*

The next I saw was one who had volunteered to speak out, so that, by comparing the following statement with the foregoing [See *London Labour*, III, 290–291], we may be able to come to some notion of the truth. The man's statement was as follows:

"I have worked as a *journeyman lumper* seventeen years. When I first began that work I was paid 3s. 6d. a-day, being employed two days and a half or three days in a week the year through. The young hands are generally knocked about and sent from one ship to another, humbugged about, and obliged to wait and wait, never getting anything for the time they have to wait. In a timber ship this is the way the work is carried on to lump her (unload her). Well, say a ship is 1,000 tons burthen; suppose her cargo is timber and with a deck load of yellow wood pine, the heaviest cargo that comes to London on deck. I'll tell you the truth if I lose my work. I don't care a fig. I can't be worse. That man you just seen hasn't told you the whole truth. He's afeard. He works out of a public-house, and daren't speak. The ships come up, and eight or nine master lumpers go aboard, and the captain may say, 'The cheapest man's to have her.' One man will say, 'I've done this ship before;' and he'll get the ship because he knows how to tip some proper party, and he tips five bob or half a sovereign. Suppose this man gets the ship; he's a master man, and he goes to a foreman, and he says, 'Get me a gang together,' and the foreman gets a gang together, and he must get a good set if the work's to be done quick. The master lumper has all the pull; the foreman doesn't get much—only his shilling a day extra. Oft enough he gets the best hands at first, and when a quantity that may be wanted is got off he puts on cheaper hands—new Irish Grecians, some people calls them, or others. Any new hands is the same. I never show those men how to work. They ruin our trade, and are ruining it more and more; they'll work for nothing.

"Each man gets 3s., the master paying the waterage. In August, September, and October, work is the best. Then we get 4s. and a pint of beer. They give us 4s. 2d., but we must pay the twopence for a pint of beer—that lies in a man's option it's said: but if a man doesn't do so, he's thought scaly. If we don't have our beer, we're done. The master lumpers who are not publicans pay at public-houses, and have sometimes to borrow the money of the publicans to pay the men, before they get their money from the shipowner. I shall lose my work, maybe, and have to go to the Mount—that is, you see, a place between the Commercial Dock and the Dog and Duck, where we walk looking out for a job—because I speak this way to you. If jobs don't come, there's the workhouse. Lots come from Ireland, and go to work, knowing nothing about it. But they'll work for anything, and so get on. [This he repeated frequently.]

"I am a married man with a family, but don't say how many, or I should be more a marked man. I wish I could write as slick as you. I'd do only head work then, and work no more. I have spent 25s. a week in drink. I ought to have as good a suit as you, when I get work as a foreman, which I do sometimes. Last week I got 20s., and took home 3s. I'm afraid to speak, I should lose my work. [This he said over and over again.] I must spend my money in drink some way, or I can't get on in any work; there's stoppages and bothers. I was told I couldn't get paid last Saturday night, for fear I should have anything to do with telling you or anybody the truth. I didn't get all my money until Sunday, and it was all gone on Sunday night. You understand; if a man gives offence, next morning he's told 'You're not wanted, there's a hand short of what we expected to want—you understand.' In less than three years a publican that contracts may make his fortune. Where these men sell a pint to a neighbour they sell three pots to a lumper. It's compulsion, as you may say—and it's no compulsion. A contractor, on a tidy job, will get his £4 profit—sometimes £10 or £15 on a good job; and he keeps moving on that way; no matter how our kids starves. Aye, and more than that, I've known contractors have £50 for a ship, and has done it for £16. I went on board the ——, for Mr. ——. He wanted to employ me as foreman, at 4s. a-day, but he wanted me to pay waterage, and I refused. I have had 6s. a-day as foreman. An average lumper will get 4s. a-day when he is at work. I was threatened to be flung out of the windows if I came to any meeting with you. When I'm out of work, the old woman has to keep me. She works at gowns, or anything. How she lives God only knows!"

The following is the statement of one who appeared to me to be both a truthful and a just man. His wife was a superior woman, and being present at his home—where the information was obtained—she acted as a check upon him, even if he had been disposed to lean either to master or workman. The man's house was comfortably furnished, evidently owing to the greater prudence of his wife, for I have found it is a rule that when the wife is cleanly and thrifty, the husband is always a higher class man:

"I have been a lumper nine years. Prices are not so good now as when I first knew the business. We got 4s. 6d. a day then; that is, the old hands did. In a year after it fell to 4s. Work was slack, and so employers could get men to work at their own prices. Three or four years back price fell to 3s. 6d. a day." My informant then repeated what I had formerly heard, attributing this further decrease to the great influx of Irish labourers, owing to the distress in Ireland, and their willingness to work for any wages whatever, which enables employers to get the old hands on easier terms.

"The lumpers," my informant continued, "are employed principally in timber and deal ships, but will undertake any work to which their employer chooses to set them. The corn-ships are all discharged by the fellowship porters; excepting the vessels in the South-west India Dock (formerly the City Canal), where the servants of the company are employed; but they must then have one of the regularly appointed meters. There is far too much drinking among us. One man I know had 14s. to receive for wages the other week, but he went on 'on tick' at the public-house, had nothing to take on Saturday night, and was 5s. in debt. It is a great disadvantage in our business that work is so uncertain. Last Christmas twelve-month, all that I earned the week before Christmas was 6d. I have now 15s. in pawn, and as we have no club nor anything of that kind, if I was to be sick there's only the parish. In a slack time I have sold Christmas carols or anything."

I will now give the statement of one of the foremen who was sent to me intoxicated by the publican-contractor, to persuade me that the system under which the working men are employed and paid is a beneficial and a just one to the labourer. The inconsistencies in the statement the reader will easily detect. He said:

"I am the foreman of a gang of lumpers. The gangs vary in number according to the size of the vessel to be laden. They vary from 8 to 26. When the gang exceeds 10 men, 2 foremen are employed, as the work is carried on on both sides of the ship at the same time. I work under a publican, who contracts with the shipowner to do the work of unlading the vessel *by the lump*; that is, so much for the entire job, without any reference to weight or measurement. I engage the men employed, anybody I please—and they are paid by the contractor. At this time of the year, when work cannot be carried on longer than from half-past seven in the morning until towards five in the evening, each man is paid 3s. 6d. for his day's work: he is paid that sum in money. He is not required to spend any of that money; nor would any man have a worse chance of work who didn't spend anything in drink at the house of the contractor. He hasn't been a publican long—about a year. We take a pot of beer a man, or twelve pots for every ten men—more usually from the house of the contractor. I consider that we are not obliged to do this.

"It is very seldom that any gang of men has a full week's work. I calculate that they are not employed above three days in the week, take the average of the year; that gives an average earning of 10s. 6d. per week. For the next three months there will be hardly anything doing in the timber-ships, on account of the ice in the St. Lawrence and the Baltic. During this slack time the men go off to any job. They may pick up a little tide-work; that is, to assist in taking a ship from a wet dock into a dry one, or any arrangement of that kind. We have no sick fund among us—no benefit club, no society of any kind. When a man's fairly beat out, his fellow workmen may subscribe a trifle for him. Drunkenness is too common among us, but I don't know that the system of working under publicans has much to do with it. My employer would as soon see his men take their money home. Many of the men are in great distress; their families are hard put to it; they are the people that have to suffer for it. The foreman, by agreement with his employer, has so much a day over what the men have, but no per centage, and nothing to do with the paying of the lumpers.

"I dare say from 700 to 1,000 men are employed as lumpers in timber ships, when work is good; lumpers work only in timber ships. There are a far greater number of men in the trade than there used to be, on account of the number of labouring men that have come over from Ireland lately. These Irishmen, when they first go to lumping, are very awkward about it, and don't soon get handy. Before they came in such lots, wages were better. They have been 4s. 6d. a day to men that knew their work. For the last three years and more wages have been no higher than 3s. 6d. a day. Of course the Irishmen, when first set to work, weren't worth so much as the old hands, but they were employed, and so wages fell down to their level. There is only one publican among the contractors for lumping. There are four principal contractors, and several small ones. I don't know the exact number. They all pay the men and the foremen alike. My employer will not allow any lumper to run up drink scores at his house to be worked out afterwards. There are too many men in the lumping business. There is no system of giving a gang of men their turn. We employ those we consider best to do the work."

I next saw two lumpers' wives. The husband of one had been fourteen years, and the other ten years, at the business. They both worked under a master who is a publican. One said, "My husband is such a strange man that he never tells me what he does get." The husband of the other, who is a foreman, according to the wife's statement, occasionally gets 5s. and sometimes 4s. 6d. a day. The first woman said, "It is a very bad principle for a man to have work out of a public-house; it makes a man spend a shilling where otherwise he would not."

The wife of the one whose husband was a foreman said, "I have had many a bitter bruise for the last fifteen years, and all through the drink. Sometimes he stops till after twelve or one o'clock. I have not had anything to eat to-day—not a taste of anything, or even a bit of fire. On draw-nights he usually comes home about ten o'clock, and I call that a very good hour for a lumper, for draw-nights are very bad nights; the men then generally spend at the public-house three parts of what they earn. On pay-night the men generally stop till the public-house is closed, and then some of them doesn't bring a penny home, but comes home in debt. When the men are in work they may go trust for anything they want. Those that drink the hardest get the most work; they are the most looked upon. If the men was to bring all they earn home—aye, or even one-third of it—it would make the family very comfortable, as there would be a few more blankets and sheets on the bed—yes, and good shoes to their wives' and children's feet. Mine are two odd ones," added the woman, thrusting out her feet; "our dog stole this one, and brought it in his mouth. The men, when they are in full work, earn 24s. per week, and they bring home upon an average 4s. out of that sum. Ah, that's about it, and there is a fourth part of them don't do that—the rest goes for what the publicans please to stick up to them."

"I know if mine brought home more than he does," said the other, "I and the children would have some flannel petticoats. I have got one thin one, but a puff of wind would blow that away. They won't take it in pawn, or it would have gone long ago." The second woman added, "I have not got anything that would get me a penny, else it would have been in pawn to fetch me over to-day. When my husband beats me it is when I am in bed; but when I am not in bed I can fly from him. I know of one woman who is in the union now. Her husband always made his 24s. a week in the spring, but he brought only a shilling or two home to her at the week's end. He was almost always drunk, and then he would knock her down and jump upon her, and leave her for dead. When he was sober he was a good quiet sort of a man. He worked out of a public-house, and that is only a part of what the women have to suffer through their husbands being entrapped by the publican into his house. The woman I speak of has gone into the union to get away from the man's ill-treatment, and to have something nourishing to keep her, for it was very little she got at home, poor thing! She is suffering in the union now. She is very bad indeed."

"I have not seen my husband," said the other one, "since last Thursday evening. He has gone away, and has not left me a farthing piece. I have taken my aprons off and pawned them for 9d., and that is all gone now. I had out of the 9d. I got 14lbs. of coal,—that is 2d.—and a $\frac{3}{4}$d. candle, and a farthing bundle of wood; that is 3d. all together. Then I had three-ha'porth of bread and half a quartern of butter, and a ha'porth of tea, and a ha'porth of sugar, and a quarter of a pound of bacon $1\frac{1}{2}$d., beside a ha'porth of onions, and a pennyworth of potatoes—that's all; and I think I laid my money out very well; and that has been all I have had since last Thursday, and now it's Sunday. Today I have had nothing at all. I don't know where my husband is gone, for the publican won't let me know. If I go and ask at the public-house they only laugh at me. Indeed, whenever a wife goes after her husband at the public-house to fetch him home, she is sent miles out of the way for a lark, so as to keep him there drinking. On the Saturday night the publican keeps the men there till the house is closed, and many of them stays there drinking far into the Sunday morning in spite of the law. Take the generality of the lumpers' wives, they are very badly off indeed." One of the women produced a bundle of pawn-tickets of things belonging to herself and her landlord. She told me that she had been obliged to make away with the blankets, sheets, and fire-irons of the lodgings that she occupied in order to live. She had kept the door shut all day (she said), for fear the landlord should come in, and missing the property, send her to Maidstone gaol.

To show the temptations that beset the poor, I give the statement of a woman known to all her neighbours as a very thrifty housewife, and an active, industrious woman. Her children's, her own, and her husband's clothing, scant and old as it was, all showed great care-taking; her home was very tidy. A few years back, a little after Christmas, she and her husband (now a lumper, but then pursuing a different calling) had been out all day, penniless, and returned to their room a little before dusk, without having earned a farthing. The wife was then suckling her first child, which was two months old. She felt very faint, and the only thing in the house on which she thought it possible to raise a penny was a glass tumbler—"that very tumbler," she continued, "which you see on the table. Everything but that had gone to the pawn-shop. Well, it cost $5\frac{1}{2}$d., and I went to —— and tried to sell it for 2d. I couldn't sell it at all, as the dealer had too many of such things. I then went to a neighbour and said, 'Mrs. B——, for God's sake lend me 2d. on this glass, for we're starving.' 'Mrs. ——,' said she, 'I'm sure you should have 3d., but I haven't 3d., nor a halfpenny.' Well, when I'd gone back it was dark, and my husband had gone to bed, such as it was—for we had neither blankets nor sheets left to cover us—as the best way to forget he was hungry and cold. We hadn't a bit of fire nor candle, but there was a bit of light came from the lamp in the street through the window. I sat down by the fire, that wasn't in, to suckle my child— poor little Bill! he's a fine lad now—and I found I had hardly any milk; and what would become of the child? All at once a thought came into my head, and I said to myself, 'Yes, I'll cut my own throat, and then little Bill's'—and I determined I would. Then I said to myself, 'No, I won't; for if I can cut my own throat, I know I can't cut the child's; so it'll be little use, I'll go to the waterworks, and jump in with him in my arms.' I got up to do it, and then another thought came on me,

D

and I laid down the child on that chair, and I shook my husband and said, 'You villain, I'll cut your throat, I will,' and he jumped up and seized hold of me, and then I felt how bad I'd been; but one's passion must have some vent, so I seized that very kettle you see there by the spout—the gas rather lighted it—and I smashed it on the floor; it was the first thing that came to hand—and broke a hole in it that cost me 2½d. to get mended. After that I felt calmed a bit, and began to see how wicked I'd been, and I fell down on my knees and cried like a child, for I was thankful to God I'd been preserved. Then I went to bed and prayed never to feel the like again." This statement was made with perfect simplicity; it came out incidentally, and the poor woman had no reason to believe that it would be printed.

III
SKILLED WORKERS

SPITALFIELDS WEAVERS

From Letter II, October 23rd, 1849

[Mayhew's general statement of his intentions and methods in this passage describes fairly accurately his procedures throughout the series. After a time, however, he visited the workers in their homes less frequently and instead interviewed them at the Chronicle offices or at large meetings.]

In my inquiry I have sought to obtain information from the artisans of Spitalfields upon two points in particular. I was desirous to ascertain from the workmen themselves, not only the average rate of wages received by them, but also to hear their opinions as to the cause of the depreciation in the value of their labour. The result of my inquiries on these two points I purpose setting forth in my present communication; but, before entering upon the subject, I wish the reader distinctly to understand that the sentiments here recorded are those wholly and solely of the weavers themselves. My vocation is to collect facts, and to register opinions. I have undertaken the subject with a rigid determination neither to be biased nor prejudiced by my own individual notions, whatever they may be, upon the matter. I know that as in science the love of theorising warps the mind, and causes it to see only those natural phenomena that it wishes to see—so in politics, party-feeling is the coloured spectacles through which too many invariably look at the social events of this and other countries. The truth will be given in its stark nakedness. Indeed, hardly a line will be written but what a note of the matter recorded has been taken upon the spot, so that, no matter how startling or incredible the circumstances may seem, the reader may rest assured that it is his experience rather than the reporter's veracity that is at fault. . . .

I will now proceed to give the result of my inquiries into the subject; though, before doing so, it will be as well to make the reader acquainted with the precautions adopted to arrive at a fair and unbiassed estimate as to the feelings and condition of the workmen in the trade. In the first place, having put myself in communication with the surgeon of the district, and one of the principal and most intelligent of the operatives, it was agreed among us that we should go into a particular street, and visit the first six weavers' houses that we came to. *[Only two interviews are reproduced here.]* Accordingly we made the best of our way to the nearest street. The houses were far above the average abodes of the weavers, the street being wide and airy, and the houses open at the back, with gardens filled with many-coloured dahlias. The "long lights" at top, as the attic window stretching the whole length of the house is technically called, showed that almost the whole line of houses were occupied by weavers. As we entered the street, a coal cart, with a chime of bells above the horse's collar, went jingling past us. Another circumstance peculiar to the place was the absence of children. In such a street, had the labour of the young been less valuable, the gutters and door-steps would have swarmed with juveniles.

We knocked at the door of the first house, and, requesting permission to speak with the workman on the subject of his trade, were all three ushered up a steep staircase, and through a trap in the floor into the "shop." This was a long, narrow apartment, with a window back and front, extending the entire length of the house—running from one end of the room to the other. The man was the ideal of his class—a short spare figure, with a thin face and sunken cheeks. In the room were three looms and some spinning wheels, at one of which sat a boy winding "quills." Working at a loom was a plump, pleasant-looking girl, busy making "plain goods." Along the windows, on each side, were ranged small pots of fuchsias, with their long scarlet drops swinging gently backwards and forwards, as the room shook with the clatter of the looms.

The man was a velvet weaver. He was making a drab velvet for coat collars. We sat down on a wooden chair beside him, and talked as he worked. He told us he was to have 3s. 6d. per yard for the fabric he was engaged upon, and that he could make about half a yard a day. They were six in family, he said, and he had three looms at work. He got from 20s. to 25s. for the labour of five of them, and that only when they all are employed. But one loom is generally out of work waiting for fresh "cane." Up to 1824, the price for the same work as he is now doing was 6s. The reduction, he was convinced, arose from the competition in the trade, and one master cutting under the other.

"The workmen are obliged to take the low prices, because they have not the means to hold out, and they know that if they don't take the work others will. There are always plenty of weavers unemployed, and the cause of that is owing to the lowness of prices, and the people being compelled to do double the quantity of work that they used to do, in order to live. I have made a stand against the lowness of prices, and have lost my work through refusing to take the price. Circumstances compel us to take it at last. The cupboard gets low, and the landlord comes for his weekly rent. The masters are all trying to undersell one another. They never will advance wages. Go get my neighbour to do it, each says, and then I'll advance. It's been a continuation of reduction for the last six-and-twenty years, and a continuation of suffering for just as long. Never a month passes but what you hear of something being lowered. Manufacturers may be divided into two classes—those who care for their men's comforts and welfare, and those who care for none but themselves. In the work of reduction certain houses take the lead, taking advantage of the least depression to offer the workmen less wages. It's useless talking about French goods. Why, we've driven the French out of the market in umbrellas and parasols—but the people are a-starving while they're a-driving of 'em out. A little time back he'd had only one loom at work for eight persons, and lived by making away with his clothes. Labour is so low he can't afford to send his children to school. He only sends them of a Sunday—can't afford it of a work-a-day."

At the next house the man took rather a more gloomy view of his calling. He was at work at brown silk for umbrellas. His wife worked when she was able, but she was nursing a sick child. He had made the same work he was then engaged upon at 1s. a yard not six months ago. He was to have 10d. for it, and he didn't know that there might not be another penny taken off next time. Weavers were all a-getting poorer, and masters all a-getting country houses. His master had been a-losing terrible, he said, and yet he'd just taken a country mansion. They only give you work just to oblige you, as an act of charity, and not to do themselves any good—oh, no! Works fifteen hours, and often more. When he knocks off at ten at night, leaves lights up all round him—many go on till eleven. All he knows is, he can't! They are possessed of greater strength than he is, he imagines. In the dead of night he can always see one light somewhere—some man "on the finish." Wakes at five, and then he can hear the looms going. Low prices arise entirely from competition among the masters. The umbrella silk he was making would most likely be charged a guinea; what would sixpence extra on that be to the purchaser, and yet that extra sixpence would be three or four shillings per week to him, and go a long way towards the rent? Isn't able to tell exactly what is the cause of the depression—"I only know I suffers from it—aye, that I do! I do! and have severely for some time," said the man, striking the silk before him with his clenched fist. "The man that used to make this here is dead and buried; he died of the cholera. I went to see him buried. He had 11d. for what I get 10d. What it will be next God only knows, and I'm sure I don't care—it can't be much worse."

"Mary," said he, to his wife, as she sat blowing the fire, with the dying infant on her lap, "how much leg of beef do we use?—4lb., ain't it, in the week, and 3lb. of flank on Sunday—lucky to get that, too, eh?—and that's among half a dozen of us. Now, I should like a piece of roast beef, with the potatoes done under it, but I shall never taste that again. And yet," said he, with a savage chuckle, "that there sixpence on this umbrella would just do it. But what's that to people? What's it to them if we starve?—and there is many at that game just now, I can tell you. If we could depend upon a constancy of work, and get a good price, why we should be happy men; but I'm sure I don't know whether I shall get any more work when my 'cane's' out. My children I'm quite disheartened about. They must turn out in the world somewhere, but where Heaven only knows. I often bother myself over that—more than my father bothered himself over me. What's to become of us all? What's to become of us all—nine thousand of us here—besides wives and children—I can't say.". . .

I was anxious to see some case of destitution in the trade, which might be taken as a fair average of the state of the second or third-rate workman. I requested my guide, before I quitted the district, to conduct me to some such individual if it were not too late. He took me towards Shoreditch, and on reaching a narrow back street he stood opposite the three-storied house to see whether there was still a light shining through the long window in the attic. By the flickering shadows the lamp seemed to be dying out. He thought, however, that we might venture to knock. We did so, and in the silent street the noise echoed from house to house. But no one came. We knocked again still louder. A third time, and louder still, we clattered at the door. A voice from the cellar demanded to know whom we wanted. He told us to lift the latch of the street door. We did so—and it opened. The passage looked almost solid in the darkness. My guide groped his way by the wall to the staircase, bidding me follow him. I did so, and reached the stairs. "Keep away from the banisters," said my companion, "as they are rather rotten and might give way." I clung close to the wall, and we groped our way to the second floor, where a light shone through the closed door in a long luminous line. At last

A Spitalfields weaver, by Kenny Meadows

we gained the top room and knocking, were told to enter. "Oh, Billy, is that you," said an old man sitting up, and looking out from between the curtains of a turn-up bedstead. "Here, Tilly," he continued to a girl who was still dressed, "get another lamp, and hang it up again the loom, and give the gentleman a chair." A backless seat was placed at the foot of the old weaver's bedstead; and when the fresh lamp was lighted, I never beheld so strange a scene.

In the room were three large looms. From the head of the old weaver's bed a clothes line ran to a loom opposite, and on it were a few old ragged shirts and petticoats hanging to dry. Under the "porry" of another loom was stretched a second clothes line, and more linen drying. Behind me on the floor was spread a bed, on which lay four boys, two with their heads in one direction and two in another, for the more convenient stowage of the number. They were covered with old sacks and coats. Beside the bed of the old man was a mattress on the ground without any covering, and the tick positively chocolate-coloured with dirt. "Oh, Billy, I am so glad to see you," said the old weaver to my companion; "I've been dreadful bad, nearly dead with the cholera. I was took dreadful about one o'clock in the morning; just the time the good 'ooman down below were taken. What agony I suffered to be sure! I hope to God you may never have it. I've known four hundred die about here in fourteen days. I couldn't work! Oh, no! It took all the use of my strength from me, as if I'd been on a sick bed for months. And how I lived I can't tell. To tell you the real truth, I wanted, such as I never ought to want—why, I wanted for common necessaries. I got round as well as I could; but how I did it I don't know—God knows; I don't, that's true enough. I hadn't got any money to buy anything. Why, there's seven on us here—yes, seven on us—all dependent on the weaving here—nothing else. What was four shilling a yard is paid one and nine now, so I leaves you to judge, sir—an't it Billy? My work stopped for seven days, and I was larning my boy, so his stopped too, and we had nothing to live upon. God knows how we lived. I pawned my things—and shall never get 'em again—to buy some bread, tea, and sugar, for my young ones there. Oh! it's like a famine in these parts just now among the people, now they're getting well. It's no use talking about the parish; you might as well talk to a wall. There was hardly anybody well just round about here, from the back of Shoreditch Church, you may say to Swan-street.

"The prices of weaving is so low, that we're ashamed to say what it is, because it's the means of pulling down other poor men's wages and other trades. Why, to tell you the truth, you must need suppose that 1s. 9d. a yard ain't much, and some of the masters is so cruel, that they gives no more than 1s. 3d.—that's it. But it's the competitive system; that's what the Government ought to put a stop to. I knows persons who makes the same work as mine—scores on 'em—at 1s. 3d. a yard. Wretched is their condition! The people is a being brought to that state of destitution, that many say it's a blessing from the Almighty that takes 'em from the world. They lose all love of country—yes, and all hopes; and they prays to be tortured no longer. Why want is common to a hundred of families close here to-morrow morning; and this it is to have cheap silks. I should like to ask a question here, as I sees you a-writing, sir. When is the people of England to see that there big loaf they was promised—that's it—the people wants to know when they're to have it. I am sure if the ladies who wears what we makes, or the Queen of England was to see our state, she'd never let her subjects suffer such privations in a land of plenty. Yes, I was comfortable in '24. I kept a good little house, and I thought as my young ones growed up—why I thought as I should be comfortable in my old age, and 'stead of that, I've got no wages. I could live by my labour then, but now, why it's wretched in the extreme. Then I'd a nice little garden, and some nice tulips for my hobby, when my work was done. There they lay, up in my old hat now. As for animal food, why it's a stranger to us. Once a week, may be, we gets a taste of it, but that's a hard struggle, and many a family don't have it once a month—a jint we never sees. Oh, it's too bad! There's seven on us here in this room—but it's a very large room to some weavers'—their's a'n't above half the size of this here. The weavers is in general five or six all living and working in the same room. There's four on us here in this bed. One head to foot—one at our back along the bolster; and me and my wife side by side. And there's four on 'em over there. My brother Tom makes up the other one. There's a nice state in a Christian land! How many do you think lives in this house? Why 23 living souls. Oh! a'n't it too bad? But the people is frightened to say how bad they're off, for fear of their masters and losing their work, so they keeps it to themselves—poor creatures. But oh, there's many wuss than me. Many's gone to the docks, and some turned coster-mongers. But none goes a stealing nor a sojering, that I hears on. They goes out to get a loaf of bread—oh, it's a shocking scene!

"I can't say what I thinks about the young uns. Why you loses your nat'ral affection for 'em. The people in general is ashamed to say how they thinks on their children. It's wretched in the extreme to see one's children, and not be able to do to 'em as a parent ought; and I'll say this here after all you've heered me state—that the Government of my native land ought to interpose their powerful arm to put a stop to such things. Unless they do, civil society with us is all at an end. Everybody is becoming brutal—unnatural. Billy, just turn up that shelf now, and let the gentleman see what beautiful fabrics we're in the habit of producing—and then he shall say whether we ought to be in the filthy state we are. Just show the light, Tilly! That's for ladies to wear and adorn them, and make them handsome."

[It was an exquisite piece of moroon coloured velvet, that, amidst all the squalor of the place, seemed marvellously beautiful, and it was a wonder to see it unsoiled amid all the filth that surrounded it]. "I say, just turn it up Billy, and show the gentleman the back. That's cotton partly, you see, sir, just for the manufacturers to cheat the public, and get a cheap article, and have all the gold out of the poor working creatures they can, and don't care nothing about them. But death, Billy—death gets all the gold out of them. They're playing a deep game, but Death wins after all. Oh, when this here's made known, won't the manufacturers be in a way to find the public aware on their tracks. They've lowered the wages so low, that one would hardly believe the people would take the work. But what's one to do?—the children can't *quite* starve. Oh no!—oh no!"

TAILORS AND SEAMSTRESSES

"Slop" Trade in General

From Letter VI, November 6th, 1849

[The "slop" or "dishonourable" part of every trade was the branch which paid wages lower than those agreed to by the Society or Union.]

I had seen so much want since I began my investigation into the condition of the labouring poor of London that my feelings were almost blunted to sights of ordinary misery. Still I was unprepared for the amount of suffering that I have lately witnessed. I could not have believed that there were human beings toiling so long and gaining so little, and starving so silently and heroically, round about our very homes. It is true, one or two instances of the kind had forced themselves into the police reports, and songs and plays had been written upon the privations of the class; still it was impossible to believe that the romance of the song-writer and the fable of the playwright were plain, unvarnished, every-day matters of fact—or, even admitting their stories to be individually true, we could hardly credit them to be universally so. But the reader shall judge for himself. I will endeavour to reproduce the scenes I have lately looked upon—and I will strive to do so in all their stark literality.

It is difficult, I know, for those who are unacquainted with the misery hiding itself in the bye-lanes and alleys of the metropolis to have perfect faith in the tales that it is my duty to tell them. Let me therefore once more assure the sceptical reader, that hardly a line is written here but a note was taken of the matter upon the spot. The descriptions of the dwellings and the individuals I allude to have all been written with the very places and parties before me; and the story of the people's sufferings is repeated to the public in the selfsame words in which they were told to me. Still it may be said that I myself may have been imposed upon—that I may have been taken to extreme cases, and given to understand that they are the ordinary types of the class. This, I am ready to grant, is a common source of error; I will therefore now explain the means that I adopted, in this instance in particular, to prevent myself being deluded into any such fallacy.

My first step was to introduce myself to one of the largest "slopsellers" at the East-end of the town; and having informed the firm that I was about to examine into the condition and incomings of the slop-workers of London, I requested to know whether they would have any objection to furnish me with the list of prices that they were in the habit of paying to their workpeople, so that on my visiting the parties themselves—as I frankly gave them to understand I purposed doing—I might be able to compare the operatives' statements as to prices with theirs, and thus be able to check the one with the other. Indeed, I said I thought it but fair that the employer should have an opportunity of having his say as well as the employed. I regret to say that I was not met with the candour that I had been led to expect. One of the firm wished to know why I singled their house out from the rest of the trade. I told him I did so merely because it was one of the largest in the business, and assured him that, so far from my having any personal object in my visit, I made it a point never to allude by name to any employer or workman to whom I might have occasion to refer. My desire, I said, was to deal with principles rather than persons; whereupon I was informed that the firm would have no objection to acquaint me with the prices paid by *other* houses in the trade. "If you merely wish to arrive at the principle of the slop business, this," said one of the partners, "will be quite sufficient for your purpose." Though I pressed for some more definite and particular information from the firm, I could obtain nothing from them but an assurance that a statement should be written out for me immediately as to the general custom of the trade, and that if I would call at any time after sunset on Saturday evening, it should be at my disposal.

I soon saw that it was useless seeking to obtain any other information from the parties in question—so, taking my departure, I made the best of my way to the workmen in the neighbourhood. . . .

Accordingly I was led, by the gentleman whose advice I had sought, to a narrow court, the entrance to which was blocked up by stalls of fresh herrings. We had to pass sideways between the baskets with our coat-tails under our arms. At the end of the passage we entered a dirty-looking house by a side entrance. Though it was noonday, the staircase was so dark that we were forced to grope our way by the wall up to the first floor. Here, in a small back room, about eight feet square, we found no fewer than seven workmen, with their coats and shoes off, seated cross-legged on the floor, busy stitching the different parts of different garments. The floor was strewn with sleeve-boards, irons, and snips of various coloured cloths. In one corner of the room was a turn-up bedstead, with the washed-out chintz curtains drawn partly in front of it. Across a line which ran from one side of the apartment to the other were thrown the coats, jackets, and cravats of the workmen. Inside the rusty grate was a hat, and on one of the hobs rested a pair of old cloth boots; while leaning against the bars in front there stood a sack full of cuttings. Beside the workmen on the floor sat two good-looking girls—one cross-legged like the men—engaged in tailoring.

My companion having acquainted the workmen with the object of my visit, they one and all expressed themselves ready to answer any questions that I might put to them. They made dress and frock coats, they told me, Chesterfields, fishing coats, paletots, Buller's monkey jackets, beavers, shooting coats, trowsers, vests, sacks, Codringtons, Trinity cloaks and coats, and indeed every other kind of woollen garment. They worked for the ready-made houses, or "slopsellers." "One of us," said they, "gets work from the warehouse, and gives it out to others. The houses pay different prices. Dress coats, from 5s. 6d. to 6s. 9d.; frock coats the same; shooting coats, from 2s. 6d. to 2s. 9d. In summer time, when trade is busy, they pays 3s. Chesterfields, from 2s. 6d., to 3s., some are made for 2s.; paletots, from 2s. 6d. to 3s." "Aye, and two days' work for any man," cried one of the tailors with a withered leg, "and buy his own trimmings, white and black cotton, gimp, and pipeclay."

"Yes," exclaimed another, "and we have to buy wadding for dress coats; and soon, I suppose, we shall have to buy cloth and all together." Trowsers from 1s. 6d. to 3s.; waistcoats, from 1s. 6d. to 1s. 9d. Dress and frock coats will take two days and a half to make each, calculating the day from six in the morning till seven at night; but three days is the regular time. Shooting coats will take two days; Chesterfields take the same time as dress and frock coats; paletots, two days; trowsers, one day.

"The master here" (said one of them scarcely distinguishable from the rest) "gets work from the warehouse at the before-mentioned prices; he gives it out to us at the same price, paying us when he receives the money. We are never seen at the shop. Out of the prices the master here deducts 4s. per week per head for our cup of tea or coffee in the morning, and tea in the evening, and our bed. We sleep two in a bed here, and some of us three. In most places the workmen eat, drink, and sleep in one room; as many as ever the room will contain. They'd put twenty in one room if they could."

"I should like to see the paper this'll be printed in," cried the man with the withered leg. "Oh, it'll be a good job, it should be known. We should be glad if the whole world heard it, so that the people should know our situation. I've worked very hard this week, as hard as any man. I've worked from seven in the morning till eleven at night, and my earnings will be 13s. this week; and deducting my 4s. out of that, and my trimmings besides—the trimmings comes to about 1s. 9d. per week—which makes 5s. 9d. altogether, and that will leave me 7s. 3d. for my earnings all the week, Sunday included. It's very seldom we has a Sunday walking out. We're obliged to work on Sunday all the same. We should lose our shop if we didn't. 8s. is the average wages take the year all through. Out of this 8s. we have to deduct expenses of lodging, trimming, washing, and light, which comes to 5s. 9d. We can't get a coat to our backs."

I inquired as to the earnings of the others. "Well, it's nearly just the same, take one with another, all the year round. We work all about the same hours—all the lot of us. The wages are lower than they were this time twelvemonth, in 1848— that they are, by far, and heavier work too. I think there's a fall of 6d. in each job at the lowest calculation."

"Ah, that there is," said another; "a 3s. job we don't have 2s. 6d. for now.". . .

During my stay in this quarter an incident occurred, which may be cited as illustrative of the poverty of the class of slop-workers. The friend who had conducted me to the spot, and who knew the workmen well, had long been striving to induce one of the men—a Dutchman—to marry one of the females working with him in the room, and with whom he had been living for many months. That the man might raise no objection on the score of poverty, my friend requested me to bear with him half the expense of publishing the banns. To this I readily consented, but the man still urged that he was unable to wed the girl just yet. On inquiring the reason we were taken outside the door by the Dutchman, and there told that he had been forced to pawn his coat for 6s., and as yet he had saved only half the amount towards the redemption of it. It would take him upwards of a month to lay by the remainder. This was literally the fact, and the poor fellow said, with a shrug of his shoulders, he could not go to be marrried in his shirt sleeves. He was told to make himself easy about the wedding garment, and our kind-hearted friend left delighted with the day's work.

A scene in front of a "cutting" tailor's shop in Whitechapel

I now wished to learn from some of the female operatives what prices they were paid, and requested my friend to introduce me to some workwoman who might be considered as one of the most provident, industrious, and best-conducted in the trade. The woman bears, I understand, an excellent character, and she gave the following melancholy account of her calling. . . .

"Upon the average," she says, "at all kinds of work, excepting the shirts, that I make, I cannot earn more than 4s. 6d. to 5s. a week—let me sit from eight in the morning till ten every night; and out of that I shall have to pay 1s. 6d. for trimmings, and 6d. candles every week; so that altogether I earn about 3s. in the six days. But I don't earn that, for there's the firing that you *must* have to press the work, and that will be 9d. a week, for you'll have to use half a hundred weight of coals. So that my clear earnings are a little bit more than 2s., say 2s. 3d. to 2s. 6d. every week. I consider the trowsers the best work. At the highest price, which is 10s. a dozen, I should make no more than eight of them in a week; that would give me 6s. 8d. The trimmings of that eight pair would cost me 1s., the candle 6d., and the coals 9d., for pressing, leaving 4s. 5d. clear—and that is the very best kind of work that can be got in the slop trade. Shirt work is the worst work, the very worst, that can be got. You cannot make more of those at 6s. a dozen than one a day, yielding 3s. a week. The trimming would be about 3d. for the shirts, and the candle 6d., as before, making 9d. to be deducted, and so leaving 2s. 3d. per week clear. I have known the prices much better when I first began to work at the business, some nineteen years ago. The shirts that they now give 6d. for were then 1s.; and those now at 2d., were 8d. The trowsers were 1s. 4d. and 1s. 6d. a pair, the best—now they give only 10d. for the best. The other articles are down equally low.

"I cannot say," she added, "what the cause may be. I think there are so many to work at it that one will underwork the other. I have seen it so at the shop. The sweaters screw the people down as low as they possibly can, and the masters hear how little they can get their work done for, and cut down the sweaters, and so the workpeople have to suffer again. Every shop has a great number of sweaters. Sometimes the sweaters will get as much as 2d. or 3d.; indeed, I've known 'em take as much as 4d. out of each garment. I should suppose one that has a good many people to work for her—say about a dozen—I suppose that she'll clear from £1 to £1 5s. per week out of their labour. The workpeople are very dissatisfied and very poor indeed—yes, *very* poor. There is a great deal of want and there is a great deal of suffering amongst them. I hear it at the shop when I go in with my work. They have generally been brought up regularly to the trade. It requires an apprenticeship. In about three months a person may learn it, if they're quick; and persons pay from 10s. to £1 to be taught it, bad as the trade is. A mother has got two or three daughters, and she don't wish them to go to service, and she puts them to this poor needlework; and that, in my opinion, is the cause of the destitution and the prostitution about the streets in these parts. So that in a great measure I think the slop trade is the ruin of the young girls that take to it—the prices are not sufficient to keep them, and the consequence is, they fly to the streets to make out their living. Most of the workers are young girls who have nothing else to depend upon, and there is scarcely one of them virtuous. When they come on first they are very meek and modest in their deportment, but after a little time they get connected with the others and led away.

There are between 200 and 300 of one class and another work at my shop. I dare say of females altogether there are upwards of 200. Yesterday morning there were seventy-five in the shop with me, and that was at eight in the morning, and what there may be throughout the day it's impossible to form an idea. The age of the females in general is about fourteen to twenty.

"My daughter is a most excellent waistcoat hand. I can give you an account of her work, and then, of course, you can form an idea of what everybody else gets. The lowest price waistcoat is 3s. per dozen, and the highest 9s. They are satin ones. She can make one satin one per day, and three of the 3s. ones. She earns, upon an average about 4s. per week; deduct from this, trimmings about 6d. for the lowest, and 1s. per week for the highest price. As we both sit to work together, one candle does for the two of us, so that she earns about 3s. per week clear, which is not sufficient to keep her even in food. My husband is a seafaring man, or I don't know what I should do. He is a particularly steady man, a teetotaller, and so indeed are the whole family, or else we could not live. Recently my daughter has resigned the work and gone to service, as the prices are not sufficient for food and clothing. I never knew a rise, but continual reductions. I know a woman who has six children, and she has to support them wholly on slop work. Her husband drinks, and does a day's work only now and then, spending more than he brings home. None of her children are able to work. I don't know how on earth she lives, or her little ones either. Poor creature, she looked the picture of distress and poverty when I last saw her.". . .

The next party I visited was one who worked at waistcoats, and here I found the keenest misery of all. The house was unlike any that I had seen in the same trade; all was scrupulously clean and neat. The old brass fender was as bright as gold, and worn with continued rubbing. The grate, in which there was barely a handful of coals, had been newly black-leaded, and there was not a cinder littering the hearth. Indeed, everything in the place evinced the greatest order and cleanliness. Nor was the suffering self-evident. On the contrary, a stranger, at first sight, would have believed the occupant to have been rather well-to-do in the world. A few minutes' conversation with the poor creature, however, soon told you that the neatness was partly the effect of habits acquired in domestic service, and partly the result of a struggle to hide her extreme poverty from the world.

Her story was the most pathetic of all I had yet heard: "I work for a slop-house—waistcoat work." She said—"I don't make sleeve waistcoats, but body waistcoats, and the lowest price I get is 4d.; I have had 'em as high as 1s. 3d. I take the run, such as they have got to give me—sometimes one thing and sometimes another in the waistcoat way. Some have better work than others, but my eyesight won't admit of my doing the best work. Some waistcoats are as much as 1s. 9d., some 2s. I have worked twenty-six years at the same warehouse. The general price for the waistcoats I have now is 6d., 8d., and 10d. I can make one a-day sometimes, and sometimes three in two days, just as it happens, for my health is very bad. Sometimes I don't earn more than 2s. 6d. a week, and sometimes I have earned 3s. 6d. and 4s. That's the most I have earned for this several years. I must work very close from about nine in the morning to eleven at night, to earn that.

"Prices have come down very much indeed since I first worked for the warehouse—*very much*. The prices when I was first employed there were as much as 1s. 9d. for what I get now 1s. 1d. for. Every week they have reduced something within these

A tailor at work

last few years. Work's falling very much. The work has not riz, no! never since I worked at it. It's lower'd but it's not riz. The masters seem to say that the work is lowered to them—that they can't afford to pay a better price, or else they would. The parties for whom I work lay it to the large slop houses. They say it's through them that the work has lowered so. I find it very difficult to get sufficient to nourish me out of my work. I can't have what I ought to have. I think my illness at present is from over-exertion. I want more air than I can get. I am wholly dependent on myself for my living, and never made more than 4s. a week. Several times I have had my work thrown back upon my hands, and that has perhaps made me ill, so that I've not been able to do anything. I am obliged to work long and always— sick or well—I must do it for my living to make any appearance at all. My sight is very bad now from over-work, and perhaps other difficulties as well—I suffer so bad with my head. My greatest earnings are 4s. per week, my lowest 2s. 6d., and I generally average about 3s. Many weeks I have been wholly without working— not able to do it. Young people that have got good health and good work might, perhaps, earn more than I do; but at the common work I should think they can't make more than I can.

"I never was married. I went out to service when I was younger, and to waistcoating after quitting service; so that I might be at home with mother and father and take care of them in their old age. I rent the house. It's where I buried mother and father from; and as such, I've kept it on since they've been dead. I let the two rooms, but I don't gain anything by it. I stand at about tenpence a week rent when I live in the top room and let the others; but sometimes it's empty, and I lose by it. Some time ago, too, a party ran away, and left £3 10s. in my debt. That nearly ruined me. I've not got the better of it yet. I've been very short—very short indeed, sir; in want of common necessaries to keep my strength and life together. I don't find what I get by my labour sufficient to keep me. I've no money anywhere, not a farthing in the house; yes, I tell a story, I've got a penny. If I were to be taken ill I don't know what I should do. But I should be obliged to do as I've often done before. The Almighty is my only support. For my old age there is nothing but the workhouse. After six-and-twenty years hard work I've not a penny to the fore— nothing to depend upon for an hour. If I could have saved, I should have been very glad to have done so. Take one week with another, I have earned 3s., and that has been barely sufficient to keep me. I've sold several things to make up, when I've come short. The things here belonged to father and mother. I've sold a great many that they left me. Many people who follow the same business I think are worse off, if anything, than I am; because I've got a home, and I strive to keep it together, and they've not."

It seemed difficult to believe that there could be found women suffering more keenly than this poor creature; and yet the gentleman who had kindly undertaken to introduce me to the better class of workpeople in the trade, led me to a young woman, almost lady-like in her appearance and manners, from whom I gathered the following pitiable tale:

She works at waistcoat business; at the best kind of work. Gets 10d. each waistcoat, sometimes 8d., and sometimes 6d. (some she has heard of being as low as 2½d.). There are shilling ones, but there's a great deal of work in them. Black satin waistcoats are 10d., stitched all round; and out of the 10d. trimmings are to be found. The trimmings for each waistcoat cost 1d., sometimes 1½d., and occasionally 2d.

"Those I am making now at 10d.," she said, "have a quantity of work in them. They would take me the whole day, even if I was well enough to sit so long at 'em. Besides this, there's half a day lost each time you take your work in. And sometimes every other day—and often every day—they'll drag you up to the warehouse for the little bit of work. They give out four at a time mostly. We have to give housekeeper's security for £5 before we can get work. Some weeks I don't do more than four. Some weeks I don't do that. Last week I had a hard matter to do four, but then I wasn't well. When I was apprentice we used to have 5s. for making the very same as those that I now get 10d. for. At 2s. a piece one might live, but as it is now, *I am starving*; if it wasn't for my friends helping me a little, I don't know what would become of me, I'm sure.

Frequently the work is returned upon our hands, and recently I have had 9s. to pay out of my earnings for some waistcoats that were sent back to me because they were kept out too long. They were kept out longer than they should have been, because I was ill; I wasn't able to make them. I sat up in my bed, ill as I was, and basted them myself, and then a girl that I got did what she could to them, and I finished them; but owing to the delay the foreman grew spiteful and returned them on my hands. I have been suffering for this ever since, and I couldn't subsist upon what I get now, were it not for some kind friends. I've got a spirit, and wouldn't like to be under an obligation, but I am forced to live as I do. While I was ill my rent went back, and I've left part of my things where I was living before I came here, because I couldn't pay up what I owed for my lodging. There is my doctor's bill to be paid—for I hav'nt paid it yet, and I have been obliged to get rid of the waistcoats that were returned to me; I sold them for a trifle, as I could, with the exception of one that I've pledged. I got 1s. upon that, and I sold the others at 1s. 6d. each, though they charged me at the shop 3s. 3d. a piece for them. I was glad to get rid of them anyhow, just then.

"The waistcoats that they pay a shilling for to have made are like jackets—they have sleeves and flaps to pockets like coats. I don't know what they are like. It would take any one two days to make them. It takes me two days. My average earnings are from 3s. to 4s. a week, and out of that I have to pay 2s. for the waistcoats returned on my hands, and about 6d. for trimmings, per week, leaving me about 1s. 6d. to live upon. Some persons say they can earn at waistcoating 14s. to 15s. per week, and they tell the master so; but then they have people to help them—girls who probably pay them something to learn the business, or who are very young, and have about 1s. per week for doing the inferior parts.

"I don't know why the prices are so low. I have found prices continually going down since I came from the west end of the town. I never knew an advance. If they took off 2d. or 1d. I never heard of their putting it on again. The prices have fallen more within the last two or three years—much more than ever they did before. I don't think they can get very much lower. If they do, persons *must* starve. It is almost as bad as the workhouse now. I was apprenticed to the waistcoating at the west-end, and was paid a little different then. I could earn 15s. a week at that time. The business has materially injured my health; yes, that it has. My eyesight and health have both suffered from it. It has produced general debility; the doctor says it's sitting so long in the house. Sometimes all night I used to sit up to work. I've known many people that have had strong constitutions, and after they've worked at it many years they've gone like I have. There are persons who get even lower prices than I do—Oh, yes, sir, a great deal lower; some I know get threepence, and even fourpence for a waistcoat."...

On my way home from these saddening scenes, I called at the wholesale slop warehouse, for the promised statement as to the prices paid by the generality of the trade. After waiting a considerable time, at length one of the principals and foreman came to communicate to me the desired information.

The usual sum earned by a person working at the slop trade is, they told me, *three pence per hour ! !*

Women working at moleskin trowsers, they said, would earn, upon an average, 1s. 10d. every day of ten hours' labour.

At waistcoats females would earn generally at the rate of 2s. per day of ten hours' labour.

The foreman and the principal then wished to know in what state I had found the workpeople generally. I told them I had never seen or heard of such destitution. "Destitution!" was the exclamation. "God bless my soul, you surprise me." "And I think it but right, gentlemen," I added, "to apprise you that your statement as to prices differs most materially from that of the workpeople;" and so saying, I took my departure.

Uniform Makers

From Letter VII, November 9th, 1849

From the slop-workers of the eastern parts of London I now come to consider the condition of the male and female operatives employed in making the clothes of the army, navy, police, railway, customs, and post-office servants, convicts, and such other articles of wearing apparel as are made either by contract or in large quantities. Small as are the earnings of those who depend for their living upon the manufacture of the ready-made clothes for the wholesale warehouses of the Minories and the adjoining places, still the incomings of those who manufacture the clothes of our soldiers and sailors, Government, railway-police, and custom-house officers, are even less calculated to support life. I thought the force of misery could no further go than with the waistcoat and shirt hands that I had visited last week. And yet, since then, I have seen people so overwhelmed in suffering, and so used to privations of the keenest kind, that they had almost forgotten to complain of them. . . .

Again, I wish the reader to understand that the following are the ordinary cases of the trade; they have most assuredly, *not* been selected for the purpose.

The first person whom I visited was a male hand, and on entering his house I certainly found more comforts about it than I had been led to expect. He lived in a back room built over a yard. It was nicely carpetted, and on one side, to my astonishment, stood a grand piano. There were several pictures hanging against the walls, and a glass full of dahlias on the mantelpiece. I could tell, however, by the "wells" beneath the two large sofas that they were occasionally used as bedsteads, and the easy-chair in which I was requested to take a seat was of so extravagant a size that it was evident it was occasionally put to the same purpose. I had been given to understand that the man was in the habit of taking lodgers, and this in a measure accounted for the double duty assigned to the different articles of furniture in the room.

"I make the soldiers' trowsers, the Foot Guards principally," said the man in answer to my questions, "get 6d. a pair, and have to find thread. The thread costs, I should say myself, at the rate I buy it, about $\frac{3}{4}$d. for a pair of trowsers. Many have to pay more, because if they can't get a quarter of a pound they have to give a greater price for a single ounce. At that rate it will take a full pennyworth to make a pair. This is the usual way in which the workpeople buy their thread, because they cannot afford to get a larger quantity at a time. The trowsers, therefore, average about 5d. each. Of course a fire must be kept for pressing the trowsers, and the expense of this has again to be deducted from the price paid. I can make a pair in five hours, but there isn't one in a hundred can do this, and it will take a middling worker eight hours to finish one pair. But then I put the seams out, and if I did them

49

at home it would take me six hours to do all myself. Without the seams I can do three pair a day. In summer I can do four, working very hard, and not being taken off for anything. I cannot get work always. Now I'm sitting still—have had nothing to do this five weeks of any consequence.

"At the best of times, when work is very brisk, and in the summer time too, I never earn more than 8s. a week. This is the money I have for my work, and from this there is to be deducted thread for the sixteen pair, and cotton for the felling of the same, and this comes to about 16d., and the cost of fire may, with the wood and altogether, be taken at 1s. Over and above all this, I have to pay 1d. per pair for the stitching of the seams, and 9d. a week for a woman to fetch and take my work to and from the warehouse. So that altogether there is 4s. 5d. to be deducted from the 8s., and so leaving only 3s. 9d. as my earnings per week at the very best of times. For weeks and weeks I don't get anything. The work isn't to be had. The year before last I was standing still full twenty weeks—couldn't get work at all at no warehouse. Last year I had full eight weeks and nothing to do all the time; and this year I have been unemployed a full month at least. During the last five weeks I have only had fifteen pair to make. It is now sealing time—that is the period when the different estimates are given in—and we are always slack then. I never keep any account of my earnings. All I know is, when the money comes in it's as much as I can do to pay my way. Taking one week with another, I'm sure I do not average, throughout the year, more than 5s. a week at the very outside; and out of this there is a full half to be paid for expenses. There's the thread and the firing and the candles, all to be paid for. (The seams I do not put out when I'm slack.) All this would come to a good half-crown, so that my clear earnings, taking one week with another, throughout the year, are 2s. 6d. per week.

"If you were to ask me what I *could* make, quick as I am, and putting my seams out—if I was full employed—I should say 12s. a week, including Sundays; and I am obliged to work more of Sundays than any other day. I scarce ever have a Sunday to myself, for Saturday is giving-out day, and they want them in on Monday morning. Monday's taking-in day (indeed, every other day is a giving-out day, and the day following a taking-in one). If we didn't take them in on Monday morning as directed, there would be no more work for us. If I was not to work on Sundays, I could get 10s. full work. But from this I should have to pay a penny per pair for the seams, and this would cost 2s. for the twenty-four I must make in the week to earn 12s.; and 1s. 8d. for the twenty pair I must make to get 10s.; and the thread and cotton would be another penny per pair—that is, as much as the seams. Then there's the coals, and wood, and candles: these would come to 16d. or 18d. at least. This altogether would amount to 5s. 4d. to 5s. 6d. to be deducted from the 12s. per week, and 4s. 6d. or 4s. 8d. from the 10s. a week. So that if I was full of work, and kept at it from six in the morning till ten at night, and carried on all Sunday as well, I couldn't possibly earn more than 5s. 6d. to 5s. 8d. per week clear—leaving out Sundays, I might get 5s. 6d. to 5s. 8d. per week. This is the most that can be made in the trade. If you were to ask many workmen, they would say it is impossible to get as much done; but I'm one of the quickest hands at the business. The ordinary hands cannot make more than one pair of trowsers in one day, which, deducting expenses, would leave 5d., to say nothing of candles, for 14 hours' labour. But even at this rate they could not earn, with their seven days, 2s. 11d., for they would lose at least in fetching the work and taking it home, which would bring their earnings to 2s. 7d. or 2s. 6d. a week, at the very outside. But this only at the briskest time; and we are generally upon an average about two months unemployed. One year we were twenty weeks without work.

"White trowsers we don't have so much for—only 5d. a pair for them—and they take quite as much thread; and without you've a good fire you cannot work at them at all in the winter, they're so cold in the hand. If the prices were to be raised, the poor would have no work at all, for then the tailors would take them. I have never had more than 6d. for the Foot Guards. For the artillery, the gunners, I have had as much as 8d.—some are 7d.; but I would sooner make the foot guards at 6d., than the artillery at the higher prices, because there is so much more work in them. At those at 6d. there has been a double cord put in within the last few years, and that has made it a great deal more trouble. You have to take two stitches where you used only to take only one; but the price never was raised.

"Never knew the price to be raised since I worked at it, and that's seven years ago. I get them from a person who gets them from the warehouse. These intermediate persons are called piece-masters, and they get a penny profit upon each garment, whether it be trowsers, coats, or great coats, and the prices I have stated are those the piece-master pays to me. They won't give them to such little hands as me. They give out a great quantity at a time, and must have them all in at a particular day— very often the next taking-in day. I fancy at one time they used to keep a stock by them; but of late years there have been so many alterations that they're afraid to do it. The piece-masters have to give security—£50 I think it is—very often; and the single hands, before they can be taken on, must be recommended to the piece-master. Notwithstanding this, a great many of the garments have been pledged. At one time the pawnbrokers used to take them in before they was made up, but now I don't think they will. The ones with the red stripes I am certain they won't. I have got my security down at the warehouse, but it takes so much time taking and fetching, and waiting while examined, that I prefer to work for a piece-master rather than the warehouseman. If they're not properly done, the foreman will cut the seam right up, and send them back, and there'll be no money till they're finished. The foremen, generally, have no feeling about the poor—that's true. I'm sure they haven't. If the workpeople can treat them with what they like, and that's liquor, they'll pass the things quicker.

"The low prices I believe to arise from the very low prices the contracts are taken at. Well, sir, look here, the soldiers, I hear, give 8s. a pair for what we get 6d. for the making of. The cloth cannot cost them more than half-a-crown. If I was to get it, I could have it for that; but they must get it considerably less from taking large quantities, which their money empowers them to do. The trimmings, including buttons and pockets, would cost about 6d., and the red stripes 3d. more, so that 6d. making, 9d. trimming and stripes, and cloth 2s. 6d., altogether 3s. 9d., and the other 4s. 3d. is profit. The piece-master, out of this, gets 2d. a pair; this is their gains for taking them in and running the risk of the people stealing the materials. The remaining 4s. 1d. is the profit of the warehouseman and the other parties connected with the trade, so that I'm sure if Government would take it into their hands, and give the clothes out themselves, the poor workpeople might have prices that would keep them from starving. If they was only so that with hard labour they could get double what they now earn, a person might live. Besides, they work, poor things, with so much more spirit. Now, it's dreadful to hear them, so it is, sir.

Many of them would sooner sit still and starve. It's useless working—it is—they cannot live by it, let them work till they drop—yes, indeed, they must. To get 4s. a week clear by my business the women must slave both night and day; but really the prices are so bad they won't even pay to have a candle to work by, so that to work at night is only to lose one's time and money. We had better go to bed and starve at once, and that's what most all are doing who are at this kind of work. The general class of people who work at it are old persons who have seen better days, and have nothing left but their needle to keep them, and who *won't* apply for relief—their pride won't let them—their feelings objects to it—they have a dread of becoming troublesome. The other parties are wives of labourers and those who leave off shirt making to come to this. There are many widows with young children, and they give them the seams to do, and so manage to prolong life, because they're afeard to die, and too honest to steal. The pressing part, which is half the work, is not fit for any female to do. I don't know but very few young girls—they're most of them women with families as I've seen—poor, struggling widows a many of 'em."

If, as you say, your clear earnings throughout the year, taking one week with another, are only 2s. 6d. a week, how do you manage to support life upon that sum?—"I couldn't do it—oh, dear no; I couldn't have held till now, nor even one month upon it. But the fact is, I let a part of my place to young men at 2s. a week, and for that I find them bed, candles, soap, towels, sheets, and the use of the sitting room and the fire, and that's my dependence. But one thing I must tell you, I can't go on with that much longer unless things alter, because I can't get my sheets out of pledge to change them, and my feather-bed I've been obliged to pawn.

"I'll tell you, sir, I was a draper's assistant formerly; lived in the first situations in London, Bath, and other places; but, of course, their salaries are small, and one is obliged to dress well on it. Well, I got a situation in the country, so that I might save something, which I could not do in town. I remained in my country situation nearly two years, and saved close upon £50 in that time. This I allowed to remain in my master's hands, thinking it would be safe, so that I might not spend it. He broke, and I lost my whole. There was not money enough to pay the law expenses, or of course I should have had my money first as a servant. Then I came back to London, I tried to get a situation, and found, as I was getting advanced in years, they preferred young men. Well, I couldn't starve, but I knew nothing that I could get a living at but as a draper's assistant, and that I couldn't get on account of my age. I can't tell you the distress of mind I was in of course, for I was very anxious lest in my old age I should be left to want. We don't think of old age when we're young, I'm sorry to say.

"Where I was lodging then, a woman made soldiers' trowsers, and as my hands were lissome, and I had occasion to use the needle frequently in the drapery trade, to tack the tickets on cloth and such like, why I thought I might get a crust by them. It was only living that I tried for, unless I'd tailor. I couldn't have done this, if it hadn't been from being accustomed to the needle. Well, I tried; and the man I did a few for was very pleased with 'em, and gave me some more. They was 3½d. a pair convicts' trousers. I soon found that, at that price, I couldn't stop in the lodgings I had and pay my way. I was paying 2s. 6d. a week. So I takes a cellar at 1s. 6d., buys a little bit of canvass, and some straw; sleeps on the floor, had a chair and table—that was all. Then the man I had done the trowsers for took me to the City, and got me some better work. He said I could do finer things. Then the warehouse gave me as many as fifty pair of artillery trowsers to make. Then I found I was living too far from my work; so I sells off my things for 4s. 6d., comes to Holborn; there was two rooms to let at 3s. 6d., and I thought I could take a lodger at 2s.; a relation of mine promised kindly to lend me the beds, which they did, and I've paid for 'em, little by little, since then. After this I scraped together somehow or other—how I did it I don't know, but it come from God's goodness, I suppose—I got enough to buy another bed, and take another lodger at the same price. The only thing that we can make a little money of is beds; but at that you lose a good deal, as well as get. And so I went, and I am where I am now.

"I've four lodgers at present, but two of those I get nothing from, as they're out of situations, and they owe me a goodish sum now; but may be I shall have it all, or a good part, when they gets into work again. My two other lodgers pay me very well indeed; they bring me in my 4s. a week, and that pays my rent; and thank God I only owe one week. But if the work don't come in, I don't know what I shall do. A little while ago I had two brothers with me ill, during the time of the cholera. I tried all I could to get them into the hospitals, but they was ill three weeks before I could. During that time I had to provide them with everything. One was obliged to have two clean shirts a day, and I was forced to pledge my feather-bed, and sheets, and blankets, to keep them. I couldn't see them lost, and let them starve under my own roof. I got them at last out of the hospital, and they've gone into the country, and I've never even heard of them. They owe me altogether, for washing, living, lodging, and food, £2 13s. 9d. I think they're honest young men, and would pay me if they could. May be they're ashamed to write to me—yes, I dare say they are, for they were good young men—though I never had their money, I'll say that of them. They was gentlemen's servants, and can't do much now. All this I shouldn't mind so much about if it wasn't for my bedding. I could get round if it wasn't for that. If I can't get my bedding back I must lose my lodgers. Their sheets has been on now nearly three months, and I'm sure they can't stand it much longer, that they won't. To my own bed I've none at all. As for myself, I ain't had a clean shirt for this month. I really can't afford to pay for the washing. I've never been able to get any new clothes since I've been at the trade. Fourpence I gave for the very coat I've got on from a gentleman's servant, and the other things has been gave to me by asking, which is very painful.

"The greater part of the things you see about here don't belong to me. This piano, now, belonged to a young man a lodger of mine. His father was a musician. The young man bought it for £3 15s. He got married, and wanted a chest of drawers for his wife (oh, good gracious, if he was to hear of this he'd kill me.) Well, I passed my word for the drawers, and he left this piano with me as security. That cat you see there now you'll say I have no business to have, if I'm so poor. She costs me $3\frac{1}{2}$d. a week, as much as half a quartern, and I grudge it, but a poor maiden lady, who's starving, brought her to me, and begged me, with almost tears in her eyes, to take care of it for her, for she couldn't afford to give it a meal—she hadn't one for herself. She's a teacher of music, and I'm sure she's dying for want of food. She's just out of the hospital, and, oh, dear, much too proud to go into the house—I wouldn't even say such a thing to her, it would break her heart. I know she's never had anything but tea—tea, tea, for months. She's a relation of the Pitt family, and the composer of several pieces of sacred music, but the plates are in pawn for 4s., and she can't even do anything with that. She's lost all her teaching, and is now in want of even the commonest food. I think the poor are not in such distress as persons in her circumstances of life. If she's ashamed to apply to the parish, you may depend she's ashamed to let any one else know how badly she's off.

"The only extravagance I have that I know of is my bird, and he costs me a farthing a week. Poor dickey! I shouldn't like to part with him. It's the only company I have. The cat I'm not very fond of. As for meat, I haven't had a taste of it for the last month."

The statement of the man was of so extraordinary a nature, that, on leaving the house, I took the trouble to inquire into his character. His landlord informed me that he was one of the most worthy, benevolent, and eccentric men that he had ever known. He was punctual in the payments of his rent, and, indeed, a most sober, industrious, and exemplary person. The duplicates of the bedding the man himself showed me, and the person who directed me to his house spoke even more highly of him than did his landlord.

I was now desirous to see a piece-master, in order that I might find out whether they really did make the amount of money that they were believed to do out of the workpeoples' labour, and found the family in the lowest state of destitution. The party lived in a back-kitchen in a house over Waterloo-bridge. It was mid-day when I got there, and the woman and her boy were dining off potatoes and some "rind" of bacon that her daughter, who was "in place," had given to her rather than it should be thrown away.

"Poor people," said she, "you know is glad to get anything." Then, observing me noticing the crockery, which was arranged on a shelf in one corner, she added—

"Ah, sir, you needn't look at my crockery ware—I'll show it to you," she said, taking down several basins and jugs. They were all broken on one side, but turned the best side outwards. "There isn't a whole vessel in the place; only nobody would know but they were sound, you see, to look at 'em. I get some of the army work— some of the common trowsers. I has a penny a pair out of them—that's the only way of living I have, sir. I get a meal of victuals now and then from my landlady. I'm a piece-mistress. I get the work out of warehouse, and give it to the workpeople. I has a penny a pair out of them. I has twopence out of some—they are the sergeants. Perhaps I'd get 40 pair out in a week, perhaps 30 pair, and may be 10— when they has them I get them. Before my husband died I've had 100 pair out in a week. God bless thee, man, many people has more—they has them out by wholesale, these large hands. I've had none this fortnight and more—only one ten pair. Some one of them takes them away in cart-loads. The piece-makers have such bundles of hands they can get a good lot done. Oh, Lord, we never had £2 a week by it, nor £1 either. The pay's very bad, sir. The most my husband ever had one week by it was about £1. He had work out of four warehouses.

"Those that has plenty of work, and gets the best, will make more by it—a good deal more. Where the piece-master draws £18 to £20 a week they must have a good profit out of that, and some of them draws more; but it's not all their own; they has their workpeople to pay out of that. So that the piece-master might draw

£3 to £4 a week at the very best time—that's when the police-clothing is out. They gets more out of that than anything else; there isn't much by these pensioners at all. They get 1d. upon a pair of trowsers, some 2d., but that's for the police trowsers, the dress ones. Upon the police coats they get 2d. some, and some 4d. out of the price, but now I believe it's only 2d. out of them. What they gets out of the soldiers' jackets I'm sure I can't say. We never had none of them. Out of the tide-waiters' coats we ought to have 6d.; the warehouse paid 7s. 6d. for them. Out of the trowsers we used to have 2d.; the price the warehouse paid was 1s. The waistcoat price was 10d. from the warehouse; we had nothing out of that. He used to have 8s. 6d. for the suit, and he used to pay 7s. 6d. for it; so he got 1s. out of them. Used to get nothing else. Used to have the pensioners' sometimes. Paid 1s. 9d., and we had 3d. out of them.

"At the time my husband lived we did pretty well. Was never out of work. If we hadn't it from one warehouse we had it from the others we worked for. He has been three years buried next Easter Sunday, and there's many a night since I've went to bed without my supper, myself and my children. Since then I've had nothing, only just a few odd trowsers now and then. I had to go into the workhouse last winter, myself and my children; I couldn't get a meal of victuals for them, and this winter I suppose I shall have to go into it again. If I haven't work I can't pay my rent. Three weeks ago I had only twenty pair to make, that's 1s. 8d. for myself and boy to live upon (my other's out in the Marine School), and my rent out of that is 1s. 6d. My boy gets 1s. 6d. a-week besides this, and only for that I couldn't live at all. And that's drawed before it's earned. I'm obliged to go on credit for my things and pay with my boy's money, and glad to have it to pay. I call it a good week if I get 40 pair of trowsers to give out. That is 3s. 4d. to me, and upon that me and my boy must both live; and there was my other boy to do the same too when I had him.

"I occasionally get a bit of broken victuals from those that know me round about. I little thought I should be so miserable as I am. That fender is not mine, I borrowed it of my landlady; nor that saucepan neither; I got it to boil my potatoes in. Indeed you may say I very often want. We should be starved entirely if it was not for my landlady, and that's the blessed truth. I belongs to Lambeth parish, and they don't even give me a ha'p'orth out of it, not even a loaf of bread. It's often we're a day and two nights without food, me and my boys together. I never did treat a foreman with rum to get any work, nor did the man ever want it from me. I'll give every one his due. He has come to see himself, and his wife, and lent me 2s.—I shall not belie any one—and often gave me a few pence when I came into the warehouse. It is not generally believed by us that the foremen are obliged to be treated in order to get the work. I never heard of such a thing, and I'm sure I never did it. The reason why I've had so little lately is because I can't get it so well done as the others. The workpeople won't do as I tell 'em. Some makes them well, and more don't.

"My husband's security is at the warehouses yet. I can't tell you how much they're for, 'cause I never seed them. He was an honest, upright man. They often trusted him as much as £100. The workpeople misses him now, but nobody misses him so much as I do. Then I could go clean and respectable, but now I don't know where to turn my head for a meal of victuals this blessed night. The workpeople I never find making away with the work. I've lost nothing by them ever since my husband died. I didn't lose a garment since, thank God. My husband used to take a security from the workpeople from their landlord, but I don't. Can't say whether the piece-masters lose much by the workpeople. If they do, they has to pay for it. I didn't hear only of one pair of trowsers being lost. My husband lost two jackets, and I had to pay so much a week for them, until they were cleared, after he died. If I'd got all the world, I haven't got a farthing of money, neither gold, silver, nor brass, nor a mouthful of victuals for myself or my boy for to-night but what's there in the plate (alluding to the remainder of the rind of bacon). I had only a penny-worth of potatoes, and that I shouldn't have had only the woman who gave me the rind gave me a penny to get some with (showing empty saucepan)."...

As I had been informed that the convict work was the worst paid of all labour, I was anxious to obtain an interview with one who got her living by it. She lived in a small back room on the first floor. I knocked at the door, but no one answered, though I had been told the woman was within. I knocked again and again, and, hearing no one stirring, I looked through the keyhole, and observed that the key was inside the door. Fearing that some accident might have happened to the poor old soul, I knocked once more, louder than ever. At last the door was opened, and a thin aged woman stood trembling nervously as she looked at me. She stammered out with a gasp, "Oh! I beg pardon, but I thought it was the woman come for the shilling I owed her." I told her my errand, and she welcomed me in. There was no table in the room; but on a chair without a back there was an old tin tray, in which stood a cup of hot, milkless tea, and a broken saucer, with some half dozen small potatoes in it. It was the poor soul's dinner. Some tea-leaves had been given her, and she had boiled them up again to make something like a meal. She had not even a morsel of bread. In one corner of the room was a hay mattress, rolled up. With this she slept on the floor. She said,

"I work at convict work, 'the greys;' some are half yellow and half brown, but they're all paid the same price. I makes the whole suit. Gets 7¾d. for all of it—3d. the jacket, 3d. the trowsers, and 1¼d. the waistcoat, and finds my own thread out of that; they're all made with double 'whitey-brown.' I never reckoned it up, but I uses a good bit of thread when I'm a making of 'em. Sometimes I gets an ounce, sometimes half an ounce. It takes about an ounce and a half to the suit, and that would be 3d. at 2d. an ounce, and then they'll have them well pressed, which takes a good bit for firing. Yes, it does indeed. I am obliged to have a penny candle—a cheaper one I couldn't see with. It'll take me more than a day to make the suit. If I had the suit out now I could get them in to-morrow evening. There's full a day and a half's work in a suit. I works from nine in the morning till eleven at night."

Here a sharp-featured woman entered, and said she wished to speak with the "convict worker" when she was alone. "She came," said the poor old thing when the woman had left, "because I owes her a shilling. I'm sure she can't have it, for I haven't got it. I borrowed it last week of her."

"In a day and a half," she continued, with a deep sigh, "deducting the cost of thread and candles for the suit (to say nothing of firing), I earns 3¾d.—not 2d., a-day. The other day I had to sell a cup and saucer for a halfpenny, 'cause crockery-ware's so cheap—there was no handle to it, it's true—in order to get me a candle to work with. Sometimes for weeks I don't make anything at all. One week, at convict work, I did earn as much as 3s. That's without deducting the cost of thread or candles, which is quite half. The convict's clothes is all one price; no one gets any better wages than this; a few has less I believe. Some of the waistcoats an't above five fardens—twopence halfpenny the jackets—and trowsers the same. I can't tell what I average, for sometimes I have work and sometimes I an't. I could earn 3s. a week if I had as much as I could do, but I don't have it very often. I'm very often very idle. I can assure you I've been trotting about to-day to see after a shilling job and couldn't get it."

The same woman again made her appearance at the door, and seeing me still there did not stop to say a word. "What a bother there is," said the convict-clothes-maker, "if a person owes a few halfpence. That's what made me keep the door locked. I suppose her mother has sent for the old shawl she lent me. I haven't no shawl to my back; no, as true as God I haven't; I haven't indeed! I'm two months idle in the course of the year." She went on again, "Oh yes, more than that; I've been three months at one time, and didn't earn a halfpenny. That was when I lived up at the other house. There was no work at all. We was starving one against the other. I'm generally about a quarter part of my time standing still; yes, that I am, I can assure you. About three shillings a week, I tell you, is what I generally earn at convict work when I'm fully employed; but then there's the expenses to be taken out of that. I've worked at the convict work for about four-teen or fifteen years—ever since my husband's been dead. He died fourteen year ago last February. I've nobody else dependent upon me. I hadn't need to have, I'm sure. I hadn't a bit of work all last Friday and all last Saturday—no, not till Mon-day. I work for a piece-master. I don't know what profit the piece-master gets. The convicts' great coats are 5d., and I can do about three of them in two days, and they will take about $1\frac{1}{2}$ oz. of thread, that's 3d.; so that in two days, at that work, I can earn one shilling clear, saying nothing of candles. That's much better work than the other." [The cat, almost as thin as its mistress, here came scratching for some of the potatoes.]

"Yes, there's people much worse off than me, but they gets relief from the parish. They tell me at the union I am young enough to work, and yet I am turned of 70. I find it very hard—very hard, indeed; oh, that I do, I can assure you. I very often want. I wanted all last Sunday, for I had nothing at all then. I was a-bed till twelve o'clock—lay a-bed 'cause I hadn't nothing to eat. There's more young girls work at the trade now. A great quantity works at it 'cause they can see better than us. They couldn't get the dresses they wears if they was virtuous.

"My husband was a file-cutter; he did pretty fairly. While he was alive I didn't want for anything, and since his death I've wanted very often; I've wanted so as I haven't had a home to put my head into. Then I slept along with different friends, and they gave me a little bit, but they were nigh as bad off as myself, and couldn't spare much. Trade is very bad now; there are a many of us starving; yes, indeed there is—the old people in particular; the young'uns make it out other ways. I pays 1s. 6d. rent. The things are my own, such as there is. I've no table; I was obliged to sell it; I've sold 'most everything I've got; I can't sell no more, for there's none now that will fetch anything. I only wish I could get a shawl, to keep the cold off me when I takes my work home—that's all.". . .

From Letter VIII, November 13th, 1849

I was conducted by one who knew the trade well to a hard working woman living in one of the close fœtid courts running out of Gray's-inn-lane. Her statement was as follows: "I make the soldiers' trowsers and jackets, and the undress white ones; also the police trowsers, the railroad cord trowsers and jackets, and the pensioners' trowsers. For the police I get 10d. the undress—and 1s. 1d. the dress ones. The one is a finer cloth than the other. They take one day each to make, from six in the morning to eight or nine at night. There's thread to find and cotton, about 1d. per pair. The soldiers' trowsers are 6½d. per pair. I can make two pair in a day, but it must be a very long day. I sew the seams myself. I don't put them out, like some. The undress white jackets are 5d. each, and they take as much thread as the trowsers. I couldn't make two of those in a day. We don't like them. They're harder work than the trowsers; then they must be kept so very clean; if we soil them, we're made to pay for 'em. The railroad cord trowsers are 1s., and they're all sewn with double thread. About half the thread is found us; so that there is about the same expense—only they're such hard work. It takes a full day to make a pair, and then your arm will ache primely, they're so very stiff. The railroad jackets are paid 1s. 9d. for. They take nearly two days each to make; there's pockets inside and out. Twopence has been took off them only lately. Before then they used to be 1s. 11d., and some would pay 2s.

"I can't say what's the cause, except that some people will have more out of the poor than others. The soldiers have to pay 8s. for their trowsers, and 8s. for their jackets—so I hears. The police dress trowsers used to be 1s. 3d., now they are 1s. 1d. The pensioners' trowsers are 6d. a pair, but there's more work in them than in the regulation, owing to the broad stripe. One seam does with the double stripe, but the broad stripe requires two, and the price is the same. These take rather longer than the other trowsers. The white duck trowsers are 5d. a pair. They take about the same time making, or a little longer this cold weather, they're so hard. The soldiers' great coats are 5d. They take much longer to make than the trowsers. Two hands must work hard to make three coats in a day. The expenses for trimmings is quite as much as for trowsers. The soldiers' lavender summer trowsers are 6½d., and, if anything, more trouble; they're all double seams, and the same expense for thread. The overalls for the horse soldiers are the worst of all; they take two hours longer to make than the others. Why, there's twelve times round the crutch piece. Oh, that's the most scandalousest work that ever was done. The seams has all to be felled down the same as a flannel would have to be. Them are the worst work of all.

"Upon an average, at all kinds of work I suppose I could earn 1s. a day, if I had it to do, but I can't get it. It's three weeks to-day since I had any work at all, and I very often stand still quite as long. It's not a farthing more than 3s. a week that I earn, take it all the year round; and out of that there's thread, candle, and firing to be taken away, and that comes to 1s. a week for coal, candle, and wood, and 6d. for thread, leaving about 1s. 6d. for my clear earnings, after working the whole week through. But that's better than nothing.

"My husband's lately been in the hospital. I was in first a month with the same complaint—inflammation of the lungs and fever. I thought it came on from this close room. My husband wanted things to strengthen him after he came out of the hospital (he'd been there four weeks), and I couldn't give them to him out of my small earnings, and he was obliged to go into the workhouse. It was only six o'clock to-night that he came out. They gave him a shilling and a loaf of bread to bring home. I don't know that any person can be much worse off than we are. I am sure I haven't anything that I could pledge. I've been obliged to pawn his tools, and if he was to go to work to-morrow he hasn't a tool that he could use. He can get a very good character. I may perhaps chance to get a bit of meat once a week—but that's a godsend."

She then took down a box, and opening it, said: "There, sir; there is the things we have been obliged to make away with in the last twelvemonth, merely to live. The last thing I pledged was his trowel—he's a mason, sir—to get some tea and sugar to take to him to the hospital. I got 9d. upon it. If he had employment, we should get on very comfortable. If it hadn't been for this illness we should have done very well, him and me together.". . .

I then directed my steps to the neighbourhood of Drury-lane, to see a poor woman who lived in an attic in one of the closest courts in that quarter. On the table was a quarter of an ounce of tea. Observing my eye to rest upon it, she told me it was all she took. "Sugar," she said, "I broke myself of long ago; I couldn't afford it. A cup of tea, a piece of bread, and an onion is generally all I have for my dinner, and sometimes I haven't even an onion, and then I sops my bread."

In answer to my questions, she said: "I do 'the looping.' The looping consists in putting on the lace work down the front of the coats. I puts it on. That's my living, I wish it was not. It's a week to-morrow since I draw'd my needle. I get 5d. for the looping of each coat; that's the regular price. It's three hours' work to do one coat, and work fast to do it as it's done now. I'm a particular quick hand; and ordinary hands it would take four hours full to do it, because I knows them as takes that time.

"I have to find my own thread. It costs $1\frac{1}{2}$d. for a reel of cotton; that will do five coats. If I sit down between eight and nine in the morning and work till twelve at night—I never enters my bed afore—and then rise between eight and nine again (that's the time I sit down to work on account of doing my own affairs first), and then work till eleven, I get my four coats done by that time, and some wouldn't get done till two. No! they couldn't, I can assure you. At the end of that time I should have made four coats, coming to 1s. 8d.; two pence I have to pay out of this for marking, and 1d. for the cotton, leaving 1s. 5d. To see the work in 'em is dreadful. Oh, dear! And I can't sit all them hours without an extra cup of tea, and the candles would come to $1\frac{1}{2}$d.; I burn out nearly two, that I do. I press in the morning, and lets my fire out at night to save my coals, so that really I make in a day and a half 1s. $3\frac{1}{2}$d., and I am thankful if I can get that. It's an hour's work going and coming, and waiting to be served at the piece-masters, so that at them long hours it takes me a day and a half hard work to get four coats looped, for which I make 1s. $3\frac{1}{2}$d. clear.

"When I first touched this work I could do eight in the same time, and be paid better; I had 7d. then instead of 5d.; now the work in each is nearly double in quantity, that it is. Let me work as hard as I can and no stand-still, and have the work gave me when I go in, I can loop sixteen coats in a week, and that would bring me in 5s. 2d., and then all my own affairs must remain till Saturday night, and I must never enter my bed till one o'clock each night in the week to do this. That is all I can get at the very best of times—that's quite true. Sometimes I am standing still for a fortnight's run. I've not draw'd my needle a week to-morrow. I've got these here, and I shall have my money on Saturday for them. I'm sure of my money, thank God. Reckoning my bad and my good time, taking the whole year round, there's so many stand-stills at our work, I'm sure I don't make 3s. a week clear. I've been working at this twelve years; I've worked ten years for one house. We used to have 7d. for what we get 5d. now. The cause of the price being reduced was on account of the pocket flaps being took off. We were much better paid when we had them on.

"I've got two boys both at work, one about fifteen, earning 3s. per week, and I've got him to keep and clothe. The week before last I bought him a top coat—it cost me 6s.—for fear he should be laid up, for he's such bad health. The other boy is eighteen years, and earns 9s. a week. He's been in work about four months, and was out six weeks. At the same time I had no work. Oh! it was awful then. I had my rent going on. I've been here seven years. I don't owe anything here now. I have been paying 1s. 6d. a week off a debt for bread and things I was obliged to get on credit then, through the both of us being out of employment." ["That's something after Dickens' style," said one of the boys to the other, in allusion to an article in *Lloyd's Weekly Miscellany*, that he was reading after his dinner. I requested to look at the paper. The story that had taken the boy's fancy was entitled "A flaw in the Diamond. A Romance of the Affections."] "This boy," continued the woman, "is only nine years of age and him I have entirely to keep and find. He goes to the Shelton School; it's a charity. The school lets him have one coat and trowsers and shoes and stockings every year. He wears a pinafore now to save his coat. It's a hanging up there, for it is such a long while till the time comes round for his new one, that this coat would be quite shabby in the winter if I did not do as much. Indeed I *do* strive very hard. The whole of us earn, when fully employed, from 14s. to 15s. a week; but I ain't half my time employed, and there are four of us to keep and clothe out of that. My eldest boy is like a hearty man to every meal. If he hadn't got me to manage for him, may be he'd spend all his earnings in mere food. I get my second bread, and I go as far as Nassau-street to get that—to save my two or three halfpence. We use dripping with it. Butter we *never* have. A joint of meat none of us ever sees. The other day the meat cost me 3d. for the whole family—it was pieces. I never buy no other, and I've got enough in the cupboard, out of what I had, to make a stew for to-morrow. My potatoes are three pound a penny. For everything I'm obliged to go a street or two away from home to save a farthing or a halfpenny. I go for my firing into Wild-street; there it's a halfpenny cheaper.

"I find it a dreadful hard time. Many, very many, are worse off than I am. What on earth should I do if it wasn't for them two boys; but then I can't expect to have them always, let them be ever so good. They won't long stop with me. When we're both out of a situation, we either starve or get in debt where we can, and then we're months struggling to pay it. Ah, sir! and it's a struggle that no one knows but the poor who strive to pay their way. No loopers are better, and most are worse off than I am, 'cause I'm such a quick hand."

Needlewomen

From Letter IX, November 16th, 1849

In my present communication I purpose laying before the public the intelligence I have gathered respecting the Stay-stitchers, Shoe-binders, Stockmakers, Cloak-makers, Upholsteresses, and Distressed Gentlewomen working at plain needle-work in the metropolis. And first of the Stay-stitchers. Here I procured an intro-duction to one of the largest wholesale staymakers in the City, in the hopes of obtaining some account of the trade. But I soon found that my time was wasted in so doing. The gentleman assured me that there were scarcely any stay-stitchers resident in London. He could get his work done so cheap in the agricultural dis-tricts, owing to the number of people out of employ in those parts, that he had scarcely any done in town; and indeed he was loath to make the least communi-cation to me on the subject and object of my visit.

Accordingly, finding it useless seeking for any information from the employer in this particular branch of business, I made the best of my way to *[a workwoman]* who had been engaged at the business for upwards of twenty years.

The following *[is her]* statement:

"I work at stay-stitching. I've worked at it these thirty years; yes, that I have, full. Well, I can't—and work hard at the work I am now having—earn more than $7\frac{1}{2}$d. a day. Now that is the kind of work," said she, drawing some drab jean ready marked for stitching, "and I can't do more than that pair and half another from seven in the morning till nine at night, and haven't time scarcely to get a meal in the meantime, and I get 5d. a pair, and if they run very large indeed I get no more. Why, sir, at the outside I can't do above nine pair a week, not if I've full employ-ment. And nine pair a week at 5d. is 3s. 9d., and that's my earnings at the very outside, if I work fourteen hours every day for six days; and sorry I am to say I'm obliged to break into the Sabbath-day to make out a living.

"They find me in thread, but I have to find candle, and they cost me $1\frac{1}{2}$d. a night now the nights are so long, or say 1d. a night, or 6d. a week all the year round, so that my clear earnings at the very best are 3s. 3d. a week. If I had the work perhaps I might manage as much as that all the year round, but I can't get it; the trade is particular slack just now—I've been very slack for this last month. I've no book where I works—they pay me as I take it in. You see I've done four pair this week, in four days; and I shan't have more than two pair done by Saturday night; so that my earnings this week will be, for the six pair, at 5d.—2s. 6d., or reckon-ing candles, 2s. clear. Last week I did five pair, and they brought me in 2s. 1d., or 1s. 7d. clear. Taking one week with another, all the year round, I think I may say I earn 3s. a week, and that is to the full extent as much as I do; or, reckoning candle, I can safely say I don't make more than 2s. 6d. clear all the twelvemonth through. I'm just able to raise a cup of tea, and that's as much as I can do out of it.

"I have my work direct from the shop. They only employ the journeywomen in the stay trade. There's no second-hand or piece mistresses in London. There's plenty there round about Deptford and Greenwich that has the work out so many gross at a time, and employs a number of young women. Some of the old Greenwich pensioners work at stay stitching for some of them. The parties has it down in bagfuls. I once used to have my work second-handed from a party as got it from the warehouse, and she employed, I think, about nine of us. She used to get 7d. and 8d. a pair at that, and she usedn't to give us more than 2½d. each pair; for the children's we usedn't to get more than 1½d. It would take us three-parts of the day to 'em. All the stays were stitched with silk in that time; but that is, I suppose, five-and-twenty year ago. It's eighteen year ago since I worked at Portsmouth for a party who is now one of the largest wholesale dealers in London, and all he gave me was 2d. a pair. They was stitched with blue cotton. I don't think he gives even so much now down there. I worked for another party, who gave me only seven fardens; but I was obligated to give the work back to him. I was starving as I am now, but I'm sure it was worse then. I can manage at least a cup of tea at present; but then I couldn't even get that. They are mostly stitched at Portsmouth now. They can get it done cheaper there than what they can here, owing to the sailors' wives round about there I suppose. Yes, it must be something like that, for no one can get a living at it.

"The party as I spoke of, who is in the City, got on, I know, in this here way. He got a number of the poor people to work for him, and made 'em all put down 5s. each before they had a stitch of work. Before you got work you must raise the 5s. somehow. Well, the 5s. laid in his hands until such time as you wanted to leave him; if you worked for him for ten years it would be in his hands all the time. The reason why I was obliged to leave off working for him was that I wanted my 5s. to make up some rent. My goods was threatened to be taken. That 5s. I knew would save them, and I applied for it. It was on a Wednesday when I did this, and I couldn't get it until the Saturday; he wouldn't give it me till then, so I lost my work of course, 'cause I have 5s. more to leave. Well, it was by the number of 5s. that he got from the people in this manner he was able to launch and take a large establishment. He didn't care how many hands he took on so long as he had the 5s., and of course he had the interest of it all. Why, he had as many as three hundred poor people; aye, more. It was said he had as many as seven hundred in his employ working out of doors, and from each he had 5s., and that was the cause of his uprising—that it certainly was.

"The downfall of the stay business was all through him and another as lived close to him. They were the first to cut down the prices of the workpeople. They sent the work into the country, to get done in the cheapest way they could, and have always been lowering the prices of the poor people. Thirty years ago I have made as much as seventeen and fivepence for my week's work. At the very commonest I could have made from 12s. to 14s. a week; and now the most I can make is 3s. 6d. Aye, that's to the full extent; and not that every week. It's about 25 years ago since the prices first began to be cut down by the two parties I speaks of. Up to that time the prices we had for stitching were about the same as those I had thirty years ago. Till then the prices had remained about the same. We could make a very tidy living out of it. But since the two parties began the prices have been falling and falling, and we've been starving while he's been a getting rich. Now all I get is 2s. 6d. a week clear, and that is to keep me and my family.

"I'm a married woman. My husband is a plasterer, but has been out of work this two year. All he's earned is 2s. for these last three months. Indeed, he's not worked for a regular master not this two years. They prefers young hands, and he's getting into years. He'll be sixty next September. He only gets a flying job now and then, and that's mostly from the landlord we live under. My eldest boy gets 5s. a week. My youngest goes to school. Seven shillings a week is all we have to keep the four of us, pay rent and all. I pay 1s. 9d. a week for my room, and that leaves us 5s. 3d. for us four to maintain ourselves upon, or live upon, if you can call it living. Yes, that's 1s. 3¾d. each a week, or not 2d. a day, to find us in food, firing, and raiment. Oh, God bless you, I am ready to drop sometimes, when I get up. I feel that faint and loss for really the common necessaries of life. I don't taste a bit of butcher's meat not from one month's end to another—no, nor half a pint of beer I don't get.

"My husband is a sober man. I hadn't a pinch of snuff for two days, until a friend gave us a bit out of his box. It came very acceptable, I can assure you; it quite revived me; that's all I'm extravagant in. I can't say but what I likes my pinch of snuff, but even that I can't get. We're never out from Monday morning till Saturday night. If I've got nothing to do it's no use going and making an uproar about, for I'm very certain there's no one about here has got nothing to give me, and I'm very certain my opening my mouth won't fill theirs. And when I've got work, why I sits hard to it, and is glad to have it to do.". . .

The next class of needlewoman that I visited were shoebinders. I found three working together in one small close attic. . . .

"It's a very poor trade, indeed," said one of the hands. "Ah! it's high time something was done for the people, for it's cruel work now. I make snow boots at present. I bind them—that is, I get them ready for the maker. The cloth and lining is cut out and given out by the warehouse. We have to stitch them together, make the button-holes, and sew on the binding and the buttons. I get seven farthings per pair, and find my own thread and cotton. That costs about a halfpenny per pair. We get about a penny farthing per pair clear when they are finished. It takes about three hours and a half to do one pair. We can't earn more than 2s. a week at our work. A person must work very hard to do three pair a day, but it's impossible to do that every day; and then there's thread and cotton to be found out of the 2s. a week, which leaves about 1s. 6d. for our clear earnings. I'm up by six, and don't leave off till twelve or one, and then I can't do more than three pair. It takes twelve hours' continual work to do three pair. The rest of the time I must mind my children and my own affairs. I generally work about eighteen hours a day. We have been working at the snow boots now full two months. Never had a book till last week. [She produced book of employer.] Three, four, and four pair, or eleven pair were taken out last week, you see. Those I finished. And four and six pair I've had out this week, in all ten. Of this I have just done five pair since Monday. I do generally about nine pair in six days and a little less than five pair in three days. The reason of my not having had a book, is owing to my master's death. His wife has recently taken to the business, and she has given books to all the hands employed.

"I also bind common lasting women's side lace boots. By binding them I mean I make them up entirely, with the exception of the sole. I have to make sixteen eyelet holes, to stitch the lasting together, and to bind them. For this I get 3d. per pair. I have to buy silk and cotton. It costs about $\frac{3}{4}$d. each pair of boots, $\frac{1}{2}$d. for silk and $\frac{1}{4}$d. for cotton. I clear about 2$\frac{1}{4}$d. per pair. Can't do a pair in much less than four hours, or three pair a day at the very outside, to work hard the day through. But we can't keep that up. By the end of the week we seldom have more than eight pair done—for getting them out and taking them in all takes time; and eight pair at 2$\frac{1}{4}$d. clear brings us in 1s. 6d. a week as our weekly earnings. Out of this we have to pay candles, and they come to 6d. a week. I know I burn a penny candle every night. That makes our clear gains about 1s. But it comes in handy. It's a few halfpence every day. We have constant employment at the warehouse. We're never standing still.

"I am a married woman. I've a very queer husband. He's a big drunkard. He's a sawyer. I'm sure if I have enough of him just to get me over Sunday it's all that I do. I can't tell what my husband gets a week. I never know what he earns any more than a stranger. After he's paid the rent I might get perhaps 4s. or 5s. of him, and that to keep me, him, and the child. Formerly I used to work at the boots in the country. Then the prices were much better. That's as much as twelve or thirteen years ago. The best 'lasting' boots were 1s. 6d. and some 2s. then; now I should get 5d. and 7d. for the same kind of work. I don't know what's the cause of the prices coming down. I find it very hard work to live. It isn't living. We've nothing but bread from one week's end to another. I know I shall have nothing to eat until I take my work in to-morrow morning.". . .

The next class of needlewoman that I wended my way to was the Stockmakers [cravats or neckties]—and here I found an instance of filial affection and almost heroism that would be an honour to any station. The characters of the parents, I should state, have been inquired into, and they are said to be worthy, hard-working, sober people:

"I work at stock work. I have the work home. I work first hand. I have 6d. a dozen for 'Albert ties,' 9d. to 1s. a dozen for 'opera ties,' 1s. 9d. a dozen for 'sham pleats,' or Albert stocks—those are the stocks with bows to them, and long ends. The 'Burlingtons'—that is the stock without ends, and waterproof top and bottom to keep the perspiration from coming through—these are 2s. 3d. to 2s. 6d. a dozen. The 'Napier' stocks are 3s. 6d. to 4s. a dozen. The Napiers have long ends hemmed on both sides, with a knob in the centre. 'Aerial' ties are 6d. a dozen: they are the new-fashioned ones lately come up. Of Albert ties, I can make about eighteen in twelve hours, or nine dozen a week. The expenses on these, including candle, cotton, and silk, would be 1s. 9d., leaving 3s. 3d. a week clear. Of opera ties I could do about nine a day, or four dozen and a half, at 9d. per dozen, or four dozen of those at a shilling, in the week; the expenses about the same, or 1s. 9d. a week, leaving 2s. 3d. to 2s. 6d. a week clear. The opera ties are worse than the Albert, for though there's more money paid for 'em, there's more work in 'em. We reckon to do about a dozen of the Albert stocks in about three days, or two dozen a week, at 1s. 9d. a dozen, or 3s. 6d. a week. The expenses are about 1s. 6d.; there's not so much cotton used in them; the clear earnings at these 2s. a week. Of the Burlingtons I couldn't do more than one dozen in three days, or two dozen per week, at 2s. to 2s. 3d. per dozen, making 4s. to 4s. 6d. for the week's earnings. The trimmings and candles come to 1s. 6d., leaving about 2s. 6d. to 3s. for the clear gains. We couldn't do more than eighteen Napiers in the week, at 3s. 6d. to 4s. the dozen. These would come to 5s. 3d. or 6s. The expenses of these, candle and all, would be 2s., leaving 4s. for the clear gains for the week. Of the Aerials about one dozen could be done in a day, or six dozen a week, at 6d., coming to 3s. The expenses are about 1s., leaving 2s. for the clear gains for the week. The Napiers are about the best work with us, and the Aerials and the Albert stocks about the worst.

"I keep one hand myself, and a little girl. I pay the hand 3s. a week, and the little girl I pay nothing, she comes with the other to learn. I give the hand her tea, and she brings her bread and butter. The expense of the tea, sugar, and milk, &c., for the week, would be about 6d., so that the hand I employ costs me 3s. 6d. I can earn, with the assistance of the two hands, from 8s. to 9s. a week upon an average, clear of trimmings and candles, and deducting the expense of the hands, 3s. 6d., I make about 5s. clear of everything. These, I think, are my clear earnings all the year round. Sometimes I get more by working extra hours. I have made as much as 7s. myself by my own hands in one week, but to get that I had to sit up about three nights out of the six; and some weeks I earn only 1s. 2d. and some nothing at all; that is when the work is slack. The work is generally slack at Christmas time and in the middle of the summer, about three months each time, so that the trade is about six months brisk and six months slack in the course of the year.

"I remember the prices of the Napiers being 8s. 6d. a dozen. They're 3s. 6d. to 4s. now. The Albert stocks used to be 3s. 6d. to 4s. when they first came up. They're 2s. to 1s. 9d. now. The Burlingtons I had 5s. a dozen for. Now they're 2s. to 2s. 3d. The opera ties I had from 2s. to 3s. a dozen for. Now they're 9d. to 1s. The Albert ties I had 1s. 9d. for when they first came up. Now I have 6d. a dozen for the very same work. The Aerials I had 1s. 3d. to 1s. 6d. for, and they cut them out for me. Now I have 6d. a dozen for them. The Albert scarfs I had 2s. a dozen for only a month back, and now I have 9d. The prices have fallen considerably more than one-half within this last year and a half. I had all those better prices that I have mentioned eighteen months ago. I can't say what is the cause. I believe it is owing to one hand having no work and going to underbid another. I myself know that one hand offered to work at a less price than I was getting, and that was the cause of my being reduced, 9d. first and then 6d. more per dozen in one article that I make. I took my work in on the Saturday, and my employer offered me 1s. 3d. for what he had before been paying me 2s. a dozen. I told him I could not do the work at that price—I really could not live by it, when a person in the shop told the master she would take the work at that price. Since, they have reduced the same article to 9d. a dozen, and this has all been done within a month.

"One of the causes of the cheap prices is, the master puts up a bill in his window to say that he wants hands, whether he does or no. This I believe is done, not because extra hands are wanted, but that the master may see how many people are out of work, and how cheap he can get his work done. Those that will do it cheapest and the best he employs, and those that won't they may starve—or something worse. In the warehouse I work for there are about 50 hands, mostly young girls. There are some married women; but I believe thirty get money by other means. I know by their dresses that they do not get the gowns they appear in out of stock work. I think it's about the same in every other house.

"I have a father and a mother dependent on my labour. I am nineteen years old on the 28th of February next. My mother occasionally helps me; but she is upwards of fifty, and cannot see at night nor to work at black things. She broke a blood-vessel nearly seven years ago, and is not able to go out to a hard day's work. My father had an accident thirteen weeks ago next Friday. He was thrown out of a cart and broke his ribs, and pressed his chest bone in. His chest is now bandaged up (showed it). He was a carter at a builder's before; but since his accident his master tells him he is unfit for the work, and he is now wholly dependent upon me for support, and I struggle hard to keep him and mother from the workhouse. I was up for three weeks. I never took my clothes off nor went to bed for the whole of that time, so that I might support him and pay the doctor's bill. The only sleep I had during the whole of that time was with my head on the table. I was at work night and day; and now I find it very hard work to pay rent, support them, and keep myself respectable without doing as the other girls do. I've been obliged to part with almost all my clothes to keep them. The doctor said he was to have port wine, and I used to have to give him two gills every day. If I hadn't got rid of my clothes I couldn't have kept him alive. We have been obliged to pledge one of our beds for £1 as well. But I hope to be able to get on still."

The cloak, skirt, and ladies' night-cap maker is another class of "hands" dependent on their needle for their living. The following may be taken as a fair average statement as to the usual earnings of persons engaged in this branch of business. The woman, I was informed by her landlord, was a hard-working, sober, and thrifty widow:

"I am a widow with four children. My eldest is fourteen—is a boy—and the youngest is a girl, four-and-a-half. My eldest boy earns 3s. a week. He is a newsboy. My second boy is out at the print colouring business. He gets 1s. 6d. a week. This is his first week of being employed. I have no other money coming in but what I get by my own needle. I am a cloakmaker—that is, I make up mantles for a warehouse in the city. My employer pays somewhat less than the other houses do, because he supplies other warehouses who supply the linendrapers, and there are, consequently, three profits to come out of his goods, instead of two, as is the usual custom. I get from 8½d. to 1s. 3d. each for such as I generally make. I have had more—indeed, I have had as much as 5s. for some, but then they take me much longer to make, so that my earnings is no more at the high price work than it is at low. Those mantles at 8½d. are for children, and very common ones. The work is so flimsy that they pay equally as well as the best. I should say, with a little assistance, I could make two of those at 8½d. in a day. With my own single hand I could make one a day, that is, if I was to sit for long hours at it. Take one day with another, I sit, upon an average, at my work from nine in the morning till eleven at night; often longer, seldom less. Fourteen hours is my usual day's labour.

"Out of the 8d. I find all the sewing materials; they come to about 1d. a cloak. It will take about ¼lb. of cotton to a dozen mantles, besides cotton-cord and hooks-and-eyes. I generally use about 1½lb. of candles in a week, and that's 7½d. I can make about six of the 8½d. mantles every week, and they'll come to 4s. 3d. Out of this there's 6d. for sewing materials and 7½d. for candles, so that at that work I can earn 3s. 1½d. per week when I'm fully employed; and the 8½d. mantles will pay better than these I'm doing now. I can earn more money at the others. I get for those I am about now 1s. 3d. each. The expenses are much about the same. I get about 1s. 2d. clear each one I make. They are children's cloth mantles. It takes two 'hands' to make one of them in a day. It would take me myself two days to make one. I have to sew eight yards of braid to every cloak, and it takes me an hour to do two yards of it. At this work I earn upon an average 7d. a day, or, deducting candles, I get a little less than 6d. clear, or 2s. 10½d. per week—that's about my earnings, taking one week with another.

"I sometimes have ladies' mantles to do. For some in the same style as those I am now making I got 2s. 6d. But they didn't bring me in any more than the children's—rather less; indeed, I was obliged to throw them up. I couldn't get a living at 'em. I couldn't meet my payments any way, and it was in the summer, too, when my expenses were less. I had 3s. 6d. for the same style of mantle at first. But another hand offered to do them at 2s. 6d. each, and so my employer refused to give me any more. I found I couldn't get a living at those prices, so I gave it up. I was not the only one in the trade who couldn't do so. I knew several myself. The 2s. 6d. ones were made of the same stuff as the children's, only lined with silk and quilted. There were thirty-six yards of narrow braid on every cloak, and twelve yards of the Algerine made into a trimming. When I made them I had four hands at work besides myself. I gave 1s. a day to three of them, and 8d. to the other. To one of the 1s. hands I gave her tea as well. I put out the frills to braid, and paid 10d. a set for them. I had ten of these sets to braid in a week. I also put out the Algerine trimming, and paid 1¼d. per yard for forty yards. With this assistance I got in as many as ten cloaks in the week, and received for them 25s. Out of this my expenses were 22s. for the wages of the hands I employed, and 8s. 4d. for the making of the frills to the mantles, and 4s. 2d. for the Algerine braiding, amounting in all to 34s. 6d.; so that I lost upon the job 9s. 6d., and my own labour into the bargain. I know it almost broke my heart, for I worked so hard and didn't get nothing for it. I was forced to sell a pattern mantle for 17s. to pay my way that week. We are obliged to take a pattern of the mantle we can make to the warehouse before we can get work. We have then to give a reference; but no security is required if the reference is approved of.

"The highest given for the making of cloaks is 5s.; and though I have had a girl, to whom I paid 1s. and her tea, hard at work with me upon them night and day, I couldn't make more than two in a week. Indeed I could hardly finish them in that time. These mantles were embroidered. They had one with another 72 yards of the Russia braid worked in flowers on each cloak, they were lined with silk and quilted, and the cuffs were turned up with satin and quilted. My expenses for silk were about 3d. a cloak, and candles were about 5d. (the evenings were longer when I made them). For the two cloaks I got 10s., and out of this I had to pay 6s. to the girl I employed, and say 6d. a week the cost of her tea, 6d. for silk for the two mantles, and 5d. for candles—in all 7s. 5d., so that my clear earnings that week were 2s. 7d., and for that I had to sit close to my work till I almost blinded myself at it. Indeed I do think if I had gone on at it till now I should have lost my eyesight altogether.

"The prices paid by the shops at the West End are much better—indeed persons can get a comfortable living at the work there. Last summer I worked for a person on the first floor here, who had employment from some shops in Regent-street, and I made from 8s. to 10s. a week, and that was second-handed. She got more for her work of course. If I could have continued at that work I could have got a very good living. I was happy enough then. When I can get a common living no one is happier than me. The shops that do not make up their own materials are supplied by the warehouses. But the shops can get them quite as cheap from the warehouses as they can make up themselves, and it's less trouble to them, so they've most of 'em given over making them for themselves. Some shops employ hands who work for them at 1s. a-day and their tea, but I can't go out on account of my young family. I am obliged to work at home. Everything gets so reduced in price now, that it is hard to find out what to work at so as to get a living by it." She produced the account-book of her employers when she was engaged second-handed for a shop in Regent-street. . . .

She then went on to say: "My eldest boy brings in 3s., so that, added to the 4s. 8d. that I get a week, makes 7s. 8d. in all, to keep five of us. Now I shall have nothing from the warehouse not before next March; so that I shall have to seek for some other employment till then. The slacks in the cloak business occur twice a year—that is to say, at the end of the winter and the summer season. The winter slack begins in December, and lasts till March: the summer slack begins in August, and lasts till October; so that there is half slack, and half brisk work. The other warehouses pay a little bit better than mine. I have also worked at the skirt work, that is, making up the flounced skirts—those that are sold ready-made at the shops. The first account that I showed you was for skirt and mantle work. I used to have 1s. 3d. for the skirts that were braided down the front, and 1s. 8d. for those with four flounces. I could earn 10s. a week regular at that, and not sit such long hours at it as I do now at the mantles. Indeed if I had that sum coming in every week I should be as happy and live as well as a person might want to live. I shouldn't crave for more than that. My husband's been dead two years the 28th of December. He was a watch finisher, and ill for two years. Lately I've been doing very badly, and before I got my good work in the summer I was doing quite as bad. I have worked at cap work as well. I've made ladies' nightcaps. I got 1s. a dozen for the best, and 6½d. a dozen for some. . . .

"Indeed I do find it very hard work to live. All of us have often to live the chief part of the week upon bread. I pay 2s. 6d. a week for rent. Thank God I don't owe a farthing. [She produced her rent-book, which was paid up to last week.] I have nothing in pledge but a Bible that my mother bought me, and I would not part with it for worlds. It has been in pledge, with two Scripture Histories, these two years, for 3s. I pay 9d. a year interest upon them. I have also a tablecloth, and a piece of merino stuff in pledge for 3s. I was obliged to pledge them when I was out of work a fortnight—that was the only fortnight I have been out of work since my husband's death. I've been out a day at a time, but never so long as that before or since. When the slack comes on, I try to turn my hand to anything I can get. I'm obliged to walk a number of miles—I'm sure, when I was last out, I walked half London through to find employment. It's very unpleasant work—they speak so sharp. All I want is a top coat to keep my boy from the cold in the winter. He never was strong."

I was referred to a person living in a court running out of Holborn, who was willing to give me the information I desired respecting the prices paid to the female hands engaged in the upholstery business. Her room was neatly furnished and gave evidence of her calling. Before the windows were chintz curtains tastefully arranged, and in one corner of the room stood a small easy chair with a clean brown holland case over it. On a side table were ranged large fragments of crystal and spar upon knitted mats or d'oyleys, and over the carpet was a clean grey crumb cloth—indeed, all was as neat and tasty as a person of limited means and following such an employment could possibly make it. The person herself was as far above the ordinary character of workwomen, both in manner and appearance, as her home was superior to the usual run of untidy and tasteless dwellings belonging to the operatives. I found her very ready to answer all my questions.

"I am a widow," she said. "I have been so for five years. My husband was an upholsterer. I was left with one child twelve years old. My husband was in considerable difficulty when he died. Since his death I have got my living by working with my needle at the upholstery business. I make up curtains and carpets, and all sorts of cases, such as those for covering the furniture in drawing-rooms. I also make up the bed furniture, and feather beds and mattresses as well. My present employer pays me for making up window curtains 2s. per pair. I have nothing to find. Upon an average I can make a pair of curtains in two days. I might do more of the plainer kind; but if the curtains are gimped, I shall do less. Taking one with the other, I can safely say I can make a pair of curtains in two days. It is impossible for me to give an estimate as to the cases, because furniture is of such various descriptions. We generally charge such things by the time they take us.

"It is the envelope that goes over the article of furniture, and protects the silk or satin that the chair, sofa, or ottoman may be covered with, that I call the case. These cases, or overalls, are generally of chintz or holland, and are made by females and sewn together. The satin or damask cover of the furniture itself is nailed on, and made by male hands. By working at cases for twelve hours I can make about 1s. 6d. a day. I do my work always at home. There are some shops send their work out, but the generality have it done at their shop. The wages given to the workwomen at the shop are from 9s. to 11s. per week, and the time of labour is twelve hours per day. I don't think any house gives less than 9s. to any one who understands the business, and 11s. I believe is the highest price to the workwomen in the upholstery business. Forewomen who hold responsible situations of course get more—they get 12s. a week. For the making of cases we who work at home are paid by time and not by piece-work. The rate is 1½d. per hour. The general price that I am paid for sofa cases comes to 2s. each, and about 3s. if I cut them out—that's a fair average. Easy-chair cases I think I get about 1s. 6d. for making, and 2s. 6d. each if I cut them out. Ottoman cases vary much in point of size. I don't suppose even a very large ottoman case would exceed 1s. 6d.—there's less work in it. A small box ottoman for the centre of a room, I think I should get about 6d. for. I can earn about 1s. 6d. a day at case work. For his carpets my employer pays 1¼d. per yard for sewing, but I find the thread. Indeed, I find the thread for everything I make, but that does not generally come to much. Carpet thread is a little more expensive. The thread for a carpet of 50 yards will cost about 4½d. I can do about 25 yards a-day at carpet work, but it's very hard work. Mattress cases are from 6d. each up to 1s., according to the sizes. Bed ticks are from 8d. up to 14d., according to size. Pillow ticks are 1d., and bolsters 2d. Window blinds are 3d. each, making. Bed furniture is 10s. for a four-post bed. Arabians generally about 4s., French beds are from 2s. 6d. to 3s. I don't think there is anything else in our line of business worth mentioning.

"If I were fully employed, I could earn about 12s. a week, but a good deal of that arises from my having been in business for myself. An ordinary hand in the trade would, if she could get enough to do, make about 10s. a week. Those who do the work at home are seldom more than half their time employed, and those who work in the shops are discharged immediately a slack occurs. There is more fluctuation in the upholstery business than in any other in London. It used not to be so; but of late years it has fluctuated extremely, from the competition in the trade. The linen-drapers have taken to supply furniture ready made. There are many large houses who do a great trade in this way, and they sell at prices that the others cannot compete with. I think the slacks are in consequence of the times and the general want of money. You see persons can do without furniture when they run short, whereas they must have other commodities.

"At one time I received from 10s. to 14s. weekly for my labour. I have had so much work that I have been obliged to have assistance to get it done in time. The upholstery line is a business of great pressure. Five years back I made about 9s. a week upon an average throughout the year. But latterly the work has become so slack that for the last two years I have not earned 4s. a week, taking one week with another; and for this last month my earnings have been nothing at all. I haven't had a stitch to do from my employer. My earnings for this last year have been so trifling that I have been obliged to do many things I never did before. I have gone back dreadfully. I have been obliged to pledge my things and borrow money to make up sums that must be paid. I *must* keep a home above my head. If it hadn't been for the Queen's intended visit to the Coal Exchange, I don't know what I should have done. It was a little bit of help to me; but, at the same time, it doesn't free me from my difficulties. Still it came like a Providence to me. I got about 35s. for what I did there. I was at work all Sunday. I was between a fortnight and three weeks engaged upon it. But I was not paid equal to what I did. I don't tell my affairs to everybody. It's quite enough for me to struggle by myself. I may feel a great many privations that I do not wish to be known. I got about 35s. in three weeks, and for that I had to work from eight in the morning till ten at night, and one entire Sunday.

"My present employer is not in the cheap trade. He is about a second-rate upholsterer. He pays to his workpeople the ordinary prices of the trade, neither above or below, and is, I think, a fair-dealing man. When I have assistance, I pay 1s. 6d. a day to those persons whom I employ. These, if active hands, might earn me as much as 1s. 9d. in the day. You see the upholstery work is always in a drive. There is never any regularity about it. It must be done by a certain time, or the order would be countermanded. The female hands employed in the business are generally middle-aged people; there are not many young people employed in it. A great many are widows, but the majority are old maids. I do believe there are more old maids employed in the upholstery business than in any other. They are generally sober steady people; in fact, they wouldn't suit if they were not. The principal part is upon very expensive materials—silk, satin, and velvets—that it requires great care and nicety. I think there are a great many—yes, hundreds—at the present time out of employment. You see the cholera frightened families away from London, and there was no orders left to be done, or anything. But just now, the gentlefolks are returning to town, and business is reviving slightly at the West-end.

"Last summer the trade was no better than it has been this. It was very bad.

The last two years have been dreadful years of business in the upholstery line. The trade is so divided, that there ought to be employment all the year round. Indeed it was so formerly. There were very few fluctuations then. I speak from twenty years' experience of the business. In the winter time, when families were in town, there was general employment, owing to the fashions altering as much in upholstery as they do in dress; and when the families at the West-end left London in the summer, they usually gave orders to the upholsterer to have their houses beautified and the furniture done up in their absence. But for the last two years this has greatly decreased. Where there has been one house redecorated there have been thirty shut up. Eaton-square, Grosvenor-square, and all those that I have had a great deal of employment from, have all been shut up; there has been nothing done. This has been the cause of a great deal of distress in the trade. I know of many cases of distress in my own circle.

"The prices paid to the workpeople have decreased materially within the last five years, to the extent of one half in bed furniture. We are now paid 10s. for making up the furniture of a four-post bedstead, and formerly we used to have £1 for the very same thing. The wages of the women working in the shops were 12s. a week till lately, now they are mostly 9s., though some are 11s. Window curtains (plain) used to be 5s. per pair, now we have 2s. And the price paid for making up the other articles has decreased in very nearly the same proportion. I don't know the cause of this, unless it be that there is less work to be done in the trade. I don't think it arises from an increase of hands, but from a decrease of work. The slacks occur much more often now than they did formerly. I think the hands are out of employ now one-third of their time throughout the year, there's such very great fluctuation in the business.". . .

I had seen all classes of needlewomen but one. I had listened to the sufferings of the widow, the married woman, and the young unmarried girl, who strove to obtain an honest living by their needle. I had also heard, from their own lips, the history of the trials and fall of those who had been reduced to literal beggary and occasional prostitution by the low price given for their labour. Still it struck me that there was one other class of needlewoman whose misery and privations must be more acute than all. It was the distressed gentlewoman—persons who, having been brought up in ease and luxury, must feel their present privations doubly as acute as those who, in a measure, had been used to poverty from their very cradle.

I was directed to one of this class who was taking care of a large empty house at the west end of the town. I was no sooner in the presence of the poor family than I saw, by the manner of all present, how differently they had once been situated. The lady herself was the type of the distressed gentlewoman. I could tell by the regularity of her features that her family for many generations past had been unused to labour for their living, and there was that neatness and cleanliness about her costume and appearance which invariably distinguished the lady from the labouring woman. Again, there was a gentleness and a plaintiveness in the tone of her voice that above all things mark the refinement of a woman's nature. The room in which the family lived, though more destitute of every article of furniture and comfort than any I had visited, was at least untainted by the *atmosphere* of poverty. I was no longer sickened with that overpowering smell that always hangs about the dwellings of the very poor. The home of the distressed gentlewoman consisted literally of four bare walls. There was no table, and only two chairs in the place. At the foot of the lady was an old travelling trunk, on which lay a few of the nightcaps that she and her daughters were occupied in making. One of the girls stood hemming by the window, and the other was seated in a corner of the room upon another trunk, busily engaged in the same manner. Before the fender was a piece of old carpeting about the size of a napkin. On the mantel-piece were a few balls of cotton, a small tin box of papers, and a Bible and Prayer Book. This was literally all the property in the place. It was not difficult to tell, by the full black eyes, olive complexions, and sharp Murillo-like features of the daughters, that their father, at least, had been of Spanish extraction. The mother herself, too, had somewhat of a foreign look, though this I afterwards discovered arose from long residence with her husband abroad.

It was not till now that I had found my duty in any way irksome to me; but I must confess, when I began to stammer out the object of my visit to the distressed lady, I could not help feeling that my mission seemed like an impertinence, and to betray a desire to pry into the miseries of the poor that was wholly foreign to my intention. I could see by the proud expression of the gentlewoman's features that she felt the privacy of her poverty had been violated by my presence, and I was some little while endeavouring to impress upon her that I had not come to her with the mean object of publishing to the world the distress of *individuals*, which I was well aware was made doubly bitter from the fear of its becoming known, even to their friends, much more to the public in general. At length I informed her that whatever she might communicate to me would be given to the public in such general terms that it would be impossible to recognise that she was the person alluded to. Upon this assurance she told me as follows:

"I work at needlework generally—I profess to do that; indeed that is what I have done ever since I have been a widow. But it is shocking payment. What I am engaged upon now is from a private lady. I haven't, as yet, made any charge. I don't know what the price will be; I did intend to ask 3d. each. The lady has been a great friend to me. I can't exactly say how long it will take me. Persons call to look at the house, and I have interruptions. They are plain nightcaps that I am making, and are for a lady of rank. Such persons generally, I think, give the least trouble for their work. I can't say how long they take me each to make. I've been very ill, and I've had the children to help me. I shouldn't like to say what I could not exactly count upon—it would be saying what wouldn't be true. I never made any before. There will be five when I have finished them all. There are three done, and this one I have in my hand is about half done. When was it we had them, my dear?" said the lady to her daughter, who stood sewing at the window.

The young lady returned no answer, and the mother continued, "I can't recollect when we had them, for we have been so much worried. Two or three times the thieves have attempted to get into the house. On last Wednesday some one tried to open the street door, thinking the house was empty. The fright has made me almost forget everything, I can assure you. Since Wednesday myself and my eldest daughter (the other goes to school) have done very nearly four of the nightcaps. But that is not by sitting to work at them continually. During that time we have made a flannel jacket as well. My daughter, indeed, made it, for I haven't been able, though of course I attended to it. The flannel jacket was for a shop. They would not have given me more than 8d., though it was lined inside with calico, and indeed was more like a coat. I found some part of the lining, though not the whole; there was a great deal of work in it—fourteen button-holes, and I charged them 1s. They demurred at the charge, and said, if they sent me another they would only give 10d., for 8d. was their usual price. I made one of the sleeves, and my daughter made the rest. We were engaged on it all the day. There were a great many seams in it, and they must have been neatly put out of hand or else the people at the shop wouldn't have given me the price; nor, indeed, would they give me any other work. Since Wednesday myself and my daughter have made one flannel jacket and just upon four nightcaps; that's all, and they will come altogether to 2s. The lady won't put the price herself upon the nightcaps, and I feel timid in asking a price of a lady that's been a friend to me. Latterly I've had no work at all, only that which I got from an institution for distressed needlewomen. They were children's chemises. I think I made seven. Didn't I?" she inquired of one of her daughters.

"Yes, mamma," was the young lady's answer. "I ought to keep a book myself," the mother went on to say—"I used to do so of all the prices. I did the seven chemises in a fortnight, and got 7s. for them. I have also made within this time one dozen white cravats for a shop; they are the wide corded-muslin cut across, and the very largest. I have 6d. a dozen for hemming them, and had to find the cotton of course. I have often said I would never do any more of them; I thought they would never have been done, there was so much work in them. Myself and daughter hemmed the dozen in a day. It was a day's very hard work. It was really such very hard work that I cried over it. I was so ill, and we were wanting food so badly.

"That is all that myself and daughter have done for this last month. During that time the two of us (my daughter is eighteen) have earned 6d., and 7s., and 2s., making in all 9s. 6d. for four weeks, or 2s. 4½d. per week, to keep three of us. I have not been constantly employed all the month; I should say I have been half the time occupied. The nine and sixpence may be fairly considered as the earnings of the two of us, supposing we had been fully occupied for a fortnight. My daughter and I have earned at plain needlework a good deal more than that. But to get more we have scarcely time to eat. I have, with my daughter's labour and my own, earned as much as 10s.; but then such hard work injures the health. I should say an industrious quick hand might earn at plain needlework, taking one thing with another, 3s. 6d. a week, if she were fully employed. But there is great difficulty in getting work—oh, yes, very great. The schools injure the trade greatly. Ladies give their work to the National Schools, and thus needlewomen who have families to support are left without employment. That, I think, is the principal cause of the deficiency of work—and many others I know consider so with me. I think that is also the cause of the prices being so low. Yes, I know it is, because ladies will tell you plainly, I can have the work done cheaper at the school. Generally, the ladies are much harder as to their terms than the tradespeople; oh, yes, the tradespeople usually show more lenity towards the needlewomen than the ladies. I know the mistress of an institution who refused some chemises of a lady who wanted to have them made at 9d. She said she would not impose upon the poor workpeople so much as to get them made at that price.

"Of course we could not have subsisted upon the 2s. 4½d. a week, which we have earned for the last four weeks. I have got many duplicates in the house to show how we *did* live. I was obliged to take the blankets off the bed, and sleep with only a sheet to cover us. I sold my bedstead for 3s. 6d. to a person, who came herself and valued it. That very bedstead, not a month ago, I gave 8s. 6d. for. It was what they call a cross-bedstead. Our bolster we were obliged to pledge. That was quite new; it cost 2s. 6d., and I pledged it for a shilling. Our blankets, too, we pledged for 1s. each; they cost me 6s. the pair; but I've taken one out since. Of course now we sleep upon the floor. Our inside clothing we have also disposed of. Indeed, I will tell you, we are still without our clothing, both my daughter and myself; and I have chewed camphor and drank warm water to stay my hunger. My pains from flatulence have been dreadful. We have often had no breakfast, and remained without food till night, all of us; and at last I have made up my mind to pledge my flannel petticoat, and get 6d. on that. Once we were so badly off that I sent for a person to come and pledge my bed. She pledged it for half-a-crown. This person told a lady in the neighbourhood what I had done, and the lady came in the evening and brought me 5s., and with that the bed was redeemed. We all like to preserve life, sir. Life is sweet when we have a family, however much we may want. Needlework is such a precarious living that we cannot subsist and clothe ourselves by it. Even in the summer it cannot be done—I have tried—no, that it can't with plain needlework. What I want is a situation for my eldest daughter. She can speak Spanish, and she works well at her needle. I myself speak Spanish and French. You won't put that in the newspaper, will you?" she asked me. I told her I would insert nothing that she wished to keep secret.

She said, "I am afraid they will guess it is I. I would rather starve than it should be known who I am. I do not wish to be made a public spectacle of. I am not ashamed to be poor, understand—for I am so through no fault of my own—but my friends would be ashamed to have my poverty known."

I told her I would do as she wished, and I assured her that I had come there to alleviate rather than to aggravate her distress. After a little hesitation she consented to the publication of what she might communicate to me, and continued as follows: "You may say my father was an officer in the English army, and my grandfather was an officer in the English army too. I have a brother-in-law a clergyman. It's not in his power to assist me. My husband was an officer in the army as well, but he was in the foreign service. He has been dead five years. He left me penniless, with three children. My son is in the West Indies. He is doing well there: he is but young—he is only 17. He has £36 a year and his board. He assisted me last year. I was in hopes to have some assistance this year. They only pay them now once a year, according to the last letter I had from him. I do feel it very hard that I—whose father and grandfather have served the country—should be left to suffer as I do. I don't consider, if you understand me, sir, that we have any merit or claim upon the Government; still I cannot but think it hard that the children of those who have served their country so many years should be so destitute as we are. All we want is employment, and that we cannot get. Charity, indeed, is most irksome to us—we may well say that. I would never emigrate to where there is greater employment—no, not as long as I live. My husband's family were all very wealthy, but they've lost nearly all in the revolutions abroad. I would not object to travel with a lady, but I could never say farewell for ever to my own country—that is what I think and feel.

"Before I came here I paid 4s. a week. I did not pay it all myself. (Here I was shown the letter of a lady high in rank, promising to be answerable for her rent.)

Now I pay no rent, and have not done so since the 19th September. The same good lady recommended me to the house-agent, and he gave me this house to take care of. I do think it most cruel that in the midst of all our distresses and poverty persons must try to enter the house. I am sure they must come to take our lives—it cannot be for what we have! We are all alone here, without any one to protect us, and we are very timid. Last night I was afraid to go to church, for I thought they would get into the premises in our absence. Several times late at night I have heard them put a false key into the door. Nobody knows what I suffer. Last Friday night—it must have been past midnight—I heard them knocking at the washhouse window, as if to take out the pane of glass, and I had the presence of mind to throw up the window of this room. We sleep on the floor. I called out, saying, Who is there? Such was my fright, that I trembled all day Saturday. I would rather go to the workhouse than stop here. But, of course, after all my struggles, I would not go there, no! though I *am* a destitute widow. Thank God, I'm not in debt—that is a great consolation to me. I don't owe any person a penny."

I hardly knew how to ask one whose narrative and manner bore so plainly the impress of truth, for proofs of the authenticity of her statements; still I felt that it would not be right, without making some such inquiries, to allow the story of her sufferings to go forth to the world. I explained to her my wishes, and she very readily showed me such papers and official documents as put her statement as to birth and the position of her husband utterly beyond a doubt.

She was afterwards kind enough, for the sake of others situated like herself, to let me see the duplicates of the different articles that her poverty had compelled her to raise a meal upon. They told so awful a tale of want, that I begged permission to copy them. The articles pledged, and the sums lent upon them, were as follows: Gown, 1s.; bed, 1s.; petticoat and night gown, 1s.; gown, 1s.; gown skirt, 1s.; 2 books and apron, 1s.; shawl, 1s.; gown, 1s.; umbrella, 1s.; petticoat and shawl, 1s.; bolster, 1s.; petticoat and shift, 1s.; ditto, 6d.; counterpane, 2s.; cloak, 3s.; a whittle, 3s.; gown, 3s.; sheet and drawers, 1s.; gown, 1s.; petticoat, 1s.; petticoat and piece of flannel, 9d.; wedding-ring, 2s. 6d. The lady also took me into the garden to show me the window by which the thieves had sought to enter the house at midnight. On the flagstones immediately beneath it, and which were green with damp and desolation, were the marks of men's hobnailed boots. . . .

From Letter X, November 20th, 1849

As a class, I must say the workpeople that I have seen appear remarkably truthful, patient, and generous; indeed, every day teaches me that their virtues are wholly unknown to the world. Their intemperance, their improvidence, their want of cleanliness, and their occasional want of honesty, are all that come to our ears. As I said before, however, I doubt very much whether *we* should not be as improvident and intemperate if our incomes and comforts were as precarious as theirs. The vices of the poor appear to be the evils naturally fostered by poverty—even as their virtues are such as want and suffering alone can beget.

Their patience is positively marvellous. Indeed, I have seen this last week such contentment, under miseries and privations of the most appalling nature, as has made me look with absolute reverence upon the poor afflicted things. I have beheld a stalwart man, with one half of his body dead—his whole side paralyzed, so that the means of subsistence by labour were denied him—and his wife toiling day and night with her needle, and getting at the week's end but one shilling for her many hours' labour. I have sat with them in their wretched hovel shivering without a spark of fire in the grate—and the bleak air rushing in through every chink and crevice. I have been with them and their shoeless children at their Sunday dinner of boiled tea leaves and dry bread, and I have heard the woman, with smiling lips, not only tell me, but show me, how contented she was with her lot, bearing the heavy burden with a meek and uncomplaining spirit, such as philosophy may dream of, but can never compass. The man and his wife were satisfied that it was the will of God they should be afflicted as they were, and they bowed their heads in reverent submission to the law. "It may be hard to say why we are so sorely troubled as we are," said the heroic old dame, "but we are satisfied it is all for the best." In my last letter, I told the story of the poor stock-maker, who, for three weeks, had never laid down to rest, so that she might save her disabled parent from the workhouse. . . . Indeed, not a day of my life now passes but I am eye-witness to some act of heroism and nobility, such as are unknown and unheard of among those who are well-to-do in the land. . . .

Those working at the lining and piecing of furs, it will be seen, are not so badly paid as many others. Of course, from the very nature of the business, the work is "slack" at certain periods and brisk at others—but still the wages are *not*, as in some trades, utterly below subsistence point when the work is brisk, and consequently they do not doom the workpeople to positive starvation immediately when the slack begins. The following statement of the earnings of two sisters may be taken, I believe, as a fair average of the incomings of the needlewomen generally employed in the business.

"I and my sister work at the fur business. I am a widow, with three young children. The eldest is nine years old; he doesn't look so old as he is; but he's lame with a diseased hip. The second is six: that's a boy; and the youngest is a girl, four years old. I live here with my sister and mother. My mother is a widow. She hasn't anything to depend upon but the earnings of me and my sister. She is sixty-five. My father has been dead these thirteen years. He was a working furrier. He was a chamber master—that is, he took the work out from the furriers', and employed hands to do it. He gave no security: it was not required. He had two women in the house to sew, and employed two or three out of doors as well. He had about six hands in his employ. Sometimes he made £4 a week, sometimes £2, according as the business was brisk or slack. After Christmas he was very often three months with nothing at all to do. But then the prices was very different to what they are now, and there was more work as well. My husband has been dead four years. He was a pocket-book maker. Sometimes he made £2 a week, and £3, and sometimes as much as £4 a week.

"I am thirty-three years of age, and my sister is thirty-six. She is unmarried. She has been of great assistance to me since I became a widow. It was under very distressing circumstances that I lost my husband. I was left entirely destitute; my husband was very much embarrassed at the time. He left his home and drowned himself. This little girl I have on my knee was born a fortnight after his death. I had then nothing to do but the fur business, which I had been brought up to by my father. Then me and my sister and my mother all worked together. Mother was then having work to do from the warehouse, but now she's not able, neither could she get it if she was, there's so many out of employ. Now she takes care of the children while we are out at work.

"We do the lining of the victorines and the capes. We also do the lining of the muffs; being brought up in the business we can do almost any part that females do. We are paid by the dozen. Victorines are from 1s. 6d. to 3s. a dozen lining. The materials are all found us except the cotton, and that costs us about 1d. the dozen victorines. We work fourteen or fifteen hours generally when we work at home. Working these hours we can line about twelve victorines at 1s. 6d. in the day, or eight at 3s. a dozen by sitting very close. We can do between three and four dozen of those at 3s. in the week, and about five dozen of those at 1s. 6d. So that at lining victorines we can earn from 7s. 6d. to 12s. a week. The capes are from 8d. to 1s. 4d. each lining. We reckon we can do about two of those at 1s. 4d. At this we can earn about 8s. at the commoner ones, and about 12s. at the better kind of ones.

"They generally do not give the muffs out to be done. These used to be 4s. a dozen stuffing and lining. About three dozen might be finished in the week; but that is what they used to be some years ago. There is the sewing of the skins together—that we do as well. The skins are cut and put together by the men, and females sew them. There are different prices for different furs. Musquash riding boas are about 2½d. each boa. Victorines of the same fur are 2d., muffs about the same. Squirrel is a little higher, about 3d. the boa. Sables are about 5d. the boa. Ermine the same. Chinchilla about the same. We can make about five of the musquash boas, about four of the squirrel, and about three of the more expensive furs. At this we can earn from about 1s. to 1s. 3d. a day; at the present time 1s. 3d. is the utmost, and we must have the best work to get that. Upon an average, at sewing the skins we can earn about 6s. a week when we are fully employed at it. Each of us can earn this.

"The expenses when we are sewing are more than when we are lining. We use thread for sewing, and it comes to about 8d. every week; and when we are lining the cotton costs us about 6d. a week. At the sewing we can make about 5s. 6d. a week clear, and at the lining from 7s. 6d. to 11s. 6d. each of us. The lining work we reckon don't last more than six months every year. There hasn't been this last summer more than three months' work to be done. We are neither particular quick nor slow hands: we consider ourselves average hands. The lining work begins about May and ends about November every year. The sewing work lasts from about March till about December. During the brisk time we are in general pretty full of work. Some seasons we are more busy than others, but in general during the brisk time we earn what we have stated. Our work begins about the middle of March, and ends about the latter end of December. During these months I should say that we each of us earn, taking one week with another, about 8s. 6d. a week clear. During the slack time there is nothing at all for us to do at home. Then the only work is at the retail houses at the West-end, where hands are engaged "repairing." The pay for this is 8s. a week. Work begins there at half-past eight in the morning, and ends at half-past eight at night.

"We have no book. We haven't had any this last year. Where we have been working lately the proprietor of the warehouse pays every week, as the work is taken

G

in; but this is not the usual practice. We worked at home this last time from the beginning of the year to the latter end of September. From Christmas till April we had nothing at all to do; and after that our earnings averaged about 8s. 6d. a week each. Since September we have been engaged repairing at a warehouse, where we have 8s. a week. This engagement, I think, will last till February; but it depends greatly on the weather. It's all according to what winter we have. After that I suppose we shall be a couple of months unemployed. The trade is much improved by dry frosty weather. There has been very little for us to do this year, on account of the alteration in the fashion. The victorines are not so much worn. They wear double furs, instead of those lined with silk. The riding boas are now more fashionable, and they require no lining, being double fur. The prices have fallen a great deal within the last five years. Every year it gets worse and worse. The prices have come down fully a shilling a dozen since 1845. We could then earn with the same labour 12s. where we now earn 8s.

"Every year we are generally three months standing still—that is the shortest time. Then there is a slackness before we get busy, and the same before the work finishes—so that altogether we may safely say that it's only for eight months in the year that we earn 8s. a week, and for the other four months we don't get more than 2s. a week upon an average. The last slack time we were obligated to part with almost everything we had. So that taking the brisk and the slack, I think we earn about 6s. a week all the year round. We are not able to save anything during the brisk time, there are so many of us—six to live on 16s. We have not been able to get back what we lost during the last slack time. We have got full £3 or £4 worth of things in pledge. We were quite three months out of work—from Christmas till the end of March—and then our rent went back, and we haven't been able to recover it yet. We owe about six weeks now. We pay 4s. a week for this one room. All my children go to school. We have one thing in pledge for 8s. The most of the duplicates is for 5s.—some are for 3s. We have no separate purses. We work together and club our money together. My sister helps me to support my children. If it hadn't been for her I don't know what I should have done. She has made every sacrifice to assist me."

In the same house that the two sisters lived in who worked at lining the furs, there was a woman occupied in embroidering the letters and figures on the policemen's coats. I found her with her young children in their bedgowns about her ready dressed for bed. It was late in the evening when I visited her. She was the type of the better kind of labourer's wife—the mother, housewife, and workwoman all in one. The cheeks of the children were red and shiny with recent scrubbing. In her arms she held an infant, and by her side sat a good-looking boy in the dress of a parish-school. By the fire sat her husband, a swarthy, big-boned man. I told them the object of my visit, and was instantly welcomed to their hearth. In answer to questions they told me as follows:

"I do the embroidery. I can work any part of the embroidery work, no matter what it is. I don't suppose any one's doing good at the embroidery, for gracious knows where it's gone to. Then there's the tapestry, that's gone altogether. That was what I learnt. We used to serve seven years at our business. I embroidered the policemen's collars and the railway guards' collars and sometimes silk work—1s. to 1s. 3d. the dress, what I used to have 5s. and 6s. for, and more than that. Why, they are paying now 2s. 6d. for cardinals that I've had 16s. for. I do the East India work for the Calcutta police; and the Liverpool police, and Isle of Man police. I work for the Penitentiary, and the Model Prison. They are the officers' coats, and indeed I do for all the prisons that wear ornaments. I work for her Majesty's yachts. I have all my work from the contractor for the embroidery. He takes it from the clothier. The clothier knows nothing about our business; he gives it to the embroiderer, who gives it to me. There are no chamber masters that I know of in our business. The contractor takes a very good shaking out of it before we has it.

"I get 6s. and 7s. a dozen for Metropolitan police dress-coat collars. I can do five a day, but we generally reckon four an average day's work of twelve hours. I can earn about 12s. a week at it. Indeed I can do more if I can get it. I have earned 29s. a week at it, but that was by getting up at four in the morning and working till ten at night; and besides, the work was much better paid for then. Then the collars was paid 8s. to 9s. a dozen—that was about five year ago. The other police are about the same; the railway and City both. The railway guards are according to the letters upon them. We are paid 4d. a dozen for the large letters. I could do about four dozen and a half a day. As they pay for that work now, a woman can't earn more than 2s. 2d. to about 2s. 6d. a day; but I've sat and earned 6s. a day at it, and that was for the small letters on the cap-bands of the railway guards, and only having 2d. a band then. For the Calcutta police I get 6d. a collar, or from 6s. to 7s. a dozen. The Calcutta police are just the same work as the Metropolitan. I do just as many of one as the other. It's a white duck collar worked with blue cord. The Liverpool police has the bird called the liver, with a branch of olive in its mouth, and a single strap and number worked in white cord upon blue. Everything used is worsted. It's been argued we work with white cotton cord, but that's a mistake. They're 6s. a dozen, and take about the same as the Metropolitan and the Isle of Man police. The ornament of that is the same as the Isle of Man halfpenny— three legs, boots and spurs. The price is the same as the Metropolitan, 6s. a dozen. I never knew them more, and they take about the same.

"The Penitentiary is a small ring something similar to the Fire Brigade. It's a small ring, and the number inside of it. They are 2d. a piece, to the best of my recollection. I can do about twelve of them a day. The Model Prison have oak leaves and acorns, with a coronet in the ring. They're worked in buff upon blue. Those I'm paid double for, 11s. and 12s. a dozen. But then there's a deal more work in them. The oak leaves and acorns requires a good deal of shaping. When they were first done they were 18s. a dozen, and that was about five or six years ago. The Metropolitan Police, when they first came up, were 16d. to 18d. a collar, and not done half so well as they are now. Dear me, there was no shape in them scarcely. The Fire Brigade is so badly paid—I think they offered me 1½d. a collar— that I couldn't work at them at all. There's the Isle of Wight work—that's the entrance to the prison gate; we have to form all the stones, and the brick-work over the arch. They are 9d. each. I've had them three or four times, but I never had a great many. We can earn about the same at that as at any other of the work. Some things I have to do are black cord worked upon blue, but I don't know what they are for; they're a small coronet in a ring. We work for the Irish police as well. It is the same as the Metropolitan, without either figure or letter. They put metal in them when they get there. Then there's all sorts of crests that we work you know— coats of arms and such like. They are mostly small orders, and don't run above fifty. We work for the Thames Police,—that's the anchor, and like the Metropolitan.

"At all kinds of work about 2s. to 2s. 6d. is what I can earn a day, working twelve hours, or 12s. to 15s. a week. There's very few hands in our business, and we can't think what's become of the work. I never had a piece of work returned in my life, and I'm generally reckoned a very good hand at the business. There can't be more than 200 persons working at it. We likewise do the soldiers' grenades on the collars of their coats. The general pay of them is 6s. a hundred, but I have never done any under 8s. 4d., because I wouldn't work upon scarlet cloth unless I had full price. I could do about 150 a week. I've worked at the embroidery and tapestry ever since I was thirteen years old. When I was first out of my time I could earn my 15s. to 16s. a week—that was before there was any regular police.

"Any one can do tapestry now from the Berlin patterns. There they are all drafted off, and I could give one of them to that child, and tell her to count her stitches and match her colours, and she could do it as well as I could; but before that the design was merely drawn in outline, and we had to shade it off according to our own judgment. I've seen 10 apprentices go away out of 12—weren't fit for the business. In those times it taught us both to paint and to draw, but now it's both painted and drawn for you. We never thought of giving a lesson in it under 5s. At that time the court waistcoats were done—a good bit of money they used to fetch. They used to come to £1 and £1 10s. They would take about four days to do. Work was paid so well for at that time. They're quite gone now; indeed, the work seems all gone altogether. I must go to Doctors' Commons to see if I can find some grenades—though that's the worst of the work. It's what I've sent back scores of times, but I must get something.

"A little while ago there was the embroidering of the gentlemen's stocks; they was worked upon the hand, and the hand embroidery has ruined the frame embroidery altogether. At these I did very well; I could make £1 a week at them easy. I've got a frame nearly half as long as this room, that I suppose I shall never want again. You see here's one of the frames—it's tied up, and no use. I've got three more, and had them all full. The cause of the stock work falling off was this: a man got a quantity of the girls out of the workhouse and put a few tidy hands to superintend the business. There was a great deal of laughing and joking about that man, for he was a butcher by trade, and the idea of his starting in the embroidery line tickled every one. He took 'em down to Cambridge-heath, and cut down the prices so low that fifty of us was forced to leave the business at once. The butcher made a failure of it, and the whole establishment was broke up, and that was the ruin of the hand-embroidery. Then there was another cheap hand, the son of a party in the trade. He undermined his father. He went to the warehouses and offered to do the work for less than half price, and ruined it altogether. I believe he made a failure too. Besides these another was going to have all the work. You see there was a good bit of money made at it then. This party sent me a shawl, a very well drawn thing. It was honestly worth 4s. 6d. to 5s. to do. I had had more money for the same. When I took it in, he had the impudence to offer me 1s. 1½d. for it. Well, this one made a failure of it too, and I have heard that his wife now is trying to pick up a bit of work anywhere.

"The military embroidery was very good indeed about three years ago. I had a great deal of it, so that I could have supported myself and four or five childen very comfortable on it. I could always keep four frames full, and now I've nothing at all to do. Last Saturday week I took 5s. 10d., and that was earnt in a fortnight, and so on about the same for many months. My weekly earnings for the whole of this year hasn't been more than 2s., take one week with another, and three years ago I used to make 15s. to 16s. a week regular, and that with perfect ease. As for the 'gold hands,' I know one that could sit and earn 10s. a day, and I don't think she knows what it is to see a bit of work now. I don't know what really has become of the work lately. All the embroidery hands are earning a mere trifle—3s. one week and then 2s.—and many has called upon me to know what's the cause of it, because they know that I generally used to be so full. Three times last week I sent that little boy to the warehouse for work, and they said, 'send in next week.' Where they're a-doing the work, or how they're a-doing it, I can't tell. Whether they're doing it in their houses or not, by young girls, I can't say; but there must be something like that, for you see as the new clothes comes round there's the work to be done, and some one must do it. Perhaps they're a-doing it in the prisons, for there's many a trade been cut up in that way; but it's a sad pity, for it was a very pretty, tasty, and clean business. My husband is engaged in flushing the sewers; he gets £1 14s. a-week regular.". . .

I now made my way to a garter-maker, and found an old maiden woman engaged at the business. Her room exhibited the utmost order and neatness. Not an article but what was in its proper place, and all was scrupulously clean. On the window-sill, which was as white as snow, stood a row of geraniums and cactuses in pots, brilliant with red-lead. The nose of the bellows was polished quite bright, and over the mantelpiece was a piece of antiquated embroidery in a gilt frame. The dress of the old maid was quite as tidy. She wore an old green stuff gown, without a speck upon it, and a little red silk handkerchief tied round her neck. Her statement was as follows:

"I make up the garters. They give me the India rubber web and I stitch the straps and the buckles on. I have 7d. a dozen pair for what I mostly do. That is the lowest price I get. The highest price I get is 1s. 7d. a dozen. If I could get sufficient I could do two dozen pair of the 7d. ones a-day, but they haven't got it for me to do; and of the 1s. 7d. I couldn't do more than a dozen. My usual time of working is from eight in the morning till nine at night. The 1s. 7d. ones are going to be lowered. They told me last time I was at the warehouse that they were obliged to sell so cheap they couldn't afford to pay that price any longer. I said I hoped they would consider of it, but I would be glad to take what they could afford to give me, as I had nothing else to depend upon.

"In the day, at the commonest work, I can earn 1s. 2d., and at the best 1s. 7d., but then I have silk to find, and that costs me 6d. a dozen for 1s. 7d. ones, and 1½d. a dozen for the 7d. ones. I think I burn half a pound of candles extra when I am at work. I have to light my candles sooner, and I sit up longer when I am at work than when I'm not. Half a pound of candles is 2½d., so that I can make clear, working at the 7d. garters, 10½d. a day; and at the 1s. 7d. I can get 1s. 0½d. clear in the same time. When I am full employed all the week at the commonest kind I couldn't make 12 dozen a week, because I should have to do for myself, and wash and clean. I make two dozen for one day—to do that I must sit close, and hardly have time to get meals, and I couldn't go on so all the week through. I might, if I could get it to do, but they haven't got trade enough for it, do 10 dozen I say in the week, and 10 dozen at 7d. comes to 5s. 10d.; then there's the deduction for the silk, which is 1½d. a dozen, and that's 1s. 3d., and the extra candles 2½d., in all 1s. 5½d. to be taken from 5s. 10d., and this leaves 4s. 4½d. as my clear earnings for the week at the commonest kind of work. Of the 1s. 7d. I think I could do about five dozen in the week, though I'm often *[idle]* for months and don't have any of that kind to do, and five dozen at 1s. 7d. comes to 7s. 11d., and then there's 6d. a dozen to be deducted. I have to find this silk for them," she said, producing a small trayfull of little 'cushions' of silk wherewith to join the clasp to the slide.

"Then deducting the silk for five dozen at 6d.—that is 2s. 6d.—from 7s. 11d., there will be 5s. 5d., and this, with 2½d. less for candles, will leave 5s. 2½d. clear for my week's work at the best kind of work to be had in the trade. I think, taking one kind of work with another, I could earn 5s. a-week, clear of all expenses, if I could get it. But I can't have it. My employer has not it to give, or else he would. I am paid as I take my work in, not at the week's end; but whenever I go to the warehouse with a dozen or two done, they give me the money for it. I have no book, and never had one. Last week I earned about 3s. clear; the week before I think I got about 4s., and the week before that I think about the same. You see I don't keep it in my memory. I believe I am considered to do them as quick as the most of the trade. I was better supplied at the beginning of the year than I have been lately, I should say I got full 5s. clear at the commencement of the year. But since August I am sure I haven't made above 4s. a week, and some weeks not that. I have the web clasps and slides direct from the warehouse.

"For upwards of twenty years I have worked for the same employer. For the last ten years I have been working regularly at the garter making. I have never found the trade slack at one time and brisk at another, in the course of the year. Some-times orders do come in and I am hurried then more than usual; but till within the last three months I have had constant employment, and made upon an average 5s. a week clear. The prices have been always the same to me. Indeed my master has been very kind to me, and not lowered the prices till now, but they are begin-ning to talk about it—they told me when I was last at the warehouse that I must do them for something cheaper, for they were obliged to sell so low. I don't know how much they intend to reduce the price. Whatever it is I shall feel the loss of it very severely. I pay 2s. a week rent, and am obliged to be very near.

"I was fifty-nine last August, and have nothing to look forward to but the work-house, unless the Goldsmiths' Company will do something for me. That is all I have to look forward to. I have not the energy I used to have, nor the spirits—oh, dear, no. I am single, and my father was a silversmith. He has been dead about sixteen years, and my mother ten. I had no rent to pay while they were alive. My father was a working silversmith, and had the pension from the Goldsmiths' Company before he died, and he had the City pension as well; and mother and me worked at the brace work. These were his things. I had no brothers nor sisters, and they came to me after his and mother's death. I've been obliged to part with some be-cause I was in need of money; and, indeed, I only see now the prospect of parting with them all. I can't maintain myself a great while longer by my work, I'm certain, and then I have nothing left but to live on them, as long as they will last, and after all to end my days in the workhouse. It's impossible for me to save a farthing. I can barely live on what I get. Indeed, the anxiety of my life at present, having my living to get, and to get my rent up, is such that I certainly would do anything I could to avoid it, but still I have such a struggle to live and pay my way that I'm tired of it.

"I have been upon my own hands about ten years, that is, ever since my mother's death. Father was afflicted with rheumatic gout for fourteen years before his death, and all I earned then went to him. I have nothing in pawn, and I owe no rent, nor any money in the neighbourhood. If there was another election for the daughters of the freemen of the Goldsmiths' Company, I should apply, but then, of course, I can't say whether I should be successful or not. All I know is, I've worked hard all my life, and been unable to get anything more than would barely keep me. As for putting by anything out of it for my old age, it was ridiculous to think: 6d. a-day is all I have had to find me in coals, clothes, and food for these ten years past. I find it very irksome that I should be forced to be a pauper in my old age, but it is impossible for me to have done otherwise than I have. I have cut and contrived every way to get a decent living out of the little I got, but now even that little is beginning to fail me. I've had my mother's clothes, you see, and they've lasted me pretty well, and I haven't had much to buy that way. I am quite alone in the world. If a place in some almshouse could be got for me that would be a real blessing indeed—worth more to me than all the money in the world."

Needlewomen Forced into Prostitution

From Letter VIII, November 13th, 1849

[Not all of the women Mayhew interviews in these letters are prostitutes in the sense of women who hire themselves out indiscriminately. In the category "prostitute", Mayhew and many of his contemporaries made little distinction between a girl "on the streets" or a professional prostitute, and a woman who simply lived with a man without being married to him.]

During the course of my investigation into the condition of those who are dependent upon their needle for their support, I had been so repeatedly assured that the young girls were mostly compelled to resort to prostitution to eke out their subsistence, that I was anxious to test the truth of the statement. I had seen much want, but I had no idea of the intensity of the privations suffered by the needlewomen of London until I came to inquire into this part of the subject. But the poor creatures shall speak for themselves. I should inform the reader, however, that I have made inquiries into the truth of the almost incredible statements here given, and I can in most of the particulars at least vouch for the truth of the statement. Indeed, in one instance—that of the last case here recorded—I travelled nearly ten miles in order to obtain the character of the young woman. The first case is that of a good-looking girl. Her story is as follows:

"I make moleskin trowsers. I get 7d. and 8d. per pair. I can do two pairs in a day, and twelve when there is full employment, in a week. But some weeks I have no work at all. I work from six in the morning to ten at night; that is what I call my day's work. When I am fully employed I get from 7s. to 8s. a week. My expenses out of that for twist, thread, and candles are about 1s. 6d. a week, leaving me about 6s. a week clear. But there's coals to pay for out of this, and that's at the least 6d. more; so 5s. 6d. is the very outside of what I earn when I'm in full work. Lately I have been dreadfully slack; so we are every winter, all of us 'sloppers;' and that's the time when we wants the most money. The week before last I had but two pair to make all the week; so that I only earnt 1s. clear. For this last month I'm sure I haven't done any more than that each week. Taking one week with another, all the year round I don't make above 3s. clear money each week. I don't work at any other kind of slopwork. The trowsers work is held to be the best paid of all. I give 1s. a week rent.

"My father died when I was five years of age. My mother is a widow, upwards of 66 years of age, and seldom has a day's work. Generally once in the week she is employed pot-scouring—that is, cleaning publicans' pots. She is paid 4d. a dozen for that, and does about four dozen and a half, so that she gets about 1s. 6d. in the day by it. For the rest she is dependent upon me. I am 20 years of age the 25th of this month. We earn together, to keep the two of us, from 4s. 6d. to 5s. each week. Out of this we have to pay 1s. rent, and there remains 3s. 6d. to 4s. to find us both in food and clothing. It is of course impossible for us to live upon it, and the consequence is I am obliged to go a bad way. I have been three years working at slop-work. I was virtuous when I first went to work, and I remained so till this last twelvemonth. I struggled very hard to keep myself chaste, but I found that I couldn't get food and clothing for myself and mother, so I took to live with a young man. He is turned 20. He is a tinman. He did promise to marry me, but his sister made mischief between me and him, so that parted us. I have not seen him now for about six months, and I can't say whether he will keep his promise or not. I am now pregnant by him, and expect to be confined in two months' time. He knows of my situation, and so does my mother. My mother believed me to be married to him. She knows otherwise now. I was very fond of him, and had known him for two years before he seduced me. He could make 14s. a week. He told me if I came to live with him he'd take care I shouldn't want, and both mother and me had been very bad off before. He said, too, he'd make me his lawful wife, but I hardly cared so long as I could get food for myself and mother.

"Many young girls at the shop advised me to go wrong. They told me how comfortable they was off; they said they could get plenty to eat and drink, and good clothes. There isn't one young girl as can get her living by slop work. The masters all know this, but they wouldn't own to it of course. It stands to reason that no one can live and pay rent, and find clothes, upon 3s. a week, which is the most they make clear, even the best hands, at the moleskin and cord trowsers work. The shirt work is worse and worse still. There's poor people moved out of our house that was making ¾d. shirts. I am satisfied there is not one young girl that works at slop work that is virtuous, and there are some thousands in the trade. They may do very well if they have got mothers and fathers to find them a home and food, and to let them have what they earn for clothes; then they may be virtuous, but not without. I've heard of numbers who have gone from slop work to the streets altogether for a living, and I shall be obligated to do the same thing myself unless something better turns up for me. If I was never allowed to speak no more, it was the little money I got by my labour that led me to go wrong. Could I have honestly earnt enough to have subsisted upon, to find me in proper food and clothing, such as is necessary, I should not have gone astray; no, never. As it was I fought against it as long as I could—that I did to the last. I hope to be able to get a ticket for a midwife; a party has promised me as much, and, he says, if possible, he'll get me an order for a box of linen.

"My child will only increase my burdens, and if my young man won't support my child I must go on the streets altogether. I know how horrible all this is. It would have been much better for me to have subsisted upon a dry crust and water rather than be as I am now. But no one knows the temptations of us poor girls in want. Gentlefolks can never understand it. If I had been born a lady it wouldn't have been very hard to have acted like one. To be poor and to be honest, especially with young girls, is the hardest struggle of all. There isn't one in a thousand that can get the better of it. I am ready to say again, that it was want, and nothing more, that made me transgress. If I had been better paid I should have done better.

Young as I am, my life is a curse to me. If the Almighty would please to take me before my child is born, I should die happy."

The next were two "trowsers hands," working for the same piece-mistress. I was assured by the woman by whom they were employed, and whom I visited expressly to make inquiries into the matter, that they were both hardworking and sober individuals. The first of these made the following extraordinary statement:

"I work at slop trowsers, moleskin and cord—no cloth. There's hands for jackets and hands for waistcoats all by themselves; every one gets their own employment. I'm a trowsers hand. I don't make army, navy, police, or railway things. Merely work for slopsellers. I work second-handed. The first-hand I work for employs only four. Sometimes she has more, but she's only four at present. She gets 6d., 7d., 8d., 9d., and 10d. per pair. 6d. is the lowest price paid by the warehouse and 10d. the highest price. Them are the prices for moleskin and cord trowsers. The party I works for is called a sweater. She gives us 4d. a pair all round, take the high with the low priced ones; that is, we have 4d. for the tenpenny trowsers as well as for the sevenpenny ones. If a pair of bespoke ones is given out to her, and she thinks they is done very nice, she'll give us 6d. for them. It takes from five to six hours to make a pair of the trowsers that we gets 4d. for, and work very quick. We must work from twelve to fourteen hours every day to make two pair; that is, allowing a little time to one's meals; and then we have to sweep and tidy our place up a little, so that we must work very hard to get two pair done in a day. She finds us thread.

"We make about 4s. a-week, but we must work till nine or ten o'clock every night for that. We never make more than 4s., and very often less. If you go of an errand, or want a bit of bread, you lose time, and sometimes the work comes out harder—it's more stubborn, and takes more time. I've known it like a bit of board. I make, I should say, taking one week with another, about 3s. 4d. a week. The sweater finds us our lodging; but we has to buy our candles out of what we make, and they cost us about 1d. each evening, or I should say 5d. a week. I earn clear just upon 3s.; that's about it. I find it very hard indeed to live upon that. We take our money every day, the 6d. or 8d.—as the case may be—and very often on Sundays we don't have anything. If we fall ill we're turned off. The sweater won't keep us with her not the second day.

"I have been married. My husband has been dead seven year. I wish he wasn't. I have no children alive. I have buried three. I had two children alive when my husband died. The youngest was five and the other was seven. My husband was a soap maker. He got £1 a week. I worked at the slop trade while he was alive. Our weekly earnings—his and mine together—was about 26s. The slop trade was better paid then than now, and what's more, I had the work on my own account. I was very happy and comfortable while he lived." [Here the woman burst out crying, and wiped her eyes with the corner of her old rusty shawl.]

"I was always true to him while he was alive, so help me God! After his death I was penniless, with two young children. The only means I had of keeping myself and little ones was by the slop work; and that brought me in about 5s. 6d. a week that was two year after his father—I couldn't afford to bury him. My sister paid first-hand. That was to keep me and my two boys. When my eldest boy died—and for the funeral. I was very thankful to the Almighty when he took him from me, for I had not sufficient to feed him. He died of scarlatina. My second boy has only been dead five months. He died of the hooping-cough. I loved him as I did my life; but I was glad he was took from me, for I know he's better now than I could have done for him. He could but have been brought up in the worst kind of poverty by me, and God only knows what might have become of him if he had lived.

"My security died five year ago, and then the house that I had been used to work for refused to give me any more, so I was obligated to go and work for a 'sweater,' and I have done so ever since. This was a heavy blow to me. I was getting about 5s. 6d. a week before then. The trowsers was better paid for at that time besides, and when I was obligated to work second-handed I couldn't get more than 4s. One of my boys was alive at this time, and we really could not live upon the money. I applied to the parish, and they wanted me to go into the house, but I knew if I did so they'd take my boy from me, and I'd suffer anything first. At times I was so badly off, me and my boy, that I was forced to resort to prostitution to keep us from starving. It was not until after my security died that I did this. Before that we could just live by my labour, but afterwards it was impossible for me to get food and clothing for myself and child out of 4s. a week, which was all I could earn, so I was obligated to get a little more money in a way that I blush to mention to you. Up to the time of the death of my security, I can swear, before God, I was an honest woman, and had the price I was paid for my labour been such that I could get a living by it, I would never have resorted to the streets for money.

"I am sorry to say there is too many persons like me in the trade—hundreds of married and single doing the same as I do, for the same reason. It's the ruin of us, body and soul—all owing to the low prices. Almost all that works for the sweaters do the same thing. I know several that's very young living in that manner. It most drives 'em mad. They're hard-working, industrious people, but they don't get sufficient price to have enough, no! not even of the coarsest victuals; and if they got more, they wouldn't think of such a mode of life. They do their work in the day, and go out in the night. They say they can't have enough by their work, and must see what else they can get some money by. In this way they make their week's money come to about 6s. or 7s.—some more and some less. I don't know any that makes a practice of walking the streets regularly of a night. They only go out when they're in distress. This is what I believe to be truth; and I can safely say as much in my conscience and before God."

The statement of the second trowsers hand was equally awful. It ran as follows:

"I work at the slop, make trowsers—moleskin and cord—any sort of plain work. I work at the same place as the other woman works at, and for the same prices. I earn, like her, taking one week with another, about 3s. 4d., and taking off the candles about 3s. every week. I have been married, but my husband's been dead eleven year. I have had two children, but I've buried them—I've got none at present—I had only one child alive at the time of my husband's death—she was about a twelvemonth old when her father died. He was a ballast getter—he got the ballast out of the river for the ships. He worked for the Trinity Company. He used to earn a good bit of money at that time. Ballast work now is very indifferent. He used to get 30s. a week at the lowest. I worked at the slop trade before I was married, but not afterwards, until my husband died. We were very comfortable, my husband and me. We had one room. He was rather given to a drop of drink.

"When he died he left me penniless, with a baby to keep. I was an honest woman up to the time of my husband's death. I never did him wrong. I can lay my hand on my heart and say so. But since then the world has drove me about so, and poverty and trouble has forced me to do what I never did before. I have been drove about by my work being badly paid. I couldn't earn what would keep me. I have always worked second-handed since my husband's death, and the money I have got by my labour has not been enough to support me. I do the best I can with what little money I earn, and the rest I am obligated to go to the streets for. That is true, though I says it as shouldn't. I can't get a rag to wear without flying to prostitution for it. My wages will barely find me in food. Indeed, I eat more than I earn, and I am obligated to make up my money in other ways.

"I know a great many women who are situated in the same way as I am. We pretty well all share one fate in that respect—with the exception of those that's got husbands to keep them. The young and middle-aged all do the same, as far as I know. There's good and bad in all, but with the most of 'em I'm sure they're drove to it—yes, that they are—I have frequently heard them regret that they are forced to go to the streets to make out their living. Why, they said, they worked so hard for so little that they might as well be on the streets altogether. I have known many who found it such a dreadful struggle to live by slop work, that they have left it and gone on to the streets entirely. I know that the low prices that are paid by the slopsellers makes women and girls prostitutes. I can answer for myself and several besides me; and had I been better paid, been merely able to live by my labour, I should have been still an honest and virtuous woman. For three or four years after my husband's death, I struggled on and kept true to his memory, but at last all my clothes were gone, and I was obliged to transgress. I actually could not make out victuals and clothes too, and I had always been used to be comfortable and appear respectable in my younger days. I know it's the lowness of the prices.

"Sometimes I'm quite tired of my life. If those who've taken to the streets as a regular practice was to come back again to work there'd be no chance of a living for them; and if I was younger I should go on the streets altogether myself. I often do say I wish I was younger. I think the women engaged at slop-work get from 6s. to 7s. a-week altogether. They cannot manage to do upon 3s., which is all that such as us can get by our labour. I speak only the truth, and I can honestly say so—that I can. Indeed, I shouldn't have told you all I have, if I didn't wish the whole truth and nothing but the truth to be known."

The story which follows is perhaps one of the most tragic and touching romances ever read. I must confess that to myself the mental and bodily agony of the poor Magdalen who related it was quite overpowering. She was a tall, fine-grown girl, with remarkably regular features. She told her tale with her face hidden in her hands, and sobbing so loud that it was with difficulty I could catch her words. As she held her hands before her eyes I could see the tears oozing between her fingers. Indeed I never remember to have witnessed such intense grief. Her statement was of so startling a nature, that I felt it due to the public to inquire into the character of the girl. Though it was late at night, and the gentleman who had brought the case to me assured me that he himself was able to corroborate almost every word of the girl's story, still I felt that I should not be doing my duty to the office that had been entrusted to me if I allowed so pathetic and romantic a statement to go forth without using every means to test the truth of what I had heard. Accordingly, being informed that the girl was in service, I made the best of my way not only to her present master, but also to the one she had left but a few months previous. The gentleman who had brought her to me, willingly accompanied me thither. One of the parties lived at the East end of London, the other in the extreme suburbs of London. The result was well worth the journey. Both persons spoke in the highest terms of the girl's honesty, sobriety, industry, and of her virtue in particular.

With this preamble let me proceed to tell her story in her own touching words:

"I used to work at slop work—at the shirt work—the fine full-fronted white shirts; I got $2\frac{1}{4}$d. each for 'em. There were six button-holes, four rows of stitching in the front, and the collars and wristbands stitched as well. By working from five o'clock in the morning till midnight each night I might be able to do seven in the week. These would bring me in $17\frac{1}{2}$d. for my whole week's labour. Out of this the cotton must be taken, and that came to 2d. every week, and so left me $15\frac{1}{2}$d. to pay rent and living and buy candles with. I was single, and received some little help from my friends; still it was impossible for me to live. I was forced to go out of a night to make out my living. I had a child, and it used to cry for food. So, as I could not get a living for him myself by my needle, I went into the streets and made out a living that way. Sometimes there was no work for me, and then I was forced to depend entirely upon the streets for my food. On my soul I went to the streets solely to get a living for myself and child. If I had been able to get it otherwise I would not have done so.

"I am the daughter of a minister of the gospel. My father was an Independent preacher, and I pledge my word, solemnly and sacredly, that it was the low price paid for my labour that drove me to prostitution. I often struggled against it, and many times have I taken my child into the streets to beg rather than I would bring shame upon myself and it any longer. I have made pincushions and fancy articles—such as I could manage to scrape together—and taken them to the streets to sell, so that I might get an honest living, but I couldn't. Sometimes I should be out all night in the rain, and sell nothing at all, me and my child together; and when we didn't get anything that way we used to sit in a shed, for I was too fatigued with my baby to stand, and I was so poor I couldn't have even a night's lodging upon credit. One night in the depth of winter his legs froze to my side. We sat down on the step of a door. I was trying to make my way to the workhouse, but was so weak I couldn't get on any farther. The snow was over my shoes. It had been snowing all day, and me and my boy out in it. We hadn't tasted any food since the morning before, and that I got in another person's name. I was driven by positive starvation to say that they sent me when they did no such thing. All this time I was struggling to give up prostitution. I had many offers, but I refused them all. I had sworn to myself that I would keep from that mode of life for my boy's sake. A lady saw me sitting on the door-step, and took me into her house, and rubbed my child's legs with brandy. She gave us some food, both my child and me, but I was so far gone I couldn't eat. I got to the workhouse that night. I told them we were starving, but they refused to admit us without an order; so I went back to prostitution again for another month. I couldn't get any work. I had no security. I couldn't even get a reference to find me work at second hand. My character was quite gone. I was at length so disgusted with my line of life that I got an order for the workhouse, and went in there for two years. The very minute we got inside the gate they took my child away from me, and allowed me to see it only once a month.

"At last I and another left 'the house' to work at umbrella covering, so that we might have our children with us. For this work we had 1s. a dozen covers, and we used to do between us from six to eight dozen a week. We could have done more, but the work wasn't to be had. I then made from 3s. to 4s. a week, and from that time I gave up prostitution. For the sake of my child I should not like my name to be known, but for the sake of other young girls I can and will solemnly state that it was the smallness of the price I got for my labour that drove me to prostitution as a means of living. In my heart I hated it; my whole nature rebelled at it, and nobody but God knows how I struggled to give it up. I was only able to do so by getting work at something that was better paid. Had I remained at shirt-making, I must have been a prostitute to this day. I have taken my gown off my back and pledged it, and gone in my petticoat—I had but one—rather than take to the streets again; but it was all in vain. We were starving still; and I robbed the young woman who lodged in the next room to me of a gown, in order to go out in the streets once more and get a crust. I left my child at home, wrapped in a bit of an old blanket while I went out. I brought home half-a-crown by my shame, and stopped its cries for food for two days.

"My sufferings have been such that three days before I first tried to get into the workhouse I made up my mind to commit suicide. I wrote the name of my boy and the address of his aunts and pinned them to his little shift, and left him in bed— for ever as I thought—and went to the Regent's-park to drown myself in the water near the road leading to St. John's-wood. I went there because I thought I was more sure of death. It was farther to jump. The policeman watched me, and asked me what I was doing. He thought I looked suspicious, and drove me from the Park. That saved my life. My father died, thank God, when I was eight years old. My sisters are waistcoat hands, and both starving. I hardly know whether one is dead or not now. She is suffering from cancers brought on by poor living.

"I am now living in service. I have been so for the last year and a half. I obtained a character from a Christian gentleman to whom I owe my salvation. I can solemnly assert since I have been able to earn a sufficient living I have never once resorted to prostitution. My boy is still in the workhouse. I have been unable to save any money since I have been in service. My wages are low, and I had scarcely any clothes when I went there. If I had a girl of my own I should believe I should be making a prostitute of her to put her to slop work. I am sure no girl can get a living at it without, and I say as much after thirteen years' experience of the business. I never knew one girl in the trade who was virtuous; most of them wished to be so, but were compelled to be otherwise for mere life."

From Letter XI, November 23rd, 1849

. . . *[I wished to convene]* such a number of needlewomen and slop-workers as would enable me to arrive at a correct *average* as to the earnings of the class. I was particularly anxious to do this, not only with regard to the more respectable portion

of the operatives, but also with reference to those who, I had been given to understand, resorted to prostitution in order to eke out their subsistence. I consulted
a friend who is well acquainted with the habits and feelings of the slop-workers
as to the possibility of gathering together a number of women who would be
willing to state that they had been forced to take to the streets on account of the
low prices for their work. He told me he was afraid, from the shame of their mode
of life becoming known, it would be almost impossible to collect together a
number of females who would be ready to say as much *publicly*.

However, it was decided that at last the experiment should be made and that
everything should be done to assure the parties of the strict privacy of the assembly.
It was arranged that the gentleman and myself should be the only male persons
visible on the occasion, and that the place of meeting should be as dimly lighted
as possible, so that they could scarcely see or be seen by one another or by us.
Cards of admission were issued and distributed as privately as possible, and to my
friend's astonishment, as many as twenty-five came, on the evening named, to the
appointed place—intent upon making known the sorrows and sufferings that had
driven them to fly to the streets, in order to get the bread which the wretched
prices paid for their labour would not permit them to obtain.

Never in all history was such a sight seen or such tales heard. There, in the dim
blaze of the large bare room in which they met, sat women and girls, some with
babies suckling at their breasts—others in rags—and even these borrowed, in
order that they might come and tell their misery to the world. I have witnessed
many a scene of sorrow lately; I have heard stories that have unmanned me; but
never till last Wednesday had I heard or seen anything so solemn, so terrible, as
this. If ever eloquence was listened to, it was in the outpourings of those poor
lorn mothers' hearts for their base-born little ones, as each told her woes and
struggles, and published her shame amid the convulsive sobs of the others—nay,
of all present. Behind a screen, removed from sight, so as not to wound the modesty
of the women—who were nevertheless aware of their presence—sat two reporters
from this Journal, to take down *verbatim* the confessions and declarations of those
assembled, and to them I am indebted for the following report of the statements
made at the meeting:

A gentleman who has for many years taken a deep interest in the subject, and
myself, severally addressed those present, and urged them to speak without fear,
and to tell the whole truth with regard to their situations, assuring them that their
names should not be divulged, and, at the same time, reminding them that the
only way to obtain their deliverance from their present condition was, that they
should speak for themselves, tell their own tale, simply, and without exaggeration,
with the most scrupulous regard to truth.

Thus admonished, the following statements were made by the parties:

The first speaker was a middle-aged woman, who stood up and said:

"I am a slopworker, and sometimes make about 3s. 6d. a week, and sometimes
less. I have been drove to prostitution sometimes, not always, through the
bad prices. For the sake of my lodgings and a bit of bread I've been obligated to do what I am very sorry to do, and look upon with disgust. I can't
live by what I get by work. The woman who employs me, and several more
besides, gets 11d. and 1s. a pair for the trowsers we make, and we get only 4d. to
5d. We can't do more than a pair a day, and sometimes a pair and a half. It's

starving. I can't get a cup of tea and a bit of bread. I was married, and am left a widow, and have been forced to live in this distressed manner for the last four years. I've been to several different people to get work, but they are all alike in taking advantage of our unfortunate situation."

Scarcely had this one sat down than another, who worked in the same house and under the same piece-mistress, rose, and spoke as follows:

"I works, sir, the goods of another person for a living. I've been married fifteen years. My husband has been dead these twelve years. I thought one place would suit me better than another, but I find them all one way; they're all much alike. The most I can earn is about 3s. 6d. a week. I get my lodgings only from the person that employs me. I'm sometimes obliged to work till twelve at night for my 3s. 6d.; and now in these short days I can scarcely earn anything. I've been obliged often to go to prostitution. These twelve years I haven't been altogether on the streets, but have been almost as bad. I can scarcely earn, sir, what I eat. I think the small number of us present arises from the shame of the women to come. But I express the truth, and nothing but the truth; and yet people are ashamed even to tell the truth. But I'm not ashamed to tell the troubles I've had through distress. Bad payment for the work obliges us to do wrong. It's against our will to do such a thing. And now for a woman of my years it's getting almost more than I can bear, sir."

The third speaker was one with scarcely any clothing upon her back. She said:

"I'm a slopworker, and have got a little boy eighteen months old, and I'm not able to do much work. I work with another woman, and get 7d. and 6d. a pair for doing trowsers. I'm often out of work, and the last fortnight or three weeks I've had nothing to do. I've got no husband, but am compelled to live with a man to support me, for the sake of my child. The father of the child is a labouring man in the docks. He helps to support the child when he can, but he is sometimes employed only two or three days in the week, and at other times not that. He hasn't left me. He gets 2s. 4d. a day when he has work. He has work to-day, and last Friday was the first he had for a fortnight. He applies daily at the docks, and can't get it; but when they're busy he gets his turn. I can state solemnly in the presence of my Maker, that I live with him only to get a living and save myself from doing worse. But if I could get a living otherwise, I can't say I would leave him. At my own work I sometimes make 2s., and at others only 1s. 6d. a week. He's willing to marry me the first day that he can afford; but he hasn't the money to pay the fees. Sometimes he is a fortnight or three weeks, and even a month without any work at all, and last week we were forced to go to the Refuge for the Destitute."

The next was a good-looking girl. Her father had driven her from home, and she could not live by shoe-binding. She said:

"Five years ago my father turned me out of doors. The shoe-binding is so low that I wasn't able to pay 1s. a week for my lodging, and that caused me to turn out into the street. Then it was three weeks before I ever was in a bed. I sat on London-bridge a fortnight before Christmas five years ago. My father took me home again three years ago, but he turned me out again, and I was forced to go back to the street. He says he can't keep us at home. He is a soap-boiler. My mother died about twelve years ago. There were nine of us when she died, and we're all living still. My father said he could not keep us any longer. I work whenever I can get it at trowsers work; but can't get it always. I used to get it first-hand till lately; but latterly I've worked for a woman who takes it in. I do a pair a day, and sometimes more. I sometimes used to make 1s. 6d., and at others 2s. a week; and when I have the best employment I can generally earn about half-a-crown."

After this another young girl rose up. She, like the last, had been turned into the streets by her parent. All she wished (she told us) was to gain admittance into some asylum for penitent females.

"I've been out in the streets three years. I work at the boot-binding, but can't get a living at it. I went with Mr. ———, and another gentleman who took me home to my father, but my father couldn't help me. If I get bread, sir, by my work, I can't get clothes. For the sake of clothes or food I'm obliged to go into the streets, and I'm out reg'larly now, and I've no other dependence at all but the streets. If I could only get an honest living, I would gladly leave the streets. But I can't earn enough at my work to get a living, and therefore I know its useless returning to it. I've been out a whole fortnight together, and not got a meal but what I got in the streets; and I've been forced several times to go into St. George's workhouse. When there I'm only five minutes' walk from my father's house, but he won't receive me. I don't know why. [A gentleman present at the meeting here said that he had gone to see the girl's father, to induce him to receive his daughter. He had to go half a dozen times before he could see him, and then he did not find him at home, but in a beer-shop, half drunk. He refused to take his daughter back, and on being told that if he persisted she must go into the streets, he replied, 'I don't care: let her do as she pleases!' The girl continued:] If I could get work that would keep me, I would give up the streets entirely.". . .

Then an orphan told us her sufferings:

"I come from Edinburgh, in Scotland. I am the daughter of a publican. I was left an orphan at twelve years old, under the care of an uncle, my father's brother. Through my aunt and uncle's cruelty I left them at the age of fifteen or sixteen, with a young man. I lived with him for ten years, and had six children. I have one boy living now, at the age of eleven. Two years ago he deserted me. I did all I could to obtain a living in Edinburgh, and through persuasion I came to London about a twelvemonth ago. I was destitute of a home. I knew no one; but as long as I had anything to pledge or sell I paid for my lodging and maintenance. I then wandered about for days together, seeking food, till some girls I fell in with near the glasshouse down here told me of the gentleman of the name of ———, and said if I would call upon him in the morning he would give me coffee and bread. I went to him for two or three mornings, and he gave me coffee and bread, and treated me very kindly. One day I saw a bill in a window in Rosemary-lane, wanting a girl to work at the needle. I went there, and got 2s. a week for three months; and I had to pay for my lodgings and find my food out of it. At last these people broke up their house because they were not married, and they quarrelled. Then I had not a home to go to, being without work. I went back to the gentleman again; he wondered to see me, and asked me why I came back, and I told him. He was very kind to me, took me into his house, and gave me lodgings with bread and coffee every morning. I was there for a week, till he found me work at the same place where I am in now. This was five months ago, and I am there now. If it had not been for that gentleman's kindness, I don't know what would have become of me, for I was without home or friends.

H

"I have not been on the town for these five months since I had work, but I was forced to do so before that. I state that solemnly, and I say it not for my own sake, but for the sake of others. I am not earning enough at the slop-work to keep me, but the person with whom I stop is very kind to me. I have paid her nothing for my lodgings, and she has given me many a meal of meat when I had not any. Could I obtain a living by my needle I would never resort to prostitution. I have got a situation to-day as a servant of all work. My boy is still living, I believe; but I have heard nothing of him this twelvemonth. He is in Scotland with his father. When his father deserted me he took the child—not at first, but I was not able to keep him, and so I sent him to his father. I do not wish to keep the child, because his father is able to keep him. I could not keep him in a proper manner. I should like to see my child sent to school, and brought up in the fear of God, and that is more than I am able to do, so that I would rather he stayed where he is. I think his father will be good to the child.". . .

This one had scarcely sat down before a woman with an infant in her arms stood up, and spoke as follows:

"I was left a widow with two children, and I could get no work to keep me. I picked up with this child's father, and thought with the little help that he could give me I might be able to keep my children; but after all, I was forced by want and distress, and the trouble of child-bed, to sell all I had to get a bit of victuals. I was forced to go into the house at Wapping to be delivered of this child. This woman (pointing to a neighbour) took care of my other children. He (the father) came to me, gave me 5s., and told me that if I could take a room he would do all he could for me. I took a room at 1s. 6d. a-week, and bought half a truss of straw; and he told me he would marry me if ever it was in his power. I could not go out into the world again; but this woman will tell you that all I have got under me and over me you may buy for 6d. I live with that man still, and sometimes I have not a bit to eat. I thought more of my little boy having a bit to eat than myself. He had been stealing some coals, and he is now imprisoned. I was forced to let him go to try to get a bit of victuals, for I had nothing more to make away with. My boy was taken up for stealing 3 lbs. of coals. He did not bring the coals to me; he was taken before he could get home. I believe he stole them for my sake; not to spend in any other way but to get a bit of bread and a bit of fire for his mother."

Another orphan then got up:

"I was left an orphan ten years ago," said she, "and took to needle-work. I took to slop-shirts, but could not get a living by that, and so I took to the seaming of trowsers. Still I could not get a living, and by that means I lost what bit of furniture I had left. I could not pay my rent, and was in arrears three weeks. My landlord turned me out, and I had nowhere to go, till I was taken to a brothel by a person that I met, but I don't know who it was. I remained in that condition till such time as I fell in the family way, and the young man I fell in that state by went away and left me destitute. I was 14 days and 14 nights and never saw a bed. It froze hard and snowed very fast, and I was left exposed till it pleased God Almighty to send the person I live with now to help me. I am advanced in the family way at present. I am living with a man now, but not in a married state. It's not in his power to marry me, his work won't allow it; and he's not able to support me in the manner he wishes, and keep himself. He has never but two meals a day—breakfast and supper. I think he would marry me if he had the marriage fees, willingly.

"It's not in my power to afford better clothing than I've got on. I hadn't a dinner to-day. I don't consider that I've tasted a Sunday's dinner for six months. I can't earn myself 4d. a day, and my partner's work don't amount to 1s. a day, taking one day with another. I've 1s. 6d. a week rent to pay out of that, and firing and food to find. Unless I was to go to other means, it wouldn't be in my power to do anything to support myself. I don't do it from inclination. I would leave it as soon as I could. I've been forced occasionally to resort to prostitution; but now I'm trying, by living on the small pittance I can get, to avoid it. I detest it: I was never reared to it. I was brought up to the church and to attend to my God. I was always shown a different pattern; but misfortune overtook me. If I could get a living without it I would leave it."

The next speaker was the most eloquent of all. I never before listened to such a gush of words and emotion, and perhaps never shall again. She spoke without the least effort, in one continued strain, for upwards of half an hour, crying half hysterically herself, while those around her sobbed in sympathy:

"Between ten and eleven years ago I was left a widow with two young children, and far advanced in pregnancy with another. I had no means of getting a living, and therefore I thought I would take up slop-work. I got work at slop-shirts—what they call second-hand. I had no security, and therefore could not get the work myself from the warehouse. Two months before I was confined, I seemed to do middling well. I could manage three or four shirts—what they call 'rowers'—at 3d. each, by sitting closely at work from five or six in the morning till about nine or ten at night; but, of course, when I was confined I was unable to do anything. As soon as I was able to sit up I undertook slop-shirts again; but my child being sickly, I was not able to earn so much as before. Perhaps I could earn 9d. a day by hard work, when I get 3d. each shirt; but sometimes I only get 2½d., and I have been obliged to do them at 1½d. each, and, with my child sickly, could only earn 4d., or at most 6d. a day. At other times I hadn't work. On the average I calculated that I have earnt 9d. a day when the prices were better. 1s. 9d. a week went for rent; and as to living, I don't call it that; I was so reduced with it, and my child being so bad, it couldn't be considered a living. I was obliged to live on potatoes and salt; and for nine weeks together I lived on potatoes and never knew what it was to have a half-quartern loaf—for the loaf was 9d. then. By that means my health was declining, and I wasn't able to do hard work. My child's health, too, was declining, and I was obliged to pawn the sheets of my bed and my blankets to procure a shilling.

"At last I found it impossible to pay my rent. I owed 7s. arrears, and my landlady plagued me much to pay her. She advised me to raffle away a large chest that I had. I did so, and gained 12s., and then paid her the 7s. I owed her; but I became so reduced again, that I was obliged to get an order to get into the 'house.' I didn't wish to go in, but I wanted relief and knew I couldn't get it without doing so. I felt it a hard trial to have my children taken from my bosom: we had never been parted before, and I can't help remembering what were my feelings then as a mother who always loved her children. I thought rather than we should be parted that I would make away with myself. But still I applied to the parish, and never shall I forget the day that I did so. I was told to go, and I would get a loaf by applying. I went in, and my heart was full at the thought of taking home a quartern loaf to my starving children. But I was disappointed; and seeing a loaf given out to other parties, I can say that I should have felt glad even of the crumbs to take home to my poor children if I could have got near enough.

"Christmas came round, and I thought, poor things, they will be without a Christmas dinner, and so I got an order to go into the Wapping workhouse. Yet my feelings were such that it was impossible I could enter, and I remained out five weeks after I had got the order, and pledged, as far as I could, anything that would fetch 2d., obtaining also a little assistance from slop-work. But I got so little that I found it impossible to live. The time came to get another order, and I went with my clothes patched from top to bottom, yet I trust they were clean. And never shall I forget that Saturday afternoon as I travelled along Gravel-lane to the 'house,' with feelings that it was impossible for me to enter, for I thought 'How can I bear to have my dear children taken away from me—they have never been taken away from me before?' I reflected, 'What can I do but go there,' so I mustered courage at all events to get to the gate; and, oh! it is impossible to describe what my feelings were as I passed through. I was admitted to a room where they were toasting the bread for the mistress's tea. A little girl was there, and she said, 'Look at these dear little children, I will give them a bit of the toast.' The children took it, and thought it very nice, but they little thought that we were so soon to be parted. The first was seven years old, the second three, and the infant was in my arms. A mother's feelings are better felt than described. The children were taken and separated, and then, oh my God! what I felt no tongue can tell. [Here the woman's emotions overcame her, and she could not proceed with her narrative for weeping. At length recovering herself she continued]:

"I was in hopes of getting my children back within a week or two, but my business could not be settled so soon. My babe took the measles; they went inwardly, and it took a deep decline. I knew it was very bad, and asked leave to go and see him. The mistress was very kind, and gave me leave. I found my child very bad, and the infant in my arms seemed declining every day. My feelings then were such as I can't tell you. I thought—'Oh! if I could only get out and have my children with myself, how much better it would be.' I hurried them to settle my business for me; it originated in a dispute between St. George's and Wapping about our parish, my husband being at the sugar-house at work. At last the dispute was settled, but the one child died, whilst the other—the youngest—was dying. I was so anxious to get out that I could not wait till my child was buried. I asked relief to be settled on me out of doors, and it was granted. I was allowed 1s. a week and two loaves. The acting master asked me if I had any place to go to. I said I would take a room. 'Have you any bed,' he asked. I said 'yes, but no bedding.' I was obliged to pledge it before I entered the house. He was a kind man, and said no doubt the overseers would get my blankets and bedding for me. 'My dear woman,' he said (for he saw I was an affectionate mother, and that I had nothing to begin with) 'here is a shilling for you.' He took it out of his own pocket, and I thought it very kind.

"The children were brought from Limehouse, and one of them was dead at the time. I went with an anxious heart to see its corpse, but I felt 'I cannot stay with you till you are buried, because I have another nearly dead; but I will come again on Wednesday to see you buried.' Well, I found my poor boy but a shadow— a mere skeleton of what he had been. I was overcome with my feelings, and I thought, 'Here is one dead, and another near death!' But I got up, and before ever I went to my room in Whitechapel I went to a doctor; but he said the boy was too far gone—that he wanted no medicine, but nourishing, for he was in a decline. I took him home, and said, 'One shilling a-week and two loaves will not support us; there are three of us, and we can't be supported by that, with this sickness. Well, I must take to slop-shirts again.' I did so. But I was not able to earn so much as I used to do. I sometimes did three a-day at $2\frac{1}{2}$d., sometimes three at $1\frac{1}{2}$d., having needles and thread to find out of that. Half an ounce of coffee went us three times, and it had to be boiled up again, which made but a scanty meal with a few potatoes. However, I was very glad to put up with it.

"And then at last I found it impossible to get on; when a man lodging in the house was anxious to get a partner, and made offers to me. I thought it better to accept them than to do worse; and by his promising to be good to me, I did comply. Soon after, it pleased God to take my other boy from me; till at last I was in trouble again, and the result was that I was in the family way, and thought, 'Now, what shall I do? My character is gone; it was good before, but now it is blemished.' The man did his part as well as he could, but the work he got was so little that he was not able to support us in a proper manner. We took a room together, and I am sorry to say some days brought home nothing—other days perhaps, no more than $2\frac{1}{2}$d. or 3d., or a few half-pence that he might pick up for carrying a letter to the Post-office, or the like, for a gentleman. Some days, perhaps, he would earn 1s., and for the next three days again often not a farthing. And I earned so little myself, that, the times going on so bad, I did not know what to do. I told the man that he and I must part; for I had seen nothing but starvation with him.

"My time was up, and it pleased the Lord that I was delivered of twins (here the poor creatures seemed visibly affected with the multiplied distresses of the speaker) and then my hands were full again. I looked at my babies, and there being two of them, felt that I could never support them, and I became delirious for hours. The doctor, a kind-hearted man, said many a lady would be glad to have two such children as these. I said, God bless them, I shall have matches to sell with them to get them a bit of bread. Before I was able I was obliged to turn out. It was winter time, and I tried slop-shirts again to get a living, and was unable to earn 6d. a day. I got 10s. behind in my rent, my landlord threatened to take my sticks if I did not pay; and at last I went into the streets with matches.

"It was on a Saturday night, and I went to Shoreditch, thinking I would not be known, and fixed my position opposite the church, before a large china warehouse, kept by a man who, it was said, would not allow any one to stand before his door. I was determined to persevere till turned away, as nothing could be done without it, and my children must have bread. I was not turned away, because I think the man sympathised with me, and I stood that night till my own and my child's pockets were full with the pence we received. At eleven o'clock my child said her pocket string had broke, and she would lose her money if she did not go away. We therefore went home, and on counting our money we had got no less than 6s. 3d., which we considered a good day's work. I said we would stop the lion's mouth with 3s., and so I paid 3s. of my rent that night. We had a meat dinner on Sunday. It was ox's cheek, with a few potatoes, and that we considered a glorious dinner. Next Saturday night I went out again to Shoreditch, expecting as good success as before, but holding my head down like a bulrush, for fear that somebody would pass that knew me.

"I had not stood long before a female companion of my early days came up and observed me; she looked at me and said, 'Susan, in the name of goodness, is that you—and what has brought you here?' I said, 'oh, Mary Ann, don't ask me, for I can't answer you—shame has brought me here.' She offered me 1s., which I at first refused to take, as she was a poor woman herself; but she made me comply, saying she wished she could afford more. Well, I did not succeed so well as I had done before, because I only got 4s. altogether, including my friend's 1s., but I felt very well satisfied, as it was much better than slop-work.

"Well, one of my twins soon after died, and was buried by the parish. I had no parish relief then, for what I had done would make me be treated like a common prostitute, and I could not bear that. At last, one cold, snowy Saturday night, I only obtained 9d., and after that resolved to go out no more. At last I consented, as the man wished me, to live with him again. But he earned very little, and I only got 2d. for what I had got 2½d. before at slop-work, and five farthings for what used to be 1½d. Utterly distressed, I thought again of making away with my children. I locked the door, with the intention of taking their lives first and then my own, but God touched my conscience, and I could not do it. I kneeled down at the bed-side and prayed God to hold my hand. I got up with a grateful heart, determined to trust in Providence.

"But I owed my landlord 12s., and he threatened to take my things. He owed £12 of rent himself, however; and when the broker took my landlord's things, he took mine. I was turned into the street on New Year's-eve—that was five years ago—in a state of pregnancy, with my little twin and my little girl along with me. I stood there till eleven, and I thought of an old lady I knew who kept a kitchen at King-street, and sent the man I was living with to ask her to give me a night's shelter. She said, 'Yes, as long as I have a roof above my head I will give you refuge.' I was very thankful; but could not expect them to turn out of their bed to give it to us, so we lay upon the floor without taking off our clothes. At last the man and I got a garret for ourselves, and, through the kindness of my friends and one of the gentlemen now present, I got a little furniture for it.

"I determined to separate from the man, being deeply impressed of the sin in which I was living. I was 8s. in debt at that time. I took to the trowsers again. My girl learned, and we got a warehouse. I was not very quick myself, and we could not earn enough to support us. I am confident we did not earn 3s. 6d. each on the average. We earnt 5s. and 6s. between us, and if we earnt 7s. by sitting up two nights a week, we felt that we had done a good week's work. A niece of mine came to me from Sheffield, about this time, and set to work with us. The three of us could earn 10s. or 11s. a week between us by sitting up three nights a week. Coal, candle, and twist had to be found out of our earnings. My niece left us, being dissatisfied with her lot. I continued in that way, away from the man, for two years, and at last found it would not do.

"I got married two years ago, and have given up slop-work, and go out charing and washing. My daughter still continues at slop-work, however; but I am sure she could not live by it if she had nothing done for her, and depended on that alone. My firm belief, before God and man, is, that three out of every four of the young women of London who do slop-work are obliged to resort to private or public prostitution to enable them to live. But I hope better things are coming at last; and God bless the gentlemen, I say, who have set this inquiry a-going to help the poor slop-workers, and I hope that public attention being now called to these matters, the oppressed will be oppressed no longer, and that the Parliament House even will interpose to protect them. But I am sorry to say the good are not always the powerful, nor the powerful always the good."

For a few minutes no one spoke. All were evidently pondering upon the tale they had just heard. At length a woman, with a half-clad, well-formed infant at her breast arose. She said:

"I lived with the father of this child. He left me when within two months of my confinement. I had no home to go to, till an old lady stuck me down beside her, and gave me victuals and drink till I was taken to bed. I left her to go into the workhouse. I was confined in the street on my way there. When I was delivered in the street, it was a very stormy day—thunder and lightning, with snow and hail. The old lady would not let me be confined in her house, for fear of bringing trouble upon the parish. I was confined in the street; an old woman brought out a blanket, and threw it over me and the baby. Mr. —— (the gentleman who was present) and his wife came over, found us clothing, paid the doctor, and gave me a shilling for a cab to go to St. George's workhouse. I came here to-night to thank that gentleman. I do nothing now to get a living, because I have no place to go to, or any friends to apply to for a character. I could work at making waistcoats, but I am quite a stranger here. The person I should work with at making waistcoats has left London. I am living now with a person down in Rosemary-lane. I have no means of living. I cannot get slop work. I used to sell things in the streets, but I cannot sell anything now, because I have no money. This child was born about two months ago. When I worked at the waistcoats, I used to make 8d. a day. I lived with a man then, but we were not married. I went with him because I could not get a situation, and I thought I had better do that than do worse."...

After this the following pathetic statement was made:

"I am a tailoress, and I was brought to ruin by the foreman of the work, by whom I had a child. Whilst I could make an appearance I had work, but as soon as I was unable to do so I lost it. I had an afflicted mother to support, who was entirely dependent upon me. She had the tic-douloureux for three months, and was unable to do anything for herself. I went on so for some months, and we were half starved, by means of my having so little work. I could only earn from 5s. to 6s. a week to support three of us, and out of that I had 1s. 6d. to pay for rent, and the trimmings to buy, which cost me 1s. a week full. I went on till I could go on no longer, and we were turned out into the street because we could not pay the rent—me and my child; but a friend took my mother. Everyone turned their back upon me—not a friend stretched out a hand to save me. For six weeks I never lay down in a bed; my child and me passed all that time in the streets.

"At last of all I met a young man, a tailor, and he offered to get me work for his own base purposes. I worked for him—worked for him till I was in the family way again. I worked till I was within two months of my confinement. I had 1s. a day, and I took a wretched kitchen at 1s. a week, and 2s. I had to pay to have my child minded when I went to work. My mother left her friend's and went into the house, but I took her out again, she was so wretched, and she thought she could mind the child. In this condition we were all starving together. No one would come near us who knew my disgrace, and so I resolved I would not be my mother's death, and I left her. She went to her friend's, but she was so excited at going that it caused her death, and she died an hour after she got into her friend's house. An inquest was held upon her, and the jury returned a verdict that she died through a horror of going into the workhouse.

"I was without a home. I worked till I was within two months of my confinement, and then I walked the streets for six weeks, with my child in my arms. At last I went into Wapping Union: my child was taken from me, and there (bursting into tears) he was murdered. I mean he was torn from me, and when I next saw him he was a mere shadow. I took my discharge, and took him out, dying as he was. I took one in my arms, and my boy, dying as he was, and we wandered the streets for two or three days and nights. I then went back to the house. The matron said she would not take my child from me. She said he was dying, and he should die beside me. He died eleven days after we went in.

"I took my discharge again. I tried again to get a living, but I found it impossible, for I had no home, no friends, no means to get work. I then went in again, and the Lord took away my second child. I came out again and went into a situation. I remained in that situation fourteen months, when I was offered some work by a friend, and I have been at that work ever since. I have a hard living, and I earn from 4s. 6d. to 5s. a week. My children and mother are both dead. The tailor never did anything for me. I worked for him and had 1s. a day. I never had one to stretch out a hand to save me, or I never should have had a second fall. From seven in the morning till one or two o'clock I work at making waistcoats and coats. I have 5d. a piece for double-breasted waistcoats, and 10d. and 11d. a piece for slop coats. I can assure you I can't get clothes or things to keep me in health. I never resorted to the streets since I had the second child.". . .

After having made these statements, they were asked what were their lowest earnings last week, when it appeared that four had earned under 1s., four under 1s. 6d., four under 2s., one under 2s. 6d. One woman said 3s. 6d. had been earned between two of them, another said she had earned 3s. 6d., while a third declared she had not earned anything. Three said they had parted with their work for food. It was the unanimous declaration of the whole present, that if the meeting had been more generally known several hundreds would have attended, who would conscientiously have made the same declaration they had done—that they were forced into a wrong course of life by the lowness of their wages.

In answer to a question whether any had other clothes than what they appeared in, the very idea of a change of garments appeared to excite a smile. One and all declared they had not, and most asserted that even those they wore were not their own. One said, "This bonnet belongs to another woman;" another said, "This shawl belongs to my neighbour;" another said, "I have no frock, because I had to leave it in pawn for 6d.;" another said, "I have been forced to sit up this afternoon and put many a patch on this old frock, for the purpose of making my appearance here this evening;" another said, "The gown I have got on does not belong to myself;" while still another added, "I had to take the petticoat off my child, for 6d. to get victuals last Sunday morning."

West-End Tailors

From Letter XVI, December 11th, 1849

[Workers in the West End of London generally belonged to the Society or Union, were best paid and had the best working conditions. The most exploited workers invariably worked for small masters in the East End, hence the distinction between the West End as the "honourable" part of the trade and the East End as the "dishonourable".]

Before entering upon my investigations, I consulted several of the most experienced and intelligent workmen, as to the best means of arriving at a correct opinion respecting the state of the trade. It was agreed among us that, first, with regard to an estimate as to the amount of wages, I should see a hand employed at each of the different branches of the trade. After this I was to be taken to a person who was the captain or leading man of a shop; then to one who, in the technicality of the trade, had a "good chance" of work; and, finally, to one who was only casually employed. It was considered that these classes, taken in connection with the others, would give the public a correct view of the condition, earnings, and opinions of the trade. To prevent the chance of error, however, I begged to be favoured with such accounts of earnings as could be procured from the operatives. This, I thought, would place me in a fair condition to judge of the incomings and physical condition of the class; but still I was anxious to arrive at something like a criterion of the intellectual, political, and moral character of the people, and I asked to be allowed an interview with such persons as the parties whom I consulted might consider would freely represent these peculiar features of their class to the world. . . .

After *[visits to a trowsers hand and a coat hand]* I visited a waistcoat hand. The male waistcoat hands, he told me, are very few, and they are growing fewer every year. In the workshop they are paid by "the log." "The log reckons nine hours for making a single-breasted roll-collar waistcoat, but we cannot do the work that is in them now in less than twelve hours, there are so many extras introduced—such as wadding to pad the breast, back straps, edging, and V cuts, which were all paid for over and above the regular charge till within the last five years, but which are now all included in the price stated by the log. Hence the waistcoats which were originally reckoned at nine hours' work take us now twelve hours to make, and are paid for only at the stated price, viz., 4s. 6d. According to the standard of 6d. per hour, we should get 6s. for the same garment as we now make for 4s. 6d. The extras were gradually reduced."

"My master," says my informant, "first objected to pay anything additional for putting on the edging. Then he refused to allow us anything for inserting the wadding in the breast. After this he cut off the extra pay for back straps, telling us

that if we did not consent to this, he would put them all out to be made; and saying that he could get them done much cheaper out of doors. When I first began
waistcoat making I could earn my 36s. every week, during the season, with ease—
and, indeed, I did as much up to six years ago. But now I must work hard to get
24s. Since the years 1843 and 1844 the prices have been gradually declining, and
the waistcoat business getting worse every year for the male hands employed in
the workshop. And so I believe it has for everybody outside the shop, excepting the
sweaters. What they get I'm sure I don't know. We never can find out their prices.
We only know they get the work done much cheaper than we can do it, for if we
murmur in the least at the price paid us, we are told by the master that he can
have it made much cheaper out.

"The reason why they can do this is, because of late years women have been
generally employed at the trade. When I first began working at this branch, there
were but very few females employed in it: a few white waistcoats were given out
to them, under the idea that women would make them cleaner than men—and so
indeed they can. But since the last five years, the sweaters have employed females
upon cloth, silk, and satin waistcoats as well, and before that time the idea of a
woman making a cloth waistcoat would have been scouted. But since the increase
of the puffing and the sweating system, masters and sweaters have sought everywhere for such hands as would do the work below the regular ones. Hence the wife
has been made to compete with the husband, and the daughter with the wife: they
all learn the waistcoat business, and must all get a living. If the man will not reduce
the price of his labour to that of the female, why he must remain unemployed; and
if the full-grown woman will not take the work at the same price as the young girl,
why she must remain without any. The female hands, I can confidently state, have
been sought out and introduced to the business by the sweaters, from a desire on
their part continually to ferret out hands who will do the work cheaper than
others.

"The effect that this continual reducton has had upon me is this: Before
the year 1844 I could live comfortably, and keep my wife and children (I had five
in family) by my own labour. My wife then attended to her domestic and family
duties; but since that time, owing to the reduction in prices, she has been compelled
to resort to her needle, as well as myself, for her living." (On the table was a
bundle of crape and bombazine ready to be made up into a dress.) "I cannot afford
now to let her remain idle—that is, if I wish to live, and keep my children out of
the streets, and pay my way. My wife's earnings are upon an average 8s. per week.
She makes dresses. I never would teach her to make waistcoats, because I knew the
introduction of female hands had been the ruin of my trade. With the labour of
myself and wife now I can only earn 32s. a week, and six years ago I could make
my 36s. If I had a daughter I should be obliged to make her work as well, and then
probably, with the labour of the three of us, we could make up at the week's end
as much money as up to 1844 I could get by my own single hands.

"My wife, since she took to dressmaking, has become sickly from over exertion.
Her work, and her domestic and family duties altogether, are too much for her.
Last night I was up all night with her, and was compelled to call in a female to
attend her as well. The over exertion now necessary for us to maintain a decent
appearance has so ruined her constitution that she is not the same woman as she
was. In fact, ill as she is, she has been compelled to rise from her bed to finish a

morning dress against time, and I myself have been obliged to give her a helping-hand, and turn to at woman's work in the same manner as the women are turning to at mine. My opinion is, that the waistcoat makers generally are now unable to support themselves and families by their unassisted labour. A number of female hands have been forced into the trade who otherwise would have been attending to their duties at home.". . .

I was desirous of seeing certain hands whose earnings might be taken as the type of the different classes of workmen in the trade. These, I had been informed, consisted of three distinct varieties: First, those who are in constant employment at a particular shop as captains. Secondly, those who are tolerably well employed during the year, and have the preference for work as leading men in particular shops. Thirdly, those who are only casually employed either in the brisk season or when there is an extra amount of work to be done. The captains have continual employment, and receive from three shillings to six shillings per week over and above their own earnings, for the superintendence of the workmen. The leading men are generally employed. They are always connected with the shop, and remain there whether there is work to be done or not. The casual men are such as are taken on from the house of call when there is an extra amount of work to be done. The casual hand is engaged sometimes for two or three days, and sometimes for only two or three hours—to the great accommodation of masters, who are certain of having their work not only done to time, but paid for by the society to which the hands belong, if damaged or spoiled by the workmen.

I consulted several gentlemen connected with the trade as to a person who might be taken as a fair type of the first class, and was directed to one who gave me the following information:

"I am a captain at an old-established house—indeed, one of the first and best a the West-end. I receive £1 19s. per week—that is, £1 16s. for my work, and 3s. extra for my duties as captain. My wages never amount to less. I have been twenty years employed at the same house, in the same capacity, and for the whole of those twenty years my earnings have remained the same. I have brought up a large family, and am landlord of the house in which I live. I pay £55 a year for it, and let off nearly sufficient to pay the rent. Four or five of my shopmates are housekeepers, and they have been in our establishment as many years as myself. It is one of the few honourable houses remaining in the trade, and may be cited as an instance of what the trade formerly was. The workmen in our establishment are all, without any exception, honest, sober, industrious, moral men; the majority of them are married, and maintain their wives and families in decency and comfort. The workmen there employed may be taken as a fair average of the condition, habits, and principles of the journeyman tailor throughout the trade before the puffing and sweating system became general.

"Ever since the alteration from day work to piece work the condition of the working tailor has materially declined. Under the day-working system a master, taking on a man from a house of call, was obliged to find him work or pay him his wages during the time he remained in his workshop; but now, under the piece-working system, a master will often keep and send for more men than he requires, knowing that he has only to pay for the quantity of work done, and being desirous to make as great a display of 'hands' as possible. Further than this, under the piece-working system, the workman has the opportunity of taking garments home to be

made; and the consequence is, being out of the master's sight, he puts on inexperienced hands to the different parts of the garment—and then, finding that by the
assistance of women and girls he can get through a greater amount of work than
he possibly could by his own unaided labour, he seeks employment from other
masters at a lower price than the regular standard, and so subsides into a sweater,
and underbids the regular workman. The masters have now learned that tailoring
work, under the sweating system, can be done at almost any price; and hence those
who are anxious to force their trade by underselling their more honourable neighbours advertise cheap garments, and give the articles out to sweaters to be made by
women and girls. By such means the regular tailor is being destroyed; indeed, a
man's own children are being brought into competition against himself, and the
price of his labour is being gradually reduced to theirs.

"These evils, I am convinced, do not arise from over-population, but rather from
over-competition. Women and children, who before were unemployed in the tailoring trade, now form a large proportion of the operative part of it. I know myself
that, owing to the reduction of prices, many wives who formerly attended solely
to their domestic duties and their family are now obliged to labour with the husband, and still the earnings of the two are less than he alone formerly obtained.
The captains of shops in the honourable trade generally make as much as I do. By
the sweating system I am satisfied the public are no gainers—the price of the
workmen is reduced, but still the garment is no cheaper. The only parties profiting
are the sweater and the dishonourable tradesman. In fact, another profit has now
to be paid; so that, though the party doing the work is paid less, still the sweater's
profit, which has to be added, makes little or no difference in the price of the garment to the public. I know myself that it is so."

The next person I sought out was one who might be taken as a fair average of
the industrious and fortunate workman. I was anxious to meet with a person whose
earnings might be considered as a type, not of the *highest* wages received by the
operatives, but of the earnings of those who are fully employed in a shop where the
best prices are paid, and where the customers are of the highest rank. I consulted
with a number of workmen as to a person of such character, and I was sent to an
individual who gave me the following statement: "I have been fifteen years
employed in the same house. It is one of the first-rate houses at the West-end. My
master pays the best prices, and I consider him a very fair man. He gives the same
price for the better class of garments as he did fifteen years ago. The only articles
for which he pays less than at the rate of 6d. per hour are the new-fashioned wrappers or paletots, and these he is obliged to reduce, much against his will, by the
competition of other houses. Gentlemen want a cheap over-coat, and tell him that
they can get it at such houses for such a price; and my master is compelled to make
it at the same price as the cheap West-end slop-houses, or he would surely lose his
customers. It is now about five years ago since my master began to make any
reduction upon the price paid for making any garment whatsoever. Before that
every article was paid for at the rate of 6d. per hour; but between the years 1844
and 1845—I cannot call to mind the exact date—my master had a consultation
with his captain as to making up the new cheap tweed wrappers, which were coming
into general fashion at that time; and he decided upon paying for them at a rate
which, considering the time they took to make, was less than the regular sixpence
per hour. He said that the show-shops at the East-end were daily advertising tweed

wrappers at such a low figure that his customers, seeing the prices in the newspapers, were continually telling him that if he could not do them they must go elsewhere. Since then cheap overcoats, or wrappers, have been generally made in our
shop, and I believe that my master would willingly give over making them, if it
were not for the extreme competition which has been going on in the tailoring
trade since their introduction.

"Amongst all the best and oldest houses in the trade at the West-end they are
gradually introducing the making of the cheap paletots, Oxonians, Brighton coats,
Chesterfields, &c. &c.; and even the first-rate houses are gradually subsiding into
the cheap advertising slop tailors. If the principle goes on at the rate that it has
been progressing for the last five years, the journeymen tailors must ultimately be
reduced to the position of the lowest of the needlewomen.

"I have kept an account of my wages for the last 16 years; but I have destroyed
several of the books, thinking them of no value. My wages have not declined since
that period, because I am regularly employed, and my master's house has not yet
become one of the cheap advertising shops—and I don't think it will in *his* time.
In the year 1833, being the first I was in London, I remember well that my wages
throughout the year averaged £1 6s. per week. I can say so positively, for I have
long been in the habit of estimating them. I never did so before that time (because I
was not out of my apprenticeship till then), and I recollect the first year particularly. Indeed, as it happens, I have the account here. I thought I had burnt it." He
then showed me an account of his earnings for the year above-mentioned. . . .

The statement of the casual hand is far different from either of the above. He
says: "I am not 'in the command of a shop'—that is, I have no regular work, but
am employed principally at the brisk season of the year. The brisk season lasts for
three months in the shop, and for two months outside of it—or in other words, the
work at the commencement and end of the brisk season is only sufficient to keep
the hands, regularly employed in the shop, fully engaged, and between these two
periods extra hands are taken on to do the work which then becomes more than
the regular hands can accomplish. I am one of those extra hands, and May and
June are the two months I am principally employed. During those months I earn
£1 5s. per week, and I must be fully employed to get as much as that. The reason of
this is, because the time required for making the garments is not fairly estimated.
After the brisk season the casual hands are mostly off trade, and have little or no
work at the honourable part of the business. From the month of July to the end of
the month of April the journeymen tailors who have not the command of a shop
are principally dependent upon what is termed 'sank work.' This consists of
soldiers', police, Custom-house, post, and mail clothing. At this work I could earn
about 6s. per week if I could get as much as I could do, but there is not enough
to keep all the men in full employment. Some weeks I *do* make my 6s.—others I
make only 4s.; then again I occasionally make only 6s. in a fortnight. I think I
can safely say my weekly earnings at 'sank work' average about 4s.; but during
the time I am engaged at 'sank work' I have the chance of the calls at my society.

"I attend at the house twice a day regularly. Since the brisk season I have not
been employed at the honourable part of the trade more than one day per month,
and I never missed attending a single call. Hence I make upon an average about
£10 by my work at the honourable part of the trade during the two months of the
brisk season; then I get about £8 16s. by 'sank work,' at 4s. per week, for the rest

of the year; and besides this I earn by casual employment at the honourable part of the trade about £3; this altogether brings my yearly income to £21 16s., which gives an average of 8s. 4½d. per week. This I really believe to be exactly what I *do* get. Those casual hands that do not take to sank work, work under the sweaters, at whatever the sweater may be pleased to give them. At the sweaters' they make more than at the 'sank work,' but then they have to work much longer hours.

"Such is the difference of prices in my trade, that during the months of May and June I make trowsers at 5s. per pair, and after that I make them at 6½d. per pair. The garments of course have not the same amount of work in them, but at those which are better paid I can earn in a day 5s., whilst I can only earn 1s. at the others in the same time. I believe the hands that cannot command a shop are similarly situated to myself. There are from 600 to 700 persons off work for ten months in the course of the year. I know this from having heard a gentleman who has paid great attention to the trade affirm that the unemployed were from 20 to 25 per cent. of the whole number of the operatives 'in union.' "

The next party whom I saw was one to whom I had been referred as a type of the intemperate and improvident but skilful tailor. I was anxious, as intemperance is said to be one of the distinguishing characteristics of the working tailors, to hear from one who was notorious for his indulgence in this vice what were the main causes that induced the habit, so that by making them public the more intelligent workmen might be induced to take some steps to remedy the evil. . . .

The person to whom I was referred gave me the following extraordinary statement: "I work at coats generally, and for one of the best houses. I am reckoned one of the most skillful hands in the trade. I might be always in work if it were not for my love of drink. Most of the foremen know me, and object to give me work on account of my unsteadiness. If it were not for my skill I should be out of work altogether, for I never would consent to work under a sweater. I would rather starve than be instrumental to the reduction of the price of my labour. As an instance of my skill I may mention that I recently made a waistcoat of my own invention, which was highly esteemed by my fellow workmen. I do not wish to particularize the waistcoat more fully, lest it should be known who it is that supplies you with this information. I am not a leading hand in any shop, but one who is casually employed. I might be a leading man if it were not for my love of drink, but, owing to that, I am only taken on when the brisk season commences.

"It is to the casual hands that the intemperance of the tailors as a class is mostly limited—those who have regular employment are in general steady, decent, and intelligent people. The intemperance for which the casual hands are distinguished arises chiefly from their being 'called on' at public-houses. A master who wants an extra number of workmen to complete his work, sends to a certain house of call in the neighbourhood; this house of call is invariably a public-house, and there the men who are out of work assemble as early as a quarter before nine in the morning to hear whether any call will be made. There are three of these calls in the course of the day: one at a quarter before nine (as before mentioned), a second at a quarter before one, and a third at a quarter before nine at night. The men off trade and seeking for employment are kept knocking about at the public-house all the day through. The consequence of this is that the day is passed in drinking, and habits of intemperance are produced which it is almost impossible to withstand. Those who have got money treat those who have none; and indeed, such are the inducements to drink, that it is almost impossible for the tailor who is not regularly and constantly employed to remain sober.

"During the slack season of vacation, there are from 50 to 100 hanging about each of the houses of call; and there are five of these houses 'in society,' and four foreign houses, or nine in all. In the vacation there must be from 500 to 1,000 people out of employ, who pass their days continually at the public-house. It astonishes me how some of them live. They cannot go home to their garrets, for they have no fire there, and if they absent themselves from the public-house they lose their chance of work. Some of those who are 'off trade' go into the country during the vacation, and others join the sweaters. But the majority remain about the public-house. They can't spend much, because they have it not to spend, but every penny they can get goes in drink, and many of the number pawn their coats and waistcoats in order to get liquor. I myself have duplicates enough to make a small pack of cards, for things that I have converted into gin.

"Ah! I like gin—you can see through it. Beer is like a fish-pond. What I hang on to is 'Old Tom;' a glass of that neat is my weakness—to mix it spoils it, to my fancy—that's true. I drink a tremendous lot. I can drink twenty glasses in the course of the day easy. I drank more than that yesterday, I am sure; I know that by 'the shakes' I have got to-day. I have them 'rattling bad' this morning. When I get another glass—or two, or three—I shall be all right. If I was to try to lift a glass to my mouth now, I should spill the half of it before I could get it there. One barman, who knows me, always puts my gin into a large tumbler for me when I go to him the first thing in the morning. I have tried to give it up, but I never shall be able. The scars on my face do not arise from the small pox, but solely from drink. When I take a great deal it flies to my nose and breaks out and about five years ago my face was one mass of sores, of which these 'pits' are the scars. When I can get it, I will drink as much as three pints of gin in the course of the day. Upon an average, I think I drink about half-a-pint of raw gin every day, and if I could get the money I should drink double that quantity. I am sure it costs me 5s. a week in gin.

"I used to be a very lucky chap at the 'DERBY SWEEPS' that used to be held at the public-houses. I have won as much as £8, £6, £5, and £4 twice; and whenever I got a prize I never did a stitch of work until I had drunk all the money away, and then I was sure to get the sack from my employer. The £8 did not last me above two or three days; I was 'roaring drunk' all that time, and afterwards I was ill for a week. I made all my companions in the same state. I am not very greedy over my halfpence, and always share what I get. The public-house got all I won.

"Another cause of the intemperance of tailors is, that the operatives are usually paid at a tavern or beer-shop. There are generally three hands employed in making one coat, and these go partners—that is, they share among them the sum of money paid for making the entire garment. It is necessary, therefore, that change should be got in order to divide the proceeds into 'thirds.' This change the publican always undertakes to provide, and the consequence is, the men meet at his house to receive their weekly earnings. I have known the publican often keep the men an hour waiting for the change. The consequence of this system of paying at public-houses is, that the most intemperate and improvident of the workmen spend a large portion of their wages in drink. I myself generally spend half (unless my

Missus comes and catches me); and on several occasions I have squandered away in liquor all I had earned in the week. My Missus knows my infirmity, and watches me of a Saturday night regularly. She was waiting outside the public-house where you picked me up, and there were three or four more wives of journeymen tailors watching outside of the tavern, besides my old woman. These were mostly the wives of the men who are casually employed. The intemperate operative tailors seldom take half of their earnings home to their wives and families.

"Those who are employed by the sweaters are as intemperate as the casual hands in the honourable part of the trade. The cause of the drunkenness of the men working under sweaters is, that the workmen employed by them are the refuse hands of the regular trade. They mostly consist of the men who have been scratched off the books of the societies through spoiling or neglecting the work of their employers from intemperate habits. I know the misery and evil of this love of drink: it is the curse of my life, but I cannot keep from it. I have taken the pledge four or five times, and broken it just as often. I kept it six weeks once, and was quite a little king at that time. I had always money in my pockets, and my wife got me a watch out of my earnings as well. Doctor Wormwald told me, when my face was bad, I should lose my nose if I continued drinking, and I said I would have my drop of gin if I had no nose at all. Any person who could prevail upon me to take the pledge, and make me keep it, would be the saviour of me. My wife is a hard-working body, and is obliged to keep me half the year round. I am a civil and well-disposed person when I am sober, but when I get a drop of drink I am a madman. I break open the doors and smash the teapot and tea things, and indeed break or disfigure everything I can lay my hands on."

The man has given me his solemn promise that, "for the honour of his craft" and "the sake of his wife," he will keep from all intoxicating drink for the future.

I now give the views of an intelligent Chartist, in the same calling, and in his own words: "I am a Chartist, and did belong to the Chartist Association. My views as to the way in which politics and Government influence the condition of journeymen tailors are these—Government, by the system now adopted with regard to army and police clothing, forces the honest labouring man, struggling for a fair remuneration for his labour, into a false position, and makes him pay extra taxes to those paid by other branches of the community; they force him into this false position by disposing of Government work at such contract prices that no man can make a decent livelihood at it. One of the best workmen, employed the whole week, cannot earn more than 12s. weekly on soldiers' or policemen's clothing, out of which he must pay for all the sewing trimmings, except twist; and having to make the articles at his own place, of course he must find his own fire, candles, &c.

"Tailors in prison are put to work by the Government at clothes that come into the market to compete with the regular trader employing the regular artisan. The public pays the taxes from which prisons are supported, and the smallest amount, even a penny a pair, is regarded by the authorities as a saving on the cost of prisons; and, indeed, they keep the prisoner at work, if he earns nothing, as the public pays all the expense of the prison. The working tailor pays *his* quota of the taxes out of which the tailor put to work in prison is maintained, and the prisoner so maintained is made to undersell the very tax-payer who contributes to his support. My opinion is, that if tailors in gaol were not employed by Government, it would leave the market more open to the honourable portion of the trade, and there would be no discreditable employing of a felon—for felons *are* so employed, to diminish the small earnings of an honest man. At Millbank they teach men to be tailors, who are always employed, while the honest operative is frequently subjected to three months' compulsory idleness; six weeks, towards the close of the year, is a very common period of the tailor's non-employment. I think that if the Charter became law it would tend to improve our (the journeymen tailors') condition, by giving us a voice in the choice of our representatives, who might be so selected as thoroughly to understand the wants of the working man, and to sympathise with his endeavours for a better education and a better lot altogether."...

I

East-End Tailors

From Letter XVII, December 14th, 1849

I believe that the facts which I publish in my present communication will lay bare a system unheard of and unparalleled in the history of any country; indeed there appears to be so deep laid a scheme for the introduction and supply of under-paid labour to the market, that it is impossible for the working man not to sink and be degraded by it to the lowest depths of wretchedness and infamy. If we wish to see the effect of this system upon the physical, intellectual, and moral character of the workpeople, we should spend a week in visiting the homes of the operative tailors connected with the honourable part of the trade, and those working for the slop-trade. The very dwellings of the people are sufficient to tell you the wide difference between the two classes. In the one you occasionally find small statues of Shakespeare beneath glass shades; in the other all is dirt and fœtor. The working tailor's comfortable first-floor at the West-end is redolent with the perfume of the small bunch of violets that stand in a tumbler over the mantel-piece; the sweater's wretched garret is rank with the stench of filth and herrings. The honourable part of the trade are really intelligent artisans, while the slopworkers are generally almost brutified with their incessant toil, wretched pay, miserable food, and filthy homes.

Nor are the shops of the two classes of tradesmen less distinct one from the other. The quiet house of the honourable tailor, with the name inscribed on the window blinds, or on the brass-plate on the door, tells you that the proprietor has no wish to compete with or undersell his neighbour. But at the show and slop-shops every art and trick that scheming can devise or avarice suggest, is displayed to attract the notice of the passer-by, and filch the customer from another. The quiet, unobtrusive place of business of the old-fashioned tailor is transformed into the flashy palace of the grasping tradesman. Every article in the window is ticketed—the price cut down *to the quick*—books of crude, bald verses are thrust in your hands, or thrown into your carriage window—the panels of every omnibus are plastered with showy placards, telling you how Messrs. —— defy competition. . . .

An offer was made to introduce me privately into the workshop of a large show and slop-shop at the East end of the town, where I might see and interrogate the men at work on the premises; but to this I objected, saying I did not think it fair that I should enter any man's premises with such an object, unknown to him. I was then told that several of the workmen would willingly meet me and state the price they received for their labour, and the unjust system upon which the establishment was conducted. This statement I said I should be very glad to listen and give publicity to.

Accordingly, three of the better class of hands waited upon me, and gave me the following account: "We work at the slop trade. We mean, by the slop trade the cheap ready-made trade. The dishonourable part of the tailoring trade consists of two classes—viz., those who are connected with show-shops and slop-shops. The show-shops belong to the cheap 'bespoke trade,' and the slop-shops to the cheap 'ready-made trade.' Many of the large tailoring houses at the East end of London are both show-shops and slop-shops. By a show-shop we mean one where the different styles of garments are exhibited in the window, ticketed as 'made to measure at a certain price.' By a slop-shop we mean one where the garments themselves are sold ready-made, and not a similar one made to measure at a certain price. In the cheap or ready-made trade a large number of one kind of garment is made up, either for home consumption or for exportation—whereas, in the show or cheap bespoke trade, only one of the same kind of garment is made up at one time.

"We all three of us work at coat-making. We are paid piece-work. The full price— that is, the highest amount paid for any coat made on the establishment—is 10s. The coat for which this price is given is a full-trimmed frock or dress coat. By 'full-trimmed' we mean lined throughout with silk and with quilted sides. The price for such a coat in the honourable trade is 18s., that is the very lowest price—the best houses would pay from 21s. to 24s. The time that such coats will take to make is four days, estimating twelve hours work to the day. They are, however, made in three days, but this is done by working over-hours at home. At dress and frock coat work we can make the most money. At this kind of work—if we could get it—we might earn 15s. a week. But there are other kinds of work which are much worse paid for, and we have to take these with the rest. If we object, we are told we shall have no more to do. The worst kind of work that we have to do consists of drab driving capes; these are made of thick 'box cloth,' or 'Devonshire kersey,' and have 'double-pricked' seams all through (the cloth is too hard to stitch, and consequently the needle has to be passed up and down or double pricked; as a shoe-maker would stitch leather); there are eighteen rows of pricking round the hand— four pockets, with flaps pricked the same as the seams—and the capes are lined entirely with silk, which is quilted all through. The price for making such a description of garment is 9s., and it will take, at least, a week making."

"I know I made one," said one of the men, "and I was more than six days over it." "Yes, that you must have been," said another, "and not an hour less. At the best houses at the West-end, the price for such a garment would be 36s. We have all worked in the honourable trade, so we know the regular prices from our own personal experience. Taking the bad work with the good work, we might earn 11s. a week upon an average. Sometimes we do earn as much as 15s.; but to do this, we are obliged to take part of our work home to our wives and daughters. We are not always fully employed. We are nearly half our time idle. Hence our earnings are, upon an average throughout the year, not more than 5s. 6d. a week."

"Very often I have made only 3s. 4d. in the week," said one. "That's common enough with us all, I can assure you," said another. "Last week my wages was 7s. 6d.," declared one. "I earned 6s. 4d.," exclaimed the second. "My wages came to 9s. 2d. The week before I got 6s. 3d." "I made 7s. 9d.," and "I 7s. or 8s., I can't exactly remember which."

"This is what we term the best part of our winter season. The reason why we are so long idle is because more hands than are wanted are kept on the premises, so that in case of a press of work coming in our employers can have it done immediately. Under the day-work system no master tailor had more men on the premises than he could keep continually going; but since the change to the piece-work system masters make a practice of engaging double the quantity of hands that they have any need for, so that an order may be executed 'at the shortest possible notice,' if requisite. A man must not leave the premises when unemployed—if he does he loses his chance of work coming in. I have been there four days together and not had a stitch of work to do." "Yes; that is common enough." "Aye, and then you're told if you complain, you can go if you don't like it. I am sure twelve hands would do all they have done at home, and yet they keep forty of us. It's generally remarked, that however strong and healthy a man may be when he goes to work at that shop, in a month's time he'll be a complete shadow, and have almost all his clothes in pawn. By Sunday morning—after the workman has paid what he has run a score for—he has no money at all left, and he has to subsist till the following Saturday upon about a pint of weak tea and four slices of bread and butter per day."

"There was a man there who came from Belgium," said one of the workmen, "I don't think he ever earned 5s. a week, and one week I know he got only 1s. 6d.— one half-pair of trowsers was all he had to do. He came up to me and begged bread by signs, for he could not speak a word of English. We made a subscription of halfpence for him round the shop, and his consul sent him back to his own country. There are five foreigners in our shop, and I can assert positively that in the last few years a great number of German and Polish Jew tailors have been brought over to work at the slop trade. I know positively that hundreds are now engaged at slop work, and every summer brings a fresh importation."

"One of our foremen is a Hungarian Jew, and he prefers foreign hands to us. We all make for ——— ———, 'the poor man's friend,'" said they satirically. "We used to have to make for him frequently, but now he has shifted to another slop-shop near London-bridge, where the same starvation prices are paid. We have also made garments for Sir——— ———, Sir ——— ———, Alderman ———, Dr. ——— and Dr. ———. We make for several of the aristocracy. We cannot say whom, because the tickets frequently come to us as Lord —— and the Marquis of ——. This could not be a Jew's trick, because the buttons on the liveries had coronets upon them. And again, we know the house is patronized largely by the aristocracy, clergy, and gentry, by the number of court-suits and liveries, surplices, regimentals, and ladies' riding-habits that we continually have to make up. There are more clergymen among the customers than any other class, and often we have to work at home upon the Sunday at their clothes, in order to get a living. The customers are mostly ashamed of dealing at this house, for the men who take the clothes to the customers' houses in the cart have directions to pull up at the corner of the street. We had a good proof of the dislike of gentlefolks to have it known that they dealt at that shop for their clothes, for when the trowsers buttons were stamped with the name of the firm, we used to have the garments returned, daily, to have other buttons put on them; and now the buttons are unstamped.

"Formerly an operative tailor's wife never helped him. He worked at the shop— brought his weekly wages home—from 30s. to 36s. a week, and his wife attended to her domestic duties, and lived in ease and comfort. This was the case twenty years ago, but since that time prices have come down to such an extent, that now a man's entire family, wife and daughters, all have to work; and, with the whole of the family's work, the weekly income is not one half what the operative could get by his own labour some years back. We are all satisfied that there is scarcely a working tailor whose wife and daughters are not engaged at some kind of slop; and that five-and-twenty years ago female labour was unknown in the trade—indeed it was not allowed. The decline in the prices of our trade arises in our opinion, from our wives and daughters being brought to work, and so to compete with ourselves.

"There is at our establishment a mode of reducing the price of our labour even lower than we have mentioned. The prices we have stated are those *nominally* paid for making the garments; but it is not an uncommon thing in our shop for a man to make a garment, and receive nothing at all for it. I remember a man once having a waistcoat to do, the price of making which was 2s., and when he gave the job in he was told that he owed the establishment 6d. The manner in which this is brought about is by a system of fines. We are fined if we are behind time with our job 6d. the first hour, and 3d. for each hour that we are late." "I have known as much as 7s. 6d. to be deducted off the price of a coat on the score of want of punctuality," one said; "and, indeed, very often the whole money is stopped. It would appear as if our employers themselves strove to make us late with our work, and so have an opportunity of cutting down the price for our labour. They frequently put off giving out the trimmings to us till the time at which the coat is due has expired. If to the trimmer we return an answer that is considered 'saucy,' we are fined 6d. or 1s., according to the trimmer's temper."

"I was called a thief," another of the three declared, "and because I told the man I would not submit to such language, I was fined 6d. These are the principal of the in-door fines. The out-door fines are still more iniquitous. There are full a dozen more fines for minor offences; indeed, we are fined upon every petty pretext. We never know what we have to take on a Saturday, for the meanest advantages are taken to reduce our wages. If we object to pay these fines we are told that we may leave; but they know full well that we are afraid to throw ourselves out of work.". . .

My next visit was to an out-door worker of the inferior description, from whom I received the following account:

"I work at the inferior work for the slop-trade. This kind of work is never done 'in doors'—that is, on the premises of the master. The inferior work consists of Shooting coats, Fishing coats, Oxonian coats, Paletôts, Reefing jackets, Pilot coats, Chesterfields, Codringtons, Bullers, Sacks, Sailors' jackets, and Spanish cloaks. The last mentioned garment is the worst paid of all the work I have to do. For making a large Spanish cloak, with a hood to come over the head, and with six holes on each side of the garment, and three banyan plaits at the hips, I get 2s. The cloak has more work in it than an ordinary great coat—indeed, it is similar in make to an old-fashioned great coat with a hood to it. It takes two days—working 17 hours each day—or very nearly three ordinary days—to make one of these cloaks. I could earn at this kind of work from 4s. to 4s. 6d., and out of this I should have to pay 7d. for trimmings and about 1s. for lighting and firing. Hence my clear weekly earnings would be from 2s. 6d. to 3s. These garments are given out only at a very slack time of the year, when they know that the men must do them at the employers' own price. About five years ago the price paid for making these garments began to be reduced. They were before that time 3s. 6d., and they have since gradually fallen to 2s.

"The best paid work that I do is the shooting coats. The Oxonians are almost as good as they are, but I prefer the shooting coats. These, I think, are the best paid of all the inferior kind of slop-work. I get 3s. for making one of these. I can make one in two days of twelve hours each; but I am a very quick hand. At this kind of work I could get 9s. per week. I could earn more by working longer time, of course. Out of the 9s. it would cost me 9d. for trimmings, and the expenses of firing and lighting 1s. My clear earnings, therefore, would be 7s. 3d. per week. Taking the good with the bad work that I do, I should say that I make on an average about 5s. or 6s. a week clear. I do make more occasionally, but then I have to work longer time to get it. By working over hours and Sundays, I manage to make from 8s. to 9s. clear. To get this much, I must begin work at six in the morning, and sit close at it till eleven at night. This statement includes, of course, the necessary loss of time consequent on going backwards and forwards, taking work in, and getting fresh work out, and having to make alterations as well. I work first-handed—that is, I am not employed by any sweater.

"I originally belonged to the honourable part of the trade. I have made shooting coats for masters at the West-end, and had 14s. for making the very same garment as I now get 3s. for. When working at the honourable trade, my average weekly earnings were about £1, including vacation. Now I don't get half that amount. It is six or seven years ago since I worked for the West-end shops. My wife did no work then. I could maintain her in comfort by the produce of my labour. Now she slaves night and day, as I do: and very often she has less rent than myself, for she has to stop up after I have gone to bed to attend to her domestic duties. The two of us, working these long hours, and the Sundays as well, can get only 15s.—that is to say, the two of us slaving night and day, and all the Sabbath long, can earn only three-quarters as much as I alone could get by working twelve hours each day for six days in the week, and that but seven years ago. I believe mine to be about an average of the condition and earnings of the male hands engaged in the slop-trade. Many are much worse off than I am, but some are better. I attribute the decline in the wages of the operative tailor to the introduction of cheap Irish, foreign, and female labour. Before then we could live and keep our families by our own exertions; now our wives and children must work as well as ourselves to get less money than we alone could earn a few years back.

"My comforts have not in any way increased with the decrease in the price of provisions. Bread, tea, meat, sugar, are all much cheaper than they were five years ago. Bread three years since this winter, was 11d. and 11½d. the quartern, now it is 4½d. and 5d.—that is more than half as cheap, and yet I can safely say I am twice as badly off now as I was then; and so I know are all the people in my trade. Our wages have gone down more than provisions: that is to say, we and our wives work more than twice as hard, and we get less food and less comfort by our labour. Fifteen or twenty years ago such a thing as a journeyman tailor having to give security before he could get work was unknown; but now I and such as myself could not get a stitch to do first handed, if we did not either procure the security of some householder, or deposit £5 in the hands of the employer. The reason of this is, the journeymen are so badly paid that the employers know they can barely live on what they get, and consequently they are often driven to pawn the garments given out to them, in order to save themselves and their families from starving.

"If the journeyman can manage to scrape together £5 he has to leave it in the hands of his employer all the time that he is working for the house. I know one person who gives out the work for a fashionable West-end slop-shop will not take household security, and requires £5 from each hand. I am informed by one of the parties who worked for this man that he has as many as 150 hands in his employ, and that each of these has placed £5 in his hands, so that altogether the poor people have handed over £750, to increase the capital upon which he trades, and for which he pays no interest whatsoever." [The reader will remember a similar case (mentioned by the poor staystitcher in a former letter) of a large wholesale staymaker in the City who had amassed a large fortune by beginning to trade upon the 5s. which he demanded to be left in his hands by his workpeople before he gave them employment.]

"Two or three years back one of the slop-sellers at the East-end became bankrupt, and the poor people lost all the money that had been deposited as security for work in his hands. The journeymen who get the security of householders are enabled to do so by a system which is now in general practice at the East-end. Several bakers, publicans, chandler-shop keepers, and coal-shed keepers make a trade of becoming security for those seeking slop-work. They consent to be responsible for the workpeople upon the condition of the men dealing at their shops. The workpeople who require such security are generally very good customers, from the fact of their either having large families, all engaged in the same work, or else several females or males working under them, and living at their house. The parties becoming securities thus not only greatly increase their trade, but furnish a second-rate article at a first-rate price. It is useless to complain of the bad quality or high price of the articles supplied by the securities, for the shop-keepers know, as well as the workpeople, that it is impossible for the hands to leave them without losing their work. I know one baker whose security was refused at the slop-shop because he was already responsible for so many, and he begged the publican to be his deputy, so that by this means the workpeople were obliged to deal at both baker's and publican's too. I never heard of a butcher making a trade of becoming security, because the slopwork people cannot afford to consume much meat. The same system is also pursued by lodging-house keepers. They will become responsible if the workmen requiring security will undertake to lodge at their house.

"Concerning the system of fines adopted at the lower class of slop houses, I know that within the last week a new practice has been introduced of stopping 1d. out of the wages for each garment that is brought in after eleven o'clock on the Saturday. By this means upwards of £1 was collected last Saturday night. This the proprietor of the shop pretends to distribute in charity; but if he does so, the charitable gift passes as his own money, and we have no means of knowing how much he collects and how much he distributes. There is also a fine of 4d. for each louse found on the garments brought in. The fine for vermin at other houses is sometimes as high as 6d., and at others as low as 3d. The poor people are obliged to live in the cheapest and filthiest places, and have, even if they felt inclined, little or no time to 'clean themselves.' If a louse is found on the garments brought in by any of the 'lady sweaters,' who are generally much better dressed than the poor

workpeople, it is wrapped up in a piece of clean paper, and presented to the 'lady' in an undertone, so that the other parties present may not be aware of the circumstance. If the vermin be found upon the garments brought in by the poor people, the foreman make no secret of it, and fine them 4d., in the presence of all in the shop. When the wife of a sweater returns home, and tells the hands working under her husband that 4d. has been stopped for a louse found upon the garments taken in, an angry discussion often arises among the workpeople as to whose it was.". . .

I now come to the narrative of a man assuredly a type of a very numerous class— a journeyman tailor, who adhered as long as possible to the "honourable" trade and the rules of the society, but who had to become *a sweater with a family*:

"I am 49, and have been a journeyman tailor for 30 years. My experience of the business in London extends over 25 years. I came to London 25 years ago, and the average of my wages was 36s.; indeed, I've many a week earned £2 and more by my own labour alone. This was the case for eight or nine years. I was very seldom out of work in those days. I was then a married man with a family; but I could and did support and educate my family well and comfortably by my own labour. After the term I have mentioned I felt a difference. Trade fell off gradually, and kept falling, dragging down men's earnings with it, until it's as bad as we find it now. Wages fell more after the change in 1834. A bad job that ever it happened—it was indeed. Wages, or earnings, kept still falling, and, my family growing up, I was compelled to become a sweater, putting my two boys and two girls to work to assist me, as well as my wife, when her health permitted. With all these five hands and my own labour I could not on slop-work, working every day and long hours, earn more than 30s. a week; and I had the best of the work that was given out.

"A man regularly employed by a slop master cannot earn more than 12s. a week by his own labour, out of which he must find his own sewing-trimmings, candles, &c. Provisions are cheaper than they were, certainly; but wages, I have found, fall faster and sooner than provisions—so cheap tea and sugar's little benefit. I worked for ——, but was only once in their shop in my life. I always sent my wife or one of my children for and with the work. I couldn't spare time to go myself. If I had only myself I could not have earned more than 10s. at twelve hours' work every day. I have no doubt that the low-priced 'ticketing' shops have brought about this hard state of things, bringing females into the trade, and forcing men to work for almost any wages. If any good soul were to leave me £100 now, or even £500, it would be no use my attempting to do any good with it as a small master. I could not get enough custom. A man could at one time live comfortably under one of them. I have not tasted spirits for seven years come Easter, but with all my endeavours and my family's I cannot save anything. My rent is 3s. 6d. a week for two rooms. If I ever ran off tippling, somebody must want.

"I left —— because I was employed to make three frock coats, lined through with silk and quilted, for which I received 10s. each (the 'regular' pay would be 21s.), and from the 30s. so earned my employer wanted to deduct 6s.—that is, 2s. on each coat as a fine. I might take less and keep my work, or be paid the 30s. and lose my work. That's the way they gradually lower wages still more. Such masters always take advantage of a slack time. What can men with families do? Men must submit."

From an intelligent man I learned how some employers still further reduced the low wages paid, by *fines*, and by *deductions* from the usual charge for garments in the case of men below the average height or bulk, saying that they must be paid for at the same rate as boys' clothing. "If I give way," said the man, "next time, perhaps, a rather bigger man's trowsers would be reckoned as boy's, and so it creeps on." On the subject of *fines*, I will relate what was told me by another workman—several representing the same thing to me as very common. His wife had taken up work at ——'s, and when she went home, some part of the stuff was found wanting; it had not been given out by the "trimmer." She went back, but could not get the stuff wanted unless she would pay for it. On her demurring, she was fined 1s.; and on the husband's going to expostulate, *he* was fined 1s., that, as he was told, he might not have the laugh against his wife! He complained to the superintendent of the shop, who told him he must put up with such things. He had his choice—pay the fines, and keep his work, or refuse to pay them, and leave it. The "trimmer" pronounced him drunk and abusive, but the man declares he went straight from his work, and was perfectly sober and civil. This same man was fined 1s. for being an hour too late with a jacket, at which he had worked all night, and had not a reasonable time allowed to finish the job. Many men complained of the utter disregard of their convenience shown by some employers or their shopmen; such as getting work in the evening, and being compelled to work all night, without a farthing extra for fire or candle.

The following is the statement of a master in the City, to whom I was referred as a very intelligent man, and one greatly respected. "I have been in business fifteen years. When I commenced I used to get good prices, but now I am compelled to give as good an article at a lower price—fully twenty per cent. lower—in order to compete with ready-made and cheap clothes shops. I have not in consequence reduced the wages of the men in my employ, so that my profits are considerably reduced, while my exertions, and those of other tradesmen similarly circumstanced, to keep together a 'connection,' which may yield fair prices and a fair remuneration, have to be more strenuous than ever. Year by year I have found the cheap establishments affect my business, and it seems to me that if the system pursued by the show and slop houses be not checked it will swamp all the honourable trade, which becomes every year smaller. Customers bargain now more than ever as to price, their constant remark being, 'I can get it for so much at ——'s.'

"When I began business the cheap system had not been started. Slopsellers formerly were those who made inferior clothing, badly cut and badly made, and paid for accordingly. Now there must be—for these great cheap houses—good work for bad wages. Some years ago a great part of the slopseller's business was to make clothes for the slaves in the West Indies, for East Indian regiments, jackets for sailors, and such like. When I began business the slop trade was a distinct thing from what is understood as the 'regular' trade of the tailor. Tailoring was then kept to itself. There were not half the good hands to be got then that there are now. A really first-rate hand was comparatively scarce. Now I can get any number of first-rate hands, as I give full wages. I could get twenty such hands, if I wanted them, in a few hours. My business, to compete with the slopsellers, requires the most incessant attention, or I am sure it would fall. I cannot now afford to give such a term of credit as formerly. My regular hands earn the same wages as they have earned all along; they perhaps average 25s. to 30s. a week through the year. My trade is looked upon as an exception to the general lowering of price and wretched payment of the workmen round about here.

"I find the effects of the ready-made trade most at holiday times, Easter and Christmas, when business used to be the best. People at those times now run to the slop-shops. I have worked my business up in my own way, but I am convinced that if I had to begin it now, instead of fifteen years ago, I could not have established myself with a body of respectable and regular customers, at fair prices; not even with more capital at my command. I must have adopted the low-priced system. As businesses 'of the old school' fall off, the customers go to the slop-sellers. Such businesses as mine are becoming fewer; tailors' shops now must be on a very large scale, or they are not to be carried on profitably at all.". . .

I was directed to one of the back streets of the Commercial-road; and there, in a small, close, and bare, unfurnished room, stretched on a bed scantily covered, I found [a] poor sick slopworker. On the floor sat a man cross-legged at work, who had no place to carry on his trade. He had come to sit in the dying man's room, and to use the sleeve-boards and irons that the invalid has no use for. On the narrow wooden mantel-shelf stood a row of empty physic bottles and an old wine glass; beside the man's bedside was a small deal table, on which was a mildewed orange, half peeled. The ceiling was browned in patches with the wet that had leaked through from the roof. The wife followed me upstairs. There was no chair in the room, and one was borrowed from below for my accommodation. She told me the house was "dreadful damp; it was never dry, winter or summer; the wet often streamed down the walls." I had seen many squalid, desolate homes, but this was more wretched than all. I asked why the sick man was not taken to the hospital. The man himself could not speak for coughing. The wife told me he could not go to the hospital, his clothes were all in pledge; they had been taken to the pawnshop for the subsistence of the family.

"If it hadn't been for that we must all have starved," she said. "This last five weeks he has been confined to his bed, and we have been obliged to make away with all we had. I have pawned all my under-clothing. I have five children; the eldest fourteen, and the youngest two years and a half old. I have pledged almost all their clothes, and if I could have taken anything else off the poor little things, I should have done it to get victuals for them."

The man himself now raised his head from below the bed-clothes. His long black hair was thrown off his forehead, and his face, which had once been handsome, was suffused with perspiration. His black unshorn beard made him look paler perhaps than he was. He breathed hard and quickly. He told me he could not go to the hospital, because he should lose his work if he did so.

"I worked at the out-door work for a large slop-shop. I did the bespoke work," said he. "Look here," cried one of his friends, dragging a coat from off the sick man's bed. "See here; the man has no covering, and so he throws this garment over him as a shelter." [It was a new pilot coat that was to be taken in that evening for the shop.] I expressed my surprise that the bed of the sick man should be covered with the new garment, and was informed that such in the winter time was a common practice among the workpeople. When the weather was very cold, and their blankets had gone to the pawnshop, the slopworkers often went to bed, I was told, with the sleeves of the coat they were making drawn over their arms, or else they would cover themselves with the trowsers or paletôts, according to the description of garment they had in hand. The ladies' riding habits in particular, I was assured, were used as counterpanes to the poor people's beds, on account of the quantity of cloth in the skirts.

"He will get 3s. for making such a coat as this," continued the sick man's friend, still holding up the garment, and out of that he will have to pay 6d. for trimmings and expenses. It will take him two days to make such a coat, working 12 hours each day. But in the slop-trade we hardly understand 12 hours work in a day; our time for labour is mostly 18 hours every day. Doing 12 hours work a day he could make 7s. 6d. a week clear at such work, and out of that he has to keep himself, a wife, and five children, and pay rent."

"I can earn upon an average," he said, "by my own labour, from 9s. to 10s. a week clear." Here my attention was distracted by a loud voice below stairs. It was one of the servants of the slop-house, come to demand a certain garment that had been given out to the sick man to make, and which he had employed a party to finish for him. It had been pawned when completed to keep the sick man's family from starving, and when the poor fellow was told the cause of the noise below stairs, he trembled like a leaf, and the perspiration again started in large drops to his forehead. "Let me drink," he said.

I asked to see the pawn tickets. They were shown me, and I was told by one of the parties present in the room, that the firm, having heard of my inquiry into the condition and earnings of the workpeople, were calling in all garments, so as to prevent my seeing the prices marked upon the tickets sent out with the clothes. The same person assured me that a servant of the house had called upon him that morning, and demanded a particular garment that he had to make for them. It was in pawn, he told me, and he had been obliged to pledge the work of another employer, in order to redeem the coat demanded. Indeed I was assured that such was the distress of the workpeople that there was scarcely one that had not work of their employers in pawn—that one coat was continually substituted for another to prevent inquiries, and that a month's interest was paid on each, though it was generally in pawn but a few days. The workpeople dreaded detection more than anything, because it was sure to be followed by the withdrawal of their security, and this was their ruin.

"I came over from Ireland several years back," continued the sick man, in answer to my questions. "I worked from a house of call for about ten years after I came to England, and then I came to this slop work, at which I have been about twelve years. When I was engaged at the honourable trade I could make three times as much as I do now. I was very comfortable then." "We are not so now, God knows" said the wife. "When I fell sick, I had 9s. a week from my society, now I have not a farthing from anybody, nor do I know where to get a farthing if I wanted it. Since I have been at the slop work I have neither been able to save anything nor to keep my children as I wanted to. I couldn't even send them to church of a Sunday for the want of their clothes. I fell ill two years ago, with a pain in my chest and side, and a bad cough. It was working long hours that made me bad. My side is quite raw from blistering. There are many men who are working at this business, who have not been outside the doors and smelt the fresh air for months and months together. In some places the workmen have only one coat to put on between six, and many cannot spare the time. The wife goes to take the work in and get the work out.

"For two years I have fought against my complaint. I never was to stay well in this house. I slept downstairs on the ground floor, and I think that was the cause of my illness. There are no drains at all to the house, and the stagnant water remains underneath the boards downstairs. In the yard the standing water is like a cesspool. I went on for two years working away, though I was barely able, and at last, five weeks ago, I was dead beat. I couldn't do a stitch more, and was obliged to take to my bed. Since then we have been living on what we pawned. There was nothing else to be done, and as a last resource we have got up a raffle. We generally do assist one another, if we can; but we are all so poor we have scarcely a penny for ourselves, any of us. I have come down to my very last now, and if I don't get better in health what will become of us all I don't know. We can't do without something to eat. My children cry for victuals as it is, and what we shall do in a little while is more than I can say."

"Consider," said a fellow workman of the man to me, "if he goes into the hospital the little employment that he has when he is well will go from him. He is afraid, therefore, to leave here." "As it is, his anxiety of mind makes him worse, for he is fretting all day long," said his wife, "about his children, and what ever will become of them all if he stops as he is much longer, I can't tell."

From Letter XVIII, December 18th, 1849

I will first proceed to give the reader a more perfect idea than I have yet been able to do of the principle of sweating. I first sought out a sweater himself, from whom I obtained the following information:

"I make the best coats, and get 16s. for frock and dress. They take me three days each to do. I have to find my own trimmings, and basting up is included likewise. I use one lamp for my own work; my missus has a candle to herself. The lamp costs me about 1s. 9d. a week, and the extra fire for heating my irons about 1s. a week. The expenses of trimmings for two coats will be about 1s. 6d., which come altogether to 4s. 3d., and this has to be deducted from 32s., leaving 27s. 9d. clear for my own weekly earnings. This is more than the generality of people can make. I make this amount of money weekly upon an average all the year round. I can do thus much by my own single hand. I employ persons to work under me—that is, I get the work, and give it to them to do.

"I generally have two men working at home with me. I take a third of the coat, and I give them each a third to do. They board and lodge with me altogether— that is, they have their dinners, teas, breakfasts, and beds in my place. I give them at the rate of 15s. a coat—that is, I take 1s. off the price I receive, for the trimmings and my trouble. The trimmings come to 9d., and the extra 3d. is profit for my trouble. They pay me at the rate of 2s. 6d. per week for washing and lodging— the washing would be about 6d. out of the money. They both sleep in one bed. Their breakfast I charge 4d. each for—if 'with a relish,' they are 5d. Their teas are 4d., and their dinners are 6d.—altogether I charge them for their food about 8s. 2d. a week, and this with lodging and washing comes to from 10s. 6d. to 11s. per week. The three of us working together can make six coats in the week, if fully employed—on an average we make from four to five coats—and never less than four. This would bring us in altogether, for four coats, £3 4s. Out of this the shares of each of my two men would be £1. The rest I should deduct for expenses. Then their living would be from about 10s. 6d., so that they would get clear 9s. 6d. per week over and above their living.

"I pay 7s. 6d. a week rent. I have two rooms, and the men sleep in the work room. I get every week for the four of us (that is for myself, my missus, and the two men—we live all together) about four or five ounces of tea, and this cost me 1s. 5d. I have 1s. worth of coffee, and about 1s. 6d. worth of sugar. The bread is 3s. 6d. per week, and butter 2s. 11d. The meat comes to about 8s., and the vegetables 2s. 4d. The lighting will be 1s. 9d., firing 1s. 6d. This will come to 30s. for the board and lodging of the four of us, or at the rate of 7s. 6d. per head. I should therefore clear out of the living of my men about 3s. a week each, and out of their work about 8d., so that altogether I get 3s. 8d. a week out of each man I employ. This, I believe, is a fair statement. I wish other people dealt with the men as decently as I do. I know there are many who are living entirely upon them. Some employ as many as fourteen men.

"I myself worked in the house of a man who did this. The chief part of us lived and worked and slept together in two rooms, on the second floor. They charged 2s. 6d. per head for the lodging alone. Twelve of the workmen, I am sure, lodged in the house, and these paid altogether 30s. a week rent to the sweater. I should think the sweater paid 8s. a week for the rooms—so that he gained at least 22s. clear, out of the lodging of these men, and stood at no rent himself. For the living of the men he charged—5d. for breakfasts, and the same for teas, and 8d. for dinner—or at the rate of 10s. 6d. each per head. Taking one with the other, and considering the manner in which they lived, I am certain that the cost for keeping each of them could not have been more than 5s. This would leave 5s. 6d. clear profit on the board of each of the twelve men, or altogether £3 6s. per week; and this, added to the £1 2s. profit on the rent, would give £4 8s. for the sweater's gross profit on the board and lodging of the workmen in his place. But, besides this, he got 1s. out of each coat made on his premises, and there were twenty-one coats made there upon an average every week; so that altogether the sweater's clear gains out of the men were £5 9s. every week. Each man made about a coat and a half in the course of the seven days (for they all worked on a Sunday—they were generally told to 'borrow a day of the Lord'). For this coat and a half each hand got £1 2s. 6d., and out of it he had to pay 13s. for board and lodging; so that there was 9s. 6d. clear left.

"These are the profits of the sweater, and the earnings of the men engaged under him, when working for the first-rate houses. But many of the cheap houses pay as low as 8s. for the making of each dress and frock coat, and some of them as low as 6s. Hence the earnings of the men at such work would be from 9s. to 12s. per week, and the cost of their board and lodging, without dinners, for these they seldom have, would be from 7s. 6d. to 8s. per week. Indeed, the men working under sweaters at such prices generally consider themselves well off if they have a shilling or two in their pocket for Sunday. The profits of the sweater, however, would be from £4 to £5 out of twelve men working on his premises. The usual number of men working under each sweater is about six individuals: and the average rate of profit, about £2 10s., without the sweater doing any work himself.

"It is very often the case that a man working under a sweater is obliged to pawn his own coat to get any pocket-money that he may require. Over and over again the sweater makes out that he is in his debt from 1s. to 2s. at the end of the week, and when the man's coat is in pledge he is compelled to remain imprisoned in the sweater's lodgings for months together. In some sweating places there is an old coat kept called a 'reliever,' and this is borrowed by such men as have none of their own to go out in. There are very few of the sweaters' men who have a coat to their backs or a shoe to their feet to come out into the streets on Sunday. Down about Fulwood's rents, Holborn, I am sure I would not give 6d. for the clothes that are on a dozen of them; and it is surprising to me, working and living together in such numbers and in such small close rooms, in narrow, close back courts as they do, that they are not all swept off by some pestilence.

"I myself have seen half-a-dozen men at work in a room that was a little better than a bedstead long. It was as much as one could do to move between the wall and the bedstead when it was down. There were two bedsteads in this room, and they nearly filled the place when they were down. The ceiling was so low that I couldn't stand upright in the room. There was no ventilation in the place. There was no fireplace, and only a small window. When the window was open you could nearly touch the houses at the back, and if the room had not been at the top of the house the men could not have seen at all in the place. The staircase was so narrow, steep, and dark, that it was difficult to grope your way to the top of the house— it was like going up a steeple. This is the usual kind of place in which the sweater's men are lodged. The reason why there are so many Irishmen working for the sweaters is, because they are seduced over to this country by the prospect of high wages and plenty of work. They are brought over by the Cork boats at 10s. a-head, and when they once get here the prices they receive are so small that they are unable to go back. In less than a week after they get here their clothes are all pledged, and they are obliged to continue working under the sweaters."

After this I made the best of my way to one who was working under a sweater, and who was anxious, I was told, to expose the iniquities of the whole system. He said:

"I work for a sweater. I have been working for such people off and on for this last eight or nine years. I 'belonged to society' before that, and worked for the most honourable masters at this end of the town. I worked in the master's shop, of course. I never did day work, but I had piece work to do. I preferred that. I was a very quick hand, and could make more money that way. At day work I should have got £1 16s. a week, but at piece work I have occasionally made 36s. in four days, but these four days were at the latter end of the week. Upon an average I could get about 38s. a week in the brisk time, which was about two months in the year. I was always employed at that time, unless it was my own fault. During the vacation, or slack, I used often to be for many months and not earn a shilling at all. I used to hang about the houses of call then, waiting for a job, which came in about one day a week throughout the rest of the year, excepting at Christmas, when perhaps I should have about three weeks' employment. I had a wife, but no children.

"Four years come this winter was the last time that I had employment at the honourable part of the trade. But before that I used to work for the sweaters when the regular business was slack. I did this unknown to the society of which I was a member. If it had been known to them, I should have had to pay a certain penalty, or else my name would have been scratched off the books, and I should have no more chance of work at the honourable trade. When working for the honourable trade I was employed about one-third of my time, and I should say I earned about £30 in the year. I was out of work two-thirds of my time. I never saved anything out of my wages when I was fully employed. I generally got into debt in the slack time, and was obliged to work hard to pay it off in the brisk. It was during the vacation, eight years back, that I first went to a sweater. Sweaters were scarcely known 25 years back, and they increased enormously after the change from day work to piece work. I could get no employment at my regular trade, and a sweater came down to the house and proposed to me privately to go and work for him. It was a regular practice then for the sweaters to come to the house and look out for such as had no employment and would work under price. I kept on for four years secretly working for the sweaters during vacation, and after that I got so reduced in circumstances that I could not appear respectable, and so get work amongst the honourable trade. The pay that I received by working for the sweaters was so little that I was forced to part with my clothes.

"When I first went to work for the sweater, I used to get 4s. 6d. for making the third part of a coat. It would take from 11 to 13 hours to make a third. I could have done as many as six thirds, but could not get them to do. The sweater where I worked employed more hands than he had work for, so that he could get any job that was wanted in a hurry done as quickly as possible. I should say upon an average I got two-thirds of a coat to make each week, and earned about 7s. Some weeks of course I did more; but some I had only one, and often none at all. The sweater found me in trimmings. His system was the same as others, and I have worked for many since in the last eight years. The sweaters all employ more men than they want, and I am sure that those who work for them do not get more than two-thirds of a coat to make every week, taking one week with another. Another of the reasons for the sweaters keeping more hands than they want is, the men generally have their meals with them. The more men they have with them the more breakfasts and teas they supply, and the more profit they make. The men usually have to pay 4d., and very often 5d. for their breakfast, and the same for their tea. The tea or breakfast is mostly a pint of tea or coffee, and three to four slices of bread and butter. I worked for one sweater who almost starved the men; the smallest eater there would not have had enough if he had got three times as much. They had only three thin slices of bread and butter, not sufficient for a child, and the tea was both weak and bad. The whole meal could not have stood him in 2d. a head, and what made it worse was, that the men who worked there couldn't afford to have dinners, so that they were starved to the bone.

"The sweater's men generally lodge where they work. A sweater usually keeps about six men. These occupy two small garrets; one room is called the kitchen, and the other the workshop; and here the whole of the six men, and the sweater, his wife, and family, live and sleep. One sweater I worked with had four children, six men, and they, together with his wife, sister-in-law, and himself, all lived in two rooms, the largest of which was about 8 feet by 10. We worked in the smallest room and slept there as well—all six of us. There were two turn-up beds in it, and we slept three in a bed. There was no chimney, and indeed no ventilation whatever. I was near losing my life there—the foul air of so many people working all day in the place and sleeping there at night was quite suffocating. Almost all the men were consumptive, and I myself attended the dispensary for disease of the lungs. The room in which we all slept was not more than six feet square. We were all sick and weak, and loath to work. Each of the six of us paid 2s. 6d. a week for our lodging, or 15s. altogether, and I am sure such a room as we slept and worked in might be had for 1s. a week; you can get a room with a fireplace for 1s. 6d. The usual sum that the men working for sweaters pay for their tea, breakfasts, and lodging is 6s. 6d. to 7s. a week, and they seldom earn more money in the week. Occasionally at the week's end they are in debt to the sweater. This is seldom for more than 6d., for the sweater will not give them victuals if he has no work for them to do.

"Many who live and work at the sweater's are married men, and are obliged to keep their wives and children in lodgings by themselves. Some send them to the workhouse, others to their friends in the country. Besides the profit of the board and lodging, the sweater takes 6d. out of the price paid for every garment under 10s.; some take 1s., and I do know of one who takes as much as 2s. This man works for a large show-shop at the West End. The usual profit of the sweater, over and above the board and lodging, is 2s. out of every pound. Those who work for sweaters soon lose their clothes, and are unable to seek for other work, because they have not a coat to their back to go and seek it in.

"Last week I worked with another man at a coat for one of her Majesty's Ministers, and my partner never broke his fast while he was making his half of it. The Minister dealt at the cheap West End show-shop. All the workman had the whole day-and-a-half he was making the coat was a little tea. But sweater's work is not so bad as Government work, after all. At that we cannot make more than 4s. or 5s. a week altogether, that is, counting the time we are running after it, of course. Government contract work is the worst work of all, and the starved-out and sweated-out tailor's last resource. But still Government does not do the regular trade so much harm as the cheap show and slop shops. These houses have ruined thousands. They have cut down the prices so that men cannot live at the work; and the masters who did and would pay better wages, are reducing the workmen's pay every day. They say they must either compete with the large show shops or go into the *Gazette*.". . .

In my last [letter] I merely hinted at the system adopted by wily sweaters to entrap inexperienced country and Irish hands into their service. Since then I devoted considerable attention to the subject, and am now in a position to lay before the public the following facts in connection with this trade:

The system of inducing men by false pretences on the part of *sweaters*, or, more commonly, of *sweaters' wives*, to work for them at wretched wages, I heard described in various terms. Such persons were most frequently called *kidnapped men*. The following narrative, given to me by one of the men concerned, and corroborated by one of his Irish fellow-victims, supplies an instance of the stratagems adopted. The second Irishman had but—as he said to me—"changed his house of bondage"—he had fallen into the hands of another sweater, his coat was in pawn, and he could not, in spite of all his struggles, lay by enough to redeem it.

The wife of a sweater (an Irishman, long notorious for such practices), herself a native of Kerry, visited her friends in that town, and found out two poor journeymen tailors. One was the son of a poor tailor, the other of a small farmer. She induced these two young men to follow her to London, immediately after her return, and at their own expense. She told them of her husband's success in trade, and of the high wages to be got in London by those who had friends in the trade, and engaged the two for her husband. Their wages were to be 36s. a week *"to begin with."*

When the Irishmen reached the sweater's place, near Houndsditch, they found him in a den of a place (I give the man's own words), anything but clean, and anything but sweet, and were at once set to work at trowsers making, at 1s. a pair, finding their own trimmings. Instead of 36s. a week, they could not clear more than 5s. by constant labour, and the sweater attributed this to their want of skill—they were not capable of working well enough for a London house. He then offered to teach them, if they would bind themselves apprentices to him for a year certain. During the year they were to have board and lodging, and £5 each, paid at intervals as they required it. The poor men having no friends in London, and no acquaintances even whom they might consult, consented to this arrangement, and a sort of document was signed. They then went to work on this new agreement, their board being this—For breakfast—half a pint of poor cocoa each, with half a pound of dry bread cut into slices, *between the two*; no butter. Dinner was swallowed, a few minutes only being allowed for it, between four and five. It was generally a few potatoes and a bit of salt fish, as low priced as could be met with. At seven, each man had half a pint of tea and the same allowance of bread as for breakfast. No supper. They slept three in a bed, in a garret where there was no ventilation whatever.

The two men (apprenticed as I have described) soon found that the sweater was unable to teach them anything in their trade, he not being a superior workman to either of them. At three weeks' end they therefore seized an opportunity to escape. The sweater traced them to where they had got work again, took with him a policeman, and gave them in charge as run-away apprentices. He could not, however, substantiate the charge at the station-house, and the men were set at liberty. Even after that the sweater's wife was always hanging about the corners of the streets, trying to persuade these men to go back again. She promised one that she would give him a handsome daughter she had for his wife, and find the new married pair "a beautiful slop shop" to work for, finding them security and all, and giving them some furniture, if he would only go back. The workman so solicited excused himself on the plea of illness.

After this the father of this youth, in Kerry, received an anonymous letter, telling him that his son had run away from his employer, carrying with him a suit of clothes, and that he (the father) should have his son written to, and persuaded to return, and the robbery might be hushed up. This was every word false, and the anonymous letter was forwarded to the son in London, and when shown to the sweater he neither admitted nor denied it was his writing, but changed the conversation. . . .

The continual immigration of foreign labour that I had discovered to be part of the system by which the miserable prices of the slop-trade were maintained, was the next subject to which I directed my inquiries, and I was able to obtain evidence which clearly proves how the honourable part of the trade are undersold by the "sloppers." The party who gave me the following valuable information on this head was a Hungarian Jew sweater. He said:

"I am a native of Pesth, having left Hungary about eight years ago. By the custom of the country I was compelled to travel three years in foreign parts before I could settle in my native place. I went to Paris after travelling about that time

K

in the different countries of Germany. I stayed in Paris about two years. My father's wish was that I should visit England, and I came to London, in June, 1847. I first worked for a West-end show-shop—not directly for them, but through the person who is their 'middleman,' getting work done at what rates he could for the firm, and obtaining the prices they allowed for making the garments. I once worked four days and a half for him, finding my own trimmings, &c., for 9s. For this my employer would receive 12s. 6d. On each coat of the best quality he got 3s. and 3s. 6d. profit. He then employed 190 hands; he has employed 300; many of those so employed setting their wives, children, and others to work, some employing as many as five hands this way. The middleman keeps his carriage, and will give fifty guineas for a horse.

"I became unable to work, from a pain in my back, from long hours at my occupation. The doctor told me not to sit much, and so, as a countryman of mine was doing the same, I employed hands, making the best I could of their labour. I have now four young women (all Irish girls) so employed. Last week one of them received 4s., another 4s. 2d., the other two 5s. each. They find their own board and lodging, but I find them a place to work in—a small room, the rent of which I share with another tailor, who works on his own account.

"There are not so many Jews come over from Hungary or Germany as from Poland. The law of travelling three years brings over many, but not more than it did. The revolutions have brought numbers this year and last. They are Jew tailors flying from Russian and Prussian-Poland to avoid the conscription. I never knew any of those Jews go back again. There is a constant communication among the Jews, and when their friends in Poland and other places learn they're safe in England, and in work and out of trouble, they come over too, even if they can earn more at home. I worked as a journeyman in Pesth, and got 2s. 6d. a week, my board, washing, and lodging. We lived well, everything being so cheap. The Jews come in the greatest number about Easter. They try to work their way here, most of them. Some save money here, but they never go back; if they leave England, it is to go to America.". . .

BOOT AND SHOE MAKERS

"Honourable" West-End Trade

From Letter XXXII, February 4th, 1850

In order to obtain a full statement from one of the most intelligent members of the West-end trade as to the causes which the journeymen shoemakers consider to have been instrumental in causing a reduction in their earnings, I consulted the Society upon the subject. Hearing that there was to be a meeting of twenty-one delegates from the various sections of the Western Division, concerning the interests of the trade, and having been informed that these delegates had been chosen, by the sections which they represented, as the most intelligent and experienced of the bodies to which they belonged, I requested that the twenty-one when assembled would select, from among them, one who could give me an account of the principal circumstances affecting the trade.

I was furnished with the address of an individual who certainly was a favourable specimen of his class. He was a fine sample of the English artisan. His children (there were three) were especially remarkable for their cleanliness, telling of the careful matron, and they played about the room, while the man sat at work, in a manner that showed little restraint in the presence of their father. Indeed it was easy to see, as well by the tidiness of the room as by the conduct of the children, that both the workman and his wife were very superior persons. The man had clearly the interests of his class deeply at heart, and spoke of such failings of his brother artisans as were alluded to in conversation with much concern and an evident anxiety for their welfare. He was tolerant, dispassionate, and almost philosophic in his tone of thought, and had a strong literary taste and a love of reflection. He talked as he worked.

"I am a *boot-closer*, working for the best shop," he said. "I am not fully employed. I have an equal share of work with my shopmates, and try to fill up my spare time with what we call 'by-strokes' (that is by seeking for extra employment at other shops). I get the best prices. In the course of last season I have made, with an apprentice and my wife's assistance, and working Sunday and all the rest of the week, and sitting up for two entire nights in the course of that time—with all this I *have* made, I say, as much as £3. How much I myself earned of that sum I cannot say—I might have done half of it. I think I could earn 35s. for one week at a time in the season, but then I couldn't keep it up at that rate. I can myself, without any assistance, earn with comfort 27s. a week when I can get it. To do that much, however, I must sit at my work for 14 hours every day. Out of the 27s.

I shall have to pay about 1s. 6d. for grindery, and 9d. for oil for my light. So that my clear week's earnings at the best would be between 24s. and 25s. When I was a single man my average earnings throughout the year came to £1 2s. 6d. per week, but I had a good seat of work all that time. I think my average wages during that time were, in the season (that is from April to July), about 26s. a week, and out of the season about £1 a week. Single-handed I think I earn about the same now.

"A great number of closers earn less than I do; some may earn a little more. I think that, to take the average of the closers generally, throughout the town, their income would be about £1 a week. In some individual instances the weekly earnings might be as low as 15s.; but I know that the accounts taken of the earnings of the whole trade, in and out of union, in 1837, gave an average of 17s. a week to each of the 13,000 individuals who then followed the business in London. Since that time wages have gone down about 15 per cent. At this rate I calculate the average wages of our body would be about 15s. per man—some, of course, getting more, and others less. But the hands generally have less to do than what they had in 1838, owing to the greater number of people working at the trade. I should say that all through the trade, taking one hand with another, each man has 10 per cent. less work to do; so that I calculate, if an average was taken of our earnings now, the same as in 1837, it would be found that we should be earning generally 13s. 6d. a week each. In 1812 the boot-makers received their highest wages. If an average could have been taken then of the earnings of the trade, one with another, I think it would have been about 35s. per man. The great decrease (from 35s. to 13s. 6d. a week) that has taken place is not so much owing to the decrease of wages as to the increase of hands, and the consequent decrease of the work coming to each man. I know myself that my late master used to earn £2 per week on an average many years back, but of late years I am sure he has not made 15s. a week. I have, moreover, often heard it said that in former times three men (with two sons each to assist them) have drawn £21 as wages in one week from their employer. This gives very nearly £2 8s. per week per man, or 8s. each per day. And now a man must work hard to get 5s., even when fully employed. But he not only has less pay now, but has less work to do.

"There are a great many causes, I think, for this great reduction in our wages and our earnings. These are chiefly—the importation of foreign goods, the increase of the Northampton goods, and the competition of the masters and the men themselves. Concerning the importation of French goods, I consider the effect they have in reducing our wages to be this: Boots and shoes are produced in France and introduced into this country at a lower cost. The English masters, therefore, in order to compete with foreigners, reduce our wages as a necessary result. The reason why we cannot produce boots so cheap as the French is owing to the difference of rents, and the mode of living in France and England. I myself lived for some time in Boulogne, and my rent there was one-half less than what I paid here. A man, if he is short of work, may take it out of his stomach—he can eat a meal or two less; but he can't have it out of his rent—*that* must go on, either asleep or awake. Again, my living cost me much less in France than it does in this country, even now. I got only half the wages there that I did here, and yet I lived more happily and comfortably. The quantity of employment that I got there was much about the same as here.

A shoemaker at work

"But these are not the only reasons why the French can produce cheaper than we can. The fact is, one workman there will have from six to seven boys (in a factory where I worked this was the case, and I knew it was generally so). I don't know what wages were given to the lads, but the workman himself used to draw from 70 to 80 francs weekly, and had full employment. Another reason why the French can produce cheaper than we can, you see, sir, is because the French have not our immense national debt to bear them down; and all these things considered, I maintain that it is impossible for an English workman to compete with a Frenchman. Again, there is a great rage for everything French, and so there is not the same employment for *us*. French goods is the fashion of the day. This is certainly not due to any superiority on the part of the workman, which is evident from the fact that an English workman readily obtains employment in France, and—in Boulogne certainly—gets half a franc more for making boots than a Frenchman. As to the injury that the introduction of French boots into England has done the English workman, I will mention this fact, that immediately the duty upon them was reduced, our wages were reduced likewise. This, I think, was in 1842 (Sir Robert Peel's tariff). Our wages then fell 15 per cent., and have never got up since, and besides this, the quantity of employment among us has decreased most materially.

"The Northampton goods injure us to an equal, if not a greater extent. They produce even cheaper than the Frenchmen, but then it is done upon the factory system. The greatest part of the boots made there are produced, as in France, by a number of lads working under one master, and this is carried on even to a greater extent than in France. In fact, it is a common saying among us that every child in Northampton has a leather apron. The Northamptoners have nearly cut the French out of the market. Most of the French boots sold in London are Northampton made—for there, from the employment of a greater number of children than in France, they produce cheaper still. Again, the rents of the Northampton people are much lower than here; in fact it is the London rents that eat the people up.

"But a greater evil than all is the competition among the masters; almost every one, excepting the most respectable of them, is trying to force a trade by underselling the others. This, of course, masters may do in two ways—either by the reduction of their own profits, or by cutting down the wages of the working-men. The cheap men may, perhaps, take a little off *their* profits, but in general they undersell their neighbours by means of taking as much as they can off *our* wages. These are always the first thing they attack. Masters tell us that their customers can get boots elsewhere at a lower price, and they must either reduce their prices or lose their customers altogether. This competition among the masters is one of the chief causes of the competition among the working-men. A workman being paid less for his work is obliged to do more, in order to get a living at his trade. Let us say that he does half as much again as he used to do—then doesn't it stand to reason that there must be less work left for the others to do; and hence, on a reduction of wages, a number must be thrown out of employ. Again, in order to gain a competency at the low-price work, an operative employs his wife, and, in many cases, two or three lads to help him, and then he finds that he can produce a greater quantity at a less price than other workmen. He then, in order to keep all the boys in full employ, offers to the employers to do their work at a less price than the usual wages. So that you see the masters compete and the men compete, and between them the trade is being ruined as fast as it can. Yes, it ultimately must come to that.

"I often lie awake and think of the evils in our trade, but can't see how it's to be altered. I trace it in this way. The cheap French and Northampton goods deprive the employers of their regular customers, and that causes them to compete with the cheap shops, and consequently to cut down our wages. Then this in its turn causes the workmen to compete, and to underwork one another, in order to obtain employment. I tell you what it is, sir, we shall shortly have the same system in London as in France and Northampton, unless something is done to stop it. A man's own children will soon be the means of driving him from the market altogether, or compelling him to come down to their rate of wages; and if we are forced to put our children to work directly they are able, they cannot receive any education whatever, and then their minds and bodies will be both stunted. Of course, that must have a demoralizing effect upon the next generation. For my own part, as the trade is going down every day, I could not think of bringing up my boys to it, considering their future welfare—and what else I am to do with them I can't say. My earnings are so small now and my income so much reduced, that I shouldn't have the means to apprentice them to any other trade. In the years '45, '46 and '47 I was in a much better condition than I am now. Then I was able to take my periodicals in. I used to have near a shilling's worth of them every week, sir. I took in *Chambers's Journal*. I took in 'Knight's Cyclopædia,' and others of the same kind. I used to have my weekly newspaper, too. But since '48 I have not had the most of them, and I now take in none at all—I can't afford it. In '45 and '46, I was able to live better than I do now. The cheap provisions have done me no good whatever."

"My husband," interrupted the wife, "has been making less since food has been getting cheaper. In '46 his work was more regular than it is now. When we were first married the wages were 1s. 4d. a pair of boots more than they are at present, and more of them to do. Two years ago the meat was very dear, I recollect, and the potatoes and bread too; but there is no fault to be found with the present price of provisions. But since they have been getting cheaper, I am sure that our comforts have been decreasing rather than increasing. Why, sir, if it goes on this way, the workhouse stares us in the face. But the intention we have is to go into a club this winter, and raise funds to emigrate to America, unless the trade improves greatly, which we see no prospect of."

"I don't see myself (said the man at work) how it is to be altered. I, like thousands of others of the working men, have been struggling hard for these many years, and yet I get no forwarder. Last year I went back in my rent £10, and how I am to fetch it up I can't say. I suppose I must go to the loan-office, and pay through the nose for the money. I should be the happiest mortal alive, and be contented, if I could be certain of a fair quantity of employment and a fair rate of wages for it, but it's vexatious in the extreme to an industriously inclined working man to go to seek work and be unable to get it."

"I was in shop (said the wife) three-quarters of an hour this morning, and only two got served out of eight. This is one of the best shops in London, and the worst time is passed now. Just before Christmas last year my husband only got 5s., and that was to pay rent and to keep six of us. I haven't had £1 from the shop in any one week since a long time before Christmas, sir."

"Not since the end of October. Last week (said the man) was the best we have had for these three months, and that was 17s. 1d. One week, a little while ago, our earnings were 9s. 2d., another 7s. 8d., and another 12s."

From Letter XXXIII, February 7th, 1850

To enable the reader to contrast the present rate of the workman's income with the past, and so to judge of the earnings of a *bootman* in the palmy days of the trade, I give the statement of a first-rate workman employed by the late Mr. Hoby. My informant is now a small master on his own account. He was what is called a *ready man*; that is, one who can work at his trade with more than average celerity.

"I got work at Mr. Hoby's," he said, "not long after the battle of Waterloo, in 1815, and was told by my fellow-workmen that I wasn't born soon enough to see good times; but I've lived long enough to see bad ones. Though I wasn't born soon enough, as they said, I could earn and did earn £150 a year, something short of £3 a week; and that for eight years, when trade became not so good. Mr. Hoby used to send out returned boots (misfits) to America, and in the slack time kept his regular hands going, making boots for the American market, and paying his bootmen 7s. 2d. a pair for them. I never sat still for want of work until he dropped this foreign trade. One week a shopmate of mine had twenty pairs to take pay for. The regular wages was 8s. 2d. for the ground-work of Wellingtons with three-quarter heels, and liberal extras. I could then play my £1 a corner at whist. I *wouldn't* play at that time for less than 5s. I could afford a glass of wine, but never was a drinker; and, for all that, I had my £100 in the Four per Cents. for a long time (I lent it to a friend afterwards), and from £40 to £50 in the savings bank. Some made more than me, though I *must* work. I can't stand still. One journeyman, to my knowledge, saved £2,000; he once made 34 pairs of boots in three weeks.

"The bootmen then at Mr. Hoby's were all respectable men; they were like gentlemen—smoking their pipes, in their frilled shirts, like gentlemen—all but the drunkards. At the trade meetings, Hoby's best men used to have one corner of the room to themselves, and were called the House of Lords. There was more than 100 of us when I became one; and before then there were even a greater number. Mr. Hoby has paid five hundred pounds a week in wages. It was easy to save money in those days; one could hardly help it. We shall never see the like again."

By way of contrast to the preceding statement, I subjoin the account of a first-class bootman of the present day, whom I saw at work in a room he devoted to the purposes of his labour. He gave me the following statement:

"I have been acquainted with the business for thirty-one years, fifteen years of it as a bootman in London. The wages I received fifteen years ago, when I was first employed as a bootman in London, were the same as they are now—or nearly the same—in the shop I have worked for until lately. I had 6s. 6d. per pair for the ground-work of Wellington boots or top boots. There are no extras in the making of top boots; they are now seldom worn except by gentlemen when hunting, and among grooms when in full dress. The best week's work that ever I had in London was £2 0s. 2d. from my own labour, but I had to work late and early, with hardly leisure for meals. With the wages I have told you, taking one week with another, I did not earn, as my book shows, more than 20s. a week on an average for the whole time I have been employed. I am now on work at 8s. a pair for the bottom work, but without any extras except sockets; take the work as it comes, so much a pair. At my present work I may average rather more than 21s. a week. I could make far more with constant work. The best workmen have often to sit idle compulsorily.

"I fear that wages will fall lower still. Many of the aristocracy get their boots from Paris, or from a French tradesman in London; but that matters little, for the French masters in London generally give fair wages—some employing no French workmen at all; so that we can't, as reasonable men, complain of them. For every pair of boots ordered from Paris, there is a man the less employed for a day or two in London; so that the labour-market is over-stocked. Through men being forced to be idle, the masters can dictate their own terms, and men must give way, or get no work at all; and so wages fall. Masters all tell us that the repeal of the corn-laws enables us to live cheaper, and so wages may properly be reduced— also that, owing to the lowness of provisions and to compete with French goods, they must either at once, or sooner or later, lower their prices. Wages always fall as fast as provisions, and where the present downward tendency will stop I cannot form a notion."

I was afterwards informed that this bootman's statement was not a criterion as to the average earnings of the trade, he representing merely the very highest class. I therefore saw several others, and give the following extract from the communication made to me by an intelligent man, as embodying the statements of them all. All attributed the falling off in their earnings not to any reduction in prices, but to the slackness of employment:

"I have been more than twenty-five years in the trade," he said, "as boy and man, and have been familiar with the London trade for nine years. At that time (nine years ago) there was decidedly more employment. I then earned 21s. a week the year through on Wellington boots at 7s. a pair (with extras). Now my work is little different as regards the prices paid to me by the employer, but my average earnings do not exceed 14s.". . .

From Letter XXXIV, February 11th, 1850

A West-end sew-round of the first class gave me the following statement:

"I have known the women's *[shoemaking]* trade ever since I was nine—about twenty-seven years. When I first worked as a journeyman on first-class sew-rounds, I could earn 32s. That's more than fourteen years ago. Take the year round I now average 24s. a week; but my work (having a turn at corks in the winter) runs up more money than other men's. The first cause of the decline in earnings is, I think, owing to the bringing in of cheap French goods, and to the number of 'slaughter shops' (slop shops) now open. There were not near so many slaughter shops open until French goods came in so cheap. Wages have fallen greatly at the bespoke shops within these twelve or fourteen years. About seven years ago, as well as I recollect the time, there was a reduction of wages paid by the best shops, amounting from 2s. to 3s. a week on the earnings of the men. I used to get 3s. where I now get 2s. 8d. for satin sew-rounds. On pump boots in my time there has been a reduction of 8d., and all other things in proportion. The cheapness of corn is certainly a great advantage to the working man; but the masters, it is generally feared, will take advantage of it, and offer to reduce wages further. When the income-tax was first put on several masters reduced the wages they paid from 10 to 15 per cent., and so more than paid it that way. It's the slackness of work in many good shops that is the injury. If men can't get regular employ there, they are forced to work, in the way of by-strokes, for lower-priced shops—and so low-priced work, well made, gets its hold.". . .

A man who is employed as a *general man on the middle (and better) class of West-end work*, gave me this information: "As to trade, though I am reckoned one of the best workmen in the business, you see how I am off." (This alluded to his room, which was very poorly furnished, while his family were very thinly clad, but well-looking and well-mannered.) "I have known the trade in London 16 years, and at that time, working shorter hours than I do at present, and on the same description of work, I made 30s. a week easy. I have earned 40s. a week then, where I can't earn 20s. now.

"I attribute the depressed earnings of working men more to the cupidity of the middle classes than to anything else; they cut each other's throats in competition, but the poor journeyman pays for it. By the change in the tariff, in 1842, I am quite certain, both from my own experience and from my knowledge of my fellow workmen, the working men in my trade were very materially injured. Captain Rous, the member for Westminster, once said in the House of Commons that a shoemaker wouldn't go to work until he had his gin and beer. Not once in a twelvemonth does a drop of gin enter my house, nor a drop of beer many a week; no, not on Sundays. To show you what I earn now, you can extract my earnings from my book; for I work very hard and very many hours. . . . That is rather more than 11s. a week on the average (but I had two or three by-strokes), and I believe the earnings of the trade in winter do not average so much. I take the year through, and compute my average at 18s. a week.

"I think the repeal of the corn-laws the greatest blessing granted to this country. Between two and three years ago if I earned 20s. in the week, 9s. would go for bread; now, with the same number in family, I pay 4s. 3d. for my bread. That makes amends for the loss I've sustained by the tariff. Some French shoes are now sold, and have been for two years, at the price that even four years ago I was paid for making such.

"Now, sir, do say a word for the sake of the labouring classes about this which I'm going to tell you of. We all suffer by the system of sub-letting—lease upon lease, and agreement upon agreement. These sub-tenants are a rent-grubbing class that speculate in houses. Such as I clothe, feed, and educate them all. I consider that in a house of this description—say this house—and that is just as the others are, the rent received by the sub-letting landlord is £80 a year; while taxes, rates, and all included, the house stands him in £35—that's an average. They are cruel men. I was once discharged for an increase to my family, the child might occasion more trouble and noise. And then it's a favour to get into their houses. They object to shoemakers—their trade is noisy. Had I only my wife and myself my room

(3s. 3d. a week) would be cheaper; 3s. 3d. is an average sum. Things can't possibly be worse for such as me.". . .

I now give a short account of *the "strong" trade*, or rather of such portion of it as is recognized as "legal," owing to its being in union. The wares made by these men are described by a correspondent, whose letter I give. Strength, so as to ensure durability of wear, is the main thing aimed at. To effect this, heavy nails (both hammered and cast) are used to strengthen the sole, which, with the upper part, is of thick coarse leather, with nails or iron tips round the heels. The work was well described to me as "downright labour;" and my informant, a "strong" man, who made light of his labour, might have added, "of the hardest kind." The threads used to sew the sole to the welt are, as was described to me by another workman, "thick enough to frighten a West-end bootman." The hands of some of the men are callous, like horn, from the induration caused by the constant friction of the threads. One hard-working man, however, after he had been obliged to be idle for a while, when he got to work again, had his hands blistered and cut by the threads in a way to inspire an involuntary shudder, the cuts and blisters being black with wax. Even in the wares of these men, however, there was a proof of the excellence to which workmanship must be carried in London. I saw a "strong" man at work, and he expended some time in polishing the sole of a very strong cheap shoe, so as to make it sightly (or as they frequently call it, *viewly*); this was the more noticeable, as the work was for no window-show, and the sole, of course, would be dirtied by the first wear; but still, with the poorest, the eye must be pleased.

I give the statement of a man familiar with the strong trade for the last 11 years: "When I first knew the trade, 11 years ago, work was good; any man who could put leather together in the shape of a shoe could get work as a strong man—with the proviso, however, that the work must be strong for wear; it must hold together firmly with wax and thread, so as not to fall to pieces. Nothing depended upon skill at that time, but on bone and sinew; a man of great physical strength might then earn his 24s. a week, by working very long hours; the average weekly earnings of the strong man at that time I reckon at 16s. My average earnings were that. The run of the work is bluchers and 'ankles' (ankle-jacks some call them), and stout leather half-boots, laced up the front. Eleven years since the best masters paid 2s. 3d. for each sort, and they found the workman in hemp and brads—the men finding heel balls, wax, paste, bristles, &c. Candles, too, had to be provided by the workman, and are a great item in his expense. It appears to me that the strong men have always been badly paid. Instead of the 2s. 3d. paid 11 years ago, there is now given 2s., 1s. 10d., 1s. 8d., and in several cases 1s. 6d., men having generally to find their own grindery. One or two employers, however—and they must have better work for it—far better—aye at least 6d. a pair better—give 2s. 3d. and grindery; but that is for the very best work. The average cost of grindery for a pair of bluchers is 2d., at least.

"The average earnings of strong men now I reckon at 12s. a week, the cost of grindery not included; but that is only when men are in full work. Men casually employed will not average much more than half that sum; in fact, things have come to such a state, that we are now going on the co-operative system; we must take to that, or men may starve to death. I believe that the masters have next to nothing left from their competition one with another—I mean nothing left in the way of profit over and above the cost of material, and fair wages, out of the price for which they sell the goods—and so they drive at profit by reducing the poor work-man's wages still lower. We are heartily sick of strikes, which, as they have been conducted generally, have been, and can be, of no permanent benefit to the men. Had we £50, we could employ all our men next month, and pay at the rate of 5 per cent. per annum interest. We could appeal to the better class of workmen, and I think could get better prices. I have no doubt of it. I know that former attempts of the kind have failed, but then they were managed by people who did not understand the business. Indeed, we are now in operation in the co-operative way, by way of a commencement, though not in so large a way as we wish and intend. There is, I consider, no class so adapted for co-operation as our class of strong men. We could appeal to the sympathies of the great body of labouring men. We have nothing to do with gentlemen's work, and don't want. France doesn't in-terfere with our trade, neither does Northampton; we are all in all among our-selves. The great impediment to our getting on has been our poverty, and the ignor-ance it carries along with it. As for what things tend to in the future, I'll tell you. I hate physical force and revolutions, but I went to Kennington-common on the 10th of April, knowing or caring nothing what might happen."

"Dishonourable" East-End Trade

From Letter XXXIV, February 11th, 1850

Having thus given the characteristics and condition of the "legal," or honourable trade, I next turn my inquiry to the state of the labouring men, women, and children employed by the slop-masters, who are distinguished from the "wages" (or legal) shops by the terms *"illegal," "scab,"* or *"slaughter-shop" keepers*. I have reason to believe that the disclosures I shall make of the patiently-endured privations of numbers of the poor people working for these masters, and of the oppressions practised on them, will probably surpass the narratives of misery, and consequent dirt and disease, which I made public concerning the tailors.

Relative, then, to the branch of the business with which I have next to deal, I give the following communications from a shoemaker, a working man, of whose intelligence I received sufficient proofs, and whose character assures me that every reliance may be placed upon his statement—to say nothing of the corroboration I received incidentally in the course of my present inquiry. . . .

". . . The system which has, I believe, the worst effect on the women's trade throughout England, is *chamber-mastering*. There are between 300 and 400 chamber-masters. Commonly the man has a wife and three or four children, ten years old or upwards. The wife cuts out the work for the binders, the husband does the knife-work; the children sew with uncommon rapidity. The husband, when the work is finished at night, goes out with it, though wet and cold, and perhaps hungry—his wife and children waiting his return. He returns sometimes, having sold his work at cost price, or not cleared 1s. 6d. for the day's labour of himself and family. In the winter, by this means the shopkeepers and warehouses can take the advantage of the chamber-master, buying the work at their own price. By this means haberdashers' shops are supplied with boots, shoes, and slippers; they can sell women's boots at 1s. 9d. per pair; shoes, 1s. 3d. per pair; children's, 6d., 8d., and 9d. per pair, getting a good profit, having bought them of the poor chamber-master for almost nothing, and he glad to sell them at any price, late at night, his children wanting bread, and he having walked about for hours in vain trying to get a fair price for them; thus, women and children labour as well as husbands and fathers, and with their combined labours they only obtain a miserable living.

—— and Co's., City, is known by many as the 'refuge for the destitute.' A slight investigation will draw out an amount of misery almost incredible. It is impossible to ascertain accurately how many men are employed on this business. It is according to the state of trade for export or home use; but in the brisk season (summer) it is, as near as I can ascertain, as undermentioned. . . .

"It is probable that, independent of apprentices, 200 additional hands are added to our already over-burdened trade yearly. Sewing boys soon learn the use of the knife. Plenty of poor men will offer to finish them for a pound and a month's work; and men, for a few shillings and a few weeks' work, will teach other boys to sew. There are many of the wives of chamber-masters teach girls entirely to make children's work for a pound and a few months' work, and there are many in Bethnal-green who have learnt the business in this way. These teach some other members of their families, and then actually set up in business in opposition to those who taught them, and in cutting offer their work for sale at a much lower rate of profit; and shop-keepers in town and country, having circulars sent to solicit custom, will have their goods from a warehouse that will serve them cheapest; then the warehouseman will have them cheap from the manufacturer; and he in his turn cuts down the wages of the workpeople, who fear to refuse offers at the warehouse price, knowing the low rate at which chamber-masters will serve the warehouse. No doubt, could the little chamber-masters find means to serve the warehouse by the gross, instead of by the dozen, they would crush the wholesale factor. So the chamber-master is a scourge to himself and a curse to the trade generally, being an active means of yearly reducing the wages of the maker, while the warehouse-man gets rich, and the manufacturer, should he be obliged to make work 2s. a gross less for warehouse, is a great gainer, because he will dock wages 6d. a dozen."

From Letter XXXV, February 14th, 1850

As an exponent of the horrors of [the chamber-master] system, let me first give the narrative of a poor shoe-binder—a widow woman—a struggling, industrious, honest creature, to whom I was directed as a fair specimen of the class. It will be seen that I found the poor creature literally starving—and that, after toiling night and day to support herself. She was without a home, and was indebted to the sympathy of friends—as poor as herself—for her share of the wretched abode where I visited her. I never yet saw so much patience under so much suffering, nor such benevolence amid such privation:

"I have got no home, sir," she said. "My work wouldn't allow me to pay rent— no, that it wouldn't at the price we have now. I live with this good woman and her husband. The rent is half-a-crown a week, and they allow me to live with them rent free. We all live in this one room together—there are five of us, four sleep in one bed; that is the man and the wife and two children, and I lie on the floor. If it wasn't for them I must go to the work-house; out of what little I earn I couldn't possibly pay rent.

"I bind shoes, or boots generally; but boot work is not to be had at this time of the year. I do the same for the shoe as the boot-closer does for the boot—that is, I prepare the upper for the maker to sew the sole to. I have 15d. a dozen for binding what are termed slippers. By a slipper I do not mean a loose easy shoe to be worn when the ordinary walking ones are off, but any kind of cheap shoe— that is what is termed a slipper in the trade. A shoe we call a tie shoe—one that ties on the instep. For binding these I get 1s. 6d. a dozen, and for the slippers 1s. 3d. I work for a slop shoe warehouse. I can only bind five pair of slippers in a day of ten hours, and to do that much I must sit close. My average earnings in a day I calculate at $6\frac{1}{4}$d. I have sometimes done half a dozen, but then I have worked a great deal by candlelight, and it doesn't pay for that. In a week I can make 3s. 1½d. by sitting close to my work—getting only up to my meals, and not being long over them. The way in which I take my meals generally is what I call worrying the victuals. I get regular employment.

"I have been twenty-two years at the business. When I first began I could earn 2s. a day, or 12s. a week, easily, by myself, and do for my family as well. To sit the hours that I do now I could earn 14s. a week well then. These slippers that used to be 3½d. a pair binding, are now come to 1¼d.; the shoes that used to be 4d. a pair are 1½d. The boots that we were paid 1s. for binding have come down to 5d., and extra work put into them as well—the closer's work is put upon the binder's work now—that is to say, the binder has now to stab the leather goloshe on to 'the uppers' of the women's boots. Formerly this was done by the closer. The binder at that time had merely to stitch the uppers together, and after that they were given out to the closer to stab on the leather goloshe. Fourteen or fifteen years ago this was altered, and the binders had to learn the stabbing and buy the tools to do it with, without any increase in the price. Before that I could have bound a pair of boots in three hours; but afterwards it took me nearly double the time to finish them. I never heard the cause of the alteration, but I know it took place immediately after a great strike among the women's men. The working men were forced to give in, and the employers immediately reduced the wages. The first reduction that took place with me was about 17 years ago, and since that time wages have been regularly going down. The employers always take advantage of the winter to cut something off our pay, saying they don't want the goods till the spring. The excuse is always that the trade is slack in the winter months, and they tell us if we don't like to do it, we may leave it. There's plenty, they say, that wants employment. I never knew the wages to rise in the spring when business is brisk—never once in the whole of the 22 years that I have been connected with the trade—that is the policy of the employers.

"When I first began the business there were but very few slop shoe warehouses. We mostly worked for the shops direct; this, indeed, was the practice for the first fourteen years that I was at the trade. After that time the slop shoe warehouses kept increasing very fast, and they supplied the shops instead of ourselves. The shopkeepers said they couldn't make them up as cheap as they could buy them of the warehouses; and so the manufacture passed from the shopkeepers to the warehouses. I only know *one* shop now that makes up the articles—formerly almost *all* manufactured their own goods. You see, there are two profits to be got instead of one, and of those the second profit comes out of the pockets of such as we who can't even afford a home. I don't think the number of binders has increased so much as the wages have decreased of late years; indeed within the last 15 years the trade has not been worth putting a person to; but I fancy the lowering of the wages is to be accounted for solely by the masters taking advantage of the slack in the winter to cut down our pay. If there is any increase of hands it has arisen from the low prices paid to the shoemakers, for now they are obliged to put all their family to work at some branch or other of their trade.

"My husband was a post-boy at a large posting-yard in Whitechapel. He has been dead five years this month. His business was cut up by the railways, and his earnings before he died were half what he used to get in better times. When he was alive, and doing well, we had a comfortable home. Our joint earnings were, upon an average, £3 a week, for a great many years after we were married. Our wages kept coming down every twelvemonth from about ten years back. However, I struggled on until he died. My husband was fond of drink, and had saved nothing in his better times. When he died I was left with my only daughter, and nothing but my trade to keep me and her. My girl was ill with a rheumatic fever, and had lost the use of her limbs. She is dead.

"After my husband's death, I could earn at shoe-binding from 6s. to 7s. a week. I paid 1s. 6d. a week rent, and I had 5s. left to keep the two of us. I did manage to make a shift with this somehow, and appear a little respectable, but it was indeed a hard struggle. We never knew what a bit of butter was, nor yet sugar, for six months round; but still, so long as I had my child, I went on happily and contentedly. At last it pleased God to take my only comfort from me. Then I went to service for a twelvemonth. My health was giving way under my work, for I had to toil night and day to get even bread. I often haven't been in bed for three nights together; and yet with all this I couldn't get enough to keep me. I was being fairly starved to death while doing the hardest work. I went to service at 1s., and had my board and lodging found me, of course. But my health had been so cut up by the little nourishment I could get while working at my trade, that I couldn't do the work of my place—so I was forced to leave it and take to shoe-binding again. Since that time I have been laid up with erysipelas, and then I was forced to part with everything I had in the world to keep body and soul together. All the little furniture I had got together, except my bed, is gone; and if it was not for the good friends I am with now I should be in the workhouse. The husband of the good woman here is a painter by trade. He has had no constant employment for this five years past. Occasionally he gets an odd job when out with his frame in the street."

"Sometimes he brings me home sixpence," said his wife. Here the man took one of the children on his knee, and the poor little thing began asking for something to eat. I happened to hear this, and on inquiring, I found that they had none to give it.

"I was obliged to sell a dish this morning, sir," said the woman, "to get the only meal of bread we have had to-day, and how we are to get another loaf I do not know." She told me she was within a week of her confinement, and not a rag of baby linen in the house. Indeed the poor things were literally starving, the whole of them.

"I give them and the little ones what I earn," said the poor shoe-binder, "and we all starve together as contentedly as we can." "I went down to the workhouse a few days ago (said the wife), to ask them to take me in to be confined, and they told me to come before the board on Friday night, but then I asked what can I do with my husband and children. They must go in too, was the answer; and so we must break up even the poor little home we have; but then you know, sir, it *is* a home; and once broken up we should never be able to get it together again. We are all under the doctor's hands. My husband is suffering from determination of blood to the head, and has been ill for this month past."

The following narrative, which I had from the lips of a man whom I have known for some few months, and whose family have been kept from starvation during the winter by the funds placed at the disposal of *The Morning Chronicle*, is a statement which forms a fit sequel to the foregoing. I can vouch for the integrity and industry of the man, for he has been long employed in making boots and shoes for the poor people who applied for relief at the office of this Journal; and a more hard-working and sober man I have seldom met with.

"I have lived at the East-end nearly two years. Some months back, I took a shop in Great Saffron-hill, Holborn; being a low neighbourhood, and having a good stock to start with, I thought in such a place we might do. I bought and sold old clothes, mended old boots, &c., for sale; but all my efforts were useless. I lived there four months; and as fast as I sold my property the money was spent to support my family. Not being able to obtain employment, we began here to feel the pinching of poverty, and got in arrear for rent. The folks we lived with were Jews; they was kind to an extreme, knowing our circumstances. I had an acquaintance in Bethnal-green, —— street, poor, but honest people, who very kindly offered an asylum for us in their house till things should mend with us. We accepted the kind offer.

"I in vain endeavoured to get work in my own line, a man's man. Then I turned my attention to women's work; it was a great struggle to get a crust for six of us. I worked in the top room with my dear friend and his family, and their privations often made my heart ache. We were too poor to assist each other. It was common for us to have breakfast about twelve, and dinner, tea, and supper last thing at night. Our two families numbered fifteen persons. When I became better acquainted with women's work, and longing to return to my own domestic privacy, my friend agreed that we should have the kitchen at 1s. 3d. per week. We lived there eleven months, but out of my scanty earnings we were not able to pay much of the rent. My friend never asked us for it. The kitchen we lived in was damp, dark, and dirty. The ceiling was six feet only from the floor. The health of myself, wife, and children suffered much here, with the bad quality of food we were obliged to eat, bad ventilation, and many hours of toil. My wife was kind and affectionate, and loved her children with that kind of affection which a mother only can feel. We used to look on those little beings with hearts ready to break. We saw them waste day after day, almost forgetting to notice the havoc that mental anxiety and the attendant miseries of poverty made upon ourselves.

"I was at this time making cloth button boots, that were said to be women's, but which were as large as men's; the foreparts must not be less than half an inch thick, stitched with a square French blade, military heels, and top pieces, braided on with copper sprigs; the price for making 1s. 5d. per pair. I was obliged to work from five to six in the morning till twelve at night. At this work, bad as the pay was, we could, by long hours, get bread and coffee, and school-money for two children—meat we could not get. I could not get Sunday's dinner. My children had, with myself and wife, been used, in our better days (formerly we kept a shop), to have a comfortable dinner, and it was months before they got used to do without. We felt much hurt when the children told other children that they had had no dinner. But at last we got them used to it. We would reserve 2d. on Saturday night to buy pudding for them on Sunday; we thought that if they told their playmates they had pudding for dinner that would do. They, with ourselves, are now so used to do without, that Sunday's dinner, and other little comforts connected with a working man's Sunday, are looked upon as things that were. I thought things could not be worse than they were at this time, but experience has taught me the contrary.

L

"I was next obliged to take slop work, women's lasting springs at 6½d. per pair; they were to be made solid and square; lasting spring-heel boots, with patent fronts, 7d. a pair—the commoner the work the more difficult and bad the stuff is to use. Common as the work was, should the bottom 'thumb soft,' or should there be the least foulness in the lasting, we must either pay for the boots or alter the work. With this miserable work, I was obliged to set my poor wife down to sew, while bread we could not buy much of. We lived upon boiled rice and hard biscuits, sold at 2d. per pound at the East-end. About this time we thought we would emigrate, if we could get the means. I calculated the time it would take to save £20, and we resolved to prolong the hours of labour, and cut short a meal a-day, and save 1s. or more each day. We commenced with a resolution to better our condition by emigration, and to obtain the means in the way described. At the end of three weeks we abandoned the idea. Our strength was spent; we were ill through over exertion, and the want of proper nourishment to keep up physical strength.

"Knowing that I was a sober man, and that none of my difficulties were brought on by my improvidence, I resolved to lay my condition before some of the noblemen of this country, feeling certain in my own mind that if the beggar and imposter could obtain money, I, with truth on my side, would be sure to find friends among them in my sad situation. I made known my past and present condition to several noblemen, in order, if possible, to obtain the means to emigrate. I have letters in my possession, which I received from some of them, but in no solitary instance did I obtain one penny. Once I had a promise from Lord —— of £1 if I could obtain the rest. My heart sickened within me; despair seemed to lay hold of me. I knew not how to turn. I next obtained work at making women's leather shoes for a retail shop, 8d. a pair; patent shoes, 9d. I took a room better ventilated, though I did not know how to pay the rent. Hope still kept me alive. I had 100 circulars printed. I wandered through wet and cold, leaving one at any house wherein I thought dwelt hearts who had a care for suffering humanity. I went from house to house like a thief, my natural independence was gone. I felt as if my heart would break, as door after door, as well as the hearts within, were shut against every appeal I made. I did not obtain one halfpenny.

"I had many things which I had purchased, which I was wont to look upon with pleasure, and felt a deep regret to part with them. My dear little ones wanted; so day after day we sold and pawned, till we became a perfect wreck. I was next advised by a friend to seek workhouse relief. My friend gave me reasons for wishing me to apply to a workhouse. After many hard struggles to screw my courage to the sticking place, I *did* go. My business being a useful one, they wished myself and family to go into the house, and would not relieve us out. I would sooner have died in the street than consented to part from my family in such a way. I returned home, and cursed in my heart such a country as England, which seemed to deny me the only privilege that I felt that I wanted—labour sufficiently remunerative to support my children without becoming a pauper. Thus, sir, every effort on my part failed, and I was obliged to settle down to do as best I could. I am waiting the will of God, and he who has so often saved me and my family from starvation, will assuredly help me out of my present difficulties.

"I reckon my average earnings this last year at 10s. per week. This last ten months I have been making women's enamelled shoes, spring heels (must be made well), at 7d. per pair. I had one seat of work, which I was obliged to take, having none else, where I was compelled to sleep and work, and pay 2s. 6d. a week rent, which, with my home-rent (3s. 6d. a week), made 6s. a week in all—so I was obliged to leave in a fortnight.". . .

[The] family system of working is one of the means by which the cheap system is maintained. The party pursuing it, though forced to resort to it for the maintenance of his wife and children, whom his own unaided labour is incapable of supporting, is enabled to produce the goods at so cheap a rate that it is impossible for a single-handed artisan to do the work at the same price, and live. Another means by which the cheap prices are maintained is the *apprentice system*, concerning which I received the following statements:

"My employer had seven apprentices when I was with him; of these, two were parish apprentices (I was one), and the other five from the Refuge for the Destitute, at Hoxton. With each Refuge boy he got £5, and three suits of clothes, and a kit (tools). With the parish boys of Covent-garden and St. Andrew's, Holborn, he got £5 and two suits of clothes, reckoning what the boy wore as one. My employer was a journeyman, and by having all us boys he was able to get up work very cheap, though he received good wages for it. We boys had no allowance in money— only board, lodging, and clothing. The board was middling, the lodging was too, and there was nothing to complain about in the clothing. He was severe in the way of flogging. I ran away six times myself, but was forced to go back again, as I had no money and no friend in the world. When I first ran away I complained to Mr. —— the magistrate, and he was going to give me six weeks. He said it would do me good; but Mr. —— interfered, and I was let go. I don't know what he was going to give me six weeks for, unless it was for having a black eye that my master had given me with the stirrup. Of the seven only one served his time out. He let me off two years before my time was up, as we couldn't agree.

"The mischief of taking so many apprentices is this: The master gets money with them from the parish, and can feed them much as he likes as to quality and quantity; and if they run away soon, the master's none the worse, for he's got the money, and can get another boy and more money; and so boys are sent out to turn vagrants when they run away, as such boys have no friends. Of us seven boys (at the wages our employer got) one could earn 19s., another 15s., another 12s., another 10s., and the rest not less than 8s. each, for all worked sixteen hours a-day— that's £4 8s. a week for the seven, or £225 10s. a year. You must recollect I reckon this on nearly the best wages in the women's trade. My employer you may call a sweater, and he made money fast, though he drank a good deal. We seldom saw him when he was drunk; but he *did* pitch into us when he was getting sober. Look how easily such a man with apprentices can undersell others when he wants to work as cheap as possible for the great slop warehouses. They serve haberdashers so cheap that oft enough it's starvation wages for the men who work for the same shops."

Akin to the system of using a large number of apprentices, is that of employing boys and girls to displace the work of men, at the less laborious parts of the trade. To such a pitch is this carried, that there is a market in Bethnal-green, where children stand twice a week to be hired as binders and sewers. Hence it will be easily understood that it is impossible for the skilled and grown artisan to compete with the labour of mere children, who are thus literally brought into the market to undersell him.

Concerning this market for boys and girls, in Bethnal-green, I received the following statements from shopkeepers on the spot:

"Mr. H—— has lived there 16 years. The market-days are Monday and Tuesday mornings, from seven to nine. The ages of persons who assemble there vary from 10 to 20, and they are often of the worst character, and a decided nuisance to the inhabitants. A great many of both sexes congregate together, and most market days there are three females to one male. They consist of sewing boys, shoe binders, winders for weavers, and girls for all kinds of slop needlework, girls for domestic work, nursing children, &c. No one can testify, for a fact, that they (the females) are prostitutes; but by their general conduct they aren't for anything. The market, some years since, was held at the top of Abbey-street; but on account of the nuisance it was removed to the other end of Abbey-street. When the schools were built the nuisance became so intolerable that it was removed to a railway arch in White-street, Bethnal-green. There are two policemen on market mornings to keep order, but my informant says they require four to keep them in anything like subjection.". . .

To show the sort of labour supplied by such boys as are to be met with at the market I have described, and the way in which it is remunerated, I give the statement of a sharp little fellow not yet 13, and little even for that tender age:

"My parents are living, " he said; "my father being a shoe-man—a man's-man. He works in a bulk (stall); but work is very bad with him. My mother makes hat-boxes for the shops at 1s. 6d. per dozen, finding the stuff—it gives her 6d. profit, and takes a day to make them. I wanted a few halfpence for myself, but most of all I wanted clothes. If I hadn't been at work this week I shouldn't have had this jacket out of pawn. I knew a boy who took me to where he worked, and I got a job there. I gave three months' work for being taught. The general thing is to give 10s. and three months' work, but my father was too poor to pay the 10s. It's about a year ago since I began to learn the trade. I can now sew a dozen pairs of slippers a day. Slippers they call them, that's the right name of them, but you would call them women's boots or pumps. The work is made ready for me, and I stitch the sole to the upper. I get three-farthings a pair, that's 9d. a day.

"I work six days in the week when my master has work, but sometimes he turns lazy after he's been drinking, and lies in bed all day. He's kind to me, and I ain't got not no missus. There are a great many boys like me, employed the same way. Some boys can make three dozen a day. There's plenty of boys can sew faster than men. Men get no more at such work than we do. I give the money I earn to my mother; she's very poor, and it's a help to her. I have had seven masters, but was never badly used. I sometimes work from six in the morning to ten at night. I can neither read nor write—I wish I could. Do you know of any school, sir, where I could learn on a Sunday?"

I now give a statement by a girl employed in the same description of work as the boy. She was 16, but showed nothing of the buoyance of youth, as if constant toil had worn down her animal spirits:

"I can make a dozen pairs of slippers (pump boots and shoes) a day, and get $\frac{3}{4}$d. a pair for them. I put the last between my knees, and hold it with a stirrup, just as you see the men work. I have parents living—they are very poor, and I put myself to this trade. I was at service as a little maid-of-all-work, but wasn't well treated, and thought I would put myself to slipper-sewing. Before I got to service I was bound 'prentice to learn lint-making for doctors' shops. I was bound till I was 21, having my board and lodging and clothes; but I left above two years ago. I was only 8 when I left. I left because my master beat me and the other girls—there was six of us; he beat us all with a strap. I was black and blue. But for that treatment, I should have been there still. My present master and mistress are kind to me. I have had other masters among slipper-making, but they were all kind to me. I got taught for only a month's work, because I was handy at it. I've seen it done so often. I live at home, and give my earnings to my mother. I am at work every day, and make 4s. 6d. a week. I like my work better than service. It's more independent."

Another of the evils of the cheap shoe trade is the chamber-master system, as it is termed. The chamber-master is a petty tradesman, who employs a number of the worst and cheapest hands to manufacture the goods on his premises. He has no shop, but is either employed directly by the warehouses, or else he makes up a large quantity on speculation at the lowest possible rate, and then hawks them round to the trade. . . .

The lodging-house system which is resorted to by the chamber-master in order to eke out his petty profits is equivalent to the worst forms of "sweating" under the cheap tailors. I now give the statement of a pale and sickly-looking man, concerning this system:

"I am fifty-three—(he looked much older)—and I work with Mr. ——, a chamber-master. I now get 8d. and 9d. a pair for the same work as ten years ago I got 2s. 6d. for at the West-end, and five years ago 1s. 3d. and 1s. 6d. at Stoke Newington. My master only employs three men now besides myself; but he generally employs eight men, and they sleep in the two rooms they work in. We all sleep in one room, two in a bed. Chamber-masters have a deal of competition to serve the great rich firms of ——, and ——, and ——. These rich men screw down the chamber-master, and the chamber-master screws down his journeymen—poor men like me—and gets some boys and girls, and cuts down our wages.

"I can now earn 9s. a week, working twelve hours a day, allowing time for meals; but of that 9s. I have to pay my employer 4s. for lodging (half a bed), tea and coffee. The lodging and beds are not so bad as in some places. Some such places are awful. I have heard men say so, but I have not yet come to the worst, though it's a wretched existence as it is. The tea and coffee is not so bad. I find my own bread. Such a room as we sleep in could be got (unfurnished) at 2s. a week, so that my employer gets 8s. a week from the four of us as profit on his room, and for the use of his bedding and a chair or two; there's nothing else, except it be what the tea and coffee cost him. I reckon that neither the tea nor coffee stands him in a halfpenny a pint; but call it a halfpenny (Sunday is free but it is laid on to the others) and that's 4d. a day, or 2s. a week—that's far too high—but take it at that, and he then gets 6s. a week profit, just out of the lodging of us; that's £15 12s. a year profit, and when he has the eight men a-going, of course it's twice that, or £31 4s.—say at least £20 a year for an average. We are paid every evening—the money for our lodging and tea and coffee being deducted. My employer is a master on his own account, and will sell retail, when he can, as well as supply the great houses. This is a very common system in this district (Bethnal-green)."

The *"strong" trade* suffer under the same grievances as those above described. Concerning the "strong" trade, as carried on in a "slaughter" house in Westminster, I give the statement of a man now employed by a firm in ————.

"I have been in the trade about 16 years. At that time I could earn 15s. a week, take the year through. The treatment of the men was always bad, but it's worse now, a great deal. I will tell what it is now, both as to earnings and the accommodation and treatment of myself and the other men employed with me. The house where we work, generally twelve of us—there were eleven to-day—was formerly a pork butcher's. The room the twelve of us work in was a hay loft, it is above the room we sleep in; it is lighted by sky-lights.

"The room where we sleep is rather smaller than where we work. The length is 20 feet, the width 15 feet, height 7 feet. The window width is 1 ft. 10 in., and its length 1 ft. 2 in. The room is very seldom washed; the walls are damp, and there is always a dreadful stench, made up of all sorts of bad smells; it's not one of them, but a lot of stinks together. No wonder I look pale. This very sleeping-room was Mr. ————'s slaughterhouse, where he killed his pigs, and where human pigs are kept now. In this room, the dimensions of which I have given you, are four beds—not such bad beds—and in them sleep eight men, two in each. There has been three in a bed. There is no ventilation, as the window will not open. From the stench I cannot, often enough, get to sleep until two or three in the morning, let me be as tired as I may. I and my mates are compelled to have from the employer what is called tea and coffee. I can't tell what the tea is, but it *is* curious tasting; it is indeed, sir; and the coffee is so bad that burnt beans, not good enough for horses, would make better. We call it 'slosh,' but that's too good a name.

"We find our own dinner, but can cook nothing on the premises, unless with the leave of the mistress, who makes it a great compliment to grant a favour, such as the loan of a gridiron. If you become too troublesome, there's a discharge ticket for you; but we haven't so very much to cook. Half-a-pound of steak between two—it costs 2½d.—is the usual thing; we call that sort of steak 'block ornaments'—what the butchers dress their blocks with—it's reckoned a luxury with us. Tea is like breakfast, only tea (as it's called) instead of coffee (as it's called), and for each meal we have to allow 1½d., finding our own bread and butter—that is when we can afford butter. The payment for the coffee and tea is exacted in this way: We are paid every night for the work we do in the day, and out of the payment due, the master every Monday stops 1s. for lodging, tea and coffee, and 6d. every night after for lodging, tea and coffee; so that there can be no arrears from the men, and that pays him 3s. 6d. a week, Sunday included. Whether I am there or not I have to pay for my tea and coffee. I must pay for it if I am miles off, if I'm employed there. If a man be off on a visit to his friends, as I know has happened, for five days, he must pay for it, though neither tea nor coffee has been made for him.

"Every man must lodge on the premises, and if a man employed be a married man, he must have a room for his wife and himself; but I have known a married man who had to pay for his lodgings with this master at another shop (for he has three) though he didn't lodge there; all circumstanced that way must pay or lose their work. That's the master's system. We work on those considerations. The men feel they are in a state of slavery. My master has the false measurement in his size-stick. We often feel languid; but shoemakers, particularly the strong men, mustn't complain when they're ill, unless they're ready for the hospital. I average, take the year through, about 9s. a week. I feel degraded by the way I'm employed, and we all do, but how are we to get out of it? It's just degradation or starvation, and I'm not quite ready for starvation.". . .

Another man, in the same employ said:

"Please to let this be made public. In the rooms where we work we sleep, making our own beds—middling flock beds, but very filthy and dirty. I saw a troop of 'Scotch greys' creeping about the quilt the other day; Scotch greys are the regular household troops there; it's a sort of head-quarters for them in that there refuge for the destitute. You understand, sir, what Scotch greys are—the vulgar call them lice, sir. Two rooms with five beds bring my employer in 21s. a week (he may pay 5s. rent for them). One of the men has a boy of 14, but very little, and though he sleeps with his father, he is charged 1s. a week.

"About fifteen years ago I was a country lad, and had two choices—to starve, or go in a place like G——'s (a similar concern). At that time I preferred water to beer or spirits; but I had no home, the refuge was no home. I could not read by any fire-side, for there was no fire-side and no chair to sit on. By degrees I made a sort of home in a tap-room; and it grew and grew until I was fond of beer, and found myself a fuddler. That's a certain evil of the system. Men must find an hour of comfort, and it can only be found in the public-house. It creates drunkenness and ruins health. At P——'s, nine men out of ten had the itch at one time, master and missus and all. Men at these places have to violate decency in a way I cannot describe to you.". . .

From Letter XXXVI, February 18th, 1850

As a further corroboration of the tendency of the cheap slop-trade to destroy not only the able artisan, but the honourable tradesman, and to substitute for employer and employed, cheats, children, and criminals, I subjoin the statement of a lady's shoemaker—a tradesman of the highest respectability, at the west end of the town, who gave me the following account concerning the way in which a fair trade is injured by the slop system, with its starvation wages:

"I remember," he said, "when there was no shoe slop-seller in London, except B——. I speak of the West-end some thirty years ago. At that time Mr. Taylor, in Bond-street, Mr. Sutton, Mr. Sly, and other first-class tradesmen (all now dead) used to carry on very extensive businesses, getting everything made by their own men, employed directly by themselves, without the intervention of any middleman system. They also gave their journeymen and binders fair and liberal wages. As it is, I pay 3s. 5d., and not at all extravagant wages, for what —— and —— pay 1s. 4d. Of course mine is an infinitely superior article; but the 'firm,' as they parade themselves, actually puff off their wares as equal to the best. I first felt the low-priced system tell upon me when the chamber-masters became numerous, and indulged in keen competition. These chamber-masters will now come to my shop and offer to sell me goods at the price I pay for wages alone.

"The low-priced goods affected my profits gradually. My books show this; first my profits fell 10 per cent., then 15, and now I reckon my profits 20 per cent. less than they were 30 years ago. I have been obliged to reduce my prices, and conse-

quently the wages; I still pay the highest wages, and this last week I looked carefully through my books to ascertain the earnings of my men. The two first weeks
in February, by an arrangement I introduced into the trade some years ago, is the
period for adjusting any change in wages, or in the trade generally, so as to obviate
the necessity of strikes. I looked, as I have said, through my books, and as an honest
man I felt that I could not reduce any one man's wages a half-penny.

"Businesses like mine are kept together by connection—by a principle of respect between tradesmen and customer, because the customer knows and perhaps
has long known the tradesman's integrity. But no business like mine could be
started now with any prospect of success. All the money at present embarked in
the shoe trade, or nearly all, is on the low-priced system. I fear that if no check
be interposed to the Northampton and slop system, matters will get worse. The
underpaid and inferior workman will drag down the able well-conducted artisan to
his level. First-rate workmen become scarcer and scarcer. The trade is falling into
the hands of an inferior craft—it's becoming slop-work, not the fine workmanship
of skilled labour—of a nice handicraft. That's another evil to all who look to
ulterior consequences. *Bad workmen have little self-respect.* We can beat the
French—it's the slop-system that is so vile. Fashion is so strong, however, that a
lady bought a pair of shoes of me, thinking they were made in Paris. In the course
of conversation I told her they were made by my own men in London, and she
has never had such a shoe from me since—much as she admired them."

As a fitting sequel to the above, I annex the statement that I received from one
of the *East-end employers*. His account is the more valuable, because it comes from
a man who has himself resorted to some of the most reprehensible practices of the
cheap trade.

"I recollect the trade before there were any chamber-masters. In 1819, I only
knew one chamber-master in London, and the number gradually spread through
this: Masters were oft tyrannical, and kept men waiting, and humbugged them all
sorts of ways, and so the men made a few sets of shoes, and sold them at a penny
a pair profit, to drapers' shops and such like; and that went on for a while, until
some wide-awake gentlefolks, that had their wits about them, like ——, and
——, bless you, they've their country houses now, and are worth thousands—
thought there was a chance to turn a penny—I mean a pound—and they opened
great warehouses and bought of the chamber-masters and of anybody in the
trade.

"These chamber-masters are often, or were often, precious rogues. They'd owe
money to the tallyman, and the chandler, and the baker, and the butcher (if they
could spring tick), and then 'made a death' in Whitechapel, and 'rose again' in
the Borough. That's what we call their leaving a place which gets too hot for them,
and leaving them that they're in debt to to whistle for chamber-masters and their
money. The chamber-masters were always sure of a market if they could stand
screwing, and didn't care for a turn at hunger now and then, and so they kept up
'deaths' here, and 'resurrections' throughout London, for a rare spin. Of course
it's nothing to the wholesale man that the chamber-master has a large circle of
weeping tradesmen belonging to his acquaintance. The more he 'does' people what
wants honest money of him, the cheaper he can live and the cheaper he can sell.
It's a system that ought to be exposed. And so you see, things is made so very
cheap that it's wonderful the *perfection* trade's brought to."

The impositions practised by the cheap shop-keeper are equally reprehensible. Some of these are injurious not only to the producers but to the consumers. Concerning the tricks resorted to by some of the most dishonourable tradesmen, in order to deprive the workman of his fair rate of wages, the following may be cited; and first of the frauds practised in the strong trade.

As to certain *frauds* practised in the different branches of the trade, I received the following information. First, concerning those carried on in the "strong" trade:

"It is common with a class of masters (said my informant) to use a false size measure stick; not above three masters use the recognised stick. To show how injurious the false size stick is to the journeyman, I will state this: a 'fives' in the fair size stick appears a 'threes' by the false one; for the pair of 'fives' in a fair measuring shop the workman receives 2s. 3d. wages; at the shop where the false size stick is used he receives 1s. 6d. Calculate each workman to make five such pairs a week, and he loses 9d. on each pair, that is 3s. 9d. a week, or £9 15s. a year. Two shops that I know employ at least six men each on this fraudulent size stick; so that each master defrauds the six men out of £58 10s. every year; and the pair of masters clear £117 between them. Now, sir, take a closer's case. For closing bluchers, by the true measure, he gets 5d. a pair, and four pairs a day will be 10s. a week. By the false size stick he gets only 4½d. a pair, or 9s. a week at the same extent of labour. My employer, an honourable tradesman, finds grindery and pays 2s. 3d. a pair (where the fraudulent size stick man pay 1s. 6d.), and yet sells his shoes, and they're better made shoes, at the same rate as they do.

"This fraudulent system cuts two ways; it robs the journeyman first, and then the customer. Many men thus employed are indifferent workmen, and feeling themselves wronged, they 'slim' the work by way of revenging themselves, and so it wears badly, and the poor man who buys it is victimised. All the profit from these frauds go into these masters' pockets; the public gain nothing; the employers sell no cheaper. By the 'false' size stick system, one master has realized a handsome country house. His system is to attack his men's wages every winter. He has done so this year.

"Now, as to the *footing*—known in the trade as *new new-footing*—there was, six or seven years ago, a great demand for 'footed' boots, and indeed there is still. Formerly the legs of the new-footed were old ones, but now they are all new leather, joined across the front. The reason of this is because the wages paid for new footing are only 1s. 7d., whereas, if closed in the regular way of new boots, the workman would receive 2s. 6d. a pair; the 'dishonourable' master coolly, and often before a man's face, runs his knife across the front of the leg, and then calls it new new-footing, and the closer has the additional trouble of closing the cut part, and receives 1s. 7d.—11d. less than if they had not been cut. The master oft enough sells them for new boots, and so again the public is not benefited by the workman being robbed. Now, one master practises this system—say four pairs a week, or 200 pairs a year—and so robs his closer of more than £9 every year by that plan alone. He has security from each man—20s., stopped at 1s. a week, as long as the man stays."

Frauds as injurious as the above, both to the workman and the customer, are practised by the cheap masters in the lighter descriptions of work as well. Among the most glaring of these impositions are the *"mock double soles"* in the women's trade, and the *"false spring heels"* in the men's trade.

As regards the *foreign labour*, I was anxious to discover, if possible, whether the same systematic importation of cheap workmen from the continent was carried on in the cheap boot and shoe trade, as I had found out was pursued in connection with the slop trade among the tailors. After considerable trouble, I was able to track out the same annual immigration. This was principally confined to the Germans. Formerly the Frenchmen were brought over to England by their countrymen who had settled in business, and who made periodic trips to Paris, in order to introduce French workmen into London before the duty was reduced on the French boots, and when there was a great demand for the article. The wages in this country have, however, declined so rapidly within the last nine years, that the number of French workmen have already decreased one-half; for now the prices paid to the workmen by some of our best shops are lower than those in France. The Germans, however, continue to be brought over annually, and are kept in such subjection by their masters, that they are afraid to make the least disclosure. The following narrative I give in the man's own broken English:

"I am a native of Chermany. I come apout six miles dis site of Frankfort: de down is named Butzbach—yes, dat is quite right. I have peen in dis country nine year. I vent over py my own account. A man had been over here, and he come over to my country and he told me as I could earn plenty money coming over here." "Yes, it is plenty money," said the wife with a derisive laugh. "Aye, a starvation life," joined in a shoebinder, who was at work upon some red morocco slippers— "I know *I* find it so." "Yes, I did vork at dis drade in my country," continued the German. "I had been apprentice to it in Chermany dree year and a half. Oh de wages is very low in Chermany, because you gets everyting a man gets—his lodging and everyting—and he gets pesites apout 5s. a veek, just as a man can vork. Vot ve gets by our vork in Chermany goes farder dere dan vot you gets here vid a pount. I call dat a very goot wages dare, only de money we gets don't look so much as it does here.

"Ven I came over here I vent to sew at one of my own countrymens, and I have mostly been vorking for my own countrymens ever since. Most of the Chermans I have vorked for have peen vot you call sveaters in dis country, because dey do make a man sveat. De vorst of de lot I ever vorked for vas von I tell you of." "Ah, he ought to have peen sent out of dis country long ago" (chimed in the wife). "He spoilt de slipper drade, he did—he was a Cherman, living down here in————. He has a cas-light in every room. He go out with his cold rings on his finkers, and his cold vatch in his pocket, and de poor man vot gets em for him sitting in de kitchin. He's cot a clock vot plays de music in his trawing-room dat cost him dirty pounds. I should like for you to step inside dat toor to see dat place and de poor man at vork for him. He von't let a poor man stay vid him vitout he vork for him on a Suntay morning while his crand musical clock is a playing. He say you von't be no goot to me. You can't get a loaf of pred." "I tell you," cried the wife, "my huspant vorked for him and never see dee outsite of de tore for dree veeks."

"He had elefen at vork for him. They most all lived in his house. He cot von room vhere he cot vour peds in it. Dere was dree married men—de rest dey vas single men. He let out his rooms, you know; de married men had dem, and de upstairs he had de peds in for de single men. Dere vas eight men sleeped in dat room vid de vour peds. He charged de single man two shilling a veek for lodging, if he vould sew for him. I had a pedroom. He charge me half-a-grown."

"It was dree pair of stairs high," cried the wife. "De room I had vas not vurnished. I pought a pedstead and seferal dings of him. Oh yes, he always sell to de men—he puy of a old proker, and de men must give him so much provit." "Oh it's very ill," said the wife, of a poor little infant that lay moaning in her lap. "I puried one not long ago, and ah dat gets any von pack. You got to vork and slave all de year round, and ven trouble come you can't pay your vay at all."

"I say de room I had of him," continued the man, "vasnt vorth no more dan eighteenpence a veek. De vurniture perhaps I could have cot for nine shilling, and he charge me vour and twenty shilling. I done all sorts of vork for him. I done some of dem poots vot is used for de Italian Opera. Sometimes de poots vas de puckskin vons vot dey use in de playhouses—pig vons up apove de knees; and he pay me only von shilling for dem vid touble soles. Any sort of vork I made—slippers, springs, vot he got from de shop—anyting. I vorked from morning five o'clock till night elefen, dwelve o'clock; yes, very near every tay I done dat in de summer. Oh! I could not make no more dan vourteen shilling in de week, Suntay and all. Den I had to pay out of dat de money for de rent, dat was half-a-grown, and half-a-grown for de tings and vurniture vot I pought of him: dat vos vive shilling. Den I used to pay for de pred and de peer. Ve had a pint every night. He always vished us to have our pred and peer of him. He vas very angry if you vent outside. Not to force you, certainly; he couldn't have done dat; put if ve hadn't done it he vould have turned us avay—yes, dat he vould, for he did give me dree or vour times notice 'cause I fetched a pint of peer outsite. Ven de pred vas outsite vive pence he charge us sixpence, and de peer vas vid him vourpence, and ve can get it alvays dreepence outside. De peer vas many times sour, and he vould make us pay twopence de pint for it. He didn't sell anyting else—he didn't sell no grindery.

"Ven I done some vork, dree or vour pair of shoes, he paid me; den of a Saturtay he took off vot I owed him for rent and tings; if I didn't have a zixpence of a Suntay he vould stop it all same; he vould say he vant to pay his rent. Sometimes I used to have to take half-a-grown, and sometimes two shillings, just as it happen. I knowed de time as I only had to take eighteenpence; and den on de Suntay I had to borrow a shilling of him for de tinner, and dat vent towards de next veek. Oh ve alvays vas in debt vid him; and ve vas in debt ven ve vent avay. I couldn't pay him, so I did gut my stick as you call it. Oh, he is de ruin of de slipper trade, because he go to every shop and say I do de vork for such and such a price. He do it a shilling a tozen less dan any von else, so dats vot cuts all de poor people out from a varehouse, because he goos in de varehouse vit a cold vatch in his pocket and dree or vour cold rings on his finkers—dats vat make him look a rebectable man, and dey tink dey can drust him.

"Now, if oder poor man comes in de shop, dey say dey vont give none—dey must have de secoority down—and pecause he takes all de vork from de varehouse, dat is de reason a poor man can't get no vork to do—so de poor man must go vork for him. He can make de slippers so much sheeper dan me, pecause he gives de poor man so much less, and gets de provit out of de lodgings and food of de men in his houze. He gets vive shilling a tozen, and gives de men dree-and-zixpence and zometimes dree shilling—dat is de vay he can get his cold vatch in his pocket, and his dirty-pound musical clock in his trawing-room. Most of de Chermans vot take out de slippers to make do de zame as dis man. Dere is von I know vot pays de men vour shilling a dozen pair vor batent leather slippers. Yes, I know dey do send for hands from Chermany ven de hands here are slack in de summer. He can't do well you see vit dose he has had pefore; dey vont come pack again, so he alvays looks for vot you call de creen hand from de country. I have knowed him send for vour at a dime.

"Most of my countrymen is prought over here by such men as he. I know myself a goot many of my vriends vot have been teceived by him. You see Chermany, since de revolutions, has had so many men vot are clad to come over, dat men like dis von can vell get dare cold vatches out of dem. Dose of my poor countrymen dat come over and cannot make de shoes he teashes to sew; if dey have money, dey give a pound, and if dey have none he vill make dem vork for a long time for him for nothing. Oh, yes! I sooner vould be pack in my own country again. All my shiltren are ill; I have dree alive, and all of dem have de cough vid de hoop. I am sure dat poor little ding vill die, and I don't know how I shall pury him."

The binder who was at work in the room was a widow with two children. She had eightpence a dozen for binding red morocco women's slippers (the largest size), and couldn't do more than eight pairs in the day; generally she could do only half-a-dozen, and for those she got fourpence—out of that she had to pay for silk, which cost a penny a skein, and a skein would do about three pair. Her earnings were not 3d. a day, and out of that she has to keep herself and two children—they were without food. "Ah!" said the woman, "the rich can do as they like with the poor people." She was at work for a Jew slop-seller. "Ah! he's a plackguard, he is," said the German's wife; "he gave me a pad zixpence vonce, and ven I took it pack to him, he say to me, 'vell you must lose dree-pence by it, and I must lose dree-pence,' and so I had to pay it him. She pinds poots for that same plackguard—lasting poots, twopence a pair." The husband of the shoe-binder, I found upon inquiry, had died of the cholera six months ago.

Concerning the French workmen, I received the subjoined statement from a native of Lille, who had been in this country nine years. He spoke with the least perceptible accent:

"Formerly the French shoemakers used to get good wages. The wages were much higher here than in France, and then there was a good demand for French workmen in London, because the duty had not been decreased. There were a great many French workmen then in London. A French boot and shoe maker at that time could earn about twice as much money in England as he could in France, when well employed. The difference between the cost of living in the two countries was about one-fifth, that is to say 20 francs in France would go about as far as 20s. (or 25 francs) in England. These extra wages were a great inducement for the French workmen to come over to this country; and a great many French masters who had started in business in England went over to Paris to engage hands, that would come over to this country. They paid their passage for them. Men that worked in Paris at men's work, at one of the best shops in the Rue St. Honoré, had 5 francs for making a pair of boots, whereas they got here then 7s. and 8s. for the same description of work. For closing, they got $2\frac{1}{2}$ francs in Paris, and here the wages were 3s. 9d. In the women's line the wages were, at the best shops, 1f. 5 sous (1s.)

for a satin sew-round, and here, for the same work, 1s. 9d. and 2s. were paid. There was at that time a very good seat of work for any Frenchman that came over to England.

"About seven years ago the Frenchmen formed a society to keep up the prices; the number of French women's men was about sixty-five, and I believe there were about as many men's men belonging to the English societies; altogether I think there were about 150 to 200 French hands in England about seven or eight years back. Now, I am confident the number is reduced at least one-half. The cause of the reduction is, that the English wages are now nearly as low as the French, and if the wages are not *quite* as low, there is at present so little work to be had of the better kind, that a man cannot earn as much here as in France. This is due to the vast increase of the slop boot and shoe trade in this country. French boots and shoes can be manufactured at Northampton and at the East-end of London cheaper than in Paris. When the French workmen first came over the work was so brisk that a great many of them got English boys to assist them, and now these English boys have grown to be men, who can work as well as themselves; and by working under price they can get the business out of their hands. A great quantity of cheap German labour," said my informant, "is, I know, brought over every year into this country. A man in —— street pays the Germans for French sew-round shoes 6d. a pair, and a man cannot do more than four pair a day. The price at the best French shops is for the same work 1s. and 1s. 3d. Some shoes of the same kind, I know, are made at 4d. per pair in the East-end of London. The Polish refugees also under-sell the French to a great extent, so that there is little or no demand for our labour in this country.". . .

I turned my attention also to the workmen employed on *men's boots and shoes for the slop shops*, to see if the abuses under which they suffered were similar in character and degree to those I have described in the case of the women's men. I found these workmen generally pale, sickly-looking men, but for the most part intelligent also, and with a manliness in their words and notions. Nearly all were indignant at the privations which they and their wives and families had to endure from the wretched wages they received. Several spoke of their employers with bitterness. One quiet-looking elderly man—I met very few elderly men, be it observed, among these slop-workers—said:

"There was Mr. —— here the other day, a very good man, and he laid it down how we ought to respect our masters, and how the middle class, such as the masters belong to, are the wealth and strength of the country. As for the wealth of the country, they may have a good deal of that among them, but as you have been among us workmen for Mr. ——, and Mr. ——, you can judge what respect *we* can have for our masters."

The average of the earnings of the men's men employed by the slop-masters was given to me at 12s. and 13s. a week, when the workman is in full work—but to get that much he must work six days, and a great portion of six nights. The average wages of the men partially employed I cannot give, as I met with men whose earnings last week were 3s., 3s. 6d., and so up to 9s. 6d. Some of the men's wives and children were wretchedly clad and lodged, and showed by their looks as well as words that they were as wretchedly fed.

"Beer," said one of these men to me, "hasn't been in my room these ten months, and I've never tasted it away from home but when I've been treated. What matters it, though, about *beer*? That little fellow there (pointing to a boy of five or six) doesn't yet know the taste of *beef*." The married men of this class generally work in their own rooms, but it is common enough for single men to work four or five in one room, as the rent is thereby lightened, and there is a saving in candle, since one of their thick candles gives light sufficient (at least what they accept as sufficient) for the whole. The practice of chamber-masters prevails among the slop men's men, but not nearly to the same extent as among the women's men. . . .

To show the system of *translating*, as it is called, I give the following narrative.

"Translation, as I understand it (said my informant) is this—to take a worn old pair of shoes or boots, and by repairing them make them appear as if left off with hardly any wear—as if they were only soiled. I'll tell you the way they manage in Monmouth-street. There are in the trade 'horses' heads'—a horse's head is the foot of a boot with sole and heel and part of a front—the back and the remainder of the front having been used for re-footing the boots. There are also 'stand-bottom' and 'lick-ups.' A 'stand-bottom' is where the shoe appears only soiled, and a 'lick-up' is merely a boot or shoe re-lasted to take the wrinkles out, the edges of the soles rasped and squared, and so blacked up to hide blemishes, the bottom being covered with a 'smother,' which I will describe. There is another article called 'a flyer,' that is, soling a shoe without welting it. In Monmouth-street a 'horse's head' is generally retailed at 2s. 6d., but some fetch 4s. 6d.—that's the extreme price. The old feet cost the translator from 1s. a dozen pair to 8s., but those at 8s. are good feet, and are used for the making up of Wellington boots. Some feet—such as are cut off that the pair may be re-footed on account of old fashion or a misfit when hardly worn—fetch 2s. 6d. a pair, and they are made up as new-footed boots, and sell from 10s. to 15s. The average price of feet (for the horse's head, as we call it) is then 4d., for a pair of backs say 2d.; the back is attached loosely by chair stitching, as it is called, to the heel, instead of being stitched to the insole, as in a new boot.

"The wages for all this is 1s. 4d. in Monmouth-street (in Union-street, Borough, 1s. 6d.); but I was told by a master that he had got the work done, in Gray's-inn-lane, at 9d. Put it, however, at 1s. 4d. wages—that, with 4d. and 2d. for the feet and back, gives 1s. 10d. outlay (the workman finds his own grindery), and 8d. profit on each pair sold at no higher a rate than 2s. 6d. Some masters will sell from 70 to 80 pairs per week, that's under the mark; and that's in horses' heads alone. One man employs, or did lately employ, seven men on horses' heads solely. The profit generally, in fair shops, in 'stand bottoms,' is from 1s. 6d. to 2s. per pair, as the article sells generally at 3s. 6d. One man takes, or did take, £100 in a day (it was calculated as an average) over the counter, all for the sort of shoes I have described. The profit of a 'lick-up' is the same, I suppose, as that of a 'stand-bottom.'

"I believe that all these tradesmen in Monmouth-street have lodgers. I was one before I married a little while ago, and I know the system to be the same now, unless indeed, it be altered for the worse. To show how disgusting these lodgings must be, I will state this:—I knew a Roman Catholic, who was attentive to his religious duties, but when pronounced on the point of death, and believing firmly that he was dying, he would not have his priest administer extreme unction, for the room was in such a filthy and revolting state he would not have the priest see it. Five men worked and slept in that room, and they were working and sleeping there in the man's illness—all the time that his life was despaired of. He was ill nine weeks. Unless a man lodged there he would not be employed. Each man pays 2s. a week. I was there once, but I couldn't sleep in such a den; and five nights out of the seven I slept at my mother's, but my lodging had to be paid all the same. These men (myself excepted) were all Irish, and all teetotallers, as was the master. How often was the room cleaned out do you say? Never, sir, never. The refuse of the men's labour was generally burnt, smudged away in the grate, smelling terribly. It would stifle you, though it didn't me, because I got used to it.

"I lodged in Union-street once. My employer had a room known as 'the barracks;' every lodger paid him 2s. 6d. a week. Five men worked and slept there, and three were *sitters*—that is, men who paid 1s. a week to sit there and work, lodging elsewhere. A little before that there was six sitters. The furniture was one table, one chair, and two beds. There was no place for purposes of decency: it fell to bits from decay, and was never repaired. This barrack man always stopped the 2s. 6d. for lodging, if he gave you only that amount of work in the week. The beds were decent enough; but, as to Monmouth-street! you don't see a clean sheet there for nine weeks; and, recollect, such snobs are dirty fellows. There was no chair in the Monmouth-street room that I have spoken of, the men having only their seats used at work; but when the beds were let down for the night, the seats had to be placed in the fire-place because there was no space for them in the room.

"In many houses in Monmouth-street there is a system of sub-letting among the journeymen. In one room lodged a man and his wife (a laundress worked there), four children, and two single young men. The wife was actually delivered in this room whilst the men kept at their work—they never lost an hour's work; nor is this an unusual case—it's not an isolated case at all. I could instance ten or twelve cases of two or three married people living in one room in that street. The rats have scampered over the beds that lay huddled together in the kitchen. The husband of the wife, confined as I have described, paid 4s. a week, and the two single men paid him 2s. a week each, so the master was rent free; and he receives from each man 1s. 6d. a week for tea (without sugar), and no bread and butter, and 2d. a day for potatoes—that's the regular charge.

"To show the villainous way the stand-bottoms are got up, I will tell you this. You have seen a broken upper-leather. Well, we place a piece of leather, waxed, underneath the broken part, on which we set a few stitches through and through. When dry and finished, we take what is called 'soft heel-ball' and 'smother' it over, so that it sometimes would deceive a currier, as it appears like the upper-leather. With regard to the bottoms, the worn part of the sole is opened from the edge, a piece of leather is made to fit exactly into the hole or worn part, it is then nailed and filed until level. Paste is then applied, and what we call 'smothered' over the part, and that imitates the dust of the road. This 'smother' is obtained from the dust of the room. It is placed in a silk stocking, tied at both ends, and then shook through, just like a powder-puff, only we shake at both ends. It is powdered out into our leather apron, and mixed with a certain preparation which I will describe to you (he did so), but I would rather not have it published in *The Morning Chronicle*, as it would lead others to practise similar deceptions. I believe there are about 2,000 translators, so you may judge of the extent of the trade; and translators are more constantly employed than any other branch of the business. Many make a great deal of money. A journeyman translator can earn from 3s. to 4s. a day. You can give my average at 20s. a week, as the wages are good. It must be good, for we have 2s. for soling, heeling, and welting a pair of boots; and some men don't get more for making them. Monmouth-street is nothing like what it was; as to curious old garments, that's all gone. There's not one English master in the translating business in Monmouth-street; they are all Irish; and there is now hardly an English workman there—perhaps not one."

TOY MAKERS

From Letter XXXVII, February 21st, 1850

A *worker in green wood* is termed a "Bristol toy-maker." The quality and nature of the *Bristol toys* are detailed in the following narrative given to me by one of the makers of those articles. In the room where I conversed with him two boys were at work, making the wheels of scratch-backs—toys used by frolicsome people at fairs, the fun consisting in suddenly "scratching" any one's back with the toy, which gives a sudden, whirring sound. One boy was an apprentice, a well-grown lad; the other was a little fellow, who had run away from a City institution at Norwood, to whom the toymaker gave employment, having known his mother. It was curious enough, and somewhat melancholy, to observe the boy working at that which constitute other boys' play. Toys were piled all over the workshop. It was not very easy for a stranger to stir without the risk of upsetting a long line of omnibuses, or wrecking a perfect fleet of steam-boats. My informant, while giving his statement, was interrupted now and then by the delivery of orders, given, of course, in the usual way and tone of business, but sounding very grandiloquent— "A dozen large steamers," "Two dozen waggons;" and then a customer had room left in his sack for "half-a-dozen omnibuses with two horses." My informant said:

"The Bristol toys are the common toys made for the children of the poor, and generally retailed at a penny. They were first made in Bristol, but they have been manufactured in London for the last 50 years. I believe there is still one maker in Bristol. Bristol toys are carts, horses, omnibuses, chaises, steamers, and such like— nearly all wheel-toys. We make scratch-backs too—that has a wheel in it. To make the toys we boil the wood—green and soft, though sometimes dry; alder, willow, birch, poplar, or ash are used. When the wood has been boiled, the toy is cut with a knife, and fixed together with glue, then painted.

"Trade is very bad at present, for when the labouring people are out of employ I feel it in my business. They cannot then buy toys for the children; unless they have decent earnings, children must go without—poor things! As all my goods go to the poor, and are a sort of luxury to the children, I can tell what's up with working and poor people by the state of my trade—a curious test, isn't it? but a sure one. When weaving is bad, Bristol toymaking is very bad. [He lived in the neighbourhood of Spitalfields.] When things are not so bad in Ireland, it's a rare time for my trade; they are so fond of them there. No cheap toys, at least in my way, are made in Ireland. When the big horses, the spotted fellows on wheels, that you must have seen, went out of fashion, it was a blow to my business. Steamers which have come up rather lately—though they have grand names painted on them, you perceive, Fire Flies and Dash Alongs, and such like—don't go off as the old horses did. Every child has seen a horse, but there's numbers never see a steamboat, and so care nothing about them; how can they? The men employed at journey work in the Bristol toy trade can earn 3s. and 3s. 6d. a day. But when work is slack, they just earn what happens to turn in in the way of work.''...

From Letter XXXVIII, February 25th, 1850

In the present [letter] I purpose dealing with those [toymakers] who manufacture the superior description of articles, such as are seen principally in the arcades and bazaars.

One among those whom I visited was a celebrated publisher of penny theatrical characters and maker of toy theatres. He is the person to whom the children of the present generation are indebted for the invention. I found him confined to his room with asthma. He sat in a huge armchair, embedded in blankets, with a white night-cap on his head. He evidently was very proud of having been the original inventor of the toy theatres, and he would insist upon presenting me with the earliest prints in connection with the mimic stage. He was a little spare man whose clothes hung loose about him.

"I am a maker of children's theatres, and a theatrical print publisher. I have been in the line ever since 1811. The first time I began to publish anything of the kind was when the pantomime of Mother Goose was performing. I was the first in the line. I think I had the business all to myself for two years. Mrs. J——, who lived in Duke's-court, Bow-street, took to it after that. She sold my prints at first, and then she began to print and publish for herself. Now, I think, there's about six in the line. I was originally in the circulating library and haberdashery line. My mother was in the haberdashery way, and I continued it. We had a glass case of toys as well, and among the toys we sold children's halfpenny lottery prints—common things that were done in those days, sir. Well, you see, my parents used to be at Covent-garden Theatre, and I took it in my head to have a print done of *Mother Goose*. I can show you the old original print by me. You shall see, sir, the first theatrical print ever published. [He here produced a bundle of impressions.] Here's the third cheap theatrical print ever published. It's numbered up here, you see—but I brought 'em out so fast after that I left off numbering them very soon. I brought out one a day for three years. The print consisted of eight characters in as many separate compartments. The first was the elder Grimaldi as Clown, the second Bologna as Harlequin, the third was the Columbine of that day. Oh dear,'' said the publisher, "what was her name?—she was a werry excellent Columbine at Covent-garden Theatre.''

The other compartments were filled with other characters in the piece. "You'll see, sir,'' continued the old man, "there's a line of foolish poetry under each of the characters. I made it myself to please the children. It runs:

'The Clown, Joe Grim,
John Bologna, the Harlequin;
Gay and merry Columbine,

With her lover, Spaniard fine;
Demon of Interest, field of gold,
Don Alvaro very old;
A poor Chinese man,
And Mr. Raymond, as Magician.'

The first theatrical print published was not very different from the third in the character of its art or poetical descriptions. There was, however, a spirit and freedom of touch about the execution that was far superior to what might have been expected.

The lines under the eight distinct characters were as follows:

'The golden egg and Mother Goose—
Prime, bang-up, and no abuse.
Here's Harlequin as feather light,
And Zany's antics to please you with delight;
Here's Mr. Punch you plainly see,
And Joan, his wife, both full of glee.
In woman's habits does Harlequin
Deceive the clown, by name Joe Grim.' "

"I brought out this print, you'll understand, to please the children. The lottery things was so bad, and sold so well, that the idea struck me that something theatrical would sell. And so it did—went like wildfire among the young folks. Shopkeepers came to me far and near for 'em. Bad as the drawing of these here is, I can assure you it was a great advance on the children's halfpenny lotteries. These two figures here in the corner, you see, a'n't so bad, but they're nothing to what we do now. This plate was done by a 'prentice of the name of Green, who worked at Mr. Simkins', an engraver in Denmark-court. He used to do them in his overtime. He was obliged to have something to look at to copy. He was no draughtsman himself, you know. This here pictur of Mother Goose he took from a large print of Mr. Simmonds in that there character published by Ackerman, and sold in Covent-garden at 2s. 6d. plain, and 5s. coloured; the others was all copied from large prints of the day. I dare say I sold right off as many as 5,000. It was printed many times over, and every edition I know was a thousand. We don't do so many now. It was sold at a penny plain, and twopence coloured.

"You had better take that there impression with you. It's a curiosity, and a bit of the history of one's country—yes, that it is, sir. Why it's 39 years ago. I think I must have been about 24 when it was published—I'm 63 in June. The success of the theatrical prints was so great, I was obliged to get three presses to print them fast enough. I brought out a new one every day, as I told you before. We only did the characters in the pantomime at Christmas time. The small ones wasn't likenesses—they was merely characters to give the costumes. We didn't make likenesses till very late. The wardrobe people at the minor theatres and masquerade people used to buy a great many to make their dresses from. Young Green only did me two plates. He was such a bad draughtsman he couldn't do anything without a copy, and I was forced to get permission of the better printsellers for all he did. I gave Green 30s. to £2 for each plate he did for me. He was very dear, 'cause he was so slow over the engravings. Well, I think I had done about seven prints—

they were bad-uns—only copies, and badly done too—all by apprentices, when Mr. Hashley, of the Hamphitheayter, sent young —— with a drawing to show me. It was uncommon well done; oh, such a beautiful picture! he got on to be one of the first-rate artists arterwards, and drawed half-crown caricatures; he did all the battle-pieces of them times—all Bonaparte's battles and Nelson's shipping. Well I gave him an order directly for the whole of the characters in the *Blood Red Knight*, wot Hashley was performing at that time. I can show you the print on it—you must see it, for it was a great adwance in my purfession, sir. I should like you to look at it, sir, cause I considers it as a matter of history like."

He here brought out another brown parcel of prints. "Look here, sir," he said, as he turned over the impressions—"here's one of the stage fronts we do now— it's only part of it, you'll understand. It's done by a real architectural designer— but *he's* dead too: I suppose I shall go next. —————— did this here stage-front of Drury-lane as it was after the fire; and he did Covent-garden for me as well, but he wasn't good at architect. This here, sir, was the first stage front we begun to make. It's the large impression; we had a small one out as well. The date, you see, is 1812—and it wasn't quite a year after I published my first print. I got liberty from the master carpenter to go and make the drawing of the front as soon as ever it was up after the fire. This here print," he continued as he turned over the different copies before him, "was done for me by a Royal Academician of the name of Mr. ——; it's Ducrow in the scene of 'the Ingun and the Vild Oss.' You see, sir, Mr. Ducrow paid for it being done by my man, and guv it away on his benefit night, and I had the plate of him afterwards. This is a late production, so you can see the improvement. There's the first plate —— did for me. It's the principal characters in *The Lady of the Lake*, as produced at the Surrey, and a great advance you see it is on the others. After that he did the *Blood-red Knight*. Here's one of his first prints of osses. It's *Baghvanho*, as performed at Hashley's. Here's the first battle he ever drew. He did it unbeknown to me on a copper of mine, thinking I would like it; but it was quite out of my line. It was that there as got him all J——'s battles to do. He showed it to him, and J—— guv him an order directly. After that he had ten pound a week from J——, and ten pounds a week from me too. He had 30s. a plate, and never did less than six in the week; and for the larger ones he had more. I found the copper. Why, I used to pay my coppersmith £70 and £80 a year for plates only. ——, the artist and scene painter, did a great many for me, and he was the only one as turned out grateful to me. All the others got such great men they wouldn't look on me.

"At first, you see, we didn't do any but the principal characters in a piece, 'cause we didn't think of making theayters then, and went on as we begun for two years. After that we was asked by the customers for theayters to put the characters in, so I got up the print of a stage front, thinking that the customers would get the woodwork done themselves. But after the stage front they wanted the theaytres themselves of me more than ever, so I got some made, and then the demand got so great that I was obliged to keep three carpenters to make 'em for me. One was a horgan builder and could make anything in machinery. I turned out the first toy theayter for children as ever was got up for sale, and that was in the year 1813. You see my father was the under property-man at Covent Garden Theatre, and I had a sister a dancer there, and another sister belonging to the fruit-office in the boxes—so we was all theatrical; and when I was about seven year old, I got my father's 'prentice in the shop to make me a wooden theayter—he was uncommon clever at carpenter work, and the painters and carpenters of Covent Garden used to come and see it when we exhibited in our one-pair back three times a week. We used to charge 2d. a piece. It was thought a great thing in those days; and so many people used to come to see it, that father and mother wouldn't allow it after a time; so it was put up as a raffle, and it was won by a young man, who took it with him to Scotland. It was that as gave me the hidea of making toy theayters for sale. After I made a few I was hobligated to make scenery, and to do the sets of characters complete.

"Nobody but me made toy theayters for a long while; nor did they do the scenery. One man used to do me three dozen theayters a week; and another man did me a dozen more of the small. The larger theayters took longer time, and I don't think I made more than a dozen of them in a year. I used to make, I think, about fifty toy theayters a week. I always had a room full of them upstairs, except at Christmas, when we couldn't turn them out fast enough. I think I must have sold about 2,500 every year of 'em. Some theayters I made came to as much as £20 a piece. I have made about four of them, I think, in my life time. They was fitted up with very handsome fronts—generally 'liptic harch fronts, built all out of wood, with ornaments all over it—and they had machinery to move the side wings on and off; lamps in front, to rise and fall with machinery, and side lamps to turn on and off to darken the stage, and trick sliders to work the characters on and change the pantomime tricks; then there was machinery to make the borders rise and fall as well, and cut traps to open for the scenery to go up and down through the stage.

" 'The Miller and his Men' has sold better than any other play I ever published. I wore out a whole set of copper plates of that there. I must have sold at least five thousand of that play, all complete. It's the last scene, with the grand explosion of the mill, as pleases the young 'uns, uncommon. Some on 'em greases the last scene with butter—that gives a werry good effect with a light behind; but warnish is best, I can't abear butter. Some of them explosions we has made in wood work, and so arranged that the mill can fly to pieces; they comes to about 4s. 6d. a piece.

"The next most taking play out of my shop has been 'Blue Beard.' That the boys like for the purcession over the mountains—a coming to take *Fatima* away—and then there's the blue chamber with the skelingtons in it—that's werry good too—and has an uncommon pretty effect with a little blue fire, though it in general sets all the haudience a sneezing. The next best arter that was the 'Forty Thieves'—they likes that there, for the fairy grotto and the scenery is werry pretty throughout. Then again, the story pleases the children uncommon—it's a werry good one I call it.

"I'll give you the date of the first likeness as ever I did; I've got it here handy, and I should like you to see it, and have it all correct, 'cause you see, as I said before, it's a matter of history, like. Here's all my large portraits—there's 111 of them. This here's one of ——. It's Liston, as *Moll Flaggon*, you see. That there one is done by Mr. ——, the royal academician. It's Mr. H. Johnston as *Glaffier*. I think the part was in a tragedy called the 'Hillusion.' That was the werry first portrait as I published. Here's one by ——, done about the same time. That's Mrs. Egerton, as Hellen Macgregor. The portraits I have just been showing you are 2d.

plain, and 4d. coloured—but they don't sell now, the penny has quite knocked them up. Then there's other people wot makes as low as a halfpenny, but they a'n't like the performance at all. You see the cheap shops makes up the dresses with silk, and tinsel, and foil, but I never did. My customers used to do some; but, to my mind, it spoilt the figures, and took away all the good drawing from 'em. Formerly they used to cut out the parts of the figures, and stick pieces of silk, and tinsel, and lace behind them. Then the boys used to make all their own dots and ornaments themselves; and I used to sell punches expressly for doing 'em, and arter that I sold the ornaments themselves. Now the ornaments are sold in large quantities by these halfpenny printsellers. They are punched out by children I think—they make them as low as a halfpenny a packet. I haven't published a new set of characters for this seven year. You see they began to make halfpenny plates—they used to copy my penny ones and sell 'em at half-price, so I thought it high time to give over. I had come down in my large portraits from 2d. to 1d., and I wasn't going to reduce to halfpenny—not I. It seemed like lowering the purfession to me—besides, the theayters themselves couldn't make a do of it, so I gave over publishing. The decline of the drama is hawful, and it's just the same with the toy theaytres as it is with the real ones.". . .

I now give the statement of a man employed in the making of rocking-horses for the toy-shops. The place where he worked presented a curious appearance; it was in an off street from a great thoroughfare. At the door lay the *torso* of a rocking-horse, discoloured from age, earless and legless, and battered apparently from hard usage. Near it, in startling contrast, was a newly-made horse of dazzling whiteness, placed out to dry. The interior of the workshop was crowded with timber, but on every side the staple of the place was horses, and these in all stages. Horses' trunks, heads, legs, tails, and manes, of all hues and sizes, huddled on the floor, piled on the shelves, or swinging from the ceiling; horses in the rough, and horses awaiting the last polish—for the rocking-horse makers make also all the smaller quadrupeds demanded in the trade. The latter, after the block has been prepared, are shaped with a sharp knife, like an ordinary pocket-knife, used very quickly. The workman at one cut makes precisely the incision or curvature he requires. The body is of pine, and the head and legs (generally) of beech. My informant remembered no change in the fashion of rocking-horses. He thus described the manufacture:

"The first process is to take a pine plank, and form it, by jointing and glueing it, into a block. It used to be made out of solid timber, old 'girters' (beams of houses pulled down), or ship masts. The jointing is the better process. The block prepared is reduced by the drawing-knife and the plane (a chopper is used only when solid timber is worked), to the shape of the horse's body. It is then what we call bevilled and morticed, to make the holes into which the legs of the horse are placed. This manufacture, I assure you, requires considerable art, the eye being almost the only guide. We make the body by measurement—the formation and proportion of the several parts is made entirely by eye. The head is shaped out of solid wood (pine), after a pattern cut out of strong pasteboard or thin plank, but we have merely the outline supplied by the pattern; what may be called the anatomy, with the eyes, the nostrils, teeth, and the several parts of the face, are carved out, the skill of the workman being directed, as I have said, altogether by his eye. To make a good head is looked upon as one of the most skilled portions of the workmanship required in the trade. The legs are shaped without pattern, the skill of the workman having again no guide beyond his eye; and the 'tenant' is then cut in the leg—the 'tenant' being a portion of wood left on the top of the leg to be fitted into the mortice hole, made for that end in the body. Next, the head is affixed, being jointed, by a great nicety in adjustment, to the body of the rocking-horse, and then the toy in its rough state is complete.

"After that it is what we call 'worked off'—that is, each part has to be duly shaped, so that all may be in accordance, head, body, and legs—without that there would be no symmetry. The 'working off' is a four hours' process (taking the average sizes), and very hard work. The first layer of composition is then applied and left to dry, which takes from eight to ten hours. The rasp is then used all over the article, and then another layer of composition is applied, and then a third; this is done to get a smooth, level surface. The last application is rubbed down with glass paper. In these several processes there must be delays, at which the workman goes to other labours. No one can make a single rocking-horse, except at a loss; it's impossible, for half his time he would have to stand idle. The horse is then painted, and the legs are screwed and fitted to the 'rocker,' or frame, which is made before the horse is finished. It is then 'harnessed'—we do the saddler's work ourselves; after that the mane and tail are affixed, and then the rocking-horse is complete, unless glass eyes have to be put into the head, as is often the case. Some gentlemen are very particular about the shape and colour of their rocking-horses. They often say, 'That thing's more fit for the plough than for a parlour'—'It's a donkey and not a horse'—and such like.

"We divide the horses into two classes, 'gibbers' and 'racers;' a 'gibber' seems to be inclined to 'gib,' a racer is represented as at the very top of his speed. Gibbers have as much call as racers. The good journeyman averages say 18s. a week. At the present time, business is middling. The men are very seldom paid by the job, unless it be something for overtime; the wages are 3s. a day. I only know two women employed in making the harness in all London; they never meddle with the manufacture of the rocking-horse. I think there is not one apprentice to the trade at present. We have no union. I have not found the slightest difference in my trade in consequence of the reduction of duties on foreign toys by the tariff of '42. We make the 'roundabouts' for the fairs; once in five years there is a demand for them. I cannot tell how many rocking-horses may be yearly made in London. Perhaps it may be calculated this way: there are 30 men employed in making rocking-horses, and each man can make two a week. That gives 3,120 a year; but as we are employed in making horses of all kinds, as well as rocking-horses, you may reduce the number by one-half, yes I think 1,500 may be about the mark."

The statement I now publish is that of a man whose room presented an accumulation of materials—paper, paste, wires, gilding, wood, paste-board, leather, and other things, mixed up with instruments for nice admeasurement. The *fancy toy maker's* appearance was that of a hearty, jovial man, and I was referred to him as being a workman alike humorous, trustworthy, and intelligent. He said:

"I am a fancy toy maker. Fancy toys are mechanical and moving toys. To describe the whole would tire you. I invent them, all that I make, even to the casting line. I can go from the clay of the model to the perfect toy. I make the model. I model the toy myself. These are all my own models." [My informant showed me several. They were remarkable for their nice art and ingenuity].

"I was out on the world" (he continued) "young, and brought up to no business—and so, having confidence in my ingenuity, I took to the toy trade, and have carried it on for 35 years on my own account, working for the warehouses. My toys, though well known in the trade for their ingenuity, are not of great cost, but are chiefly within reach of the middle classes. They include animals of all descriptions—donkeys, horses, cows, cats, elephants, lions, tigers (I could make giraffes, but they're not in demand), dogs and pigs. Here is a toy of my own invention. This boy is flying a kite, and you see how, by the cranks and wires, the boy appears to advance and the kite takes the air. Here is a boat. These model men fix on here. By movements which I have contrived, they row the boat. I forget many of my inventions; the inventions in my calling are generally made in a slack time, when we have leisure to devote to the subject. It's slack now.

"Any man going into my trade must have great readiness as well as ingenuity—be quick as well as inventive. A man who hadn't those qualities would have as good a chance of succeeding in my trade, as a man who wrote badly and spelt worse would have in yours, sir. We are all working men, sir—you'll not be offended by my saying that. I started the figures on the donkeys, and the donkeys had a good run for a good while, and I hope they'll not leave off running for a good while longer, especially if they've good masters on their backs—I mean employers like Mr. G——. The boats with the men rowing in them had as good a run as the donkeys. The donkeys beat, though.

"There are very curious phrases in my trade. A boy who looked in at my workshop window, said, 'I'm blessed if I know what trade they are, but I heard them talk about cutting off three dozen donkeys' heads.' Donkeys' heads, you see, are made of papier-maché [I was shown a very good specimen], and the head is affixed so as to move—so are the ears, and the tail too, if demanded. I invented that donkey. The ass is made entire, and then the head is cut off to be refitted, with the faculty of moving. Here's an elephant—he moves his tail as well as his trunk. If I think of inventing a new toy, I often can't sleep from thinking of it. I assure you I have actually *dreamed* the completion of a new toy—of one that required great thought I went to bed with the plan working in my brain, and that led to the dream. I talk about it in my sleep.

"I consider that I am not at all well paid for my labour. No toy-maker is *well* paid for his mere labour, let alone his ingenuity. I can't state my average earnings, there is such a casualty about the work; it is often a speculation. I have to pay for so many things for my experiments, and for colours and varnishes, that my earnings are really very low. Two pound a week, do you ask if I make? Not one, sir, though I'm the top of the trade. My trade is a sort of individual thing; a man finds he has a turn for it, and so he takes a turn at it. There are no women in the trade that I'm aware of, except a young woman known as 'the mechanic' for her remarkable taste and ingenuity. The introduction of French toys at a lower rate of duty (in 1842 I think it was) affected my trade. I had far fewer orders after that, and prices fell. I should say it has made fifty per cent. difference to me generally. Many of the inventions or patterns that I have originated have been copied in Germany. Sometimes I get a hint from them, in return for all they borrow, so to call it, from me. They rob me, and I take from them. The fashion in penny toys is very variable; but toys of twenty years back often come into fashion again. It's so with mechanical toys—chiefly such as I make—moving figures. Some things that I invented long ago have recently come into fashion again—the working blacksmiths and sawyers, for instance. They say that 'luck's all;' in my trade 'fancy's all.' "

A statement was given to me by a man whose workshop, as he explained, had one peculiar characteristic; *for copper toys of the better sort*—or perhaps, he added, of any sort—it was the workshop of the world. He bears an excellent character, and the appearance of his wife and children was highly creditable to an artisan of his limited means. He worked in a small room on a ground floor, devoted to the purposes of his trade. He said:

"I have known the trade in copper and brass toys since I was a child. I am only 23, but when I was four or five years old, my father, who was in the trade, and indeed invented it, set me to work to clean the toys off, or punch holes, or do anything I could. We knew nothing but industry, and so were never driven to the streets; but my father might have made a fortune, with steadiness. At present I make chiefly copper teakettles, coffee-pots, coal-scuttles, warming-pans, and brass scales (toy scales); these are the most run on, but I make besides brass and copper hammers, saucepans, fish kettles, stewpans, and other things. I am now, you see, making copper teakettles and saucepans. There are sixteen pieces in one copper teakettle—first the handle, which has three pieces, seven pieces in the top and cover (lid), one piece for the side, two in the spout, one for the bottom, and two rivets to fix the handle, in all sixteen. That's the portion of the trade requiring the most art. Copper toys are the hardest work, I consider, of any toy-work. The copper is this dull sheet copper here, eight square feet in a sheet of it. I use generally a four-pound sheet, costing 13d. a pound. I make six dozen tea-kettles out of one sheet. The copper you see must be 'planished,' that is, polished by hammering it with a steel-faced hammer on a steel-faced 'head,' four inches square, to make it bright.

"I make, on the average for the year, eight dozen tea-kettles every week; that is 4,992 a year. I make all that are made in London—yes, in the world. Here's the world's shop, sir, this little place, for copper toys. My father and I (when he worked at the trade) had it all to ourselves; now *I* have, for my father is on other work. He is now helping to fit up a ship for California, belonging to a gentleman who is going to send out his son to settle there as a bottled-porter merchant. An uncle of mine once *did* make a few. I make as many scuttles in a week as I do tea-kettles, for I'm always at it, and as many coffee-pots; altogether, that's 13,976 teas, scuttles, and coffees. Of the other sorts, I make, I know, as many as I do of teas, coffee-pots, and saucepans. They're all fit to boil water in, cook anything you like—every one of them. You can make broth in them. They are made on exactly the same principles as the large kettles, except that *they* are brazed together, and mine are soft-soldered. Altogether, then, I make 27,952 of copper toys in a year. I sell my copper toys—all sorts, take one thing with another—at 36s. a gross. All my toys are retailed at 6d. each. I think I can earn 20s. a week, if my wife and I work early and late, which we do when we've call, there's so much work in those things. Sometimes we earn only 10s. I calculate it as an average of 15s. the year through. That's but little to keep a wife and two children on—one only just born a month ago last Monday, and another is only just buried. It's little to earn for making all the copper toys, as far as I know, in the world.

"I think I could do well in New York, where my trade is not known at all. I have all the art of the trade to myself. It was very good once, but now it's come down very bad in this country, and I should like to try another. People here haven't got money for toys; besides, mine last too long; they ought to break quicker. What my father once had 20s. for, I now get 5s. When these toys first came up, an Irishman cleared £1,400 in five years by selling them in the streets. That's twenty years ago; and he's now thriving in America." "If my husband wasn't steady, good, and careful," said the wife who was present, "my children and I might see the inside of the 'large house.'" "Things get worse," resumed the husband. "Almost every time I go to the warehouses they say, you must work cheaper; but it's not possible if a man must live, and see his family living."

I visited a *pewter toy-maker*, a man who explained to me that he could account for the bareness of the room in which I saw him (and which was, he said, beyond the cobbler's stall in the song—for it served him for bed-room, and parlour, and workshop, and kitchen, and all) by too sad a cause. The illness and death of a child, lately buried, had compelled him to part with many of his things. It is not difficult to describe the contents of his room. A bed occupied a sort of recess, and the other contents (I avoid the word "furniture") of the garret were—pewter. There were trays of bright pewter tea-cups, ready for the final "working off;" trays of tea-pots, and of other articles of the "tea service," which he manufactured. Pewter was everywhere. He had the pale and subdued look which I have often seen in mechanics whose earnings are limited and uncertain. I may add, that he worked for the pewter toy-makers, whose "statistics" (as he called them) I give from him, and he took time and pains to state them with correctness.

"I am a pewter toy-maker," he said, "and make only toys, sets of tea services, such as these I show you, sir, which consist of twenty-three pieces—six cups, six saucers, six spoons, sugar tongs, milk-pot, tea-pot and lid, and sugar basin. I make only tea services, and can make three dozen sets in a day, that is 828 pieces—that's not a few, and that would require ten hours' good work. Each piece is cast in a mould, and I will show you how. Here I sit before the fire, with the melted pewter in this pan on the fire before me. I hold the mould in my hand, and dip my ladle into the melted pewter, and fill the mould with it. The mould, of course, is different for each piece. I often scald my fingers and hands—here is an old burn, and here another. I mix my own pewter—tin, and lead, and spelter. The spelter is to give it a colour. The commonest pewter would not answer my purpose. The mould is all brass, and, when filled with the metal, is at once dipped into water to cool; then the metal is turned out, and it has to be pared and trimmed ready for use afterwards. To make one set by itself would take me full two hours. You may cast a number before you even get the right heat. As it is, I cast one lot by itself—go on casting tea-pots, and then any of the other parts of the service. As fast as they are cast, I apply this knife as if opening an oyster, and open the mould, and out comes the article.

"Last year I made, one week with another, six dozen sets a week, or 3,744 in the year, that is 86,112 pieces, reckoning them singly and by the year. I think you'll find that right. The set is retailed at $4\frac{1}{2}$d. and 6d., according to the prices of the shopkeeper. I get 3s. for a dozen sets—sometimes only 2s. 6d. Reckon that I make six dozen sets a week, and that's 18s.; but the material, including coal, costs me nearly 9s. out of that 18s.—so that I have but 9s. for myself. My trade is bad, and is generally bad for a while after Christmas. I think it's improving. Easter and Whitsuntide are the grand times, for us, on account of the fairs. There is another man in the trade who, with the help of eight men he has, can make three gross of tea or dinner services a day. He makes largely for shipping—to America and Ireland principally, where I've heard they're not up to toy-making. I suppose that, one week with another, the year through, he may turn out a gross and a half of tea and dinner services. He makes other things, but in the tea services that's 216 sets a week, or 11,016 sets a year, which is—mind, sir, we don't drop a few thousands—303,358 single pieces a year. There is another worker in pewter toys, or rather a family, who may make half as many as the person with eight men, so that those two and myself turn out 551,149 pieces in a year—over half a million; as many farthings as it's over, would make me a happy man. I reckon there are twice as many (in pieces) made of the other pewter toys—such as gridirons, fire sets, kitchen sets, carts, horses, omnibuses, steam-engines, soldiers, sailors, drummers, milkmaids, cats and kittens, dogs with baskets in their mouths, shepherds and shepherdesses, and some more. So, if you'll calculate—and it's as near the mark as a man may come, and nearer than it often comes—for I know it all by practice—it comes to 1,102,298 pieces a year in my trade in London—quite within the mark, shepherdesses and all included.

"I haven't got full work, or anything like it, and can't get. I reckon my earnings last year—a clear 9s. a week—to have been less by 3s. than the other workmen in my way. My wife is a reel winder, and she earns as much, or nearly as much, as I do. There was an acquaintance of mine—a joking sort of man—said to me last week, 'Well, will you pewterers show anything at the Grand Exhibition of Industry, next year?' 'I don't know much what it's about,' I said, 'but mine's too small a way.' 'So,' says he, 'I hope something will be done for the honour of the toy trade.' 'Good earnings, I think, sir, would honour it best,' was my reply."

A *basket toy-maker* gave me the following information. His room was very poorly furnished, and was chiefly noticeable for its heterogeneous admixture of trades. The twigs used in basket-making lay on shoemakers' lasts; a bird-cage rested on a sieve; half-made toy-baskets were mixed with scraps of leather. All told of a dreary poverty: but the basket-maker's tone was cheery, and he told me he had felt the folly of repining uselessly.

"I was bred and born to basket-making," he said, "my father's and my uncle's trade. I've known the basket toy making for seventeen years. I follow it in the summer. There is little chance of selling basket-toys in the streets in bad weather. But in summer the children are walking out with their mothers, and the children are our best friends, for they tempt the mothers to buy of us. Besides, as to summer and winter, the country travellers (hawkers) don't go out in the winter. My goods are chiefly for fairs. I was very fortunate for a time. No one at all interfered with my trade in small baskets with pincushions in them. The pincushions are made of crimson velvet, and sawdust; a few times I have used pink velvet, but that soon fades, so I stick to crimson. In the winter I take a turn at shoemaking, which I learned from an acquaintance. I myself am the only man in all the world who makes the penny pincushion-baskets. It's just a pincushion in a little basket, you see; but I started it. I sell it for a penny now with the cushion. Sixteen years ago I could sell more—ah! that I could, a great deal, and the same size—without the cushions, than I can now sell with them. But in that time a penny article of a nicer sort was a rarity, and so it went off. But now there's penny books, and penny papers, and penny numbers, and penny everythings, and nothing's so scarce that way as the pennies themselves.

"When I first made my baskets they was little things. Oh! here I've found a little basket, one of what I may call the first generation. But now this is the size. [The 'first generation,' as he called it, was about half the size of the 'present generation.'] My wife and I can make eight dozen a day; we made no more of the little ones, only the bigger ones take rather more time. That's a good day's work is 8 dozen— 6 dozen is a fair day's work, what I call a 12 hours' day—as much as any man ought to work; but shoemakers must work 18 hours. It's no matter if we can make ourselves happy in our lot. Last year, from June to the end of October, I made three gross a week, that is, I did with my wife's help, she assisting at the cushions; that's 15 weeks at 432 a week, or 9,072 for the 21 weeks of the season. That's correct. The warehouses have the regular profit; they screw down. I can only get 7½d. a dozen, or rather 7s. 6d. a gross, for baskets with pincushions. Formerly warehouses laid in a stock of my baskets before Easter. Now they don't until they are asked for. There is such change in fashion that shopkeepers is afraid to lay in. For all that, if I had capital I would now make a stock of them, and take my chance; but what capital can I raise, working for 1s. to 1s. 6d. a day on slop shoes, and with a family.

"I have made every kind of basket toys. Penny wicker carts, which pay the worst, go off the best. I can't make 1s. a day at long hours at them, or I would be carting now. The cushion-baskets was my regularest trade—the pennies; but I have made them of very fine basket work. They were sent out to Jersey, and to the repositories at the fashionable bathing places in England, and indeed all over the country. They were 6d., and some higher, according to the work, to shops. In the last season I only got 1s. 9d. clear profit on six dozen, or 10s. 6d. a week. It's an awful trade. My only chance is at a fair, anyways handy, but that's only a shilling or two extra, and fairs is few and far between, and then there's travelling expenses to come out of that and fatigues to stand. I wish I knew where I could get a few velvet cuttings cheap— that's a great advantage to me."

A person to whom I was referred as a very ingenious workman, gave me the following information concerning kites:

"I am alone in the trade," he said, "the only man in the world who makes kites after my peculiar scientific principles. This kite here, you see, folds up and will go into a case like an umbrella case, so that you can carry it in your hand. Instead of paper it is of fine cloth, as it is called in the trade—but it is fine glazed calico. By the management of the strings attached to the frame, the kite can be altered so as best to suit the wind as ascertained previous to flying, just as a sail on board ship is regulated. The tails of my kites have a series of 'cups,' or 'cones,' also of glazed calico. I hook them on or off, and there is no time lost. The introduction of the peculiar tails of my kites trebled their sale. I have made kites 12 feet high, which have drawn a four-wheeled chaise holding two persons. Such kites (12-foot kites) are mostly used in drawing boats along the Rhine and other rivers. They have amazing power. A pocket-handkerchief even, when held up in a wind, will be found to influence the motion of a boat. I have known even a 5-foot kite go to the full extent of the string, which was 1,700 yards, a few yards short of a mile. We calculate that two miles is the greatest distance a kite can be made to fly, but that is only when one kite is attached to the string of another already high in the air. No one could hold a kite flown so high; a post, or something of that kind, must be used.

"I have made kites for carrying meat into the air to test the state of the atmosphere during the rage of the cholera. I made 5,000 kites last year, but mine is a peculiar trade. Numbers take up kite-making without any instruction in the art. I suppose there are not above 25 kite-makers in London. Each, I should think, may make on the average a gross of kites in a day, which is 864 a week, which is 17,280 each man for the 20 weeks the season lasts, or altogether 432,000, and with more 437,000; of the farthing kites a man may make two or three gross a day, but some require labour, and a gross is a fair average. Average the cost of the kites to the public at 4d.; and my best 12-foot kites sell at £2, and a good 6-foot kite is fairly worth 6s. without the tail. I sell no kite under 1s. 6d. with the tail, and that will give £7,283 6s. 6d."

A woman who had known the *fancy ball business* for "well on to thirty years," she said, gave me the following information:

"I make only the better sort. Here is one; made of different coloured cloths, you perceive, in diamonds of different lengths and widths. The joinings are covered over with this light gilt wire. That toy, sir, is my own invention, I may say. I invented it with six quarterings, and now it has thirty-six. I make such like in velvet. They are really beautiful. They're stuffed with the softest and finest seal's hair; so soft, the best hair is, that with a child's strength it wouldn't break a window, unless it was very bad glass, even if flung right against it. They're drawing-room balls. I work, sir, sometimes, for the Royal Family. The order comes to me through a warehouse, but I supply the article direct. I charge the warehouseman the same as usual; what he charges is no concern of mine. I look at it this way: if a shopkeeper pays a fair wage to let workpeople live decently, and not be beat out by the first rainy day, why, let him get as good a price as he can. These balls, you see, are coloured leathers, without gilt wire, but well made. Each diamond is cut out according to a nice iron pattern. These are common things which I'm forced to make for the low shops. They won't wear. As to the cheap shops, I myself have seen ——, in the ——, mark balls, that he had paid 4d. a piece to me for, at 2½d. in his window, before I'd left the place. He must make it up somehow, that's clear.

"What my returns in this business are, I can't tell; for my husband, who cuts out and such like, has another trade, and all the money goes together; we keep no separate accounts at all: but I do very well. We sell, I think, about a gross and a half a week, fancy balls. There are two other persons carrying on the trade, and the two together may make as many balls as I do. That's three gross a week, or 22,464 balls a year? Very likely. I pay no regular wages, as the trade is carried on by my own family; occasionally we have a little help. You can, if you like, reckon what the toys I make amount to this way: Say 1s. a dozen in the lump, for though I only get 5d. a dozen for some, I get 30s. for others. That's £561 12s. a-year. The other makers together may take half that. The two sums added together come to £842 8s. A good deal of money that, to be spent every year in fancy balls."

I had the following statement from a Frenchman, who took no little pride in his art. He is the only person who carries on the making of *papier-maché toys* (as they have been called), which are covered—or, more properly, and that was my informant's word, *clothed*—with fur or hair. These toys display great taste and ingenuity. Some rabbits were as large as life—he brought different specimens to

show me—and they looked natural enough, the body of the animal being made of paper formed by an art and a process (according to his own account) peculiar to my informant. A French accent was perceptible throughout the entire conversation, but was only very remarkable in rapid speech or in a dash of excitement. He said:

"Papier-maché was made before my father was born, or before my father's grand-mother, but improvements took place twenty-five year ago. I can make you, if you please, the biggest animal in the world, waterproof, and that nothing can never break, of paper or papier-maché. Anything may be done with the paper, but I now use a composition as well—it is my secret of what he is made. I make only animals. I make them both way, for the ornament of the chimney and the amusement of the children. I make every domestic. There is none but I manufacture him with natural hair and wool. French poodle dogs have the call; rabbits is good; lambs go very well; goats is middling. All the world can be supplied, from 3d. up to £5, with the French poodles. I do not make the lions, nor the tigers, nor those creatures—I make only in domestic animals, but I *could* make the lions and the tigers as well. I make forty dozen domestic animals a week. Why you come here to ask?

"Lately my trade has been bad. I employ women and girls only, at so much on the dozen. I do not like to tell at what. It cannot be necessary. I cannot tell what relates to my secret. I will not. The skins for the poodles and the lambs I dress myself, or they would be stink. The cost—oh, I will not tell, they cost too much. I have been here for twenty-one years. I get the stink-lambs for skins. Last year I used 4,800 lamb skins, and 5,000 some year. I employ eight English women. The dogs is all lamb skins—their outsides. I use nearly as many rabbit skins. I do not never admit persons into my work-room. It is a very artful ingenuity. I can beat the French—indeed, I have beat my countrymen at home, for I have exportation to Paris; but the Germans come in cheap, cheap, and ruin the trade.

"This is a barking dog. I have made him, his bark and all—you see; yes, and you hear. The penny barks is no good; what barks can you expect for a penny? There's no get fat about him at 9d. This rabbit, you see, has a different skin to this other— the skin is the great cost with me. He have, too—the spring in his ears and tail, so that he lift them when the wheels go round. The earnings of my women? Oh! never mind; but I am not ashamed to tell. They earn 7s., and 9s., and 11s. a week, and never not less than 4s. My late wife could earn twenty and two shilling a week in this trade; but then she had the talent. Oh, no, none can now earn like that—they have not the talent—they have not the art in it—the nature—the interest. The work can only be done best by a relative of the master, one that has the interest in the making. The toys are not exactly papier-maché, which is fluid for mouldings, they are paper, common paper, in a solid form. The *how* it is made is my secret. None other persons are in my trade. I cannot open the secret any further. Pardon my reserve, for which I have account to you. How you say, sir, four dozen domestic animals a week, that's quite reasonable as to the arithmetic of it, and he makes 22,960 domestics a year. Yes, that at least and my women do not work hard. They might work harder. They work hard if they want new dresses for the Sundays. What will the twenty thousand and odd toys bring in in money? The price vary, you com-prehend, according to sizes and qualities, and arts and beauties. Yes, you can say 1s. each. How much, £1,148 in a year for all the domestics. Yes; but I shall not tell prices or secrets."

From Letter XXXIX, February 28th, 1850

. . . concerning the *wooden dolls*. I called upon a maker whom I found ill in bed, suffering from rheumatism. In his room were piles of the bodies, and collections of the arms and legs of dolls; they caught the eye on every side. This doll-maker regretted the decline of art in some branches of his calling. A description of cheap wooden dolls that used to have their noses carved were now made, through the demand for lowness in price, with the nose but a little elevated on the counten- ance——"nothing to call a nose," he said; but, though the man was conversible enough, I did not think it proper to persevere in my inquiries with him in his sick state, and so visited another, whom I found at work, assisted by his daughter. He was an elderly person, who had known the trade many years, as his narrative shows. He said:

"I make the jointed wooden dolls. The turned work (the body) is the work of the turner's lathe. I do it myself, and the faces of the commoner dolls are a com- position put on afterwards. I go in for beauty as much as I can, even in the lower priced dolls. These dolls, now, are carved, after having been turned out of the wood. The 'carving' and 'drawing'—making eyes, eye-brows, and lips in colours with a fine brush—are the fine touches of the trade. Nice lips and eyes set the article off. The lower-priced dolls have wooden joints at the middle, by which the legs are fastened to the body. We don't go in for symmetry in the commoner sorts of legs; nor, indeed, for any calves at all to them. They are just whitened over. The better ones have nice calves, and flesh coloured calves too. They are more like nature. The joints of the two sorts are made on the same principles. I buy their ringlets— it's generally ringlets, but, sometimes, braids or plaits, ready made—and have only to fit them on. That's not very different from human nature, I take it. The arms are stuffed leather, made by others.

"The best time for my trade was from 1809 to 1816. In every one year that I have named, I made 35 gross of dolls a week: but they were little creatures, some of them 4 inches long, dwarfs of dolls. I don't deal with the little creatures now. I'm in the larger line, as you see. A namesake of mine at that time made 100 gross a week. That's 1,060,880 dolls a year, is it? Look at that, now, for us two only. The little things I spoke of used to fetch a penny, now it's a farthing. I make now, I believe, two gross of dolls one week, and one another. The larger dolls require more time, which accounts, independent of the demand, for the difference. My dolls are sold to the public at 3s. and 1s.: that's the retail price, mind, and small are my profits. Wooden doll making is generally confined to families, so we can't speak of journeymen's wages. There are eight other doll-makers, and perhaps each may make twice as many as I do, but as they make so many more of the smaller sort, the cost (to the public) wouldn't be more than mine, perhaps about the same—but I can only guess. I have felt a great falling off on the demand since the last tariff—at least one quarter less is now made. When the duty was highest I knew a gentleman who now and then would venture £1,000 in buying foreign toys. It was, he said, a speculation, but he generally got £2,000 for his £1,000, and the toy trade was benefited, for variety and new fashions were seen, and there was a better demand for toys."

Now of the *sewed dolls*. The following statement will give the reader a slight insight into the earnings and condition of those who contribute so much to the pleasure of the young of the metropolis. It was given me by a man whose whole appearance showed grinding poverty. His cheeks were sunk more than I remember to have ever seen in any previous instance, and altogether he seemed, from grief and care, like a man half dead. His room, as well as I could see it by the light of one small candle—for it was late at night before I could visit him—was bare of anything to be called furniture, except only a very poor bed, a chair or two, and a table or bench at which he was at work with his paste and paper. In one corner was an oblong object, covered with an old quilt. It was a coffin containing the body of his child, a girl four years old, who had died of the hooping-cough. There were four living children in the room—all up, late as it was, and all looking feeble, worn, and sickly. A baby of four months old was asleep in the arms of a little girl of five or six. A baby of fifteen or sixteen months apparently, was in the arms of another girl, who in vain strove to quiet it. The mother was absent with some of her wares. The man's manner was meek and subdued, and he did not parade either his grief or his poverty. He merely answered my questions, and to them he said:

"I make the *composition heads for the dolls*—nothing else. They are made of papier-maché" ("paper mashed" he called it). "After they go out of my hands to the doll-makers, they are waxed. First, they are done over in 'flake' light (flesh colour), and then dipped in wax. I make a mould from a wax model, and in it work the paper—a peculiar kind of sugar paper. My little girl, fifteen years old (I have her besides these four young ones), and myself can only make twelve or thirteen dozen a day of the smallest heads. For them I get 4d. a dozen, 4s. the gross, and the material I reckon costs me 1s. 10d. If I make 2s. 6d. in a day, I reckon it a good day's work—and what is half-a-crown for such a family as mine? I pay 4d. per lb. for paper, and am so poor that I am forced to buy it all retail. I make, of all sizes, four gross of heads a week, the year through. That is 29,952 a year. I do not make 12s. a week on the average, take the year through. Besides, doll making is a precarious trade; and then there's fire and candle extra when you must work in a hurry. The dark must do when I'm forced to be idle. There are five more in the trade, and each may do more a year than I do, but I cannot tell. Some of the warehouses, moreover, get their heads made on their premises by boys at 5s. or 6s. a week, and that knocks us out altogether sometimes. They think only of cheapness—it's nothing what such as I may suffer.

"My poverty is grievous enough, as you see; and as you asked, I tell you. My wife makes a few dolls' arms of stuffed sheepskin; sawdust is used. She only gets seven farthings a dozen for them, and has very little employment. My trade was far better. Only two years ago I had from 1d. to 2d. a dozen better prices for my heads—a great difference to me—and my wife had 5d. a dozen for her arms some years ago. They get the bodies now stuffed with sawdust at 2s. 6d. a gross, and they did pay 5s. It's starvation work—stuffing 144 bodies for half-a-crown. Ah, sir, the children of the people who will be happy with my dolls little think under what circumstances they are made, nor do their parents—I wish they did. Awful circumstances in my room. Death there now (pointing to the coffin), and want here always." [This was really said most plaintively, because most naturally.] . . .

From the very ingenious inventor of the *speaking doll*, a tradesman in High Holborn, I had this statement:

"I am the only person who ever made the speaking doll. I make her say 'papa' and 'mamma.' I haven't one in the house now to show you. I have sold the last. I sold one to be sent to St. Petersburg—it was damaged on the passage, and when landed couldn't say either 'papa' or 'mamma,' and the gentleman who bought it couldn't get it mended in all Russia. I could have told him that before. For the Exhibition of 1851 I believe there will be something equivalent to what I tell you of, but there will be something of everything. The invention of the speaking doll took me many experiments and much study. The thought first struck me one day on hearing a penny trumpet—why not make a doll speak? Science is equal to everything. Some time ago a ventriloquist came over from Dublin to me; he could imitate everything but a baby, and he came to consult me about a baby's voice. I put him in my show-room, and said 'You stand in the corner and hear it.' I made the doll speak, and he said 'that is the thing;' he gave the two guineas for the price of the machine (not a doll), and went away quite glad. I have taken the apparatus to a party and made him speak on the stairs; a young gentleman I did it to tease turned quite white, as he could not tell who or what was coming.

"After I determined to try and manufacture a speaking doll, I persevered day by day, thinking of it when doing other things, and completed it in three months. I often dreamed of it, but never got a hint of the speaking doll in my sleep, though I have in other discoveries. When I heard my first speaking doll call me 'papa'—which she very properly might—I said in a sort of enthusiasm—it was with feelings of the greatest gratification—'I've got her at last.' I sell rather more than a dozen in a year at £6 6s. each. Many a time in my show room have the children looked out for the baby when they heard my doll. I had a rascal of a parrot once who could say 'papa' and 'mamma' as well as my doll herself—the parrot learned it from the doll. Many doll-makers have dissected my speaking doll to get at my secret. I knew one clever man who tried twelve months to copy it, and then he put his work in the fire. I laugh—I don't care a fig. I have the fame and the secret, and will keep them; the profit is but small—and as for the fame, why that's not for me to talk about.". . .

A *toy drum and tambourine maker* gave me the following account:

"The first process in making a tin drum," he said, "is to cut the tin the size required, solder the ends together, and colour the body. We then paint the Royal Arms on it, or a crown and V.R. The hoops are then cut (they are beech) and coloured, and then what we call the 'twig' is cut, and the parchment for the top of the drum being sewn to it, the twig is fitted to the tin body, and attached to it by the strings, which are tightened or slackened by leather braces, for the weather affects the drum. A best toy drum goes thirty-five times through our hands before it is finished, as time must be given in the working for the parts to dry and set. I don't make the sticks, the toy turners do them. I and my four boys could make a gross of small wooden drums in a day, but only a dozen of the best large tin drums, highly ornamented. Of wooden drums, I make a gross a week, the year through—and 52 gross, at 3d. a piece (retail) gives £93 12s. There are other makers in London, who may make about as many as I do; giving altogether £187 4s.

"We make very few tin drums now to what were made—the foreign toys have affected us so. I may make half a gross of them a week through the year, and taking the average price at 1s. (the big ones making up for the sixpennies), it gives £185 14s., which you can calculate as with the wooden drums—double it

N

for other makers—and it's £371 8s. for London-made drums. Tambourines are made after the same fashion, but have only a limited sale. I only make about three dozen a week, and the public may buy them (retail) say at an average of 9d.—that's £70 4s. I can hardly tell you what the other makers sell. Whether the same calculation as with the drums would be correct or not for the tambourines, I can't say. I *have* heard an uncle whom I succeeded say—and he employed eleven men where I have four boys at apprentices' wages—that the war time was the time for the toy drum trade."

A *gun toy-maker*, whom I found at work, his wife assisting him, gave me this statement:

"I was born to the business of toy gun, and pistol, as well as of tin toys, which consist of mugs and trumpets; but the foreigners have got all the trumpet trade now, what we got 30s. a gross for we now get only 7s. The other tin toys—such as horses and carts, got up by machinery for a penny—are made in Birmingham. None are made in that way in London; they're but *slop toys*. The tin toy trade at Birmingham is the factory system with children; think of children working hard at toys—poor little things to whom a toy is a horror! A gun is made in this manner. The wooden part, the stock, is made ready for the gunmaker's use by any carpenter; it is of pine. The next process is the making of the wire spring, then the barrel (tin). These different parts are then put to the stock, the lock is made by ourselves; they are of solder, and cast. The spring is placed inside the barrel, a ring is placed at the end by which it is drawn out, fastened to the pin (like the nipple of one of your deadly guns), and the weapon is ready for discharge.

"I make the week through three gross, which is 22,464. There is one other toy gunmaker in London, and he may make as many as I do, which will be 44,928 made in London. Reckon a third retailed to the public at 4d. (called pistols), and reckon those retailed at 6d. in the proportion of 6 to 4 in number with those retailed at 1s., and you have the sum of £1,238 4s. The foreign trade has injured my business greatly, both as to quantity and price. I first felt the effect in 1844 and 1845, and my business has kept getting worse and worse until now. I do not make half so many guns as I did before the change in the tariff, and the price is worse to me by 3s. out of 21s.—that was the price formerly of a gross of such as these, now they are 18s. only. The trumpet trade's quite blown away from us—I may as well have my joke about it. Of tin mugs I make 10 gross a week the year round, which is 74,880.

"There are three other makers, who may turn out one-half as many as I do, the three of them together—that is 111,320 in all. They are all retailed at 1d. (I have 7d. a dozen), and so the public pay for tin mugs, made in London annually, £468 6s. 8d. In war time, bless you, that was the time for my business—there *was* a demand for guns then I can tell you! I sold eight, then, to one that I sell now, though the population's increased so. These pistols, which I get 1s. 6d. a dozen for now, I had 3s. 6d. a dozen for then. I remember the first botched-up peace in 1802. I can just recollect the illumination. My father (I heard him say so) thought the peace would do no good to him, but it didn't last very long, and the toy-gun trade went on steadily for years—with a bit of a fillip, now and then, after news of a victory; but the grand thing for the trade was the constant report that Bonaparte was coming—there was to be an invasion, and then every child was a soldier. Guns *did* go off briskly at that period—anything in the shape of a gun found a customer in those days. Working people could then buy plenty of toys for their children, and did buy them too. The men in the trade earn 12s. a week. The warehouses send out quantities of my guns and pistols to the colonies, especially to Australia—the duty keeps them out of the United States. The slop toy trade goes down here now."

An Italian gave me the following account of the *detonating cracker business*. His parlour, as well as the window of his workshop, presented an admixture sufficiently curious. Old foreign paintings, religious, mythological, or incomprehensible, were in close connection with unmistakeable Hogarth prints. Barometers (for these also were "made and repaired"), showed that it was "set fair," and alongside them were grosses of detonating crackers. Of frames and mouldings there was a profusion, and in all stages, from the first rough outline to the polished gilding. He said, in pretty good English with a strong Italian accent:

"Yes. I make de detonating crackers, and am de only man in England skilful to make dem. It is a grand secret, mine art. It live in my breast alone—de full, entire secret. I will show you de pulling crackers. Dey go in wid de pastry-cook's things at de parties of de rich. A gentleman say to a lady, so I have heard, in de pleasantness of de party, 'please to pull.' Yes, indeed, as they write above de bells. And so de pretty lady pull, and de cracker goes bang—a sudden bang—and de lady goes 'Ah-h-h!' quite sudden too, of course, dough she must have known before dat de crack was to come. Ah! sir, dey seldom tink of de Italian artist who make de pulling cracker dat has brought out her nice 'Ah-h-h!' for 3½d. de gross—dat is all we gets for de dozen dozen.

"I dare say de rich fashionable pastrycook get a great deal for dem. I don't know how much. Dey are sold at de retail shops, dat are not high shops, at a halfpenny a dozen. Den de detonating—them what are trone down on de stones, and go bang, and make de people passing go start. Do dey cause many accidents do I tink? Bah, nonsense. It is de play of de boys: it keep dem out of mischief. I sell fifty gross, one week with another. I can make, if required, wid my boy, eighteen gross a day. All last year I sold, as near as I can tell, fifty of de pulling, and fifty gross of de detonating. Dat is—yes, no doubt—14,400 a week, or 748,800 a year. How curious! More dan seven hundred dousand bang-bangs made in dis little place. Dere is danger, perhaps, in de make to some, but no to de right artist. At a halfpenny a dozen, dat is £260 paid by de public—dat is only part of my business; but den de pastrycook charges may make de amount double, and double again, and more dan double dat again."

A very ingenious man, who resided in two spacious rooms at the top of a high house, gave the following statement concerning *camera obscura* making. I may here remark that I have always found the intelligent artisan—who could easily be made to understand the purport of my inquiries—ready to give me the necessary information, not only without reluctance, but with evident pleasure. Among the less informed class I am often delayed by meeting with objections and hesitations; these, however, are always obviated by having recourse to a more intelligent person. My present informant said:

"I have known the camera obscura business for twenty-five years or so; but I can turn my hand to clock-making, or anything. My father was an optician, employing many men, and was burnt out; but the introduction of steam machinery has materially affected the optical glass grinder—which was my trade at first. In a steam-mill in Sheffield, one man and two boys can now do the work that kept sixty men going. I make bagatelle boards—there's no great demand for them—and targets—they go off very fair. The only improvement I remember in the making of the common cameras is this: Formerly the object glass was a fixture in the wood of the box, and immovable, and of course could only take an object at a certain distance, whereas, by applying a movable brass tube, with the glass in it, you can command objects at any distance, adjusting it precisely on the principle of a telescope. Too much light obliterates your object, and too little light won't define it. Last year I think I made three gross. Here is the stuff of the box body, cedar; all blacked in the inside, so as to exclude any false light. The bottom is deal, and the natural colour of that or of the cedar would obliterate an object by giving false lights. The small cameras are 2s. 6d. (retail), the next size is 5s., and so by half-crowns, generally up to 20s. or 21s. I make more than one-half 2s. 6d. ones; they sell well in the summer season. I don't get more than 6d. a piece out of the 2s. 6d. ones. Perhaps I make two gross smaller, and the other sizes, of the third gross, in about equal proportions; altogether £126 19s.

"There is no other maker for the toy-shops in the camera obscura trade, to my knowledge, beyond myself. In making my cameras I test them from this door to objects at a distance. It gives every line of those tiles, every shape of those chimney pots, and every tumble of those tumbler pigeons. So I detect any error in the focus, and regulate it. I must test them at a good height, with a good light. A fog gives you only a fog—no defined object. The perfect adjustment of the focus, and, indeed, of every portion, is the nice art of my trade."

A very ingenious and intelligent man to whom I was referred, as the best in his trade, gave me the following account of magic lanterns. His parlour behind the shop—for he had risen to be a shopkeeper in some kinds of toys and other articles, known as the "fancy trade," was well furnished, and in a way that often distinguishes the better class of prosperous artisans. A fondness for paintings and for animals was manifested. On a sofa lay two very handsome King Charles's spaniels. On a chair were a fine cat and kitten. Outside his parlour window was a pigeon colony, peopled with fine large birds, a cross between those known as a "carrier" and a "horseman." Books, of no common class, were abundant enough, and his periodical was not wanting. He said:

"I have known the business of magic lantern making thirty-five years. It was then no better than the common galantee shows in the streets, Punch and Judy, or any peepshow or common thing. There was no science and no art about it. It went on so for some time—just grotesque things for children, as 'Pull devil and pull baker.' This is the old style, you see, but better done." [He showed me one in which, to all appearance (for it was rather obscurely expressed), a cat was busy at the wash-tub, with handkerchiefs hanging on her tail to dry; Judy, with a glass in her hand, was in company with a nondescript sort of devil, smoking a pipe, and a horse was driving a man, who carried the horse's panniers.]

"Bluebeards were fashionable then—uncommon blue their beards were, to be sure; and Robin Hoods—and Robinson Crusoes with Fridays and the goats, and the parrot, and the man's footmark on the sand—and Little Red Riding Hoods, as red as the Blue Beards were blue. I don't remember Ali Babas and Forty Thieves, there were too many of the thieves for a magic lantern—too many characters; we couldn't very well have managed forty thieves—it's too many. There were things called

'comic changes' in vogue at that period. As the glasses moved backwards and forwards, fitted into a small frame like that of a boy's slate, a beggar was shown as
if taking his hat off, and Jim Crow turning about and wheeling about, and a black-
smith hammering—moving his hammer. There were no theatrical scenes beyond
Harlequins and Clowns.

"About thirty years ago the diagrams for astronomy were introduced. These
were made to show the eclipses of the sun and moon, the different constellations,
the planets with their satellites, the phases of the moon, the rotundity of the earth,
and the comets with good long tails. What a tail 1811 had! and similar things that
way. This I consider an important step in the improvement of my art. Next, moving
diagrams were introduced. I really forget, or never knew, who first introduced those
improvements. The opticians then had the trade to themselves, and prices were
very high. The moving diagrams were so made that they showed the motion of the
earth and its rotundity, by the course of a ship painted on the lantern—and the
tides, the neap and spring, as influenced by the sun and moon. Then there was the
earth going round the sun, and, as she passed along, the different phases were
shown, day here and night there. Then there were the planets going round the sun,
with their satellites going round them. How wonderful are the works of the
Creator! The comets, too; that of 1811, however, with a famous tail, as he
deserved. His regular course—if you may call it regular—was shown. I saw him
when a schoolboy in Wiltshire then. There has not been a comet worth calling
a comet since. The zodiac made very pretty slides—twelve of them, each a sign.
These things greatly advanced the art and the demand for magic lanterns increased, but not much for some years, until the dissolving views were introduced,
about eighteen years ago, I think it was.

"But I should tell you that Dollond, before that, made improvements in the
magic lantern; they called the new instrument the phantasmagoria. Mr. Henry,
who conjured at the Adelphi Theatre some eighteen years ago was one of the first—
indeed I may say *the* first—who introduced dissolving views at a place of public
amusement. Then these views were shown by the oil light only, so that the effect
was not near so good as by gas, but even that created a great impression. From that
period I date what I may call the popularity of magic lanterns. Henry used two
lanterns for his views; but using them with oil, and not on so large a scale, they
would be thought very poor things now. Then the Careys introduced the gas microscope, up in Bond-street. The gas miscroscope (the hydro-oxygen it's sometimes
called) is the magic lantern, and on the principle of the magic lantern, only better
glazed, showing the water lions and other things in a drop of stagnant water.
Thames water may do.

"I now introduce insects and butterflies' wings in my lanterns—real insects
and real wings of insects on the slides. I make such as fleas, bugs, pig-lice (an
extraordinary thing, with claws like a crab, sir), and so up to butterflies—all between glasses, and air tight—they'll last for ever if necessary. Here's the sting,
tongue, and wing of a bee. Here you see flowers. Those leaves of the fern are really
beautiful—of course they are, for they are from the fern itself. This is one great
improvement of the art, which I have given in a more simple form than used to be
the fashion. You can magnify them to any size, and it's still nature—no dispropor-
tion and no distortion. Butterflies may be made as big as the wall of this room,
through one of my magic lanterns with microscope power attached—but the larger

the object represented, the less the power of the light. Gas, in some degree, obviates that fault. No oil can be made to give a light like gas. After this the question arose as to introducing views with the lime light, but the paintings in the lanterns were then too coarse, for the light brought them out in all their coarseness. Every defect was shown up, glaringly, you may say. That brought in better paintings—of course at a greater cost. The Polytechnic has brought the lime-light for this purpose to great perfection. For the oil-lights the paintings are bold, for the lime-light fine and delicate. Next the chromatrope was introduced, revolving stars chiefly—the hint being taken from Chinese fireworks. Mount Vesuvius was made to explode and such like. That's the present state of the art in London.

"The trade is five or six fold what I once knew it. Landscapes, Fingal's caves, cathedrals, sea views, are most popular now. In the landscapes we give the changes from summer to winter—from a bright sun in July to the snow seen actually falling in January. I make between 500 and 600 a year, say 550; I think I make one half of those made. The lowest price of a well-made lantern is 7s. 6d., and so on up to £20, dissolving and double lanterns. About a third of the lowest price are made, but people often go on from that to a superior article. I sold last year about 100 of the best of single lanterns, retailed at £10. Calculate a third at 7s. 6d., and 100 at £10, and the intermediate prices in—I think we may say—equal proportions—and you have the amount. Average the middle lot at 30s., suppose—that is £1,469 14s. I think that the other magic lanterns made, though they may be double my quantity, will not realize more, as so many lower-priced lanterns are made; so double the amount, and we have £2,939 8s. for London-made magic lanterns. I think I can, and shall, introduce further improvements.

"There are slop magic lanterns; they are slops, made, I believe, but I am not sure, in French Flanders; and I believe more of them are sold than of our own. What is worse than slop art, sir? These slop lanterns are generally retailed at 1s. 6d. each, with 12 slides. The tin part is neatly made; but, altogether, it is sad rubbish. I have been told by persons who bought them—and I have been often told it—that they could make nothing of them. The only good that they can do is, that they may tempt people to buy better ones—which is something. The admission of foreign toys at a low rate of duty has not injured the magic lantern business, but has rather increased it."

DRESSMAKERS

From Letter LXXV, October 24th, 1850

[Though the connection between Mayhew and the Morning Chronicle *was severed early in October, 1850, the letters from "The Metropolitan Correspondent" continued until the end of December, 1850. In* London Labour, *Mayhew claimed authorship of a number of these later letters, including those on dressmakers. Whether he wrote all the letters which appeared after his break with the newspaper is not known positively, but the probability is that he did. Therefore, a few interviews from these last letters are included here to serve as a kind of appendix to Mayhew's investigations of skilled workers.]*

. . . From an *improver* and an *apprentice*, both in superior houses, I had statements of sufficient kind treatment and good meals, with fair hours of labour generally. The improver, who was from the country, and had paid a premium of £15 for two years' "improvement," had merely board and lodging. The apprentice, with whom a premium of £25 was given for three years, had also board and lodging.

A day-worker stated to me that her business was greatly affected by the system of taking improvers, as they did the work for nothing beyond board and lodging, which must otherwise be paid for. As much as 1s. 6d. a day and her tea is sometimes given to the day-worker, but this is a rare occurrence. The usual payment under the best employers is 1s. a day and tea. The hours are from eight to eight, or nine to eight—indeed the hours vary—but the day-workers at least *expect*, if they do not always *receive*, overpay for overhours. One young woman, a day-worker, who lived with her mother, a poor widow, told me that she earned 7s. a week eight or nine months of the year, and not 1s. 6d. a week the three or four months she was not at her usual day-work. "There are," she said, "several respectable tradesmen who get day-work for their daughters, and who like that way of employing them better than in situations as assistants, because their girls then sleep at home, and earn nice pocket-money or dress-money by day-work. That, again, is a disadvantage to a young person like me who depends on her needle for her living. The most of our day-workers are from twenty to thirty, some from fifteen to twenty, and a few between thirty and forty; but I know of no old woman who is a day-worker in the superior trade. You must be quick and have good sight. You never, or very seldom, see a milliner or dressmaker wear glasses, unless she's quite young and does it to preserve her sight, or because she thinks she looks better in them, or unless she's a first hand and is independent and doesn't care. I have gone from my work to my mother's at all hours of the night, as I always endeavour to work overhours if I can, and I never was insulted in the streets. I have heard, and a very good thing it is, that if any young person is insulted by any bad drunken fellow in the street, the police-inspectors, if she tells them she is a dressmaker going home from her work, and they are satisfied she is so, are instructed to call a cab and send her home in it, and the Association pays the expense."—[I ascertained that this was the case].

Concerning late hours I had the following statement from a trustworthy source:

"I was *second hand* at Mrs. ——'s. I had £20 a year, or at that rate for as long as I stayed, and board and lodging. In the busy time I worked, and so did six others of us, to twelve at night, and then had to get up again at four the next morning, and work again till twelve. This happened four times a week, or eight or nine times in the season, as nearly as I can recollect. We had only ten minutes or a quarter of an hour allowed for any meal—even for dinner. The rest of the time was spent at work. I have dozed over my work and have wakened from a sort of dream with a start, and have felt quite cold, though the room was hot from the gas lights. If I complained, or if any of the others complained, we were told 'Oh, it's only for an occasion; it's a sudden order, and we can't get hands in a moment;' but the sudden orders came very often. My health suffered very much. My back ached from long sitting, I had flying and severe pains in my chest and sick headaches, and no appetite. I have sat working for twenty hours two or three or four days in a week. When business was slack we worked from eight to eight, or nine; or from nine to eight, or seven, or six. In the busy time six hands certainly did work enough for nine. We cannot, even if we wished, put in inferior work, for we are told often enough that ladies are good judges of work, and their maids are better, and good work they must have. It can only be the wish to make money by any means that makes employers over-work young persons. Improvers work the same hours; but apprentices don't. They are too young. It would kill them. I have often walked home, about a mile and a half, on a Saturday night at twelve o'clock; we never work later, nor on Sundays, and I could hardly walk so far. It was only over-work that I suffered from. Often on a Sunday I could not eat the nice dinner at home, though I went home only once a week, and my mother got alarmed, and the doctor said I must either give up my place or go into a consumption. The dread of such a thing is shocking. So I gave up my situation, and have enjoyed some rest and country air, and now I am quite well."

Concerning diet, also, I was informed in several quarters that there was a great improvement within these four or five years, but there are still many instances of very insufficient diet being given. From a dressmaker, filling a responsible situation in a fashionable house I had the following statement:

"The quality of the meat we have is good, but the quantity is sadly deficient. I have sometimes to send out for a mutton chop and get the cook to dress it, in addition to my dinner, though my appetite is delicate. This is always the case if I have to carve, as I have sometimes, for really I feel for the young persons who are so poorly fed, and I leave hardly a bit for myself. For breakfast we have poor tea (I sometimes put some of my own in the pot to make it palatable), and bread and butter, and not enough of either. For dinner, at one, nineteen of us will sit down to dine off a leg or a shoulder of mutton that weighed 7, 8, or 9 lbs. before it was put down to be roasted; for we have roast meat oftener than boiled. I don't know what it loses in cooking. If it's pork, however, that is generally boiled. Along with it we have vegetables in quite insufficient quantities, when vegetables are cheaper

A dressmaker, by Kenny Meadows

than potatoes, and potatoes when they are cheaper than vegetables. For pudding, or with the joint if we choose, we have plain boiled rice—nothing with it. The mistress is generally present and pretends to make her dinner with us, eating the least of all, and leaving a little in her plate, and always saying what beautiful meat it is. Sometimes, but very seldom, it has been tainted; but that was the butcher's fault, or the cook's. I have really felt for hearty girls coming from the country. They look on the little joint and the number at table, quite frightened. In time they lose their appetites. I have known girls with good appetites spend almost their whole salaries in buying little things that they could eat, and say that they must do it or be famished. Tea is the same as breakfast. For supper we have each a small slice of bread and a small bit of cheese—the two may cost a halfpenny—and a glass of table beer. I can't eat cheese, so I may eat dry bread. The beer is very good when it's fresh, but it gets partly or quite sour before we've got through the barrel; but we must drink it through before another can be bought. There is a dinner on Sunday, but only odds and ends, to deter anybody from having a Sunday's dinner, for we are asked every Saturday night if any one dines at home on Sunday. In our house nearly all are improvers or apprentices, which makes bad diet worse, when such young girls have to put up with it."

From Letter LXXVI, October 31st, 1850

To show the wretched remuneration paid to mantle-makers, and its rapid reduction, I give the following statement from a mantle-maker of the skilled class, who had, in the winter of 1849–50, received from a West-end house the higher rate of remuneration mentioned:

"I worked," she said, "for a house which does not go to the expense of purchasing the fashionable patterns, but depends upon the few who do send to Paris for them, by giving those who work for the houses having patterns from Paris mantles to make to those patterns. I applied as usual, but was informed that they could get them beautifully made for little better than half what they had been accustomed to pay for them last season, and so I was obliged to take them, as half a loaf is better than none. These houses find no difficulty in getting them done, as those persons who employ a number of young people will take them at any price. If you remonstrate with the draper, and say that it is impossible to do them at the price, the answer is, that you must pay your work-people accordingly, which is about as much as to say—'Go into the streets, you and all you employ, and make it out that way. What do we care what you do? What is it to us so long as we make money out of you?' "...

A pale woman, with a feeble look, whom I found at work making caps, gave me the following account. Her room was a small attic, and its principal furniture was a Waterloo bed, with its decent curtain. There were also two tables, six chairs, a painted chest of drawers, and some other articles of furniture in much greater profusion than is usual in the rooms of the poor. This was accounted for by the husband being a bedstead-maker, and having made the other furniture partly himself, or having bartered bedsteads for it. She said:

"I got married out of a place where I had saved a few pounds, between four and

A dressmakers' workroom

five years back. My mother was a milliner, working for a cheap shop; so I was taught the use of my needle for cap-making and such like, before I went to service. My husband's earnings won't keep us both. He doesn't clear 12s. a week the year through, at least not more than 12s. at his trade, and no man works harder; but then he works for what they call a slaughter-house. I have 4½d. per dozen for making these plain fronts. I find nothing but thread, and a pennyworth will make three dozen fronts, which I can make in a day, from seven in the morning to seven or eight at night. I reckon I clear 1s. a day on whatever work I get from Messrs. ——, my present employers. I am not fully employed, but I earn 4s. a week, not less, all the year through. Our rent is 1s. 4d. a week, which is considered cheap for this room, and there is again 1s. 6d. a week for part of a room where my husband works with another man, a chair maker, as there's not room for his work here, and the landlord would object to it. These caps are what we call 'fronts and whiskers.' [The "front" was a ribbon with blonde round it, the "whisker" fully frilled blonde.] I sometimes, when I'm not on for shop, make some on my own account. They used to be called 'lappets.' They are made up plain, because some customers like to trim them themselves; but the trimming's never so well done after the cap's made; but customers such as I mean will half cover them with flowers or ribbons. It takes 2½ yards of blonde to make one of these fronts. At three-farthings a yard, that makes the stuff cost 2d. all but half a farthing; then there's thread and making, there's 2d. say for candles, and a shopkeeper will offer 2s. 6d. a dozen for them, or as low as 2s., which is the price of the stuff. They are not so well made as those I am doing now—nothing like it. I can make half as many again in the time.

"If a capmaker takes in plain caps a shopkeeper will say, 'They are never asked for now; only trimmed caps.' If we take in 'trimmed,' then he says, 'Plain caps are more wanted; people like to trim them themselves;' all to beat down the prices, and I don't think the public's any cheaper served. My trade would be far better if there wasn't so many respectable young women, living with their parents, who work at it for next to nothing, just for pocket-money, and because it's better than being idle, and they consider themselves too good to go to service, or too delicate to 'make place' (fill a servant's place), and so they earn 3s. or 4s. a week at cap or bonnet making. It buys them clothes perhaps. I live a good deal on tea. My husband has tea, too, three times a day, four days in the week, and sometimes with beef sausages, or a rasher, or a bit of fish with it. Always a meat dinner on Sunday, and a pint of beer, but beer at no other time. Fire at my husband's work-place and here where we live costs 2s. 6d. a week, but he only wants a fire sometimes. I can't work without one, I get so chilled if I do. If my husband fell sick and continued sick two or three weeks, or less, there's only the parish to look to. We make both ends meet as it is, and that's all. If I had any family I don't know what we should do."

HATTERS

From Letter LXXVII, November 7th, 1850

The earnings of the *finishers* and *shapers* [*of hats*] are higher than those of the body-makers, in the proportion of 40s. to 30s., or thereabouts; so that a clever body-maker generally aims at following one or other of those branches. From a shaper I had the following statement:

"I served my apprenticeship in London, and have been a journeyman, off and on, in town, for twenty-two years. I could earn three guineas a week twenty years ago, and seldom earned less than £2. I saved money then, and might have saved more, but I am well satisfied as it is, and needn't have much fear when a rainy day comes. The trade is not what it was, but I make from 35s. to 40s. still in a busy time, and from 20s. to 25s. or 28s. in a slack. Hatters are an independent set of men still, but they were more so. If a master said a word that wasn't deserved, when I first knew the trade, a journeyman would put on his coat and walk out, and perhaps get work at the next shop. It's different now. The 'fouls' have become more numerous, and we are afraid of letting them into good shops, though I don't know why we should be afraid, for few of them can work well enough. None indeed can work well enough on the best stuff. There used to be far more drinking among hatters when I was a lad. I have known some of them be steady and industrious for the week, and on a Saturday night order 'a bottle of wine in a white bottle' (decanter), just for themselves. A man was almost forced to drink a lot of beer at that time in a workshop, or he would be counted a sneak. Now we do just as we like in that way. I am now a shaper in silk, but I am master of all branches of the business. There has been very little change in the fashion the brims are worn in, during my time. Not in the best work. If you see hats with odd shapes in a shop window, marked 'the slap-up,' or 'the Corinthian,' they're slop-made things generally, and don't take. Working hatters have been greatly affected in the way of their earnings from the French hats. In my opinion they've been reduced in their earnings beyond what good they get from cheap provisions. There's less employ, for one thing—as a man will make three good silk hats, and some will make four, in as short a time as he can make two good stuff hats. But we must just make the best of it.". . .

From a highly respectable woman, whom I found at work, assisted by one of her daughters, a young girl of 17 or 18, I had the following account of hat binding, which may be taken as a correct statement of the average earnings of the out-door workwomen in the fair trade:

"I have been a binder," she said, "for twenty years. I was brought up to it by my friends, who were in the line, and soon after I worked for myself I got married. I have worked at it ever since, except when the care of my children prevented me. I married a journeyman hatter. He is now on three days' work a week, and earns 13s. or 14s., or a little more, in those three days. I think most hat binders marry hatters. I have earned 30s. a week fifteen or eighteen years ago, but now I must work hard indeed to earn 10s. Sometimes, when work is slack, I earn 6s. a week. Out of that I have to provide my own thread, which costs 2d. to 3d. for a dozen hats. Prices for binding have fallen gradually and gradually since the silk hats came in, and there have been more hands brought in or come in as binders. Ten years ago, or rather more, I had 6s. a dozen for binding and lining, where I now have 2s. 6d. or 3s. I once left a shop because I was paid only 4s. and 4s. 6d. a dozen, and now they are done for that shop at 2s. 6d. and 3s.—poor women under-sell one another so. They go to the masters and offer to do binding at next to nothing, and so prices have fallen.

"I generally work ten, and sometimes thirteen hours a day. I believe it's women who have not been regularly brought up to the hat binding that undersell us. I have heard that some of them are on the streets, but I think not any who were brought up among their friends as hat-binders. They would suffer much before that, I'm satisfied. I have 3s. 6d. a dozen for binding these hats (pointing to a heap), which are the largest size; smaller sizes run 2d. or 3d. a dozen less. Most shops have some difference in their prices to trimmers. When silk hats first came in it was very hard work for the fingers—it was like sewing through a piece of board; now it's quite easy in comparison. We are forced to put up with such prices as we can get—even the best hands among us are, and there's a great difference both in neatness and quickness; for if I myself, for instance, refused to take a lower price, there's plenty will jump at it. So we injure one another, and make rich people richer. With our family my husband and I did better when wages was good and work plenty, and bread and meat dearer, than now that bread is cheap and wages and employment fallen off. With what we earn at present we couldn't have clothed and educated our children so decently as we have.". . .

I have already spoken of the little masters. They are divisible under two heads. Some, and for the most part elderly men, are little masters, working for the general public, or rather for a "connection" (though with no shop or even a window for display); and they employ from one to seven hands, or carry on their business by their personal labour, altogether unaided, in the slackest times. In those times they work both on their own account and on speculation; providing their own material, when speculating in their labour, and hawking their manufacture for sale to the lower priced hatmakers, or to the better hatmakers inclined to give a tolerable price—or what they account tolerable—for skilled labour. They speculate prin-cipally in silk bodies; some, however, finish the hat. From one of the better class of little masters I had this statement. My informant was an elderly man, residing in a comfortable house, and had known the trade familiarly for many years:

"I started as a little master," he said, "about 20 years back. I supply the trade with bodies sometimes, and find my own material. Mine is very uncertain work—it's mostly a summer trade. I work for my private customers, or for the trade, on order; and I make bodies to carry out to the trade for sale on speculation. I only do the best work in bodies to carry out. I have earned £3, £3 5s., and £2 18s., when a journeyman at ——'s. If a man didn't earn his £2 a week in those days, he was reckoned not worth his plank room. That's far better than being a little master, as far as money goes, for I consider that one week with another, for all I have a connection, I only make 22s. I mightn't have started for myself, but I fell in with some overbearing masters and foremen.

"I've had as many as four journeymen working up stairs, and four down stairs, for me in this house; now I've only myself; but the brisk season's over. I get 10s. 6d. a dozen for my bodies, and am oft enough bid 8s. 6d., because bodies can be bought for less than that, but they're rubbish. The stuff costs me 5s. There's Mr. ——, he'll give 8s. a dozen always for the better sort of bodies, and I've gone to him sometimes in a pet, and as a last resource. Though mine are real good bodies, a master or foreman will 'star them' (crush them), pretending to examine their quality, but just to show his power—foremen are worse than masters that way—and I then have to make them over again partly. Out of six dozen I've taken into ——'s, I've had three dozen starred, and had to take them back. It was nothing but to show power.

"I can make a dozen of my bodies in a day and a half. A young fellow by working very long hours may make a dozen, but they're only fit for the lowest gossamers, the 'four-and-nines.' They're bad work; there's too much water used in them. There's such a difference in trade, that I could keep a wife and five children better nineteen years ago—my youngest is turned 19—than I can keep myself now. I think little masters are increasing. I used to reckon that master hatters got 12s. a hat profit on the best stuff, and that was one thing to tempt me to start for myself; but a little master can't command a trade in the best articles. I reckon there's 2s. profit a hat in silk; but at this part (Walworth), if you walk out, you'll see 500 silks to 20 stuffs. A stuff will wear two silks at least. A four-and-nine can be supplied to a shopkeeper at 3s. 6d."

The other, and by far the most numerous, class of little masters I have already described. From one of the class I received the following account. He was a pale, weak-eyed looking man, with a stoop, as if contracted by leaning over his work. When I saw him he was busy at work in the garret of an old and apparently frail house, the narrow stairs seeming to bend under the tread. The walls of his room had been recently white-washed. A penny sheet almanac was pinned over the fire-place, and was almost illegible from the smoke it was exposed to, "when the wind was in the north," the man said. The furniture was a small bed, covered by a thin but clean rug, on a heavy old frame, a table, two chairs, a stool, a hatter's plank, fitted below the small window, a kettle, a gridiron, and a few pots and pans.

"I was a weaver in the north," he said; "never mind where. I left home in a bit of a scrape, but for nothing dishonest, and so we'll say nothing about that. I was a fool, and that's a fact. I had £9 or £10 to call my own, fairly, and I came to London, as fools often do. I found I could as soon have got work at being a lawyer as at my own trade—so, as I had an acquaintance a hatter, he said to me, 'learn hatting.' I bargained with him, and wish I hadn't. I paid my friend, for learning me a bad trade, two guineas; he wanted £3, and then 50s. It's between three and four years ago, and I worked for him a month for nothing, finding myself. Before my month was up my money ran taper, and I was afeard I shouldn't have enough left to start me, but I had. I took this very room as you see me in, and gave 30s. for the sticks, just as an old cobbler, that died in that very bed, had left them. The landlady took his traps for burying him. She's really a good soul. That was £2 2s. gone; and two hat irons, one 14lb. and the other 10lb., cost me 2s. 9d. at a sale. They are old things. Here they are still. But they cost 3d. a pound new.

I got twelve blocks at 1s. a-piece second-hand. They cost 4s. to 5s. a-piece new, and they would have been about as cheap new, for they wasn't just in the fashion; two of them in particular, and I paid 2s. a-piece to get them 'turned down' again, and put into the fashionable shape, for you must work fashionable. A plank and a table cost me 4s. 9d., second-hand of course. I paid 5s. for the calico and gums to make my first twelve bodies to begin with, and I set to work. The bigger fool for it. It took me a day and a half, or 19 hours to make the dozen—I can do it in 13 or 14 hours now—and I took them to Mr. —— for sale. I asked him 8s. 6d., as I thought he would reckon that low, and it would recommend me, for my friend got 10s. Mr. —— said 'Pooh, I can get better at 7s.,' but I got 7s. 6d. for them; and if I had asked him 7s., he'd have said 'I can get better at 6s.' I carry on this way still.

"I had a bit of a demand the autumn before last for bodies, and I got a man to help me, and I made 18s. a week for four weeks, and 16s. for the next week, and the next week to that only 4s. I can't tell what made the brisk, exactly; but I thought I was doing rarely, and I took an apprentice; his parents is poor people, close by. I gave him nothing. I was to teach him his trade—there's no indenture or anything of that sort—for two months, and then he was to have half of what he brought me in; but he and his father and mother cut away after I'd had him three weeks, and I've never seen him since. I've gone on this way all along, living from hand to mouth very often. I'm not treated like a Christian by some of the shops I take my bodies to. Last winter I was often starving. I've gone out with half-a-dozen bodies in a morning, and have brought them back at night, without a farthing in my pocket: of course I couldn't break my fast. I've gone to bed to try and sleep off the hunger—gone there at four o'clock, as I had neither fire nor candle, and have kept waking every hour, a dreaming that I was eating and drinking. I suppose it was the gnawing at my stomach that caused the dream. I was three weeks in arrear for rent, too, at 18d. a week, but my landlady's very good.

"I hardly know what I make a week, take the year through; perhaps 6s. or 7s. a week; some weeks only 4s., some weeks 10s. or 12s., or more. I've been rather in luck these three or four last weeks as I haven't made—that is, I haven't cleared —less than 10s. 6d. a week. But if I do make 10s. at this time (October), what is it? Fire costs me 5d. a day—say for six days. I'm out the rest of the week, when I'm busiest. That's 2s. 6d.; candles is 1s. for the time I'm at work; rent's 1s. 6d., and 3d. extra to rub off an arrear that's out this week. How much is that?" 5s. 3d. "Then there's 5s. 3d. left to live on. I live mostly on coffee, three times a day, with bread and butter. If I can't afford butter, I toast the bread. I gave ½d. for this old fork to do it with. It's better that way than dry. Sometimes I have one or two, or three, fresh or salt herrings for dinner, that cost 1½d. or 2d.; or sometimes only 1d., or ½ lb. of beef sausages, that cost 2d. common, or 2½d. better; but what's ½ lb. sausages for a man like me, that, when it's wanted, gets out of his bed at daylight, and goes to his plank? That sort of living costs 7d. or 8d., or 9d. a day. Beer I very seldom taste. Tobacco 2d. for three days: it puts off the hunger. I've always worked by myself, but perhaps I could do better at working with two or three mates. Sometimes my bodies have been starred, and I've had to set to work, half starving, on a Sunday, to make them good again; but that hasn't happened lately."

From an elderly man I had the following account of his "going on tramp"

22 years ago. I give it to show what the system then was; there is comparatively little of it at present:

"There's no doubt," he said, "that many a hatter went on tramp, and got to like the life, when he needn't have gone, if he'd looked out fairly for work. When I started from London, I needn't have gone if I hadn't liked it, if I'd exerted myself; but I wanted a change. I made for Lancashire. I had 1½d. a mile allowed then, and a bed at every 'lawful town.' Sometimes, if the society's house, which was always a public-house, was small, and full, I had half a bed—for other societies used the house, and I have slept with tailors, and curriers, and other trades on tramp. Sometimes the landlord bedded me out. It was a pleasant life enough. You saw something new every day, and the fresh air and exercise made a man as strong as a horse. I know plenty of men in different trades that wouldn't thank you for work—they liked tramping better.

"I got good work at Oldham, and after that came to London, or I might have become one of that sort myself. When I went to work at first, after tramping, I didn't feel quite settled for a week or so. I've seen some queer doings among tramps. One was regularly joined by a woman as soon as he left a town, and she quitted him just before he went into one, if it was a small place, though a 'lawful town,' or she might be noticed with him. She sold laces, and was no better than she should be, so tramp money went to help to keep her. A tramp's was a jolly life enough, but it's different now. But I reckon I should be very sorry to see the allowance to tramps done away with, for I think it helps to keep a man more independent, and prevents many a hand from having to work at under wages as he might be driven to do otherwise.". . .

IV
MERCHANT MARINES

SEAMEN AFLOAT

From Letter XL, March 7th, 1850

I purpose directing my attention in this and the following letters, first, to the state of the *seaman afloat*—after which I purpose following him *ashore*, and describing the impositions which are there practised upon him. . . .

A man who was much more than bronzed—as he was actually red in the face and neck—gave me the following statement. He had free and jovial manners, but sometimes evinced much feeling, especially when speaking of the emigrant ships. He wore three shirts—a clean one over two which were not perfectly clean—for he could not bear, he said, to show dirty linen. This happened only, however, he told me, when he was "out on the spree," for then he was in the habit of buying a clean white shirt as soon as he wanted "a change," and putting it on over his soiled one, in order to obviate the necessity of carrying his dirty linen about with him; so that by the stratification of his shirts he could always compute the duration of "the lark." He wore only a jacket, and felt inconvenience, when on the spree, in having a dirty shirt to carry about; and to obviate this he adopted the plan I have mentioned:

"I was *boatswain of an emigrant ship [to Australia]* last voyage. They were Government emigrants we had on board. The ship was 380 tons according to the new mode of measurement, and 500 tons according to the old mode. She had eight able men before the mast, four apprentices, a second mate, steward, cook, first mate, and captain. In addition to these, there were eight supernumeraries. You see, sir, all the Government emigrant and convict ships are obliged to take out four men and a boy to each 100 tons. We were near upon 400 tons burden; so we were obligated to have 16 able seamen and four boys; but, as I told you before, we had only eight able seamen. To make up the deficiency, we shipped eight supernumeraries. These supernumeraries were no sailors at all—not able to go aloft—couldn't put their foot above the shearpole. They were mostly men that the Government had refused to assist to emigrate. The shipping masters had put them on blue jackets, and told them the names of ships to say they had served in, so as to get them a berth. The shipping masters will get them a register, ticket and all; and these are the men who are taken in preference to us, because they go upon nominal wages of a shilling a month. I tell you what it is, sir. I saw to-day half a dozen of these fellows taken instead of six good able-bodied seamen, who were left to walk the streets: that's the candid fact, sir. It's a shameful thing to see the way we are treated. We are not treated like men at all; and what's more, there's no dependence to be placed on us now. If a war was to break out with America, there's thousands of us would go over to the other country. We're worse than the black slaves; they are taken care of, and we are not.

"On board ship they can do anything with us they think proper. If in case you are a spirited man, and speaks a word against an officer that tyrannicalises over you, he will put you in irons, and stop your money—six days for one: for every day you're in irons he stops six days' pay, and may be forfeits your whole wages. There's as good men now before the mast as there is abaft of it. It ain't the same now as it used to be. Our fathers and mothers, you see, gives us all a little education, and we're now able to see and feel the wrongs that are put upon us; and if in case people doesn't do better for us than they do now, why, they'll turn pirates. The navy is just as much dissatisfied as the merchant seamen. If a war was to come with France, we might turn out against them—for we owe them a grudge for old times past. For myself, I can't abear the hair of a Frenchman's head. It would never do not to stand by the little island again the Mounseers; but, again America, I'd never fire a shot! They have got feeling for a seaman there. There's no people running after you there to rob you. The pay's a great deal better, too, and the food twice as good as in the English ships. There's no stint of anything; but in this country they do everything they can to rob a seaman. They're cutting our allowance of bread down from one pound to three-quarters, and our sugar is reduced from one pound to three-quarters as well; and they're trying to cut down our wages to 35s. a month besides. But what's it matter what they give us? They can trump up any charge they please again us, or they can tyrannicalize over us till a man's blood can't stand it, and then can stop as much as they like, and we can't say nothing again it.

"I was out thirteen months and a half. I went away last Christmas-eve twelve-month, and I arrived in London the 8th of February last; and what do you think I got, sir, for the whole of my service—for risking my life, for working all hours, in all weathers—what do you think I got, sir? Why, I had £10 2s.—that's it, sir—for thirteen months and a half. I ought to have received about £32. My wages as boatswain were £2 10s. a month. I have had £4 and £3 10s. for the same duty. But the little petty owners is cutting down the wages as low as they can, till they're almost starving us and our families. The rest of the money that was due to me was stopped, because I spoke out for my rights; and five of the other hands was served in the same manner. The owners saved near upon a hundred pounds in this way; and, what's more, they were not satisfied with this. The owners (I give you my word) stopped one pound more out of the little that was coming to us, for a charitable institution as they called it. What it was I don't know. The petty owners take every advantage on us they can. They can build their new ships—one or two every year—and they gets them all out of fleecing us. I tell you what it is—such men will be the ruin of the country, sir; for the tars that kept the little island in old times is now discontented to a man.

"The reason why the owners stopped our pay was because we spoke out when the ship was short of hands. There was only four able men in her, and there should have been eight; so we had to do double work all of us, night and day. We complained to the captain that the ship was short-handed. But, you see, the wages for able seamen is more in foreign countries than in England; so, to keep the ship's expenses down, the captains object to take on fresh hands in foreign ports. Well, the captain promised us to get some new men at Sydney, but he went to sea short-handed as we were. So we axed him again to get fresh hands, as the ship was leaky, and we wanted our full complement of men; but he refused to do so, because the wages at the next port was nearly double the pay in London; and then we told him we wouldn't do any more work. This he called a mutiny, and our wages was stopped to near upon £20 a man.

"The usual rate of pay in an emigrant ship for an able seaman is £2 a month. The tonnage varies from 200 to 1,000. Ships of 200 are not safe to go as far as Sidney or New Zealand; but that the owners don't trouble their heads about, so long as they can get their ship full of emigrants. The greater number of emigrant ships are about 500 tons. To understand how many emigrants can be comfortably accommodated in a ship, I should first tell you that in the best ships the emigrants are divided—that is, the single people are separated from the married; the single men are for'ard, the married people are 'midships, and the single women aft. In a vessel of such an arrangement not more than sixty emigrants to every 100 tons can be taken out with comfort. I have known near upon 100 emigrants taken out to each 100 tons—that is to say, I have known a ship of 380 tons have as many as 380 emigrants on board." (A carpenter, who had made his two last voyages in emigrant ships, here said "That is too often the case, I am sorry to say.") "A ship of 380 tons could take conveniently about 240 or 250 emigrants."

The carpenter corroborated this, and told me that it is his duty to go down between decks each day, to open the scuttles and ports, so as to ventilate the ship, and he has frequently seen a man and his wife and three or four children all huddled up and almost stifled in a double berth (only a berth for two people). The death of some child has occurred almost every day in the ship. In bad weather, when the hatches are kept on and tarpaulined over, often for two or three days at a time, the heat between the decks of an emigrant ship is as bad as the hold of a slave ship in the middle passage. The usual allowance in an emigrant ship of the best class is six foot by two foot. But "I have often seen," the carpenter said, "the poor people, in some of the worst ships, stowed away for'ard so close that you might have said they were 'in bulk.' There were thirty people in thirty feet space. I know, as a carpenter, that many of the emigrant ships are not fit to bring home a cargo; though, as the owners say, they are quite fit to take emigrants out. I have seen right through the top sides (the timbers above the copper-sheating) of many of them—the planks have warped with the heat of the sun. A man has often to carry an emigrant ship in his arms, from one port to another, for the hands are always at the pumps. It may astonish the public that so many emigrants are lost, but we ships'-carpenters are only astonished that there are so few."

The boatswain here continued: "The carpenter has told you nothing but the truth. In the worst class ships there is scarcely any separation of the sexes. A partition is certainly run up between the sleeping-berths; but as these do not reach the top, any one can make it convenient to get over, or look over, the partition into the next berth. There is scarcely a young single woman who emigrates that keeps her character on board o' ship, and after that she mostly makes her appearance on the town in Sidney. I'm speaking of those who go out unprotected; and what else can be expected, sir, among a parcel of sailors? The captains and doctors often set the example, and the mates and the sailors, of course, imitate their superior officers. There has been no chaplain on board the emigrant ships that I have been in. Some captains read prayers once on a Sunday, but many don't; and I have often known a ship go right away from London to Sidney, without divine service ever being performed. The Government emigrants, I believe, usually pay about £7 per head, and those who are not sent out by the Government pay from £18 to £20 for the passage. For this sum they are found in provisions. There is a certain scale of provisions allowed; but this is almost nominal, for the greater number of emigrant ships carry false weights, and the allowance served out is generally short, by at least a quarter." (I could hardly credit that the spirit of commercial trickery had reached even the high seas, and that shipowners had taken to false weights as a means of enabling them to undersell their brother merchants. On inquiring, however, I was assured that the practice was becoming *common*.)

"Again, the quality of the food is of the worst kind. There are regular Government surveyors to overhaul the provisions of such ships; but, Lord love you! they are easily got to windward of. The captain, under the directions of the owners, puts some prime stuff among the top casks, and all the rest is old condemned stores—rotten beef and pork, that's positively green with putrefaction—and the biscuits are all weevilly; indeed they're so full of maggots, that the sailors say they're as rich as Welsh rabbits, when toasted. The poor things who emigrate have no money to lay in their own private stock of food, and so they're wholly dependent on the ship's stores; and often they run so short that they're half-starved, and will come and beg a mouthful of the sailors. They're not allowed above one-third of what the sailors have. *We* have one pound and a half of meat, and they don't get above half a pound, and that's several ounces short from false weights. They have three quarts of water served out to them every day, and that very often of the filthiest description. It's frequently rotten and stinking; but, bad as it is, it's not enough for the poor people to cook with, and make their tea and coffee morning and evening. I have seen plenty of the emigrants hard put to with thirst —they would give anything for a drop to wet their lips with.

"From all I have seen of the emigrant ships, I believe it's a system of robbery from beginning to end. There are gentlemen shipowners who treat their men and the passengers justly and fairly. These are mostly the owners of the largest ships; but of late years a class of petty owners has sprung up—people who were clerks of the large owners a few years back—and they take every opportunity of tricking all in their pay. These men, I say again, will be the ruin of the country, unless something is done to protect the sailors against them. They're driving the tars out of the country as fast as they can. Convicts, when taken out, are very well treated; *the owners are obliged to take care of them*; there's a captain of marines to look after them, and it's quite wonderful how differently they fare to the poor emigrants. I never knew the convicts to be badly treated on board of ship, but I've known the emigrants to be so continually. You see the emigrants are poor people, and have no one to look after them."

From Letter XLI, March 11th, 1850

I had the following narrative concerning the *South American trade* from a sedate and intelligent man, who had all his "papers" with him, his watch, and was well-dressed, and with every appearance of what is called a "substantial" man. Previous to the voyage from South America, he had served on board Australian emigrant ships, and fully confirmed what was told me by others, as to the practice of giving short weight on board many of those ships, and as to the conduct of some of the captains, surgeons, and officers towards the unprotected female emigrants. I have, however, been at considerable pains to inquire into the truth of the statement given in my last letter. This I have thought it just to do, in consequence of a communication, received from a shipowner, denying the whole narrative. The result of my inquiries is, that I find the boatswain's account borne out most fully by persons of the highest respectability and the greatest experience. I have made a point of seeing one of the mates whose duty it is to serve out the provisions, both to the emigrants and crew. I am assured that the meat is often one-third short weight, and that the men are sometimes excited to acts of insubordination on purpose that a part of their wages may be stopped:

"I have been a seaman eighteen years," he said, "and my last voyage was to Port Phillip and Callao. I served on board a barque of 642 tons on the voyage from Port Phillip. I reached that place in another ship, and there I shipped for Callao. We had twelve able seamen before the mast, two ordinary seamen, steward, cook, first and second mates, carpenter, boatswain, and master. By rights, I consider that we ought to have had two more able seamen, but for all that she was better manned than ships usually are. They do leave the port of London so short-handed, that many accidents, and great loss of life rise from it. You see, a seaman doesn't know how many hands are to be shipped until he comes to sign the articles, and it's too late to say anything again it then. So they oft enough ship cheap foreign fellows at any foreign port, and a good man has to bear everything. That sort of thing, I can tell you, and from my own knowledge, gets worse and worse. They'll often try to knock off a good man to save his wages, or, to spite him, put him to jobs that they think he'll refuse; and they put him to them just to make him refuse, and so save the owners' money, and get favour with them. We are so treated that we are all dissatisfied; we talk of it on board ship. Plenty say that if a war broke out they would not fight for such a country as this; far more say they would rather fight against this country in an American ship than against America in an English or any ship. I fought for the country at St. Jean d'Acre, under the Hon. Captain Waldegrave, and I would fight for it again, bad as it is, but there's ten to one the other way. I have had many a dispute about it on board ship, and have been many a time abused by the hour together by my shipmates for saying I was willing to fight for the country.

"In my last voyage from Port Phillip to Callao, and then to London, I had £3 10s. a month as able seaman. I consider that I ought to have had £4 for going round the Horn on a homeward voyage only. From London to Callao and back £3 a month would be fair. In my last voyage we had very good provisions, and a fair proportion of them. In my voyage out the provisions were very bad. We had, last voyage, neither false weight, nor any imposition of that sort, but I know that such things are common. They do so try to cheat the seamen that way, that it oft causes great disturbances. We had a good captain, but a strict man in regard of duty. He had worked his way from the 'hawse-pipes aft,' and knew every branch. He was a seaman, every inch of him. But I have met with many an officer not fit to be trusted with either life or property at sea. In my last ship there was really nothing for a reasonable man to complain of, except in the berths, which were both too small and too large, as some were meant for double berths. We shipped a sea off

the Horn, and the forecastle was drenched, and we had to sleep on wet beds three
or four nights. The captain offered to give us a sail, and let us sleep on the guano
that we had on board. In the small berths we were scrouged up like pigs in a stye—
hardly room to move. We brought home a cargo of guano from the Chinqua
Islands. We first got sufficient guano to ballast the ship, and for that we discharged our old ballast.

"The way the guano is put on board is this. The guano is in cliffs—we call it
'the mountain'—it runs to a certain depth, and it's all stone at the bottom. From
the sea it looks like a rocky mountain; there's nothing green about it—it's the
colour of stone there. They say it's the ordure of birds, but I have my doubts about
that, as there could never be birds, I fancy, to make that quantity. Why, I have
seen as much guano on the Chinqua Islands—they're about two degrees south of
Callao, on the coast of Peru—as would take thousands of ships twenty years to
bring away. There are great flocks of birds about the guano places now, chiefly
small web-footed birds. Some burrow in the ground like a rabbit. Among the
larger birds are pelicans, plenty of them. A flock of them has a curious appearance.
I have seen hundreds of them together. There is plenty of penguins, too, and
plenty of seals, but the British ships are not allowed to capture them. I believe
the Peruvian Government prevents it. A Peruvian man-of-war, a schooner, lies
there.

"The guano is put on board this way: We have two 'shoots.' A shoot is made
of canvas, equally square on all sides. The diggers bring the guano a quarter of a
mile, to the shore. A place is prepared on the side of the guano mountain, by the
sea, railed off for security with what you would call a hurdle, but it's very strong
bamboo cane. There the diggers empty their bags, through an open place into
the shoot which is spread below, and held by ropes. The shoot is then lowered
down from the guano mountain by the diggers, and the seamen who hold the
ropes to regulate it must keep the lines a moving, to keep the guano from choking
(going foul) in the shoots. We must regulate it by the pitch of the ship. The ship
is moved alongside, and so the shoot is emptied down the hatchways at a favourable moment. There is a very strong smell about the guano mountain. It oft makes
people's noses bleed. The diggers on shore and trimmers in the ship have to keep
handkerchiefs round their noses, with oakum inside the handkerchiefs. It affects
the eyes, too; no trimmer can work more than fifteen or twenty minutes at a time.
The seamen are not employed in digging or trimming; they used to be in trimming
in 1843. The diggers and trimmers are labourers who live on the guano mountain
(it's an island), to do that work. I believe the trimmers have two dollars a day
when at work. The diggers have so much a bag. I don't know how much, as we
weren't allowed on the island, except with the captain's leave. They have built
huts of sticks on the mountain; the diggers have covered them with flags—that's
a sort of bulrush that grows on the coast; others are covered over with mats. There
were a few women there, but no bad women.

"The diggers are chiefly foreigners, but there are a very few English and Scotch.
Perhaps there's 100 of them in all. They don't look sickly. Nothing grows on the
guano mountain; there is not even a sea-weed at the water's edge. Guano is an
unpleasant cargo until you get used to it on board ship. At first the ship smelt
as if she was laden with hartshorn. I have picked large lumps of salt, like smelling
salts, out of the guano." I may add that a cargo of guano was being unladen at

the West India Dock on one of my visits there. It was hoisted out of the hold in bags, and had altogether the smell of very strong and unsound cheese. The whole atmosphere of the ship was cheesy. Some of the guano, which had been spoiled by salt water, had the appearance of yellow mud or slime.

A seaman, who was recommended to me as a trusty and well-conducted man, gave me the following statement as to the *African trade*:

"I have been fifteen years a seaman, and my last voyage was to the *Gold Coast, in Africa*. I sailed in a brig of under 200 tons. We had five able seamen, first and second mates, cook, steward, captain, and an apprentice. I was second mate. The able seamen had £2 7s. 6d. a month, which I think not sufficient, and they had to find their own stores besides, though they were charged a fair price on board. Men are generally dissatisfied, and a great many say they would never fight for such a country as this, 'specially not against America, nor stick to the country at all if they could get away. I am a married man myself, and so I suppose I must fight for the country if a war broke out. It's a great hardship on a married man that his wife cannot be allowed a portion of his wages during her husband's absence; but there's hardly an owner in London will allow monthly notes for the wives, and some that do allow them don't pay them, or pay them irregularly. I know one young married woman who had nothing for eighteen months her husband was away at sea. What's to become of such women? Half of them left that way go on the town to keep them from starving.

"Ours was a ship of the best sort as regards its management and accommodation—no false weights and no humbug about fines or such like, to cheat the men and please the owners; but there's a great deal of it about. Messrs. —— are good men to have to do with, and the owners in the African trade are good men generally. It's your cheap owners mostly in other trades that pluck every feather out of a seaman if they can, and they always can somehow. Provisions were good and plenty in my last ship; grog at the master's option. Very few ships now give it as an allowance. When we reached the Gold Coast we put ourselves in communication with a consignee. We took out a general cargo, and brought back ground-nuts, ivory, gold dust, and palm oil. The great thing is palm oil. The consignee trades with the natives, giving them cowries—they're shells that are the money there—cloth, beads, cotton, iron pots, and other things, in exchange for the cargo home.

"We very seldom went on shore on the west coast of Africa, on account of the surf. It's very few places where you can land with a boat. I have known that coast for five years, and I have been on shore. The place was green enough, but was very sickly. The natives come on board in their canoes; as they are all naked, they get through the surf in their canoes well enough, and if the canoe be capsized they swim ashore, for they are like fish in the water. They come to sell yams, or birds, or anything they have, and some of them are good hands, rather, at a bargain. No women come with them, and the seamen are not allowed to visit the women on shore. If a man be ashore a day or two he generally has the fever when he gets on board again. Masters go off the quickest, as they are most ashore. I don't think they drink. There were some fine strong fellows among the natives; some had a few words of English; all that knew any English could swear; they soon pick that up; it's like their A B C among sailors.

"I never was up any of the rivers. We generally leave the cargoes at different

places along the west coast. There is no regular harbour on the Gold Coast, not,
I believe, until you get down to the Bight of Benin. We may lie a week or ten days
where we discharge most cargo, and then the men can't get ashore; plenty would
if they could, but I think it's not worth the risk. We often had talk on board
about African travellers, such as Mungo Park. Sailors are more intelligent than
they used to be. It's a dull coast. It seems mountainous in some parts, and with
valleys in others, but all looks dull and dead. Indeed, you can't see much of the
coast, for you see it chiefly at the forts. The mortality there is great; the white
people die the quickest. I heard a captain say that out of twenty-one clerks he
had taken out there seventeen had died. It must be a very profitable trade to
those on shore who can stand the climate, or they wouldn't stay there, leading
such dull lives. Many seamen won't go there. We get no provisions from the
shore but a pig a week (generally), or what they call a sheep, but its neither one
thing nor the other. It's not woolly, but hairy, like a goat—though it *is* a sheep.
It weighs perhaps from 15 lb. to 25 lb. I once killed one that was 13 lb. The flavour
is pretty good, but there is no fat about the ribs; between the ribs, indeed, there's
just the skin, like a pig's bladder. We generally make a mess of a whole sheep, with
the yams; what we call sea-pie. I now like yams as well as potatoes. I brought over
one yam that weighed 18 lb.

"The great dissatisfaction of seamen generally, is the lowness of their wages.
Look how the Americans are paid, and then look at this. In the African trade, and
other trades, a man may be employed nine months out of the twelve, and if he
averages £2 2s. a month, which is a liberal reckoning, why he has £18 18s. a year,
and perhaps a wife and family to keep. What's £18 18s.? I would never go to that
African coast again, only I make a pound or two in birds. We buy parrots—grey
parrots chiefly—of the natives, who come aboard in their canoes. We sometimes
pay 6s. or 7s. in Africa for a fine bird. I have known 200 parrots on board; they
made a precious noise; but half the birds die before they get to England. Some
captains won't allow parrots. There's very little desertion on the African coast.
Seamen won't land to desert and wait ashore there for another ship. It's more
than their life is worth."

A very fine looking fellow, as red as a hot climate could make him, with bright
eyes, black curly hair, and a good expression of countenance, next gave me the
following information concerning the *West India trade*:

"I have been at sea," he said, "nearly eleven years, and my last voyage was to the
West Indies—to Kingston, Jamaica. The vessel was a barque of 240 tons. We had
a crew of fourteen, being five able seamen, one ordinary seaman, two boys, cook,
carpenter, steward, chief and second mates, and captain. The wages of the able
seamen were £2 5s. a month. £2 5s. is now the general rate for a voyage to the
West Indies, but I think it isn't sufficient; indeed I'm sure of it. I have had £2 10s.
and £2 15s. for the West Indies from the Clyde. In the Scotch ports and in
Liverpool it's never less than £2 10s. I reckon that London is the worst paid port
in the country. I account for it, because there are so many men here, and some
of them scamps enough to take anything; and then the foreigners that want to go
back will go for anything. I have often sailed with foreign seamen, but never with
a Jew seaman in my life. I see *them* only in the bum-boats in England. The
steward had £2 10s., the cook the same, the carpenter £4, the chief mate £4, the

second mate £2 15s., the ordinary seaman £1 15s. The boys were apprentices.

"The crew were all foreigners, or from British colonies, except myself, the ordinary seamen, the captain, and the boys. Two of the foreigners were very good seamen. They spoke very little English. We agreed very bad—not the foreigners and us—but the captain and us. When we left the Downs, we had very bad weather in the Channel, and two men were laid up sick, and sometimes three. The captain, because he couldn't get the ship worked to his liking, kept calling all hands a 'parcel of d—d soldiers.' She worked very hard with too few hands, such as the complement we had, and dreadful hard when three were laid up. The captain swore terribly. He didn't read prayers—swearing captains do though oft enough—by way of a set-off they say. Nobody can respect prayers from such people. I do from good men.

"I am a Scotchman. My last captain was a good seaman, though not much of a navigator. He pretty well ran the ship ashore in coming into the English Channel off the Scilly Islands. He nearly ran ashore, too, on the French coast, and with a fair wind right up the Channel. From the ignorance I have seen in officers, I am certain it is wrong to let anybody command a ship without his being examined as to his fitness. Young fellows often get the command through favour; they're relations of the owner, or something of that kind, and so they are trusted with men's lives. Our second mate was appointed by the owners, and hardly knew how to knot a yarn. At Kingston the men could go ashore every night, but no women were allowed on board. We took out a general cargo, and brought back a cargo of log-wood, fustic, and black ebony. Me and a darky stowed it all.

"The men that were slaves in Kingston are starving. Those that were working on board our ship had only 2s. a day, and for such work 3s. 6d. is paid in England. It is all stuff that they won't work. They'll work hard enough if anybody will employ them. I have seen 100 of them come down to our ship the last voyage, a few weeks back, and beg for a crust. Me and my mates gave them half our grub to get rid of them, and because we couldn't bear to see them starving. I have heard hundreds of them say, and many a hundred times—for I've been four voyages to the West Indies—that they were far better off when they were slaves, but I never heard them say they wished they were slaves again. There are thousands of blacks in Kingston seeking for work and can't get it. They work pretty hard when at work, but not like an European. No man in the world works harder than an European. There seems no trade in Jamaica now, and all the people is ruined.

"In my last ship our fare was very bad. We had pork and beef—and regular mahogany, you see—1¼lb. of each, and ¾lb. of bread each—for the bread was allowanced—but ¾lb. of bread is too little. We had also rice and flour, but not enough. Grog was at the captain's option. There was no splicing the mainbrace; a glass of grog now and then, when we reefed the topsails, and sometimes not then. I'm sure grog does a man good on board ship, especially in hard weather. To show what things sometimes go on in merchant ships, I will tell you this—a man daren't speak a word for his rights on board ship, or all the officers are down upon him. The pay gets worse, and the accommodation worse still. To show you what may go on in merchant ships, I'll tell you what I know. We were once, and lately too, off the Chinqua Islands, round the Horn, laying for a cargo of guano, just astern of a Bristol full-rigged ship. On a Saturday, as is a usual thing with merchant ships, we sent there for a 'Saturday night's bottle' to drink 'Sweethearts and Wives,' and the skipper said he'd be d——d if he'd give it. His own men persevered in asking him for the bottle, and he went below and came up with a brace of pistols. He fired at one man, and the ball grazed his forehead, and took a bit off the top of his ear; that was the first pistol fired. He was not drunk. He then fired the other pistol, and shot a man dead through the breast. That man took no part at all. The man that was shot never spoke after. We heard the two shots on board our ship. There was then a cry of 'mutiny,' from all the ships in the harbour—about a dozen—a cry of 'mutiny on board the Eleanor, and the captains sent off their officers and crews, with arms, to make peace. Afterwards the captains went aboard and held a council of war, and two men who had threatened to take the Bristol captain's life for shooting their shipmate where chained to the mizen topsail sheets—I saw the men there myself. Our boat and another ship's boat next day took those two men to the Peruvian man-of-war schooner on the station, and what was done in the matter I never heard; but the Peruvian man-of-war and the Bristol ship came together to Callao when we were there, and there we left them. The best way, sir—aye, and the only way, too—to stop desertion, is better usage and better pay, and more to eat, and then never a man would grumble, and there'd be no bad language either—unless when allowable. You may register and register, and go nibbling on, but I tell you it's the only way. In my last ship I had no berth: there was no room in the forecastle to hang up hammocks except for four. The cook slept there every night; he couldn't be disturbed; and the rest took their turns, turn in and turn out, but I never turned in at all, because others had the turn before me. I slept all the time on a water-cask. In the West India trade I have worked 13, and 14, and 16 hours a day, though from six to six is the law of England, and there was no necessity for longer hours, only it was the captain's whim, that was all. A quick voyage was wanted, but good seamanship and good usage—and they often go together—are enough to do that without distressing the men, who are neither so well paid, or so well treated, or so well fed, as to care about the interests of the owner. What's the owner to me? He doesn't care for me, or very seldom; if he did, I'd care for him.". . .

A short man, but evidently of very great strength, brawny and muscular, and with a very good frank expression of countenance, gave me the following account as to the treatment on board the *American ships*:

"I am a *Scotchman* born, but am now *in the American service*, and on board a transit (merchant) ship trading from New York; not a liner, which runs only to one place. I have been in the English service, and was brought up in it. I have served on board one of your English ships that was not fit to go to sea, when she started for Callao. Off the Horn she leaked 350 strokes at the pump an hour. We couldn't sleep in the forecastle for the wet. Some of my shipmates were half dead before we got to Callao. We were always in danger in her, and there's no back way out at sea. The captain and his usage of us was very bad, striking men at the wheel; he once gave her up and cried like a child. She was above 800 tons. The English Consul at Callao wouldn't interfere, and told us, when we complained to him of the state of the ship, that he would do nothing for us, and, for anything he cared, we might all die in the streets. The captain had to ship three crews between Callao, the Clinches—that's the guano mountain—and the port of London. The old crew, all but two or three, were left at Callao. Well, sir, when this ship was at last got to the West India Dock she was patched up, and was then thought good enough for an emigrant ship, and was sent out to Australia with emigrants.

"I have been, off and on, in the American service these last 5 years. It's a far better service than the English—better wages, better meat, and better ships. No half-pounds of meat short there; eat when you're hungry, and the best of grub. What goes into an English ship's cabin goes into an American ship's forecastle. The Americans are fast getting the pick of the English navy. I have now 15 dollars a month, or £3 2s. 6d. No trouble about bonded stores or such like. You take your tobacco with you from any American port, where it costs 3d. or 4d. a pound; and tea, and coffee, and sugar, and rum are found you. The very best tobacco is 20 cents, that's 10d., in America; but that's for chewing. The six cents tobacco, or 3d. a pound, is as good as you pay 3d. an ounce for here; so there's a pound for an ounce, you see. There's a lot of the American tobacco smoked in England; plenty of it puffed away at 3d. a pound all round the Custom-house. For the same sort of service in an English merchant ship I might get £2, or £2 5s., and starving all the time, unless I chance on a good employer, but they are scarce. The sleeping berths are far better in the forecastles of the American than the English ships— more room, and better fitted up. Why, of course, the English seamen flock into the American service as fast as they can, petty officers and all.

"I see a lot of foreign seamen in London now. I suppose a 'Dutchman'—that's what any foreign lubberly fellow is now called—is shipped for every English seaman driven out of your fine ports. These Dutchmen will put up with anything whatsomever—kicks and hits, and all. As for want of grub, they'll starve before they'll ask for it, and the English captains know that well, and so prefer those fellows; and the English seaman may go to America, or where he will, for what they care. In every respect, both about registry and everything else, the American service is better than the English. The English service is fast coming to be only fit for Dutchmen—that's about it, sir, you may depend. There's very little else but English seamen in the American ships. Our crew is nineteen, and only four are American born; fourteen are British subjects. If a war broke out—I could answer for myself and for hundreds besides—I wouldn't fight for England against America, but for America against England. I'll not fight for a country that starves and cheats you. I'll never fight for short weights and stinting in everything, not I. I left an English ship at Quebec, which is the greatest place in British America for sailors deserting. The living is so bad that men won't put up with it. They can easily hide in Quebec, and so go overland into the States. Nothing will check desertion in the English service but better wages, better treatment, and better food. The discipline is much the same on board the American as on board the English ships. An English seaman is very little thought of in his own country, but he's well thought of in America. He's a man there.". . .

From Letter XLII, March 14th, 1850

A tall, well-looking man, exceedingly bronzed, with an appearance of high health, and evidently possessed of great bodily strength, gave me the following account of an *East Indian voyage*, just completed:

"I have been at sea twenty-two years, and am now 34. From that age to 40 a seaman is considered in his prime. I have been at sea all these twenty-two years, merely excepting the times the ship was in port. I never was cast away in my life, but having a good character [to prove this, he showed me different papers] I have been generally fortunate in getting good ships and good masters. Good masters can always command the very best men. I have always found it so, and so their ships are always safest. Tyrannical and ignorant masters have often enough to put up with such men as they can get. We naturally avoid such ships if we know the character of the masters." [By masters, he meant the captains of the vessels.]

"My last voyage was to Aden, and from there to Colombo in Ceylon, and Cochin on the Malabar coast. The vessel was 400 tons, and carried a crew of seventeen—the master, mate, second mate, carpenter, steward, cook, seven able seamen, two ordinary seamen, and two apprentices. An able seaman is a man capable of doing every part of the duty required on board ship; an ordinary seaman can only do part of it. My wages, as an able seaman, were £2 a month; the ordinary seamen had, one 30s., and the other 25s.; the cook had £2 7s. 6d.; the steward £2 10s.; the second mate £3; the carpenter £4 10s.; and the chief mate £4 10s. The captain had, I believe, £12 a month, and two per cent. on the cargo. We took out coal and government stores to Aden, leaving that place in ballast. At the other two ports we took in cocoa-nut oil, coir rope, and junk (short pieces), bee's wax, coffee, and cinnamon. My opinion is, that £2 a month is not a sufficient payment for an able seaman, considering the nature of his work, and that he must be sailmaker and everything on board a ship. Then look at the hardships we endure on board ship—I have been kept up forty-eight hours, all hands on deck, without a minute's rest, and with hardly time for meals. Certainly there was great danger then, but we had a good captain. Masters never show any allowance for a man having been up all night on account of the weather; he must do his work all the same. I am quite satisfied, from the talk I have had with seamen situated like myself, that it is our general opinion that the wages ought to be higher; but if we tried to get better there was always some one, and good seamen too, ready to jump into the place, and take even less, especially when times are bad.

"In my last ship the provisions were by no means good. The biscuit, flour, beef, and pork, were all the remains from the stores of her former voyage from Ceylon. The peas and barley only were fresh at starting on the voyage. The biscuit was full of weevils (a small black insect), and we had to bake it in the oven before we could eat it. It eat better then; the baking made it crisp instead of tough, as it came out of the barrels, and killed the weevils—but we had to eat the dead bodies of the things that didn't crawl out. We made great complaints about it, but were told there was no help for it; we must eat through the bad to get to the good. There was no help unless we kicked up a row, and that wouldn't do at all. The pork and beef were both very bad, as rancid as could be. A piece of pork weighing 5lbs. used to lose about 2lbs. in boiling. We complained, and the master weighed it himself on deck; but he told us there was no help for it, he eat the same himself. We had three half pints of pretty good tea each, night and morning. Sugar was scarce, only $\frac{3}{4}$lb. to each man a week. At each meal we have as much bread as we like to eat, unless the ship be on short provisions. Grog was given out at the captain's option, sometimes one glass a day, sometimes two, three, or four, according to the day's work, as well as a glass every Saturday night to drink 'Sweet-hearts and wives,' and another glass after dinner on Sundays. On Sundays—I ought to have told you—we had two fresh meals: on going out a pig was killed, for one, and the other was bouilli soup, from preserved beef in tins; and in coming back a pig was killed every Saturday, and, little or big, the crew had half of it on Sunday. No one can call me a drunken man, but I think grog encourages a man to do his work well—just what is fit to revive him when he flags. Too much is worse than none.

"In my last ship we had two forecastles, one above (the gallant forecastle), and one below (the lower). I was in the lower forecastle, which was pretty good and middling for room, though in some ships it's very bad. My berth was 6 feet by 3. I am 5 feet 10¾ in. in height. I have slept in a berth only two feet wide, so that I could hardly get into it, and, when in, couldn't slew round or anything. The gallant forecastle was very leaky, the water coming in continually in rainy weather, and wetting all the men's beds. The carpenter couldn't stop it, the ship was so slightly built, though she was only four years old. She was built at Leith. The master was a good officer, without being too severe; but the mate was a domineering, ignorant fellow; and, indeed, sir, these ignorant fellows are always the worst; he used to run tattling to the captain and make mischief fore and aft. We had two or three rows in her, and all through him. I consider there is a decided improvement in merchant ships of late. Lime juice and vinegar is a great improvement in southern-going ships. It is a very common fault in all the ships I know, to have no place to keep the bread in. It's kept in bags, and they are put anywhere—anywhere down below. No care at all is taken of it, and the damp gets to it and causes maggots and weevils. The last voyage, when we eat through the old bread, two cwts. of the new was found to be so mouldy that it had to be heaved overboard. The bags often come up so rotten with damp that they fall to pieces, and the bread falls out. I think if the bread were kept in barrels, as the beef and pork is, or in tins, it would be much better and healthier. I don't know how they manage the bread on board a man of war—I never was on board one; but they'll take care of it there you may depend.

"In the East India ports that I have visited lately, the native women are not allowed to come on board so freely as they were, but the men have more liberty to go on shore. I think there is not so much swearing and cursing on board ship as there used to be. If the officers swear, they always make men swear. We had prayers on board my last ship in fine weather, but I wouldn't go—for we had our choice to go or to stay—because it was a mockery. The captain began swearing the moment he'd done praying. I think masters should not be permitted to take out bread, or other stores, that had remained from former voyages, and were bad in consequence. They might be sold for pig-meat, and the biscuit is often fit for nothing else. My last captain was a good navigator, or we might have been lost, as the mate couldn't be depended upon for navigation. I think, too, that six pints of water a day, our present allowance, is too little—it ought to be a gallon. The water is generally good now, being all filtered, at the principal ports at any rate, before it is shipped. As to advance notes, I think they had better be done away with, and have the plan they have in the States (United States). There, when a seaman gets a ship he goes to a shipping-office and receives the advance money agreed upon from the master of the shipping-office without any note, whatsomever. The man you lodge with, to whom the advance-money is paid, is security for you to the shipping-office, in case you run away. He will then have to make it good. The master of the ship repays the shipping-office master. That's a simpler plan than ours."

P

I shall now contrast the above statement with one that I had from a seaman in the employ of Mr. Green, the eminent shipowner. High as the man speaks in praise of his master, I am happy to have it in my power to state, that all I have heard fully bears out this most honourable eulogium. . . .

"I have been to sea about four or five and thirty years, I expect. I was apprenticed in the West India trade, in 1814 or 1815. I remained in the West India trade for ten or twelve years. Then I went to Sydney for three or four years. After that I was sailing in small craft from St. Thomas's to different ports in South America and to different islands in the West Indies, till 1840. Since that time I have been sailing out of London to the East Indies in Mr. Green's employ. When I first joined Mr. Green, in 1840, his Home, for the sailors in his employ, was not open, but on my return from Calcutta it was. Before that time I had been in the habit of living in the Home in Well-street. This was opened about 1832 or '33, I can't recollect exactly which. I know I shipped out of it in 1840 to join Mr. Green's company. I had £2 a month on first joining Mr. Green's ship. In other ships I had £2 5s.; but I had heard that Mr. Green gave better employ and better usage, at £2 a month than others at £2 5s., and so I thought I'd be one of his men. I had heard of Mr. Green being one of the best masters out of the port of London, and I felt anxious to join him. I knew I should lose 5s. a month by so doing, but what I lost one way I was convinced I should gain in another, and I found such to be the fact.

"Of all owners I have ever shipped with I have found Mr. Green to be the best. Why, sir, in the first place, when a man comes back there is a place for him to go—a home, sir. I call it a real home, sir; and there is no other shipowner that I know of that cares so much for his men. I am a single man. I have been ten years in Mr. Green's service, and I can conscientiously state that a better master to his men I never knew." (I endeavoured to impress upon the man that, if he had anything private to communicate, his name could never transpire, nor would he be in any way injured, and he again assured me that Mr. Green was a gentleman who had invariably shown a disposition to benefit his men, and that the men had the same feeling towards their master as he had towards them; they would do all they could to serve him.)

"My last voyage was made in the Northumberland, from London to Madras, and from Madras to Calcutta. She was about 800 tons. Mr. Green has one ship over 1,400 tons, and that is the largest he has in the East India trade. There are larger ships, and they run perhaps 50 tons more. In the 800-ton ship that I went out in last voyage we had 33 men and boys in the forecastle, and four officers abaft, and about eight middies. Besides these, there were carpenter, boatswain, sailmaker, ship's cook and baker, captain's cook, steward, and cuddy servants. We had about five or six passengers. It was in the winter time. Had it been in the summer we should have had double or treble that number on board. We took out soldiers as well, about 150. I should say we had six soldier officers on board. We had only about five or six soldiers' wives with us. We had full weight of provisions, always good, and plenty. We had sufficient of good water—well filtered and sweet. We had salt beef and plums and flour one day, and pork and peas the next—as much as we could eat. We had plenty of room on board Mr. Green's ship, and plenty of air. The midshipmen's berth had a port-hole and scuttle, and was a very large and airy cabin; so, indeed, were all the berths.

"We touched nowhere on our outward-bound voyage till we got to Madras. We had no tomfoolery at the line; no hailing of Neptune over night, and shaving of the greenhorns in the day time. No ships lie at Diamond Harbour now. We went up to Calcutta. We lay just below Fort William. Every Sunday and every night the men were allowed to go on shore, upon the condition that they came on board in the morning. I didn't know that any man deserted—it would be matter of dishonesty on a man's part to leave a master who treats his men so well as Mr. Green. A man loses more than he gains. No women were permitted to come on board—that is not allowed now; they used to do so, but we have improved much in these few years. When I came home I had Mr. Green's Home to go to. Had I belonged to any other owner I should have been uncared for. I came home ill— ill with the liver complaint and with ulcers in the stomach—and I was received into his sailors' home, as if I had been a person worthy of being looked after. Had I belonged to any other owner I should have been left a prey to the land-sharks of London. I think that if all owners were like Mr. Green there would be fewer men to leave the merchant service of this country. What the merchant seamen generally require is to be well treated, and then they would be sure to be good men. Mr. Green has a school for the children of sailors. It will hold more than 300 I have heard, and I know the sailors love him for his regard to their little ones, and so indeed does all Poplar. I have been in ships that are as badly found and the men as little cared for as those of Mr. Green's are well provisioned and the men truly regarded; and I can conscientiously say that if all owners were like Mr. Green, our merchant service would be the envy of the world. The masters lay the blame upon the men, but from what I have seen I can declare that it is not the men's fault, but the captains or the owners, as to how the men behave themselves. I never knew any act of insubordination to occur on board of Mr. Green's ship, and I attribute this solely to the good treatment of the men. What man can speak again a master like that? There is a good home and a good bed always to go to, and I only wish such masters were more general, and then the country would be safer I can tell you.". . .

To show the opinion of a *chief mate* as to the men in the merchant service, I give the account of a very intelligent man, whose last voyage was *in the Mediterranean*:

"I have been at sea for 30 years—from 15 to 45 years of age—and my last voyage was up the Mediterranean to Constantinople, and then up the Black Sea, and into the Sea of Azof to Kertch. She was a brig of 240 tons, with a crew of twelve—captain, chief mate (myself), eight able seamen, and two apprentices. Within my own knowledge I can vouch for a far better state of things now existing on board ship. Little, however, has been done for the better accommodation of the men. There is still shocking crowding in the forecastles; and the deck over the forecastle is often so leaky that in rainy weather the men may really sleep in the rain— go down wet, and come up wetter, oft enough. I have seen them—aye and often— come smoking like a steam apparatus, up from the forecastle. Talk of sanitary regulations, sir—have them afloat as well as ashore. The men are constantly suffering from cold, and frequently from ague, as I have seen.

"In respect to cleanliness, there is decidedly a great improvement; and even that might be increased by making the men air their bedding when the weather permits, which they seldom do now. Perhaps the bed-clothes in the berths are not changed once in a whole voyage, or the bed aired. The want of something for the purposes of a water-closet is also a very great defect in our merchant ships at present. There *is* something of the kind. The head-rail is used for such purposes; but when it blows very hard and heavy, men cannot go to the head-rail—many men have been lost by going there in stormy weather. The officers have conveniences, and the men could easily have the same. In my last voyage the able seamen had £2 a month each. My opinion, as an officer, is that it ought not to be less than £2 5s. for any long voyage—men deserve it. The officers had the usual rate. We discharged our cargo, bale goods and manufactured iron, at Constantinople. The men were allowed to go ashore on Sundays. No women are admitted on board, on any pretence, in any of the Mediterranean ports.

"To have examinations of the officers in merchant ships, as to their nautical knowledge and their sobriety, and certificates after passing examinations, will, in my opinion, be a very great improvement. Many a bright vessel has been lost through the ignorance or drunkenness of her commander. When a master is ignorant, his crew soon find it out, and all take advantage of it; there is no good discipline; while in case of peril, the men have no confidence in their master, and the danger is greatly increased. In one of my voyages, through not having a chronometer on board chiefly, we made Scilly two days before we expected even to see land. If it had not been fine summer weather we must have gone bump on shore among the wreckers. Every vessel, as a regulation, ought to have a chronometer on board, and the master ought fully to understand its use. Fines on board ship would, in some respect, be proper. Confinement does no good; it's ridiculous, for one man in a fault is confined and idle, and another, in consequence, is overworked, for no fault of his.

"As to wages, I think that, in justice to the seaman, wages ought to commence from the time of signing the articles; as it is, a seaman has often to wait eight or ten days before his vessel sails, and, as his wages only reckon from the sailing of the vessel, he is compelled to be eight or ten days idle, and unless a very steady man, soon gets through all his means. Why not have the men on board? It would save their lodging, and save them all sorts of temptations, and it would be no loss to masters or owners, for they have to pay riggers and labourers as it is. A better way of keeping the log, so as to answer regularity and accuracy, is very desirable. I have seen a log where the mate put down the vessel as steering N., and the wind in the other column as N. by W., as if the vessel lay within a point of the wind, while she was not within 5½! There can be no doubt that there ought to be some readier means of recovering wages due to seamen's representatives. I mean seamen who have died on the voyage. I think it would be better, as regards wages generally, that there should be an uniform rate of wages, as in the United States. It would be found a great improvement in this country. In some ports here £2 is given for the East Indies; in Liverpool it is £2 5s. Men would know what to expect with an uniform rate—indeed, they could reckon it with certainty. In the United States there is an uniform rate, the men being engaged at shipping offices. An able seaman has $15 a month for Europe, and $12 a month for the East Indies and China. No wonder so many Englishmen are in the American service—the pay is better, the provisions are better, and the accommodations are better. Now, a better and more uniform rate of wages in English ships would prevent many men deserting at New York, and other cities in the States, where they are tempted naturally by the better state of things among the Americans. Do what anybody will, sir, the only true way to check desertion is to pay the men better, and to accommodate them better. That goes to the root of the matter."...

From Letter XLVI, April 3rd, 1850

I now give the statements of *[a]* long-experienced *[man]* on board *steamers belonging to the foreign trade of the Port of London.* . . . The fire-man was very well-informed, and produced his papers, when necessary, to vouch for the truth of what he stated. His appearance was not that of a strong man, and his narrative accounts for it:

"I have been 20 years fireman in steam-vessels," he said, "and have acted as engineer. When I first knew steam-vessels the boilers were larger than they are made now, as the cargo was less an object then than the conveyance of passengers. As to the berths, and the accommodation generally, it's worse now than it was 20 years ago. They care nothing where we are crammed—in any hole. If you complain, there's plenty of men out of employ will jump at it.

"I have been employed in steamers in all parts of the Mediterranean (in Government and merchant service), from Gibraltar to Odessa; in the West Indies; on the French, Belgian, and Dutch coasts; to Hamburg, too; also the Baltic, and to Spain and Portugal. I was in Don Pedro's expedition, and didn't make so badly out of it either—I served in the Royal Tar, Captain M'Dougal (Admiral Sartorius commanded the squadron)—and in the coasting trade of England, Scotland, Ireland, and the Channel Islands. Twenty years ago I served in a steamer which plied between London and Boulogne. I had 30s. a week, finding my own provisions. Now, if I were in the same trade, with twenty years' experience at my back, I should have 24s., instead of 30s. The engineer twenty years ago had £3 a week in that trade, finding his own provisions; now he has from 38s. to 44s.; the last is the very highest.

"My last voyage was to Marseilles, and I had then at the rate of 20s. a week, as fireman, for taking the vessel out, but provisions were found to us. The first engineer had, I believe, £20 a month, and the second £16. I greatly prefer finding my own provisions (but that can only be done in short voyages)—for those found us by the masters are often very bad and very salt, and eating that stuff with constant fire and steam about one is terribly trying. In a hot climate we work at 190 degrees at least, in the engine-room of a steamer. Now look at this; in all this heat I have had to chop my meat; it was like a salt board, and with proper tools I could have carved and cut it into 'baccy boxes; that I'm sure I could. My health of course suffered from this. There is another grievance—no merchant steamer, that ever I knew or heard of, carried lime-juice; and that's the very thing wanted by men in my capacity; it's better than all the grog in the world. I don't know why the law don't make merchant steamers carry lime-juice. Grog, you see, revives one only for the time, but lime-juice cools you without inflaming you.

"I have told you the berths are not what they were on board steamers. The iron boats are the worst for accommodation. The iron is always wet and cold, and the cold is always in the berths, and into them such as me have to go from the heat of the engine-room. A man to stand it should have the constitution of a negro by day, and an Esquimaux by night, especially in bad weather. The water keeps always working its way between the iron plates of the vessel, and so into the forecastle. I have been drenched so in bad weather that it has brought on four weeks' rheumatics. In our berths there is (as a general rule) no ventilation, except by the very hatch that you come into the place by. A lamp is generally there night and day, however, or there would be no light. I can't complain of having been so much cramped for sleeping-room in steamers; the berths are mostly 6ft. 2in. by 2ft. Some of the engine-men, in some steamers, have to sleep in the engine-room, and there we cannot sleep from the heat, and from the damp caused by the steam. There are mostly swarms of bugs too, helping the heat and the damp to keep one awake. I hardly knew what bugs were, in comparison, on shore, but their head-quarters are in the engine-rooms of steamers (I don't say of all steamers).

"There is another thing I must tell you of. When new machinery is put into a steam-boat, the engineer of the factory puts his own man on board the steamer as engineer, to manage the machinery, which the makers generally warrant for twelve months. The captain of the vessel has nothing to do with the appointment of the men in the engine-room (except in the Oriental and Peninsular Company), and the engineer selects his own men. The engineer from the factory, ten to one, has never been to sea before, and is very often sea-sick when we get out to sea—not able to take care of himself, let alone of a pair of engines. And the other men selected by the engineer are no more seamen than he is, and they are sea-sick too, and laid up, and the vessel may take her chance. I have known the seamen sent down from the deck to do the work of the engineer's people below. A bad system prevails as regards boys. An engineer, or a captain, will employ boys in the place of men, who must stand idle while boys are underselling them, and the boy is registered as a fireman, and the registrar can't help it if the captain applies.

"The way the work on board a steamer is carried on by us in the engine-room is this: The engineer has the charge of the engines, and is to attend to the commands of the captain and the pilot, as to 'stop her,' and any such order; he is looked upon as the responsible man. The business of a fireman, or stoker, is to keep up the supply of steam, by regulating the water pumped into the boilers, and by keeping the fires up to the required height. A great deal of responsibility as to the safety of a ship depends upon the fireman. In voyages of more than twenty-four hours' duration, there are two engineers generally, and firemen according to the length of the voyage and the power of the boat. I have worked in a West India boat with twenty-eight firemen, seven coal-trimmers, and five engineers. The engineers relieve each other every four hours; only the head engineer in a West India boat keeps no regular watch, and the others may relieve each other oftener if they choose; the firemen keep their regular hours the same. The work is very exhausting. We must have something to drink, and ought really to have lime-juice, for it gives an appetite. In the Gravesend and Richmond boats there is no relief; one engineer and one stoker does the work; but they are not considered in our class at all. In the above-bridge boats there is generally nothing but a parcel of boys, had cheap.

"The stokers are not at all satisfied. I have served on board an American steamer, and know what good reason we have to be dissatisfied. None of us, I believe, if a war broke out, would fight against America. In the American steamer I was in we were all Englishmen, captain and all, but three. We were 136, or near that, in crew. I wish I was in the American service again. Better pay, and better provisions, and better accommodation. They know how to behave to a man, in America, and I would never have left them but for family matters. As to the quantity of coal consumed in steamers, I can only give it, as near as I can, according to horse-power. A vessel of 300-horse-power will, on the average, burn 120 bushels of coal an hour. Steamers may average that consumption at sea eight months in every year—120 bushels an hour, day and night." (Considering, then, the horse-power of the whole of the steam-vessels of the United Kingdom to be estimated at 92,862, we shall find that they will consume 216,628,473 bushels, or 6,017,456 chaldrons of coals per annum.)

"I have known great carelessness on board of steamers," continued the fireman, "and wonder that there are not more accidents and explosions. There is often great carelessness from drunkenness by the engine-men—ten minutes' neglect might blow a vessel out of the water. I have often known short weights given in steamers. The way we are provisioned, both the seamen and the engine-men, in some long voyages, is this: the provador (steward) of the steam-vessel has perhaps to provision thirty or forty passengers, and what's left out of the cabin dinner is sold by him to the crew at 9s. a week generally, we paying him that for our board out of our wages. The steward hands over what's spared out of the cabin dinner to the cook, who serves it out to the crew. If there's not enough, we ask the cook for more; and he will say 'I have none to give,' and so there's a sort of a row; and as of course we pay for full provisions, and come short oft enough (a general thing, indeed), it's the same as cheating us by giving short weight. If you complain you are called 'mutinous.' The provador has the greater profit that short-feeding way, and can pay a larger sum to the owners for his situation, for he buys his place. I have known a provador pay £300 for his place for the summer season.

"In the Mediterranean trade the fireman has £3 a month, and salt, *very* salt, provisions found him. On board a man of war a fireman has £2 6s. a month, with lime-juice after forty-eight hours at sea. In an American merchant seaman there's lime-juice always to your command, as well as sugar. I had at the rate of from 36s. to 40s. a week, on board the Yankees, and capital provisions found. A good engineer will have, I believe, from £18 to £20 a month in the Yankee steamers, and is treated like a gentleman there. In the Dutch and Belgian trades, and in all short foreign voyages, the fireman has 24s. a week, and the engineer 44s., all finding their own provisions. The same in English and Scotch coasting, except that one company gives firemen only from 15s. to 20s. a week, but allows them beer. In the Irish trade 20s. a week is paid a fireman, and 44s. or 46s. an engineer. Can you tell me, sir, why it is that we stokers have to pay 1s. a month to the Merchant Seamen's Fund, and have never had any benefit from it? I never heard of a stoker ever getting anything from it. A fireman cannot be admitted into the Sailors' Home, either, in Wells-street—and why not, for we are more liable to accidents than seamen?". . .

I shall now proceed to give instances of the condition of the men on board the vessels employed in . . . *[the]* coasting trade—beginning with the *"Colliers"*:

A man, as clean as if he had never seen coal-dust, gave me the following intelligence:

"I have been nearly twenty years at sea, and was brought up in the coal trade. I'm a native of Sunderland. I have been in the coal trade all the time, except three

voyages to North America. Since I knew the service there have been many changes
in it. When I first went to sea the coals were put on board in the Wear out of
keels; they're a sort of lighters. You've heard of 'Weel may the keel row'—that's
it. The coal was shovelled out of the keels at that time through the port-holes into
the hold—or rather out of the keel on to a stage, and so into the hold—just as
they put in ballast now. In Sunderland, now-a-days, the coal is mainly lifted out
of the keels in tubs; a keel contains 21 tons, or eight tubs. A steam-engine, fixed on
shore, on the Wear, lifts a tub out of the keel, heaving it up like a crane, and
the bottom it let go, by being unclasped, and so the coals are shot into the hold.

"Twenty years ago I was bound apprentice for seven years. I can't read or
write. I was never taught navigation, and don't understand it now. I had £45
apprentice wages for the seven years, with 8s. a week for board when the ship was
at home, and 12s. a year for washing money. I found my own clothes. Those are
the payments to apprentices in the coal trade still. I think all seamen ought to be
taught navigation. I have a brother now master of a London ship in the coal trade,
who knows no more of reading, writing, arithmetic, or navigation than I do. When
I was first at sea, an able seaman had £3 a voyage from Sunderland to London in
summer, and £4 to £4 10s. in winter. Twelve voyages in a year is an average, though
more are made sometimes. Take the average wages, twenty years ago, at £3 15s. a
voyage, and calculate that, you'll find it comes to £45 a year. Now the wages of
an able seaman are (from Sunderland to London) £3 a voyage in summer, and
£3 7s. 6d. to £4 in winter, but £4 very seldom. Reckon twelve voyages a year at
£3 5s. a voyage, and it comes to only £39.

"We generally have the best of provisions in colliers—always fresh meat—boiled
beef mainly. We are not allowanced. There is no grog; only small beer. In a gale
of wind the captain *may* give us perhaps a glass of grog. We are often very short-
handed in crew—more often than not—and then certainly it *is* slavery. We pay to
the Merchant Seamen's Fund 1s. a month, but I never met a man who knew what
became of it. To be sure I have known widows at Sunderland have 2s. a month,
but that's only when their husbands had paid twenty years to the fund. The seamen in colliers don't complain of their treatment nor of their food—they can't
reasonably; but they do complain of bad wages. I can't say whether they would
fight for the country or not in a war. Education would be good for seamen; I wish
I had education, and I might be a captain. I have been mate often enough. Drunkenness is not common among the seamen in colliers. It's a very hard trade. Off Yar-
mouth is about the worst place between the North and London; there are so many
sands. We have often had to heave the coal overboard to lighten the ship."

Another person, a very smart and intelligent man, in the same trade, gave me
the following further information:

"The coal trade has made excellent seamen. It was called a nursery for the navy,
and it bears that character still—the men in colliers are so numerous, and they
must know every branch. The boys are continually heaving the lead, which is a
most important part of seamanship, and doing handreefing and steering besides,
in all coasting. In a dark night, in the narrow channels, they have little beyond the
lead to trust to. A seaman brought up in the coasting trade is the best man at a
push; though he may not be so good at dandy work in the rigging, such as graft-
ing, splicing, and knotting. The apprentices are always at sea, and receive no education through the care of the masters or owners, while in the coasting coal trade.

In a foreign voyage with coals, from the north country ports, the boys are taught navigation, and reading and writing, if they look for it, not without. But boys and captains in the coal trade are generally ignorant. One half are captains one voyage, cooks the next, then mates—then before the mast—and then, may be, round to be captains again. They are no navigators, but capital coasters; blind as they are as regards education, they know every set of the tides and channels from Newcastle to London. If they lose sight of land, they are regularly at sea, as the saying goes, and always steer west. That's sure to bring them in sight of land, and then they know where they are in a minute. Or else they hail any ship they meet, and ask where the land bears. They never ask about latitude or longitude; that's no use to them.

"Boys are more used in manning coal vessels than ever, if you can call it *manning*. It's done for cheapness. A boy may have £20 or £24 for four years. I had £34 when apprentice, but that's sixteen years ago. I know a collier manned entirely with prentice boys—captain, mate, cook, and all—every one of them—boys; the oldest apprentice is the captain. When the heavy North American ships lay up at home for the winter, the owners take the boys out of them, and put them on board colliers from the north to London. The cost of all hands on a voyage in a collier of eight keels may be £29 or £30. When boys only are employed, the saving to the owner will be above £20 the voyage, at the very least. Boys' labour is fast displacing men's. That's one reason there are so many idle seamen about.

"The way in which the colliers are disposed when they reach the port of London, is this: The master goes ashore at Gravesend to the harbour-office with his papers. The office instructs him where to lie; whether to go to the Pool or not. I have known colliers three and four weeks in the river before their turn came for the Pool. Only a certain number of vessels are admitted into the Pool at one time; and while out of the Pool they can't unload or sell the cargo. Why that's allowed, I don't understand. It's nothing but a monopoly to keep up the price for the rich merchants. At the north-country ports, too, there is the 'limitation of the wend'—I think they call it. Each ship there must wait for its turn; that's the general practice. That's another way to lessen the supply for the London market—all to serve the owners and merchants, I can tell you. Look what happens. Freights go down, in consequence of the supply being limited, because so many vessels are lying idle; and our wages go down with freights; so the men are thrown adrift. Now, suppose there was no limit to the supply of London, why, coal would soon be half the price that it is, and then there would be double and treble the quantity consumed. Compare a public-house fire in Newcastle with one in London; why, they burn four tons there to one here. I can't tell how people put up with dear coals. Without the limit there would be twice and thrice the quantity of coals to bring, and twice or thrice as much employment for seamen and for ships, and then up would go freights and wages. There would be also a great increase in the coal trade for foreign ports. There wants a little stir about it.". . .

SEAMEN ASHORE

From Letter XLVII, April 11th, 1850

[In the following interviews, Mayhew surveys the accommodation available for sailors when they are in port.]

A middle-aged man, of very sedate appearance and residing in the *[Sailors']* Home, gave me the following statement:

"This is my fourth visit to the Sailors' Home in the course of nine years. I consider it an excellent institution for seamen. We have good strong grub, but we don't look for so many hares and things as at some boarding-masters'. At breakfast, at eight o'clock, we have always corned beef, salt fish, bread and butter, and coffee. For dinner, at one to-day, we had bouilli soup, roast and corned beef, meat-pie, and vegetables, with a pint of beer a man. That's the usual style of our dinners here. We have hot dinners on Sundays. For tea, at six, bread and butter and tea, with water-cresses. For supper, at nine, bread and cheese, with a pint of table ale. At half-past ten another pint of table ale is served out to each man, and then we can smoke till eleven, and go to bed. We can smoke as we please all day in the hall. They close the doors at eleven, and never open them on any account. We have prayers regularly every morning and evening. I generally attend, but we are not compelled; Roman Catholics go to their own places. The savings-bank at the Home is a very good place, for it makes a man more careful. I received £33, and put it in the bank. I draw it out as I want it, by 5s. and 10s.

"I've known rogues of boarding-masters who would have made me drunk, and have left me without money next morning. I knew a man who found himself the next day after a voyage, without a penny, and the boarding-master, when he told him he was robbed, said he was 'slewed' the night before, and came home without a penny. He was a shipmate of mine, and I saw him home to his boarding-house, and I'm sure he had the money about him then. He and I believed the boarding-master had robbed him when dead-drunk—that's five years ago. He made no stir about it; he had no evidence. The boarding-master kept him a few days without any charge, and then he got a ship.

"If a man's sober and steady, he can keep himself happier and cleaner here than in a boarding-house. Here we have all cabins to ourselves; in many boarding-houses, but not those of the best sort, we sleep two in a bed. Our friends can come and see us here, but not any female friends; though a man's mother or sister may sit down and talk half an hour to them—not by themselves privately, but in the hall, or up-stairs in the dining-room. I think the steadiest-going seaman will always speak well of the Sailors' Home—I've found it so. If we have no money to stay longer, we must go, and can be admitted, if we are destitute, into the asylum below; but that's reckoned bad; it lowers a good man. I should be very badly off before I went there—very hard-up indeed. I could stay here a week or ten days after my money was out; but if I leave then—and leave I must—without getting a ship, I must leave my chest of clothes until I can get money to take them out. I don't know how long they keep the chest for any man leaving in debt. No grog is allowed in the Home, and men are better without it. We all agree very well here. After staying out all night, a man can go back next morning as usual."

I shall complete the present description of the better kind of Homes for Seamen with an account of a seamen's boarding-house (of the best class), for such it was described to me on excellent authority. The house was of the description known as a "gentleman's house;" it stood at the top of a street, not a thoroughfare, and behind it was a spacious garden, with out-houses where the more cumbersome luggage of the lodgers was stowed, and a very clean piggery. The garden walls were well covered with vines, and there were broad gravel walks, on which the seamen sauntered and smoked their pipes. At the end of the garden was an arbour, in which a sailor's old sea chest did duty as the seat. In an open recess built out from the kitchen window, the top of which was on a level with the ground of the garden, hung six hares, four ducks, a joint of beef, a shoulder of mutton, and ham—tolerable specimens of the seamen's fare. I was told that the boarding-master was enabled to afford what may be accounted sumptuous dinners—considering that 14s. per week, the same amount as is paid at the "Home," is the charge for board, lodging, and a fair proportion of washing—by going himself to the same markets, and making his purchases on the same terms, as a wholesale dealer in game or poultry.

On my visit some lodgers had just arrived from sea, and were refreshing themselves at a well-furnished tea-table. Four meals a day are supplied to the boarders, meat being given at three of them, whilst the supply of green vegetables, such as watercresses, is abundant at breakfast and tea. The inmates are single men, or those whose wives, home, or friends, are in other ports. The grand staple of the furniture of the house I speak of was shells. They were in every room, as if the owner of the house were studying the conchology of the East. They had been presented to him as little tokens of respect or remembrance by his guests. Some nautilus shells were specimens of exquisite beauty, while other shells were remarkable for their size, or for the delicacy, richness and iridescence of their colours. Mixed with the shells were masses of coral in different forms. In one of the best rooms, where the lodgers could resort to write their letters, or where they could see any visitors, the grate was filled with a large mass of coral and shells, and curiosities of all kinds covered the mantelpiece and side-tables. With these, too, were mixed the teeth of the whale, on some of which were carved, or scratched, drawings relative to a seaman's life. The house I am describing could accommodate thirty boarders, for whose use eight sleeping apartments were provided, a separate bed being allotted to each man. . . .

I will now give the statement of the *Boarding-house Master* himself, merely observing that I was referred to him by gentlemen of the greatest experience, as a fair sample of the better class, and as a person upon whose word every reliance might be placed:

"I have had seven years' experience in keeping a boarding-house for sailors. I charge 14s. a week for board and lodging, supplying four meals a day, with meat

or poultry at three meals. When the hare season is in I cook upon an average 20
hares a week, my boarders being in number about 30. Sometimes they tire of hares.
When on shore, seamen are, however, generally fondest of hares, or rabbits, or
poultry, and such things as they seldom get at sea, but I always provide roast and
boiled joints as well. I find also to each man a pint of beer at his dinner and
supper. . . .

"I may be said, in some sense, to act as banker to my lodgers, so far as this:
When any boarder comes from sea he will place his money in my hands for safe
keeping, and will draw it out in small sums as he requires it. I keep it in a book this
way." [He showed me the book, which was kept with perfect system and regularity, some of the boarders testifying to the accuracy of the accounts.] "I never
advance a man a farthing when he's drunk—not one farthing. Every morning I call
over to each man a statement of his account, and if the boarder be not able to read
and write, I call upon his shipmates to look at the book, and explain and satisfy
him that it *is* right. The book always lies on a table for anybody's inspection.

"I mostly see my old customers, voyage after voyage, and they often bring their
shipmates with them. My lodgers are of the better sort, and are well-conducted
men, all things considered; by that I mean, that if a small tradesman or mechanic
were suddenly to find himself in possession of £10 or £20, or more pounds, after
having known many hardships, he would be more likely to commit greater excesses
and offences than a sailor does. The sailor is, as a rule, a manly fellow, and I never
knew any one of my lodgers strike a woman, unless aggravated by women of the
town when drinking. These things, however, come very little under my observation, unless when sent for to help any of my lodgers out of a scrape; for in my
house no disorder or bad language is allowed. Men who do not behave themselves
must go. The board at houses like mine I consider to be better than at any other
place, as we consult the men's tastes more than they can do at places carried on
strictly by rule. The charge is the same as at the Home.

"I would very gladly undertake to carry on the Sailors' Home, and pay servants'
wages and *rent* into the bargain (which they do not, the building having been
raised by subscription), and every other expense, and make a handsome thing of
it too, without any charitable donations or subscriptions, or anything of that kind.
As to the destitute men, who are now sent from the Home to the Seamen's Asylum,
I should deal with them as I do with the men in my house who get through their
money before they leave. I keep them until they can get a ship. I have lost very little
indeed (and that chiefly by death) by men neglecting to pay me on their return from
a voyage for what I let them have on credit. I have had post-office orders for such
payments from all parts of the kingdom. If a man has left in my debt, and his first
voyage afterwards is a bad one, I wait till the next, and almost always get paid.
When men come to my house straight from the ship I advance them 5s. a piece, or
if it's a steady man or an old customer 10s. They pay me when the ship is paid off.
As to advance notes, I cash them for my regular customers without any charge.
To those who are not regular customers I charge 5 per cent., but if the advance note
is in payment of what they owe me I charge them no per centage, and may advance
them something beyond the payment of the note.

"If the men be not all in my house at eleven—and sometimes they are not if they
have gone to Astley's, for instance, or any place of amusement—I keep open till two
in the morning; but I will open my doors at any time rather than subject any

lodger to lose his clothes, as he most likely will if he be locked out all night. I have known men who have been out all night 'skinned' as it is called; that is, they have lost everything, shirt and all. Perhaps a woman of the town will come or send to me—every day may be it happens—and will bring a pawnbroker's ticket for a seaman's clothes pledged by her, the man having been drunk sometimes. The woman demands so much money for the duplicate of the clothes; if the duplicate be for 10s. she will ask 3s. or 4s. more than the 10s. If I threaten to take her before a magistrate, as perhaps the clothes have been pledged unknown to the man, she may give up the ticket, but not if it be only for 5s., as a magistrate then won't interfere. I have known the men—plenty of them—lose their clothes in the middle of the day. The Home closing at eleven has subjected many men to lose their clothes to my knowledge. I have known men locked out of the Sailors' Home come to their ship-mates at my house for a night's shelter. If they have no money left, they may either walk the streets all night, or try and get a lodging with a friend, or go home with some girl who is tolerably certain to rob them of their clothes, and this while they have plenty of money in the Home.

"As to clothes, my lodgers employ any tailor they please, and I pay any strange tailor's bill if instructed so to do. Seamen will very well bear talking to when I tell them what fools they are to throw away their money as they often do, without any reasonable enjoyment for it. I have known great bearded men cry like children when I have reasoned with them as to their extravagance and tomfool-eries; but they can't bear any threat of exposure or anything like compulsion."

From Letter XLVIII, April 19th, 1850

The Sailors' Home, however, has many other defects [than the early closing hours]. The foremost of these is the system of touting for custom, carried on by the runners of the tailors in connection with the establishment. Of this touting I had the following account from a man who spoke from personal knowledge:

"There are three tailors—or outfitters generally, for they supply shoes, hats, shirts, &c., as well as clothes—who reside in the neighbourhood of the Sailors' Home; and the conductors of the Home do not willingly allow any other tailors to enter the establishment, and would demur to paying a bill, out of a seaman's cash in their hands, to any other tailor. These three outfitters employ at least 11 regular runners or touters, at 30s. a week each, or £16 10s. altogether; besides that, some of the principals and their families tout also. I have seen as many as 14 runners on board an East Indiaman, all trying for the custom of the sailors. Sometimes we board the ship at Gravesend—sometimes lower than Gravesend, well down to the Nore—and sometimes at Blackwall. If we get aboard a Quebec or West Indiaman, or any two or three months' ship, we mustn't waste time there, as the crews of such ships have no great sum of money to receive, but we must hurry off to a Calcutta ship, if there be one. When on board, the runner inquires as to the money the men have to receive, generally asking the mates and appren-tices such questions as, 'Has So-and-so been the whole voyage?' 'Will his pay be stopped, or any of it?' And, when the answer is satisfactory, the runner goes to work.

"When the ship reaches the dock we go on shore with a seaman that we have stuck to like wax, telling him that there's no place like the Sailors' Home. 'No robbery there,' we say; 'no! there men are taken care of, and the best of victuals.' We go touting as for the Home, but it's for our employers' interests. If the ship come up on a night's tide, too late for the Home, as is often the case, we get the men who are bound for the Home a night's lodging, paying the cost of it; or if they are inclined to go on the spree, then we plant them on some woman or other that we know, pay the expenses, and then look them up in the morning to convey them to the Home. On our way we generally have a glass with them. I can say that there are runners connected in this way with the Sailors' Home, who are drunk five days out of six. These runners for the Home are generally dissipated people, and drink hard. Our first object is to get a seaman to one of the Sailors' Home tailors. We are employed by the tailors and not by the Home, but the Home people know—they *must* know—how we are employed by the tailors to get men to the Home, for we are all introduced by our employers to the superintendent there. I have seen eight tailors' runners (all belonging to the three firms) plying in the Home at once, to the great annoyance of the men, whom I've heard say, 'D— you, I won't be bothered. I'll go where I like.'

"A runner's is a miserable life—we're looked upon as anything but respectable when we get aboard a ship; but aboard you must, as it's all in the way of business for employers. A seaman just landed of course wants a little money. He can't get any at the Home if he arrives after six in the evening, though he's charged for a day's boarding—so he gets all he wants of the tailors. This used to be charged as cash, and is still charged as cash, if advanced by the tailor after six at night; but if a man be regularly installed in the Home, and want a pound or two, or £3, to buy any useful thing at a good shop, he's asked by the cashier at the Home what he wants the money for. They won't advance money unless they are satisfied that the money's worth will be in the man's possession when he returns to the Home. But if a seaman wants a sovereign for any purpose of his own that he don't wish there to be any prying into, he goes to the tailor, and says, 'I want a pound for this, or for that;' and the tailor says, 'Well, I can't let you have money, you know it's against the rules, but I can, as you're so pressing, let you have what you want and charge it as a garment, and put it down with a per centage.' So said, so done. I have known a seaman, when the tailor or his man took in his bill to the cashier at the Home, say 'I've never had those trowsers'—and I have been behind the man myself, and have whispered, 'the money, you know' (I can't say that the superintendent heard me), and the man answered, 'Oh, yes, I remember, now.' The tailor's bill was then paid; but it wouldn't be paid unless the sailor had money in the bank to meet a fortnight's board.

"The three tailors with their profits and extent of business can afford to run risks and give credit; knowing their position with the Home, they must do it; but they can charge accordingly. I once had 25s. a week, and 5 per cent. commission, from an outfitter, for touting, and have under that agreement received from £2 10s. to £3 a week. My commission has been often 35s. on £35 custom, carried by me in one week from Sailors' Home men to the tailor who employed me. I have known £120 worth of clothes supplied in one week by one man to different men at the Home, nearly half being profit. Take £3 as an average price for a 'round suit' (cloth jacket, waistcoat, and trowsers) for this I reckon that 38s. at most would be the

A scene in 'The Sailors' Home'

prime cost, but the outfitters try for cent. per cent. I believe that they pay for making a jacket from 4s. to 4s. 6d.; trowsers (two shops pay more than others), 2s. 6d. to 3s.; waistcoat, 2s. The cloth is not to be complained of. Some round suits of the better sorts are charged £4. Sometimes one of these tailors has from sixty to seventy sailors to clothe in a week, but for three or four weeks he may have nothing, or next to nothing, to do. I should say that three out of four sailors want suits when they land after a longish voyage.

"After a long voyage, a man in the Seamen's Home is allowed to draw £1 before he is paid his wages; after short voyages, he has a smaller sum, in proportion. If he has been a long voyage he is sure to want more than £1 before he gets paid off, as, perhaps, he has £25 or £30 to receive; and he runs to the tailor to get an extra advance, and pays for it as I have told you, and that seems to me one reason why the Home is of more benefit to the tailor than the sailor. Many a seaman has been sucked uncommonly dry by persons connected with the Home. Some of the officers of the Home have watches to sell them, and then they may buy them back of their customer, if he happens to want money afterwards—as is a common case—at half-price. An officer too will sell clothes that he's bought cheap of some former lodger who was out of funds, to any new comer wanting them.

"A respectable boarding-master feels bound, for the sake of his character, to keep his lodger until he gets a ship; but that is not the case at the Home. There, after a man's money in the office or bank is run out, they sometimes give him a week's grace, but not until they are certain, from the waiter who has care of the dormitory where the man is lodged, that he has a chest and clothes sufficient to pay for a week's board. In case the man don't get shipped in the course of the week, his clothes are taken from his cabin and put into the store room, and then the poor fellow is refused a meal's victuals and turned into the street. The officials say it's the rule, and must be enforced. Then the man must get to any place he can, and when he gets a ship he of course must pay the person who was kind enough to take him in and supply him with board; after that he may not have enough to pay the Home out of his advance; he goes to sea, and is away perhaps eighteen months or two years, and when he returns and inquires at the Home what has become of his chest and clothes, he is informed they were sold. I'm told that's against the law, but the sailor don't know there is any redress. Such a case as I have described is of common occurrence at the Home: seventy or eighty forfeited chests and clothes are sold every second year." [According to the last year's account the sale of seamen's effects and old stores amounted to £13 13s.]

"Then the officers of the establishment are not allowed, by the rules, to have any perquisites. But I will tell you how it's managed. When men come to the Home they are entered on the books, and then the waiter, who knows his business very well, has perhaps a nice watch to sell, which he 'bought cheap of a man before he went to sea.' This of course yields a good profit. It's the same with any other article; or the waiter may recommend a tailor, for which he gets a commission. Then comes the doorkeeper, and he gets plenty of pickings. The doorkeeper, of course, knows his customers, and would like to drink their healths; they'll ask him to have a glass with them; but the doorkeeper can't stir out, and would rather have the money; the sailors of course can't think of giving a respectable-looking man 2d. for a drop of beer, so they give him 6d. or 1s., and as much as 2s. sometimes. The seamen, when they require money, get cheques from the superintendent on the cashier, but if the office is closed the doorkeeper lends money on them at very good interest. I have known when the clerks have been in the office they have been denied, just for this lending of money and getting of interest. I don't suppose that the committee knows anything about these things.

"The chief officers of the Home are licensed shipping agents. When the Home is quite full—say 300 in it—not more than half that number will sit down to dinner, as sailors won't be tied to hours ashore, when they've money of their own; and that must leave a good profit. If the lodgers come in after mealtimes they can get something to eat in the kitchen, that is if they don't mind the steward's black looks. Men are so sucked, as I have told you from my own knowledge, by runners, and tailors, and the servants of the Home, that I'm satisfied £20 in a sailor's pocket will go further at a boarding-master's than at the Home. The tailors expect their runners to look sharp after the seamen that they've had as customers, and get them ships before all their money is done, or they may be troublesome to the tailors when they want money or such like. The tailors' runners will follow a ship from Blackwall to the London or St. Katharine Docks, coming up by the railway, though I'm told that going on board ship and touting that way is contrary to Act of Parliament. The tailors' runners do all the touting for the Home, which now has only one agent of its own for that purpose, but *he's* not seen at work more than one tide in a week perhaps.

"The Home professes to cash advance notes at 5 per cent. This is the way it's done: if a sailor wants his advance note cashing, an officer of the Home perhaps will say, 'Well, what do you want the money for?' and the man may answer, 'Why, for clothes, I want 30s.' Then says the officer, 'Here, ——, send for so-and-so, and let him supply 30s. worth of clothes.' The Home won't give money if it can be avoided, in such cases; and as the tailor sends in the clothes, why he, and not the Home, runs the risk if the man shirk his engagement."

From Letter L, May 2nd, 1850

In my present Letter I shall treat of the worst class of boarding-masters, known by the name of *"Crimps."* Concerning the practices of these persons I had the following account from one well acquainted with the subject:

"The men who keep the worst class of lodging-houses for sailors are often lumpers—men who are employed by the stevedores to stow the cargo of a ship. They are not fully employed, and, having idle time, look out for lodgers. Those who supply them with lodgers are often runners or touters, but some tout for themselves. The keepers of these low houses are generally of the lower order of the Irish. They hang about the docks, infesting the bridges as ships come in, and getting hold of men who have come home from a voyage. If these men haven't houses of their own to take seamen to, they take them to the lower lodging houses for seamen, kept by others. For taking men to these lodging-houses they will receive from 5s. to 20s.—as much as 30s. I have known given—but the price varies according to the voyage, for on this depends the amount the sailor has to receive, and this the crimps always endeavour to find out. They are generally

Q

dressed in the garb of a rigger—that is, a canvas jumper (a sort of spencer slipped on over the head), canvas trowsers—both so dirty that you can't tell what was their colour when new—and a sou'-wester. That sort of dress doesn't attract the notice of the officers. The lumper, or whoever keeps the low lodging-house, asks for the cook, and inquires if he has any fat to dispose of. This they do as a pretence, as it's against the act of Parliament for them to go aboard; so they get into the galley, and inquire as to the sums the seamen have to receive, and pump as to the 'green uns' (men who have not been in London before). They look out for stupid fellows—though some of the old ones are worse than the young ones.

"These crimps often take a drop of rum or gin in a bottle in their pockets, and treat Jack, who thinks them good fellows, and will go with them. They offer to carry the men's clothes, or to do anything to recommend themselves, or will lend a hand on deck to pull or haul, or help the ship's service as she comes into the dock. This sort of going on further removes the suspicion of the captain or his officers. Suppose they offer to act as a sailor's porter, and to carry his clothes anywhere, the sailor may say, 'But I've no place to go to.' Then the crimp—or whatever he is called—says, 'I'll take you to a good boarding-house,' and he takes him to some boarding-master who will pay him—if the crimp has no house of his own. The crimps' lodging-houses are chiefly in courts and alleys in the lower part of Shadwell, Wapping, St. George's, and East Smithfield. The courts are unpaved; they have been better cleansed lately, but they are very bad still; and a sensible seaman might be frightened at the look of them; but they don't want sensible seamen there, and so don't look out for them. The beds are bad. Men, women, and children pig together. I have known smart-looking young fellows go there, but they are generally frequented by men who haven't much money. Such boarding-masters soon get rid of their lodgers. They say: 'By dad, they'll eat their heads off; we must quit them in a jiffy.'

"Most of the men lodging in these houses come from St. John's, New Brunswick —some are from Nova Scotia, and some from Newfoundland; but they are from North America mainly. The sailors have the character of being soft, and think themselves cunning. They are often fine-looking fellows. They charge these men 14s. a week for their board and lodging, and give them very frequently red herrings or a bit of coarse beef for their dinner, or a bit of salt fish—not much fresh meat—but only what they can get cheap. Once a man went home drunk to one of these places—I've heard it from a person who couldn't be deceived—and when the man recovered from his drink he felt hungry and asked for his supper. The boarding-master, however, had greased his lips when asleep, and on hearing the seaman on waking ask for his supper, said, 'Well, by J——, haven't you supped already? Arn't your lips greased with the fat of the good meat you tucked in, and isn't the bones alongside of you!' The bones had been put there accordingly. This I know for a fact. Tricks of that kind are not uncommon when men have been drinking, and the men are encouraged to drunkenness and all kinds of debauchery.

"Another class of the lowest boarding-masters keep women in the house who live with the seamen, or they more generally have a house next door, where the women live, with a communication to the lodging-house. These houses are far more decent than the others as to cleanliness. A girl pays for a furnished room on the ground floor from 6s. to 9s. a week; upstairs from 4s. to 7s. for front rooms. For the ground floor back room from 4s. to 5s.; for the upstairs back room from 3s. to 4s. In these places a sailor's money is gone before he knows well where he is. If the lady be in arrear £2 or £3 for rent, he has to pay it, and to meet every expense for himself and his 'wife,' as she is called, besides a new cap for the mistress of the house, and some clothing for the children, and other expenses into the bargain, if the seaman be at all flush of money. As soon as his money and clothes are gone (he very seldom saves his clothes), he must go; and then he must resort to his shipmates at the more respectable boarding-masters'. I never heard of men being hocussed in those places. The girls are not of that class. These sort of houses are not so numerous as they have been. Some are carried on by a man and his wife; others by girls on their own account; and some of these girls keep lodging-houses for seamen as well, but they are getting very cautious about it, and I know but four or five of such places. There are more, no doubt. If a man have a good deal of money when he goes there, the people in the house never lose sight of him. If he wants to go to any place of amusement, 'Jack and his mistress go,' or somebody's got to go with him, and he's stuck to until he hasn't a farthing left. I know some women who keep beer-shops—along with lodgings for sailors—which are of the character I have described. The women keeping these beer-shops act as the men's wives; and indeed some have been married in church three or four times. The sailors often marry such people for the spree of the thing."

Three young men, employed as *"porters for seamen"* (so they described themselves), gave me the following statement concerning the tricks practised by ships' porters generally, in which they all concurred:

"It would be much better if such as we were licensed; we look after porter's work, carrying sailors' luggage ashore. Last ship we were aboard some coal-whippers were there, and were sarcy, and were turned out, and we were turned out as well. We go aboard to carry the sailors' goods ashore; but some porters—for there's two classes of us—go aboard for thieving, or to take men away. We work two or three together that we may save the goods from thieves by keeping watch. Perhaps if a ship comes into dock there'll be more porters go on board than there are seamen; twenty-five we've seen on board one ship, but not more than six were regular porters. There are regular porters at each dock—perhaps nearer forty than fifty in all. Four times that number do it for jobs. People that work about the dock, work as ships' porters. Dock labourers often leave their work to go on board a ship. If they hadn't done so this afternoon, we should have had a dinner tomorrow (Sunday). The coal-whippers look out as well as the dock labourers.

"When we get goods ashore one must always keep watch; we can't work singly. If nobody watched, somebody would sling the chest on his back and walk off with it. Besides, there's often so many things, that we can hardly keep watch enough. I saw a man the other day on board a ship pull off a pair of old boots, and slip on a new pair, that was put on the deck to be carried ashore. Such practices are common with jackets. The seamen look to us to be honest with them in bringing their things on shore."

One man, who said that he had been 25 years at the trade, off and on, gave me the following account:

"From the West India Dock to Shadwell or Ratcliff-highway, a porter will receive 2s. or 2s. 6d.—2s. from the West India Docks will satisfy us, and 2s. 6d. from the East. The worst class of porters will do it at 1s., making up the difference by cribbing. Besides, they'll run away with the seaman, if they can, and sell him. They sell him to anybody—to any bad boarding-master. The price of the man depends upon what money he may have. One man was sold the other day by the porters; there was a good power of them, and they took him—he was a black man—to one of his countrymen, but he wouldn't buy him, but Mr. —— bought him at 6s. 6d. If we take a man to a decent boarding-house, we get 1s. or so for our trouble. A bad boarding-master will regulate his price to the porters according to what clothes the seaman may want, for one thing. We've heard of £1 being given for a 'Chinaman.' A two years' voyage man will fetch £1 at ——, or ——, or ——, or any crimp's. If we took a man to a respectable house, we might get 1s. for beer; so, to be paid, we must take men to lower lodging-houses, who will pay us.

"The way to stop this sort of thing is to license men like us. Men who are employed by the low boarding-masters will knock you down if you interfere with them. They treat the men if they get them ashore, and carry gin and rum aboard with them. Ashore they run off with the chests and things in a truck, and the sailor may follow. They go where the boarding-masters pay best, and the boarding-masters that keep half-brothels, or find women for the men, can afford to give higher prices for seamen than the respectable houses. We know a boarding-master who has, we believe, fourteen brothels. He may buy his sailors at £1 a piece, but he employs his own men. He has five cabs; we saw one at the West India Dock to-day, taking two men's things away, and hindering regular porters of a job. It's hard to say how many porters or runners he has, but we know two of his constant hands. His men are allowed in the dock, for they dress respectable, with gold chains as thick as your finger, and rings on their fingers; so these runners get in when we can't.

"The brothels for sailors are chiefly in East Smithfield. A man who went to a low boarding-master's with near £40 in his pocket—he was a ship's carpenter who had been away some eight or nine months—wasn't a fortnight before he was cleaned out—regularly 'skinned' of his clothes and all—and we found him in the streets without a shilling. He is a quiet, nice fellow, too. The boarding-master pretended to read the list of payments and money that the man had before he left, and the carpenter said, 'Yes, that's it,' and he was turned out directly. He was drunk all the time, and they give him shilling or fourpenny bits, and said they were sovereigns. He didn't care as long as he had gin. He used to take a farthing for a shilling to spend at a public-house. One boarding-master furnishes rooms for prostitutes, and recommends them to the seamen who lodge with him.

"The low boarding-masters usually buy the sailors' clothes for them, getting them second-hand often, and charging them as new, or else putting down for them—as much as the Sailors' Home tailors, who have to pay lots of money to their runners, and so you know must put on a little extra. The Sailors' Home tailors have many runners, who do us harm by getting jobs from us. There are two classes of boarding-masters—good and bad; the good treat their lodgers as well as the others use them badly. One boarding-master kept a man six months once, after his money was out. Scores of times we've heard seamen say, when the runners have asked them to go to the Sailors' Home, 'Go there, to be sent to the straw-house

A sailor just off the boat and on his way to the Sailors' Home

when our money's done? No! No! A boarding-master will keep us when it is done.' By licensing the porters and boarding-masters good must be done, for then half that carry on those trades would never get a license. None of the bad class of porters like to hear of a license. The worst sort of boarding-masters are Irish, and foreigners more than others. There are not many Jews. There may not be more than twelve regular boarding-houses of the worst class. More than fifty take occasional boarders—two or three; but they are generally the very worst of all. The charge is 2s. a day with all of them."

A well-spoken and good-looking sailor told the following story of the proceedings as regards himself in a low boarding-house:

"I came to London last Wednesday," he said, "and was on my way to Mr. B——'s, a respectable boarding-master, whom I have known for eleven years. He had changed his residence in the five years that I had been away in India, China, New Zealand, Sydney, and other places. [The man, I ascertained, bore a good character.] Well, I was going along the Highway, with a little drop of drink in my head, sailor-like, you know, sir—half seas over, that's about the size of it— excited quite on getting ashore, and thinking how I would surprise them at home (that's what I always call Mr. B——'s), when I met with a young woman, and she asked me if I was looking out for anybody? I told her I wanted Mr. B——, and she said, 'You had best come to my house; he's gone away.' I answered, 'Well, I don't mind; short reckonings make long friends.' If I hadn't been tipsy I shouldn't have been carried off by such a craft.

"She took me to a house—I remember it was up a dark passage—there's plenty of ins and outs in the streets about here—and we had something more to drink. Next morning I found myself 'skinned'—that's about the size of it; and about 50s. was the value of the 'skin' I lost. A pair of old canvass trousers was left for my own good cloth ones, but all the rest of my clothes were gone, and the young woman was gone too. I never got served out so before, but I was catched on the hip this time. About Bluecoat-fields—that's the name of the place where I was taken to—is called 'Skinner's Bay,' because men are mostly served there as I was.

"When I awoke in the morning I thought at first I was at Mr. B——'s, but I soon found the difference. Instead of a comfortable bed-room, I was in a small, poor, dirty room, with a few halfpenny pictures over the mantel, and two or three broken cups or saucers in the room. The young woman told me overnight that I might as well stay at her house as at Mr. B——'s, for that I should only be charged 14s. all the same. In the morning I met with an old woman, when I looked out for the master of the house or somebody, and I soon found her a country-woman of mine. She would give me no information, but wanted me to board there at 14s. a week, saying I might save money by it; and meaning, I suppose, that the people there would supply women or drink regularly, or any foolery a sailor was after, and all for the fourteen shillings. But I said—feeling I was a fool in the morning, though I thought myself a smart man overnight—'No, no, none of that; I'll be off.' So I walked away in my canvass trowsers and blue shirt, like a collier going nor'ard, bucket on one side and broom on the other. I got to my old boarding-master's, and then got clothes and help. If I'd stayed, as I'd money coming, I might have lost another skin. It's no use prosecuting the people. I shan't be any poorer a twelvemonth's hence."

I was told by an experienced person that seamen are not robbed in this manner so frequently as they used to be—or so frequently, perhaps, as people generally imagine. It is commoner to pawn the man's clothes than to steal them. The police warn a seaman if they see him led to a boarding-house that is known to be half a brothel, and so will the better sort of sailors' porters. Often, however, seamen will not state where they have been "skinned," having a greater feeling of shame in the matter now than they once had.

Concerning the practice known as *kidnapping*, among the worst class of boarding-masters, I had the subjoined statement from a person intimately acquainted with the subject:

"The desertion of foreign seamen in this port is very great, particularly among the Prussian and Russian ships. The system is this. On the arrival of a Prussian or Russian vessel it is closely watched by certain lodging-house keepers, about half-a-dozen in number, who entice the foreign seamen to leave their vessels, the lodging-house keepers pretending that they will get them berths in English ships with better wages. Two of these lodging-house keepers are foreigners, and they can all express themselves so as to be understood by a Prussian or Russian. One of these men can make himself understood in four or five languages. They assist the foreign seamen to smuggle their clothes out of the ship, generally at night; or, as the principal place for this traffic is at the Commercial Dock, the clothes are sometimes taken out piecemeal, in the daytime, hid in some adjacent by-place—perhaps under a hedge—and then carried away at night, or early in the morning, to the lodging-house. One of those houses had a place fitted up in the back yard for the reception of the seamen to be concealed, and the place was so contrived by sliding panels as to present the appearance of a dead wall, or of some building unconnected with the lodging-house.

"Here, and in similar places, the kidnapped people were detained until the sailing of their vessel—that is, if no reward had been offered for their apprehension by the master. By the laws of many foreign countries the master of a merchant ship is under a heavy bond to return the seamen to their native country. If the reward be offered, the man is restored to the ship, and the money paid as the reward is deducted by the captain from his wages. Should no reward be offered, the lodging-house keepers, knowing from what ship they have stolen the sailors, wait upon the master, telling him that they have heard his men are missing (much after the fashion of the street dog-stealers). Ultimately, perhaps, the captain will agree to pay something to have his men sent back to the ship. This is only done when the seamen kidnapped are penniless, and the lodging-house keeper thinks it better to try to get £5 from the foreign captain that wait for a £2 advance note from a British ship.

"When the lodging-house keeper has bargained in this way with a foreign captain, he returns home and informs the poor fellows whom he has deluded that he has got them a British ship, with good wages, good living, and all the rest of it. The seamen are then taken to some convenient river-stairs, where the assistance of the Thames police inspector has been secured; he at once places the men in his boat and conveys them as prisoners to their own ship. Sometimes the men have been rowed right into the river without knowing they were in custody. When the men are returned to their own ship the crimp receives an order on the broker for the reward, or the amount agreed to be paid.

"In order to convince myself of these facts I called at a broker's office, and saw in the books an entry of £31 odd having been paid to a crimp, who had returned some foreign seamen to their ship; one of these men (there was six in all, £5 a piece being the money paid) was seen in the crimp's house, but no one had any power to interfere and compel the man to return to his duty. One of these lodging-house keepers was lately summoned at the Thames Police Court, at the instance of the Swedish Consul, charged with kidnapping a foreign seaman. The man was enticed away from his ship (a Swedish vessel) by a lodging-house keeper, and placed on board an English ship. He received an advance note for about £4, and the whole of this was taken possession of by the crimp. At Gravesend the Swede's own vessel dropped down at the time the British ship that he was on board of was at anchor there. The man swam, during the night, from the British ship to his own. He appeared as a witness at the police-court for the prosecution, and detailed these circumstances with the aid of an interpreter. After much discussion between the solicitors employed, the case was dismissed, the magistrate having no jurisdiction—the Merchant Seamen's Act applying only to 'subjects of her Majesty,' and the Merchant Seamen's Protection Act to the 'seamen of this kingdom.' "

I have already given the opinion of an intelligent and experienced officer on the necessity of improved *sanitary regulations* on board ship. I now give . . . . [a] narrative, bearing closely on that important subject. . . .

"I joined the —— as seaman, at Bombay, on the 15th of October, 1849, and sailed from that place about the 22nd of that month for London; no spirits were allowed. I have been in temperance ships before, and no cases of scurvy have arisen. The lime-juice was served out generally daily, and was always taken by the crew. Sheep and pigs were taken on board at Bombay; one sheep died, and one was killed to save its life. The one that died was cooked for the pigs, the one that was killed was made into a sea-pie; some of the crew eat it. I tasted the dough, but could not eat the meat. The pigs were all kept for the captain's table. About the 27th of November we had some bad weather, and the long-boat, containing the pigs, sheep, and poultry, was filled with water. From that time they were removed into the forecastle, in which we slept; the stench from them was very bad—particularly from the pigs and the dead ducks. They all remained there till they were required to be killed. The captain did not have the same water as we had, which was very bad; but after all the cuddy water was gone, himself and mates were obliged to turn to ours.

"One man died with the venereal and scurvy; he only worked a month and ten days after he joined. An apprentice boy was the next who was taken ill. He first caught cold. He was kept up in the cross-trees all day naked in the wet and cold by the captain, who said he was too long over his work when aloft. The scurvy afterwards came on. The apprentice boy died first, then the man, and three others shortly after. They all complained of hunger. The salt meat was stopped, and no substitute was given to us. Two pigs were then left, one of which we brought to England; so there was enough and to spare. The sugar was stopped when any of us were taken ill, because, as the captain said, it was getting short; but those who could work had their proper allowance, for the captain always said we were shamming sick, and he would starve us out. He refused to give us anything but what we signed articles for. The vessel was built of iron. We felt the cold very much; out of the sixteen bunks (sleeping places) eight only were fit for use; the water ran into the others; they were never cleaned out from the time we left Bombay, neither were they touched there. Not even a drop of vinegar was given to us, to sprinkle the bunks with, when the men died. We clubbed together, and out of our allowance we used to get a little for that purpose.

"In the forecastle it was very close; there were no ventilators. Before the pigs were put into the place amidships, there was a door on the starboard side that we could open, but it was afterwards fastened up; the door on the larboard side was never opened. The hawser-holes run in amidships, so we did not even get the air that would have come through them. On arrival in the channel we had but three of the foremast hands who could do duty, and I think the master ought to have sent on shore and obtained other hands, at Scilly or Falmouth; he did take in six fresh hands in the Downs, about three hours before the steam-tug took us, but then none of the crew could stand on their feet."...

V
TIMBER TRADE

SAWYERS

From Letter LIX, July 4th, 1850

[At this point, Mayhew changed his general organizing principles. He abandoned the classification of "skilled and unskilled labour" and decided to survey all the occupations of the trades connected with a single raw material, in this case timber. His letters on the timber trade thus reported interviews with semi-skilled workers (dock labourers and sawyers), with skilled workers (turners, joiners, and some carpenters), and with the artisans who made furniture.]

I shall now give an account of the earnings and condition of each of the different classes of sawyers . . . beginning with those engaged in the cutting of timber and hard wood. . . . To this I shall append a statement . . . concerning the effect of machinery upon the working classes generally. In doing this I trust I need not remind the reader that the opinions there expressed are those of the *working men* themselves, who have been allowed to state their sentiments, because, suffering severely from machinery, it was considered to be but fair to express their thoughts and feelings upon this subject. It is right I should add, that I have found not one man in the trade opposed to machinery, in the abstract. The main objection of the operatives appears to be, that machinery benefits the capitalist, at the expense of the working man.

From "a pair" of deal or general sawyers, whom I found at their work, I had the following statement. The "pitman" said:

"I have been above thirty years a sawyer and a pitman; that is, the sawyer who works in the pit. We work in pairs—the topman and the pitman. The topman's part is the most difficult certainly, as he directs the saw to do her work (we always call the saw a *she*) according to the line. Every piece of timber is lined (chalked). When I first knew the trade things was much better. Me and my mate could earn between us then, £4 10s. a week easy. Top and pit men is paid alike, and has always been so. Now it is with great difficulty that we can make £3 a week the pair on us; and when we earn £3, we receive only £2 15s., for 1d. out of every shilling is deducted. The employer stops the 1d.; it's called 'pence,' for the finding of tools, all of which the master now provides for us." [Another man gave me a full account of this "pence," and calculated the amount of profit made by it.] "That wasn't the case till machinery got into full operation, twenty years ago, or somewhere thereabout."

"I believe" (said the other man, the top sawyer), "the first steam saw-mill was started at the foot of Westminster-bridge by a man named Smart, thirty-five years ago, or so. We thought nothing about that then. Smart sawed deals. Master

233

got harder and harder upon us. Our last strike was in the first year of the cholera, in 1833 I believe. We are paid for a twelve-foot deal 3¼d. a cut. Other deals are paid at the same rate. They do it cheapest at saw-mills, but not the best for working purposes, as carpenters can't 'bring it up' so well; that is, it's not so well adapted for work, because the machinery can't humour the grain. You see, sir, machinery is a ruining of all of us. Where there was 200 pair of sawyers there's not 50 now. We struck to keep up the prices of that day, which was 3½d. a cut in our yard, but the masters got so many hands in from the country and other cheap ways, even if the fellows knew nothing about a saw before, that we was obliged to give way. Ours is very hard work; the general hours is from six to seven. The year through the utmost we average a man is 25s. a week when the pence is paid. We are obligated to drink beer to keep our strength up, and that to from 6d. to 10d. worth a day; but there's no compulsion in any way as to beer. Some drink more than 10d. worth in a day, but that's more than sufficient. Our men can't afford to be what you may call drunkards (but p'r'aps one can't call them exactly sober men). The lazy fellows somehow—and I don't know how—do manage to get drunk pretty often.

"The wood we saw now is cut much greener than it used to be, and is worse to manage. We get English wood as it falls—oak, ash, beech, elm, and sycamore—them's the principal; and we have to trim it, knock the knots off and the bark off, but the oak comes to us stripped. For trimming the wood we're poorly paid. For ash, elm, beech, and all trees we have 6s. per 100 feet; the masters agree it's worth 1s. more. A man couldn't make 20s. a week at that, and the 'pence' to be stopped out of it. I've been a top man for more than thirty years—I should say about thirty-five. Top and pit sawyers very seldom change places, only for a make-shift. The top-man, though it's the most difficult part, gets no more than the pit man, not a morsel, and he has to keep the saw in order, and he's answerable for all work to the master. The easiest wood of all to saw is American pine; it gives to the saw easiest. English timber (elm, beech, and sycamore) is the hardest. Oak's another thing; it's difficult to get it ready to fit it for sawing, but not harder to saw than elm. With a log of mahogany the top-man must humour the saw so as to cut to the master's orders, and masters are very exacting. If we vexes 'em, they puts us on spruce deals, which are the hardest deals to cut. We can't make above 2s. 6d. a man a day of it, and they keep us at it as long as they think fit. In spruce deals we have to cut what the saw-mills can't well cut; they can cut it, certainly, but they charge higher; for there's only one cut (two boards) in a spruce fir, and it takes them as much time to cut one cut as to cut ten.

"I've known, in 1821, when George IV was crowned, 80 pairs of men in two sawpits, where now there isn't a single one. The pits, all of them I think, is coming to a close, and the business is going to the dogs, or the sawmills, for it's all one. Many sawyers is now glad to go in for labourers to saw-yards, for piling and placing the timber, at 3s. or 4s. a day—perhaps only with two days' work a week —because they can't get employment at sawing. One of our saws—they run from five to seven feet—will cost £1 for five feet, and on to 30s. for seven feet, without the frame, which may cost 10s. The weight of a 7-foot saw is from 60 to 70lbs., for two men to pull up and down all day, at the rate of, say ten strokes, or seventy feet, a minute, or 4,200 feet an hour; and that's, as you say, 42,000 feet in a day of ten hours—so that we lift upwards of half-a-hundred weight nearly eight miles high in our day's work. The resistance of the saw—as it pulls like so many hooks coming down and catching—is not an easy calculation. A scientific man— it's ten years ago, I think—calculated, and reckoned that each down stroke (for the up stroke is only a lift up of the saw, like) was equal to lifting 86lb. My opinion is, and I judge by experience and by lifting weights, that he was right; others think so, too. I don't know what he calculated it for." [The man then, at my request, went into another calculation as to weight, of course with my assistance with the figures.]

"A force of 86lbs. is required for each down stroke: 10 in a minute is a force of 430lbs. put out by each man every minute, and that's a power of 25,800lbs. an hour. In a day of ten hours, the whole amount of power is equal to 258,000lbs., or more than 18,428 stone; and divide that by 8, and that'll show how many hundred weights—more than 2,303, or upwards of 115 tons a day. The strength's put out equal by the two sawyers, top and pit, generally; and it ought to be always, when each man does his part properly, and like a workman.

"Provisions has been cheap for some time, and that's a great thing for working men. If we says a word about better pay, or the grievance of the 'pence,' masters stops our mouths with machinery. A 'pair' of sawyers will do three dozen cuts of 12 feet deals a day, or four dozen of battens. A 'cut' is nine inches through in a deal and seven in a batten. The saw may go ahead half an inch a stroke as near as may be. Sawyers is generally healthy men and not short-lived."...

A man whom I found residing with his wife and children in a little place of apparently two rooms made the following statement as to cooper's stave sawing. He lived, with many others of the same class, in one of very many alleys that run from the river side, behind the site of what was once the Globe Theatre, to Guild- ford-street, Southwark. The alleys are built with the utmost economy of space; some of them are almost too narrow for the passage of a horse. I saw nothing, however, to call filth. Abutting on one of the narrowest of these alleys are high dark wooden palings, from behind which come the smell and lowing of cows, a circumstance rather in contrast with the thick packing of human habitations on all sides:

"I have been twenty years a cooper's stave sawyer," he said. "We use different saws to those of the deal sawyers. They are smaller in the teeth, and only four feet long. A saw and frame will weigh 50 lb. on an average, and I reckon that we pull 60 lbs. weight every stroke. We make 50 strokes a minute up and down. I'm sure of it. We work very quick. That's 200 feet a minute, or 4,000 yards an hour— about 2¼ miles. We are top-sawyers and pitmen. Both are paid alike, though the topman has the hardest work. When I first knew the business times was much better. I could then earn £2 a week, and my mate the same, comfortably, the year through. Now we can each of us earn 25s. on an average the year through. We are paid by the piece. For 6-foot Dantzic or Memel straight cut staves 1s. 7d. per dozen cuts is paid us. We may have one or two cuts in each stave. For Quebec staves of the same length, or even if not quite so long, 1s. 8d.; Quebec hogsheads, 1s. 4d. They run about five feet; Dantzic hogsheads, about 4 feet, 1s. 2d.; brandy pipes, about 5 feet, 1s. 4d.; barrel straight cuts (for beer barrels), between 3 and 4 feet, 1s.; if we cut them into 'doublets'—and in doublets it's easier work for the cooper, for we thin the stave for his purpose—we have 2d. a dozen extra. The master gets more profit by it, but we have only 2d. a dozen, and other sizes in proportion, up to 4d. These are the principal staves; the others are for vinegar kilderkins and small barrels (9 or 18 gallons), and paid in proportion.

"We work two or three different sorts of timber, but all of them oak; all foreign, Baltic or American. We saw the staves from the timber as it's brought by the ships; it's cleaved (cleft), or chopped, to our purpose abroad. In the winter of '47–8 we were on strike sixteen weeks, but only me and two mates stood out for that time. They reduced us in the doublets 6d., from 1s. 11d. for the long staves to 1s. 5d., and for straight cuts to 1s. 4d., while others were reduced in the same proportion. We formed a committee among ourselves and got our prices back again, however. We did it in a month, after forming a society, though some staveyards didn't manage it for six or nine months. The masters gave way when they got busy. Our masters can get their staves sawn cheaper at a steam-mill by 6d. a dozen the bigger ones, the straight cuts; but the machine can't make all the turns wanted in the stave—thank God for that. For straight cuts they are working us out. We haven't many straight cuts now to what we had; less by the working sawyer from 10s. to 15s. a week wages. Some masters—mine's one—don't like to send their staves to steam-mills for straight cuts, for if the timber for the staves be crooked we can cut them to more advantage to the master than the steam-mills can.

"We take our money in the counting-house. I have been paid, in another employ, at a public-house, and we were obliged to take our beer from there every day, but when we formed our committee we put a stop to all that bad system. It was time, for some of us had to go home with nothing on a Saturday night. Sawing is very hard work, and requires four pints of beer a day to support a man, but many drink a great deal more. The public-house system made men drunkards —I'm sure it did, sir. I confine myself to four pints, which is enough for me. I know of no teetotallers among us. Accidents are common with sawyers. I've fallen many times, and have been cut all to pieces, so to say, by the saw." [He showed me some scars on his arms.]

"We have a sick fund. Take sawyers altogether, they're fond of a drop, but I don't think them rougher than other people when they're in liquor. We are nearly all married men with families. Families seems a sort of gift to poor men, instead of to rich ones. I have known sawyers working at 70 years old, hard work as it is. We live as long as other people, I think. We pay no 'pence,' but have to find our own saws. A saw may cost from 7s. to 10s., and the frame 5s., when a new frame is wanted. A frame will last five or six saws. A saw will last us about five or six months in average use.". . .

Concerning the operation of the steam saw-mills upon the working men, I had the following statement from two picked men: they were general sawyers. One, who was 55 years old, had been 40 years in the trade; and the other, who was 49, had had 35 years' experience in it. "I can recollect," said the younger, "when I could save more money in a week than I can now earn in the same time. Ah! then, if a man was a goodish sawyer, and out of work, he would have twenty or thirty people after him. Often, when I've been going along London streets, with my saw on my back, a timber-merchant or a cabinet maker would hail me, and cry, 'Halloa, ho, do you want any work, my man?' and often they gave a sum of money for a good sawyer to come and work for them."

The elder man said, "My father was a sawyer, and often I've heard him say that the trade was better in his younger days than even it was in mine. He used to speak of what it was seventy years ago; the wages weren't better in his younger days than they were in mine, but the work was—there was fewer hands, you see. I have heard him say that him and his mate has earned one pound a day. He became a timber merchant afterwards, and he's told me that he'd paid a pair of sawyers that he had in his employ £24 in the month. They were veneer sawyers, and that was the finest and best paid work in the trade—now that's *all* gone from us. There an't one regular veneer sawyer left in the trade. All veneers are cut at present by machinery. Thirty years ago, when London wasn't half so big, there was three times as many sawyers as there are now, and one pair in every ten out of these used to cut veneers. In every timber yard the 'first pair' was generally employed cutting veneers. In the neighbourhood where I live, the sawyers are not half so many as they were. At R——'s yard, where they used to keep nine pair, they hasn't more than three, and yet the work's increased to that extent that it would keep twenty saws going where only nine was employed before. At S——'s there used to be nineteen pairs of sawyers constantly at work, and now there's not employment for one pair. I think I have heard my father say that there was as many as 3,000 pairs in the metropolis. Why, not more than twenty year ago one master sawyer used to have as many as five apprentices. In the year '26 it was about as good a time for sawyers as ever it was—there was a good demand for men, and good wages."

"I can remember it better," said the oldest of the two; "but, never mind, that's the last time that the trade's been what you may call good. It began to decline between '26 and '27—just about Fauntleroy's bankruptcy. I remember the saw mills began to get more general from that period. I can't recollect when the horse saw-mills was fust put up. Several cabinet-makers used to have hand-mills of their own, which consisted of circular saws in a bench, and worked by a couple of labourers. One of the horse-mills—I remember it was over about Pedler's-acre—was said to kill a horse a day. The first steam-mill that was set up was at Battersea. It was a Frenchman (Brunel) that took out the patent for cutting veneers by steam—that's above forty years ago. The steam-mill had been up two or three years when I first came to London, and that was in 1810. I recollect seeing some shortly after I got to town. They was cut more true than any sawyer could do them, but not half as well as they are done now. The first that was done was eight in the inch, and now they can cut 14, as thin as a wafer, and that's impossible for the best sawyer in the world to do. I have cut as many as eight in the inch myself, but then the wood was very shallow—eight or nine inches deep. The general run of veneers cut by hand was about six in the inch. It wasn't until some five or six years after the first steam saw-mill for veneers was set up that one was erected for deals, and some time after that they were used to cut timber. About 1827, they began to get general, and as fast as the saw-mills have been starting up so we have been going down. We only have the rough work, and what the saw-mills can't or won't do. We get chiefly 'one cuts' to do, because the saw-mills can't do that kind of work so well as we can. A sawyer formerly took apprentices."

"I was an apprentice for seven years," said the younger man. "And I worked along with my father," said the other. "It was a rule in our trade that the eldest son was entitled to his father's business. Now I don't see a sawyer in London who has an apprentice. Formerly we would allow no man to work at our trade

R

unless he had been apprenticed or articled for three years; now it's open to any man, and yet none that I know of come into it. Many that I am acquainted with have left it, and many more would be glad to get away from it. I was one of the enumerators at the taking of the last census in the district in which I now live, and now I think there are not more than half as many sawyers as what there were then; the old hands die off, and no young ones fill up their places. Some few sawyers perhaps put their boys to the trade because they haven't the means to apprentice them to anything else, and the boy, you see, by working with his father, will bring in something at the end of the week. All that the two earns then goes to one home. I know many sawyers that have emigrated, and among them have been some of the best workmen, and some of the most intelligent.

"The trade, we think, will keep dwindling and dwindling every year; but machinery, we think, will never be able to take it all from us. I haven't been at work not a day this week. Some times we are worked to death, and sometimes we are picking our fingers. At the beginning of the week we are often obligated to have extra hands, and at the end of the week we are standing still, may be. There may be some few in large firms who may have constant work; but the most of our trade is idle more than half their time. It puzzles me how they live, some of them. Twenty-six years ago, my average wages was 35s. a week all the year round. Now I should say that this last year my wages hasn't been above 18s. a week all the year through. I don't think the average wages of our trade, take the good with the bad, are above £1, and formerly it was full double that. Why, twenty years ago we used to have a trade dinner every year, somewhere out of town, and to go up to the tavern—wherever it was—in grand purcession, with bands of music and flags flying (we had a union jack that cost forty odd pound then), and the dinner for the whole of the districts used to come to near upon 50 guineas.

"After all this I leaves you to judge what our opinion is about machinery. Of course we looks upon it as a curse. We have no chance to compete with a machine; it isn't taxed, you see, as we are. I look upon machinery as an injury to society generally, because if it drives the hands out of our trade they must go into some other, so that working men is continually pressing one upon another. If machinery can cut the wood cheaper than we can, it's a gain to the timber merchant, he is enabled to reduce the price, and so some part of society may be a gainer by it, but we think society loses more than it gets. Supposing a machine to do the work of 100 pair of sawyers, then of course it throws 200 men out of employ; and these 200 men have families, and they are all benefited by the employment of the working man's labour. But in the case of machinery only one man is benefited" [this I found to be the common opinion of the operatives]; "the money all goes to him and the others are left to starve, or else for society to support, either as paupers or felons, so that society, in the present state of things, after all, loses more than it gains. We see that as science advances the comfort of the working man declines. We believe machinery to be a blessing if rightly managed. It only works for one class at present, but the time *will* come when it *will* work for all parties. . . .

"Let machinery go on increasing as it does, and there will come a time when the labour of the many will be entirely done away with; and then what will society gain when it has to keep the whole of the labouring classes? We can see machinery improving every day, so that there is less work for the people and more paupers. Our bread is being taken out of our mouths, and our children left to starve. I am quite satisfied that those who have nothing but their labour to depend upon get up every morning less independent than they went to bed. The many long heads that are scheming how to deprive men of their work is quite sufficient to bring that about. It's no use emigrating either. Let a working man go where he will, machinery pursues him. In America it's worse for sawyers, if possible, than here. There the sawing is all done by water-mills, and wood is so plentiful and so cheap that if they spoil a bit, it ain't no matter. Working-men is much disheartened at the increase of machinery, when they're a standing at the corner of streets idle and starving and see carts coming out of the yard filled with planks that they ought to have had. You see, sir, when some are injured by any alteration, they gets compensation; but here is our trade cut up altogether, and what compensation do we get? We are left to starve without the least care. I have paid 1s. 10d. for a quartern loaf before now, and I could get it much easier than I can now. When I get up in the morning, I don't know whether I shall be able to earn a 6d. before nightfall. I have been at work ever since I was eight years old, and I'm a pretty good example of what the working man has to look for; and what's the good of it all? Even the machines, some of them, can't hardly raise the price of the coals to get their fire up. When they first set up they had 6d. a foot for cutting veneers, and now they have only 1d. Machinery's very powerful, sir, but competition is much stronger."

CARPENTERS

From Letter LX, July 11th, 1850

I shall now proceed to give the statements of the men employed at the several branches of the "honourable" trade. . . . The following information I received from a highly respectable journeyman carpenter working for the best shops at the best prices:

"I have known the London trade between twenty and thirty years. I came up from Lancashire, where I served an apprenticeship. I have worked all that time entirely at carpentering. No doubt I am a pure carpenter, as you call it, never having worked at anything else. Before I got married, eighteen years ago, I tried to make some odds and ends of furniture for myself, but I couldn't manage them at all to please myself, except in the frame of a bedstead, so I got a cabinet maker to finish my chairs and tables for me." [My informant then described the nature of the carpenter's work, and expressed an opinion that to have it executed in the first style a workman should do nothing else.]

"I have always had 5s. a day, and in busy times and long days have made 33s. and 35s. a week, by working over time. I have always been able to keep my family, my wife and two children, comfortably, and without my wife's having to do anything but the house-work and washing. One of my children is now a nurse-maid in a gentleman's family, and the other is about old enough to go and learn some trade. Certainly, I shan't put him to my own trade, for, though I get on well enough in it, it's different for new hands, for scamping masters get more hold every day. There's very few masters in my line will take apprentices; but I could set him on as the son of a journeyman. If I'd come to London now, instead of when I did, I might have got work quite as readily perhaps—for I didn't get it within a month when I did come; but then I was among friends; but I should have had to work for inferior wages, and scamping spoils a man's craft. *[Another word used to describe slop carpenter work is 'scamped work.']* He's not much fit for first-rate work after that. I am better off now than ever I was, because I earn the same, and all my expenses, except rent, are lower. I have a trifle in the savings bank. But then, you'll understand, sir, I'm a sort of exception, because I've had regular work, twelve months in the year, for these ten or twelve years, and never less than nine months before that. I know several men who have been forced to scamp it—good hands, too—but driven to it to keep their families. What can a man do? 21s. a week is better than nothing.

"I am a society man, and always have been. I consider mine skilled labour, no doubt of it. To put together, and fit, and adjust, and then fix, the roof of a mansion so that it cannot warp or shrink—for if it does the rain's sure to come in through the slates—must be skilled labour, or I don't know what is. Sometimes

240

we make the roof, or rather the parts of it, in the shop, and cart it to the building to fix. We principally work at the building, however. There's no rule; it all depends upon weather and convenience. The foremen generally know on what work to put the men so as best to suit, but in no shop I've been in has there been a fixed and regular division of the carpenters into one set as roofers, and another for the other work. Our work is more dangerous than the joiners, as we have to work more on scaffolding, and to mount ladders; but I can't say that accidents are frequent among us. If there's an accident at a building by a fall, it's mostly the labourers. I'm satisfied that the carpenters on the best sort of work are as well conducted and as intelligent as any class of mechanics. With scamping masters character is no recommendation, or very little. A very good hand I know was sometime out of work, and applied to a scamping master, and said, 'Mr. —— would vouch for his being a good workman and a sober man.' 'D——n your soberness,' was answered to him, 'what do I care for that? What I want is plenty of work done.' Men get not to care for their character when they come to be knocked about by such masters. I myself know three men, at least, that were sober and respectable when in good work: they're scamping it now, and drink all they can get. One of them's a married man, and his wife has to go out washing, and his family's in rags.

"We find our own tools, and a first-rate kit of carpenter's tools, with duplicates and everything proper, may cost new, and at first hand, on to £30; but perhaps not very many have more than £15 worth, and some have to get on as well as they can with from £5 to £10 worth, or less than £5; but then, of course, they must keep renewing them. It's generally all up with a carpenter if he's popped his tools, and has to get them from his uncle's when he wants them. If they are in heavy, he hardly ever gets a fair start with them all again. I never knew one do it, and I have known very industrious men forced to pledge almost all their kit. We use saws a good deal, and sharpening them is a great cost to us. Wear and tear of tools I reckon at well on to 2s. a week. That's for six days' regular work. In the winter there's mostly a slack, as building, of course, ain't so freely carried on in heavy rain, and frost and snow, and dark short days. Some carpenters have nine months of it, and not a few either have six months' work of it in a year; others just what they can catch."

A very intelligent man gave me the following information as *to the best description of joiners' work*:

"I have been twelve years a journeyman joiner in London. I consider a joiner a man who works in a building, and usually at a bench, at everything the plane goes over, such as doors, windows, sashes and frames, closets, skirting, flooring; but that's generally sawn and planed at the mills, and we merely lay it—in fact, the joiner is the preparer, fixer, and finisher of a building. The other work is the carpenter's such as the roof, &c. I have been ten years in one shop, in the honourable trade, where we have as good wages and as good usage as in any shop, and where between 400 and 500 hands in all branches are employed. The wages paid us are 5s. a day for ten hours, from six in the morning to half-past five. Half an hour is allowed for breakfast, an hour for dinner, and half an hour for tea, but that is generally waived, and so we leave work at half-past five. For over-hours we are paid at the same rate, 6d. an hour, unless it be after ten at night, when we have 9d. an hour. On Sunday double time is allowed—that is, 1s. an hour, as is the case in repairing Somerset-house, the Admiralty, and other Government offices, where Sunday labour is resorted to not to interrupt business. I never knew any man to object to work on a Sunday. I would not if I felt it to be a matter of necessity. If it was not a necessity I would object.

"In our firm over-hours are not frequent, but in some few shops the men now work until eight o'clock. The trade is greatly opposed to over-time, because it keeps many men out of employment, but sometimes it is unavoidable. We prepare the doors, &c., which we make in the workshops (I speak of large and honourable firms), and then take them to the building to be fixed. In each workshop there is a foreman, whose business it is to see that the work is properly done. In a very busy time in our firm he has an assistant, and does not work himself. He overlooks all the men, whether forty-six benches, as in our shop, which is a double shop, or in an establishment where there may be only eight to ten; but smaller masters, or jobbing or speculative builders, frequently act as their own foremen, having sometimes 'a leading hand,' who works like the other men, but may have 2s. a week extra. He 'sets out' the work, and works himself when not so employed. We have no control—I mean our society has none—over the number of apprentices, or rather boys or youths a master chooses to take. Some take an unconscionable number. At ——'s they had to every one man five or six boys or youths, not apprenticed, but learning the trade. That firm's knocked in the head now, but the same system prevails, though not so extensively. In our shop we have only one apprentice and three other boys (one is my son). We never think now, though it was the case, of requiring seven years' apprenticeship for admission into our society. The men's sons had always an exemption from this rule.

"One of the great evils of the trade, as regards working joiners, is the system of the masters having 'improvers.' These are young men, generally out of their time, who want 'improvement' in their business, and who often come recommended from the country, where the master joiners have many customers; or they are connected with friends of the master, and so are put on. These 'improvers' are paid from 18s. to 24s. a week, of course superseding experienced hands at the regular wages. 'Improvers' are very seldom worth the money they receive; indeed, their object is to learn their business perfectly. The foreman don't trust them with the finest and nicest sort of work, such as the frame, the sash, and the staircase, unless he sees they have great capabilities; so that after all, seven-eighths of them don't 'improve' much, but the public don't know good work from bad, and in consequence it appears cheap; and so wages get dragged down, and good hands are superseded. We seldom in our firm work by contract, but it's coming on; it's forced on the master—but then our work is very superior. Competition is ruining fine work, what you may call skilled labour, for there's not the time allowed to do it. Now, for a contract for a large building, honourable masters, treating and paying their men fairly, will take it say at £20,000. Another firm will undertake it at £14,000 or £15,000 (just look at the *Builder* about that). To make up the difference, they must use—the cheap contractors must—inferior timber, put together anyway, inferior and under-paid workmen, 'improvers,' and boys. The clerk of the works sees to the safety of the building; some are easy, and pretty easily managed; others are very strict. All Government work is done by contract, and at the lowest rates—slop wages generally. The Woods and Forests allow 28s. a week, and if an 'honourable' master gets the job he has to pay 30s., as society men won't work under. The new Houses of Parliament are, however, an exception to this rule. The best hands are in society. I have regular work, and have nothing to complain of that way; but for all that I would like to leave the country, for there's worse times coming.". . .

An experienced man gave me the following statement concerning greenhouse work:

"I have known the hot-house building, and similar branches of the trade—often called 'decorating'—for three or four years, and before that I was a joiner. There is no difference, I have ascertained, in a horticultural joiner's trade, as regards wages, for the last twenty or thirty years. The wages are the same as the joiners', and the same hours. Our work, for gardens, is more a matter of taste than house work, in which certain plans are laid down and must be observed. In hothouses the chief distinctive work is the framing, as the sashes are pure joiners' work. We make also cucumber-frames, summer-houses, conservatories, greenhouses, forcing-houses, lattice and trellice work for the training of climbing plants, and for ornamental purposes—in short, everything connected with gardens. Within these few years, say seven years, there has been a great increase in the demand for this kind of work, especially in greenhouses and conservatories. Not one-tenth of the men employed in this kind of work have been apprenticed to it solely; they are mostly joiners, for men when out of work must turn their hands to anything.

"Machinery affects our trade, in the preparation of sash bars, which contain the glass. They are chiefly 'stuck,' made by machinery. We can't compete with it. They charge 7s. to 8s. per 100 feet run for bars, finding the material, and having all ready prepared for use. The material, the timber, will cost two-thirds of that sum, and the labour would be, on an average, 3s. 6d. Our work, however, is considerably truer than their's. We can work with our tools to a great nicety, and that can't be done by the machine. None of their mouldings are perfectly regular. If the timber be crooked, the machine works it crooked to the timber, but we don't. Nearly all the mouldings for cucumber boxes and for general purposes are prepared by machinery. The manual labour so superseded is in my opinion one-fifth; and that drives men to undertake any job, and to go in as day workmen, and then look out for another job. Ours is chiefly outdoor work, and is very uncertain, as we can't 'fix' in wet weather.

"Within seven years iron and metal (composition) roofs, for hothouses and conservatories, have come into rather general use, having a lighter appearance than wood. Perhaps, however, there are nearly twice as many wood as iron or metal roofs made. Metal roofs (they're generally all called so) are fixtures usually. Another system of ventilation is pursued in them, either by a general ventilator at the top of the roof, which is the commonest way, or by perforated glass, the panes then overlapping one another, with an interval between to admit the air. In the wood work, we have sliding frames for ventilation, the upper frame being pulled down over the bottom sash, which is a fixture, the top being then left open for the admission of the air. I have been engaged in constructing hot-houses for nursery grounds and gentlemen's gardens both, from 100 to 150 feet long, for all purposes. The nurserymen have generally the larger hot-houses. There is a sort of mania for them now, and more especially since the improved system of heating by hot water came in, within these five or six years. A large-sized boiler, 24 inches diameter, is calculated to heat 1,000 feet run. If for a pinery, this heat is from underneath, in pipes fixed in brick archways, and is forced upwards. If for grapes, the hot-water pipes are laid on the ground, and the same for flowers. Only for pines, or fruits of any kind are the pipes laid underground. The heat may be regulated; it may be concentrated in one part, or may be diffused through a hot-house or any adjacent buildings by means of stop valves, which can be opened or shut at pleasure. This process is better for ripening fruit than sunshine, as it is more regular.

"We have no society, and I don't know the number in the trade. Our average employment for regular hands is not more than eight or nine months in the year; for those nine months the wages are 30s. in the week. Many, however, get only employment at this work two or three months in the year, and then they look out for any kind of wood work. I know of none regularly doing horticultural work cheaper, but there is slop work got up for the trade, and that can only be done by parties taking less than the regular wages; and that's almost always by inferior workmen. A good hand can get his wages. Slop masters palm off inferior work as the best, and in the long run they'll drag us all down to bad work and bad wages. It's influencing us now. Masters say, 'I can get this done at this or that low rate,' and I have to drive on to meet their views. Masters are beaten oft enough by the slop-masters, and bad men are ruining good ones. Few persons are judges of work. Only to-day a gentleman called wanting a hot-house to be built; he said he could get it done, when the price was named to him, at so much less at ——'s. He was told that one great job which had been done at this cheap slop house had all to be re-done.

"A great part of the bad work is brought in by slop-masters, but the public themselves, even gentlemen, go about asking prices and cheapening tradesmen in my line, who, to meet the times, must put in, and do put in, inferior materials and use machine labour, even when it's not suitable at all. Gentlemen will offer from £1 to £8 less than a fair price for a hot-house. I have known one who wanted a green-house, call at our place, and state that he could get the fixing done cheaper than we could. He offered for the wood work what was the cost of the material alone. 'There's the duty off timber,' said he, 'and the duty off glass.' He was told that wages were the same, and he replied, 'Well, then, you should reduce them too.' (Hothouses are lower since the duty was taken off glass.) He was then told that to work at his price either the timber-merchant or the working man must be robbed. He replied, 'I'll call to-morrow and tempt you with another guinea, and show you the money, and then I know you'll take it.' He is a man worth £20,000 a year and more, and left his carriage at a distance to pass as a humbler man."

From a sash-maker, one of the best hands, I received the subjoined narrative:

"I have worked at sash-making ten years, regular. I have done very little else all that time. For nine years I was solely employed at making sashes. In most of the large shops they let the sash-work now to what is termed a task-master, and then he employs his own hands. This is done in many shops where the best prices are paid. The sash-maker in a shop is a party who makes nothing else but the sashes and frames. I have been in London 25 years; sash-making was not a distinct branch of the trade then—it is only since there has been so much contract work, and the master-builders, large and small, have taken to letting the different parts of a house out to different hands, that separate men have been employed for sash-making. By giving the different parts out to different hands, the work, I think, is done in half the time, because a man has all his tools ready and set, and in general work a great deal of time is lost in shifting from one kind of work to another. The tools require to be altered for each class of work. When a man is always doing one job, he can do it almost without noticing his tools. The sash-maker, to whom the work is let, is never paid by the day, but always by the piece; the price is so much per foot for the different kinds of sashes. Common 2-inch or $1\frac{1}{2}$-inch sashes, are about $4\frac{1}{2}$d. per foot (either 'scribed' or 'mitred'); the better kind of deal sashes (which run about $2\frac{1}{2}$ inches) are 6d. the foot. These are the prices in good shops— they may be a halfpenny more or less in different places.

"The party to whom the sashes are let at these prices is called the taskmaster; and he seldom does anything himself except setting the work out and superintending. The work itself is done by men whom he employs, and these he always pays by the day. The taskmaster in good shops generally gives 5s. a day, and I knew one hand who had as much as 6s., but this was an exception rather than the rule. Usually the taskmasters try to cut the workman down as much as possible. Frequently they will give only 28s. a week in the best shops. The taskmaster generally works in the shop of the employer the same as the men, and the employer seldom troubles his head about what he gives those who work under him. A taskmaster will generally have from three to five, and sometimes as many as twenty hands at work for him. The taskmaster will often make 5s. out of the labour of each of the regular sash-makers that he employs under him. I have known one taskmaster to make as much as £10 a week out of ten men that he had working for him. We, of course, could measure the work as well as he could, and calculate what he got out of our labour. The taskmaster system is a very bad one for the working men, or, indeed, any system is bad where one working man is put to make money out of his fellows, for he must either employ cheap or very ready hands to get anything out of the job. It either leads to strapping—that is to making men work unusually hard—or else to making them work at unusually low prices. This is one of the reasons why a man cannot find work directly he turns the middle age. Nothing but young strapping hands will do for the taskmasters.

"The cause of this hurry and scurry, and scramble, and scamping of work, and reducing of wages, is the contract system. First of all, gentlemen and others will have the work done as cheap as possible—the lowest estimate has the preference in contract work. Then masters go to work cutting under one another, just to get the job; and after that why, of course, they must make it up out of the men's muscles and bones. Before this contract system there was no such thing as letting and sub-letting of work, and one journeyman living and preying upon another. When I first came to town, such a thing as piece-work was hardly known, and if a man got a job that way, he was pretty well ousted from society for it—but now piece-work is as common as day-work; so much so, that the usual question among journeymen is whether they have the job by the day or piece. Piece-work is the worst of all things to be introduced into a trade. It has been the great evil, and will be the downfall of our trade; for directly men are paid by the piece, then of course they can employ others to assist them at lower wages than the regular pay, and then begins all kinds of scheming, strapping, and ultimately, starving of the men."

From Letter LXI, July 18th, 1850

I shall now proceed to set forth the effects of each of [the] several causes of low wages *seratim*—beginning with the means used by the more honourable masters, and concluding with an account of the practices pursued by the speculative builders. First, of the *"strapping"* system. Concerning this I received the following extraordinary account from a man after his heavy day's labour; and never in all my experience have I seen so sad an instance of over-work. The poor fellow was so fatigued that he could hardly rest in his seat. As he spoke he sighed deeply and heavily, and appeared almost spirit-broken with excessive labour:

"I work at what is called a strapping shop," he said, "and have worked at nothing else for these many years past in London. I call 'strapping,' doing as much work as a human being or a horse possibly can in a day, and that without any hanging upon the collar, but with the foreman's eyes constantly fixed upon you, from six o'clock in the morning to six o'clock at night. The shop in which I work is for all the world like a prison—the silent system is as strictly carried out there as in a model gaol. If a man was to ask any common question of his neighbour, except it was connected with his trade, he would be discharged there and then. If a journeyman makes the least mistake, he is packed off just the same. A man working at such places is almost always in fear; for the most trifling things he's thrown out of work in an instant. And then the quantity of work that one is forced to get through is positively awful; if he can't do a plenty of it, he don't stop long where I am. No one would think it was possible to get so much out of blood and bones. No slaves work like we do.

"At some of the strapping shops the foreman keeps continually walking about with his eyes on all the men at once. At others the foreman is perched high up, so that he can have the whole of the men under his eye together. I suppose since I knew the trade that a man does four times the work that he did formerly. I know a man that's done four pairs of sashes in a day, and one is considered to be a good day's labour. What's worse than all, the men are everyone striving one against the other. Each is trying to get through the work quicker than his neighbours. Four or five men are set the same job so that they may be all pitted against one another, and then away they go every one striving his hardest for fear that the others should get finished first. They are all tearing along from the first thing in the morning to the last at night, as hard as they can go, and when the time comes to knock off they are ready to drop. I was hours after I got home last night before I could get a wink of sleep; the soles of my feet were on fire, and my arms ached to that degree that I could hardly lift my hand to my head. Often, too, when we get up of a morning, we are more tired than we went to bed, for we can't sleep many a night; but we mustn't let our employers know it, or else they'd be certain we couldn't do enough for them, and we'd get the sack. So, tired as we may be, we are obliged to look lively somehow or other at the shop of a morning. If we're not beside our bench the very moment the bell's done ringing, our time's docked—they won't give us a single minute out of the hour.

"If I was working for a fair master, I should do nearly one-third less work than I am now forced to get through, and sometimes a half less; and even to manage that much, I shouldn't be idle a second of my time. It's quite a mystery to me how they do contrive to get so much work out of the men. But they are very clever people. They know how to have the most out of a man, better than any one in the world. They are all picked men in the shop—regular 'strappers,' and no mistake. The most of them are five foot ten, and fine broad shouldered, strong backed fellows too—if they weren't they would not have them. Bless you, they make no words with the men, they sack them if they're not strong enough to do all they want; and they can pretty soon tell, the very first shaving a man strikes in the shop, what a chap is made of.

"Some men are done up at such work—quite old men and gray with spectacles on, by the time they are forty. I have seen fine strong men, of six-and-thirty, come in there and be bent double in two or three years. They are most all countrymen at the strapping shops. If they see a great strapping fellow who they think has got some stuff about him that will come out, they will give him a job directly. We are used for all the world like cab or omnibus horses. Directly they've had all the work out of us we are turned off, and I am sure after my day's work is over, my feelings must be very much the same as one of the London cab horses. As for Sunday, it is *literally* a day of rest with us, for the greater part of us lays a bed all day, and even that will hardly take the aches and pains out of our bones and muscles. When I'm done and flung by, of course I must starve.". . .

I now come to treat of the system pursued by the speculating builders of the metropolis. . . .

In order, however, that I might not be misled by the journeymen, I thought it my duty to call upon some master-builders of the "honourable trade"—gentlemen of high character—as well as upon architects of equally high standing. I found the same opinion entertained by them all as to the ruinous effects of the kind of competition existing in their trade to a master who strives to be just to his customers and fair to his men. This competition, I was assured, was the worst in the contracts for building churches, chapels, and public institutions generally.

"Honesty is now almost impossible among us," said one master-builder. "It *is* impossible in cheap contract work, for the competition puts all honourable trade out of the field; high character, and good material, and the best workmanship are of no avail. Capitalists can command any low-priced work, by letting and subletting, and all by the piece. Most of these speculating and contracting people think only how to make money; or they must raise money to stop a gap (a bill perhaps to be met), and they grasp at any offer of an advance of money on account of a building to be erected. Their proceedings are an encouragement to every kind of dishonesty. They fail continually, and they drag good men down with them."

Strong as these opinions are, I heard them fully confirmed by men who could not be mistaken in the matter. "Advertise for contract work," said another gentleman, "and you'll soon have a dozen applicants at all sorts of prices; and all tradesmen like myself, who calculate for a contract at a rate to pay the regular wages, and not to leave either the timber-merchant or anybody else in the lurch, and to yield us the smallest possible per centage for our risk and outlay, are regarded as a pack of extortionate men.". . .

Such are the opinions of the honourable masters in connection with the building trade, as to the ruinous effects of the slop or contract system. I shall now subjoin the statements, first, of the foremen, and lastly, of the workmen in connection with this part of the trade:

"I am foreman to a speculating builder. My employer is not in a very large way: he has about ten carpenters and joiners. He does not let the work, he employs all the men by the day. The highest wages he gives is 28s. a week; this sum he pays to three of his men. He gives 24s. to three others; and two more have £1 a week. Besides these he employs two apprentices. To the oldest of these he gives 15s. a week, and to the youngest 6s. The men who have 28s. are superior hands—such men as at either of the C——'s would get their 6s. a day. The 24s. men are good skilful carpenters, fairly worth 30s.; and those in the receipt of £1 are young men fresh from the country—principally from Devonshire. The wages in the west of England are from 12s. to 15s., and these low wages send a lot of lads to town every year, in the hope of bettering their condition. They mostly obtain work among the speculating builders. I suppose there are more carpenters in London from Devonshire and Cornwall than from any other counties in England. At least half the carpenters and joiners employed by the speculating builders here are lads fresh up from the country. Apprentices are not employed by the speculators as a rule.

"Most of the speculators have no fixed shops. Their work is carried on chiefly in, what we term, camp shops—that is in sheds erected in the field where the buildings are going on, and that's one reason why apprentices are not generally taken by speculating builders. The speculators find plenty of cheap labour among the country lads. A hand fresh up from the West of England can't get employment at the best of shops, unless he's got some friends, and so, after walking all London, he generally is driven to look for a job among the speculators at low wages. What few good hands are employed by the speculators are kept only to look after the countrymen. As a rule, I think young hands are mostly preferred, because there is more work in them. It is one of the chief evils of the carpenter's trade that as soon as a man turns of forty masters won't keep him on.

"The master whom I work for pays much better prices than most of the speculators. The average wages of the inferior hands employed in building is about 15s.; that is, I think, one-half of the hands don't receive more than that, and the other about 24s. But day-pay is the exception with the speculators. The way in which the work is done is mostly by letting and sub-letting. The masters usually prefer to let work, because it takes all the trouble off their hands. They know what they are to get for the job, and of course they let it as much under that figure as they possibly can, all of which is clear gain without the least trouble. How the work is done, or by whom, it's no matter to them, so long as they can make what they want out of the job, and have no bother about it. Some of our largest builders are taking to this plan, and a party who used to have one of the largest shops in London has within the last three years discharged all the men in his employ (he had 200 at least), and has now merely an office, and none but clerks and accountants in his pay. He has taken to letting his work out instead of doing it at home. The parties to whom the work is let by the speculating builders are generally working men, and these men in their turn look out for other working men, who will take the job cheaper than they will, and so I leave you, sir, and the public to judge what the party who really executes the work gets for his labour, and what is the quality of work that he is likely to put into it.

"The speculating builder generally employs an overlooker to see that the work is done sufficiently well to pass the surveyor. That's all he cares about. Whether it's done by thieves, or drunkards, or boys, it's no matter to him. The overlooker,

A carpenter at work

of course, sees after the first party to whom the work is let, and this party in his
turn looks after the several hands that he has sub-let it to. The first man who
agrees to the job takes it in the lump, and he again lets it to others in the piece. I
have known instances of its having been let again a third time, but this is not usual.
The party who takes the job in the lump from the speculator usually employs a
foreman, whose duty it is to give out the materials, and to make working drawings.
The men to whom it is sub-let only find labour, while the 'lumper,' or first contractor, agrees for both labour and materials. It is usual in contract work, for the
first party who takes the job to be bound in a large sum for the due and faithful
performance of his contract. He then in his turn finds out a sub-contractor, who
is mostly a small builder, who will also bind himself that the work shall be properly
executed, and there the binding ceases—those parties to whom the job is afterwards let, or sub-let, employing foremen or overlookers to see that their contract
is carried out.

"The first contractor has scarcely any trouble whatsoever; he merely engages
a gentleman, who rides about in a gig, to see that what is done is likely to pass
muster. The sub-contractor has a little more trouble; and so it goes on as it gets
down and down. Of course I need not tell you that the first contractor, who does
the *least* of all, gets the *most* of all; while the poor wretch of a working man, who
positively executes the job, is obliged to slave away every hour night after night
to get a bare living out of it; and this is the contract system. The public are
fleeced by it to an extent that builders alone can know. Work is scamped in such
a way that the houses are not safe to live in. Our name for them in the trade is
'bird cages,' and really nine-tenths of the houses built now-a-days are very little
stronger. Again, the houses built by the speculators are almost all damp. There is
no concrete ever placed at the foundation to make them dry and prevent them from
sinking. Further, they are all badly drained. Many of the walls of the houses
built by the speculators are much less in thickness than the Building Act requires.
I'll tell you how this is done. In a third-rate house the wall should be, according
to the Act, two bricks thick at least, and in a second-rate house, two bricks and
a half. The speculators build up the third-rates a brick and-a-half thick, and the
second-rates only two bricks, and behind this they run up another half brick, so
that they can throw that part down immediately after the surveyor has inspected
it. Many of the chimney breasts too, are filled up with rubbish, instead of being
solid brickwork. The surveyor is frequently hand in hand with the speculator,
and can't for the life of him discover any of these defects—but you know there's
none so blind as those that *won't* see.

"And yet, notwithstanding all this trickery and swindling, and starving of the
workmen, rents in the suburbs do not come down. Who, then, are the gainers
by it all? Certainly not the public, for all they get are damp, ill-drained, and
unsafe houses, at the same prices as they formerly paid for sound, wholesome,
and dry ones. And most certainly the working men gain nothing by it. And what
is even worse than all is that the better class of masters are obliged to compete
with the worse, and to resort to the same means to keep up with the times, so
that if things go on much longer the better class of mechanics must pass away
altogether."

Concerning ground rents, I had the following account from one well acquainted
with the tricks of the speculators:

"The party for whom I am foreman has just taken a large estate, and he contemplates making some thousands of pounds by means of the improved ground rents alone. There are several with him in the speculation, and this is the way in which such affairs are generally managed. A large plot of ground (six or seven meadows, may be) somewhere in the suburbs is selected by the speculators as likely to be an eligible spot for building—that is to say, they think that a few squares, villas, and terraces about that part would be likely to let as soon as run up. Then the speculators go to the freeholder or his solicitor, and offer to take the ground of him on a ninety-nine years' lease at a rent of about £50 a-year per acre, and may be they take as many as fifty acres at this rate. At the same time they make a proviso that the rent shall not commence until either so many houses are built, or perhaps before a twelvemonth has elapsed. If they didn't do this the enormous rent most likely would swallow them up before they had half got through their job.

"Well, may be, they erect half or two-thirds of the number of houses that they have stipulated to do before paying rent. These are what we term 'call-birds,' and are done to decoy others to build on the ground. For this purpose a street is frequently cut, the ground turned up on each side, just to show the plan, and the corner house, and three others, perhaps, are built just to let the public see the style of thing that it's going to be. Occasionally a church is begun, for this is found to be a great attraction in a new neighbourhood. Well, when things are sufficiently ripe this way, and the field has been well mapped out into plots, a board is stuck up, advertising 'THIS GROUND TO BE LET, ON BUILDING LEASES.' Several small builders then apply to take a portion of it, sufficient for two or three houses, may be, for which they agree to pay about five guineas a year (they generally make it *guineas* these gentlemen) for the ground-rent of each house. And when the parties who originally took the meadows on lease have got a sufficient number of these plots let off, and the small builders have run up a few of the carcases, they advertise that 'a sale of well-secured rents will take place at the Mart on such a day.'

"Ground-rents, you must know, are considered to be one of the safest of all investments now-a-days; for if they are not paid, the ground landlord, you see, has the power of seizing the houses; so gentlemen with money are glad to lay it out this way, and there's a more ready sale for ground-rents than for anything else in the building line. There's sure to be a strong competition for them, let the sale be whenever it will. Well, let us see now how the case stands. There are fifty acres taken on lease at £50 an acre a year, and that is £2,500 per annum. Upon each of these fifty acres fifty houses can be erected (including villas and streets, taking one with the other upon an average). The ground-rent of each of these houses is (at the least) £5, and this gives for the 2,500 houses that are built upon the whole of the fifty acres £12,500 per annum. Hence you see there is a clear net profit of £10,000 a year made by the transaction. This is not at all an extraordinary case in building speculations.". . .

As regards "Improvers," I had the subjoined information from a very intelligent and trustworthy man:

"I am a joiner, receiving the regular wages. I am familiar with all the systems carried on as regards 'improvers.' These improvers are frequently the sons of carpenters and joiners, who have been instructed by their parents, and then seek to complete their knowledge of the business without going through a course of apprenticeship. Or they are often the sons of tradesmen in the country, who come to town for the name of the thing, and that they may put on their signs—'So and So, from Messrs. ——, London.' A certain class of young men have been apprenticed, but not being perfect in their business, also go as improvers. The wages of improvers vary greatly—from 10s. to 23s. or 24s. a week. They generally have some interest to get into a shop. They know some friend of the master, or something of that kind. Then there can be no doubt that there are such things as *bonuses* to foremen.

"No doubt the introduction of these improvers is detrimental to the well-doing of the journeymen, who are driven, especially if they are past their prime, to work for lower wages. Masters don't like old men at all. Many masters are partial to improvers, and keep them on when they discharge journeymen. In the scamping (slop) shops, masters best like strong hearty young fellows from the country as improvers—men they can get plenty of work out of. Scamping masters soon discharge their improvers if they lose any of their strength and capability of hard work. Few improvers are kept on, as improvers, after they are twenty-five. Their ages run generally from sixteen to twenty-four. I have never known an improver become a journeyman in the shop in which he worked as an improver. Masters seem to distrust them. In speculating builders' employ there are generally more improvers than journeymen—thrice as many more. Speculating builders keep on only as few as possible journeymen, and those just to keep the work in decent order. Improvers can't be trusted by themselves. With some speculating builders the improver works by the piece, and is then ground down very low in price. A man of 22 will then not make above half wages, 15s., and work more than the regular hours to do that. Improvers find their own tools, the same as journeymen.

"I believe that twenty years ago there was not such a thing as a scamping master in London. Ten years ago one in ten might be scamping masters, and now quite one-third are so. Take masters altogether at 1,300, and 430 of them are scamping masters. Some of them are in a very large way, and employ occasionally 200 hands; and altogether I fancy they rank, as to the number of hands, with the honourable trade. I think the system gets worse and worse. Mr. ——, one of the best builders in London, is now obliged to give way to competition, and get up a more scamping sort of work, instead of the fine and beautiful work that he used to supply."

The next point to be noticed is the system of letting and subletting the work. From an experienced carpenter and his son, also an experienced man in his trade, I had the following account:

"I may say," said the father, "I have been seventy-five years in the carpentering trade, for that's my age, and I was born in the business. I worked nearly fifty years in Somersetshire, chiefly as a journeyman. Forty years ago the wages were 3s. a day in Taunton—that was the highest wages for the best men. When I left five years since, it was a good man who got 2s. 6d.; many got 2s. a day. The decrease took place about thirty or thirty-five years back, when the competition and cheap estimates for contract work began. I remember the time, because a man came from Wellington and undertook some work which no tradesman in Taunton would undertake—the building of a market-house, which was put up to competition by the trustees. Immediately after that wages fell, for cheap contract work spread all over the neighbourhood. The man from Wellington cut down the wages directly; many worked for him at 2s. a day. Trade was dull then. It went on continually on the low system, and continues on that system still. The men that the market-house contractor employed were mostly inferior labourers, and he got them cheap. Of course it's the cheaper and worse labourers that first force the superior workmen to come down. Contracts had reduced good men as regards wages to the level of bad men, and good men must scamp it, for scamping is the rule now. I came to London five years ago to join my family, who were settled here. My family were then at work on a contract for a lawyer."

"I knew nothing of the lawyer," said the son of my first informant, "but I saw a notice up that the carcases of six houses were to be finished, and made fit for inhabitants, and tenders were to be sent in; the lowest bidder of course to be accepted. The solicitor, that my brother and I had the contract from, was the agent of the ground landlord, who was anxious to have buildings erected on his property. The ground landlord had advertised that the land would be let on building leases, and that advances would be made, according to the usual dodge —for dodge it is, sir. A builder was soon found, one with little or no money, for money in such cases is no matter—that's an every-day affair. He agreed to erect six houses, and £250 was to be advanced for each house, something more than half as much as would be required to complete each of them. The builder got the carcases up, and then the agent put the stopper on him, and seized the houses for the ground landlord. Each house, in the manner it was left by the builder, when he was stopped, had full £300 expended on it of *somebody's* money, and materials. For this the builder became bankrupt and he was sent to prison. The houses were then advertised for sale and sold, the agent buying them, and just for the amount advanced—£1,500. So that after full £1,800 had been expended on the houses the agent got them for £300 less. The wages paid to the men employed on the building were as low as contract work usually is, and some carpenters there earned only 2s. 6d. a day of twelve hours. The work was let— brick-work, smith's-work, and all—and at a very low rate. Had fair living wages been paid to all employed the value of the six carcases would have been at least £2,400; so that the lawyer, you see, gains £900 by this mode of management. These are the parties who thrive by the contract system. The public gains nothing, for the house is not let for a farthing less rent than if built on a fair wages system; but the owner or his people may get 15 or 16 per cent. for their money.

"There is the same system now being carried on, and to a very great extent, all over the same neighbourhood. Some as good mechanics as ever took a tool in hand work from four in the morning till eight or nine at night, and earn only 4s. a day. Before the contract system it was 5s. a day of ten hours. Now on this contract system men grow rich on the degradation and suffering of the working man, and on the swindling of the timber merchant, the iron merchant, and the other tradesmen out of the materials. Nineteen out of every twenty speculating builders become bankrupts." [I may add, that in the bankrupt lists of last year, 51 are returned as builders; the largest number in any trade, except drapers and victuallers.] "So that," continued my informant, "notwithstanding all the money that these speculating builders wring out of the men, they keep failing every day. The agent I've been speaking of stuck boards up over the neighbourhood, stating that the finishing of the carcases, as I've said, was to be let to the lowest bidder,

on certain terms; advances were to be made on the surveyor's report, among
other conditions. I knew, if a low figure wasn't sent in, it was no use trying for
the job, so my brother and I bid for the work at the lowest possible sum. We
reckoned on our own labour being serviceable, as we could do so much among
ourselves, and save the expense of a foreman and such like. We hoped to make
something, too, out of the extras, that is for extra work not included in the
specification, for the specification is never correct. Men now bid very low in
hopes of making their profit in this way. My father, my brother, and myself,
didn't realize more than 4s. a day, working on an average 13 hours. If we'd been
employed by a contractor, who took it at the rate we did, our wages couldn't
have been more than 3s. a day, and that was the reason of our bidding for it. The
journeymen in that neighbourhood now get 3s. a day, all the work being let and
sub-let. A journeyman will undertake work to pay himself 4s. a day, and will hire
men under him at 3s.—or even less—14s. or 15s. a week. One man takes the
windows, another the skirtings, another the doors, another the dwarf and high
cupboards, another the stairs, another the mouldings, another the boxing shutters
for the windows, and another the floors.

"The average price for labour in contract work windows is 6s. an opening for
25 feet, and according to Skyring's prices (which are low) the charge would be
10s. Doors, double moulded, are paid 2s. 6d. on an average, and they ought to be
5s.; of course, they must be scamped. On this work I must make two doors a day,
while one properly made is a good long day's job. Some of these doors don't last
above ten years. Staircases are done at £3 a six-roomed house; it ought to be
from £5 to £5 10s. For boxing shutters £1 4s. is the price, instead of from £2 10s.
to £3. It's a fortnight's work to do it well; it's 40 feet work, a fair price (Skyring's)
being 1s. 4½d. a foot. At Notting-hill, twelve years ago, I had £2 10s. for this
same work. Floors, on contract, are 2s. 6d. a square, though that's above the
average, and they are honestly worth 5s.; Skyring gives 6s. 6d. Skirtings, which
they take by the house, are 15s., and ought to be £2 10s. Mouldings, which are
taken by the hundred feet sticking (working) are 1s. 6d. the hundred, running
measure, the regular price being 4s. 2d. The dwarf and high cupboards are a
shameful price by contract—2s. 6d. each, with shelves, folding doors, hanging,
and everything complete. These prices are what I know of by my own experience;
but when there's a further sub-letting by a journeyman contracting under the
contractor, and so getting hands at the lowest possible rates, they are even less
than I have specified.

"Contracting altogether is a bad system; it's carried on for the benefit of a
few at the cost of the working men, and out of their sweat, and at the cost too of
respectable tradesmen many a time. Government contracts are carried on just the
same way. I myself have worked at the Post-office, and the man next me had only
18s. a week. Since the present contractor has had it, only 12s. is paid; so you can
see what it must all lead to. I reckon that there are from 18,000 to 20,000
working men in my trade in London; and I believe that full two-thirds of them
work at under wages. One half of the two-thirds will get 4s. a day, and the other
third 2s. 6d. In London, as you have stated, sir, no doubt there are 6,405 houses
built every year; and at least 6,000 of them are built by contract work, and
speculating and scamping builders. All in the suburbs are. These would average
(reckon the new houses erected to be chiefly in the suburbs) from £30 to £35

a year rent. One carpenter could frame and finish two such houses a year. That would give employment at the cheap built houses to 3,000 men. These houses are raised on the reduction of the working men's wages, and that reduction, as they now get 20s. where they did get 30s., makes the loss to each working man as much as 10s. a week, or £25 a year, and that amounts in all to £75,000 per annum, which somebody or other gets out of the journeymen carpenters alone. That *somebody* is not the public—that's very clear, for rents are as high if not higher, and since the majority of speculating builders become bankrupts, it's clear that the ground landlords, their solicitors and agents, are the only men benefited by the system.

"The effect of this reduction on the working men is, as I said, very bad indeed. Respectable masters, who would be fair and honest, are so cut down by competition, that they would almost as soon be without trade as with it. The consequence is, half of the men are unemployed, and when employed get not much more than half wages. If people only knew how the 200 miles of streets that have been built in London in the last ten years had been run up—through what sufferings to the working man and his family—they wouldn't think it quite so grand a thing."...

CABINET - MAKERS

From Letter LXIII, August 1st, 1850

A good-looking man, who spoke with a hardly perceptible Scotch accent, gave me the following account of his experience as a *general cabinet-maker* of the best class. His room was one of the sort I have described in my preliminary remarks:

"I am a native of ——, in Scotland," he said, "and have been in London a dozen years or so. My mother was left a widow when I was very young, and supported herself and me as a laundress. She got me the very best schooling she could, and a cabinet-maker without some education is a very poor creature. I got to be apprenticed to Mr. ——, who took me because he knew my father. I got on very well with him, and lived at home with my mother. When I had been five years or so at the business I went with my master to Lord ——'s, a few miles off, to do some work, and among other things we had to unpack some furniture that had come from London, and to see that it wasn't injured. My lord came in when we had unpacked a beautiful rosewood loo table, and said to my master, 'you can't make a table like that.' 'I think I can, my lord,' said my master, and he got an order for one, and set me to make it as I had seen the London table, but he overlooked me, and it gave great satisfaction, and that first made me think of coming to London, as it gave me confidence in my work.

"I had only occasional employment from my master when I was out of my time, and as my mother was then dead I started off for London before I got through my bit of money. I walked to Carlisle and was getting very tired of the road, and very footsore. What a lot of thoughts pass through a countryman's mind when he's first walking up to London! At Carlisle I had about a month's work, or better, as an order had just come in to Mr. —— from a gentleman who was going to be married, and the furniture was wanted in a hurry. I gave satisfaction there and that encouraged me. I walked to London all the way, coming by Leeds and Sheffield, and Leicester, and the great towns, where I thought there was the best chance for a job. I didn't get one, though. In my opinion, sir, there ought to be a sort of lodging-house for mechanics and poor people travelling on their honest business. You must either go to a little public-house to sleep, and it's very seldom you can get a bed there under 6d., and many places ask 9d. and 1s.—or you may go to a common lodging-house for travellers, as they call it, and it would sicken a dog. Then, in a public-house, you can't sit by the fire on a wet or cold night without drinking something, whether you require or can afford it or not.

"I knew nobody in London except two or three seafaring people, and them I couldn't find. I went from place to place for three weeks, asking for work. I wasn't a society man then. At last I called at Mr. ——'s, and met with the master himself. He asked me where I'd worked last, and I said at Mr. ———'s, of ———, and Mr. ———'s, of Carlisle. 'Very respectable men,' said he, 'I haven't a doubt of it, but I never heard their names before.' And he then asked me some more questions, and called his foreman and said, 'R———, we want hands; I think you might put on this young man; just try him.' So I was put on, and was there four or five years. I had many little things to learn in London ways, to enable a man to get on a little faster with his work, and I will say that I've asked many a good London hand for his opinion, and have had it given to me as a man should give it. I do the same myself now. A good workman needn't be afraid: he won't be hurt.

"I work by the piece. I have been very fortunate, never having been out of work more than a month or six weeks at a time—but that's great good fortune. These are my earnings for the last eight weeks. I've only lately begun to keep accounts, all at piece-work, and a busy time: 32s. 2d., 41s. 3d., 40s. 1d., 36s., 29s. 6d., 28s., 35s. 10d., 35s. 9d. An average of near 35s. is it? Well, no doubt I make that all the year round. I can keep a wife and child comfortably. I wouldn't hear of my wife working for a slop tailor. I'd rather live on bread and water myself than see it. Slop means slavery. In my opinion, if the black masters, or the slaughtermen, as they call them at the other end, didn't keep men always going, or didn't force them to keep always going, they'd be troubled to get hands. But when men are always struggling for a living, they have no time to think or talk, and so they submit, and, indeed, their wives and families make them submit.". . .

Bedstead making is, as I have stated, a distinct branch of the cabinet-maker's business. It is, however, generally carried on in the same premises as the other branches, but in some establishments bedsteads are the principal manufacture. The bedstead-maker has not to cut out his material in the same way as the cabinet-maker, as the posts are fashioned by the turner or the wood-carver ready for his purpose, and the other portions of his work are prepared by the sawyers in the sizes he requires. He is the putter together of the article, in every part, except the insertion of the sacking bottom, which is the work of the porter.

From a well-informed man, a member of "society," I had the following statement, which embodies information (which I found fully corroborated) of the social condition of the men, and the fashions of the trade. I am informed that in the society of bedstead-makers there is not one unmarried man.

"When I first knew the business, 40 years ago, I could earn at bedstead making, by hard work, 50s. or 60s. I have heard men brag in a public-house that they could make more than 60s., and masters got to hear of it, and there was great dissatisfaction. We always work by piece, and did so when I was an apprentice in London. The prices paid to society men are, on the whole, the same as in 1811. We all find our own tools, and a good kit is worth £30. I consider the bedstead-makers an intelligent, sober class. I'm speaking of society men—gentlemen I may call them. I don't know much of the others. The majority of us are members of literary institutions, and some of us have saved money.

"There is great improvement since I first knew bedstead-makers, in point of temperance. There used to be hard drinking and less working. In 1810, when we met for society purposes, our allowance of fourpence a night per man that had to attend was drunk in an hour; now it's not consumed in the course of the meeting. Several of us are house-keepers, and can support our wives and families comfortably. I don't think one of the wives of the members of our society work in any way but for the family. I have brought up seven children well, and now five are working at other trades, and two girls at home. Very few good hands now earn less than 30s. a week, and some 8s. or 9s. more. I do that, and I've been very rarely out of work. There is no importation of French bedsteads now; there used to be, but they didn't stand. When I first made bedsteads, tents, four-posters, and half-testers were the run; now half-testers and tents are never asked for. Then came the Waterloo bed, which turns up with a curtain over it. The French bedstead next came in, with and without canopies. The Arabian bed is the present fashion. It resembles a half-tester.

"The iron-work has interfered greatly with my trade. I remember when there were no iron bedsteads at all; now —— sends out 60 or 70 in some weeks. The iron bedsteads came into more general use about ten years ago. People fancy they're free of vermin, but I have had to take some to pieces, and have found them full of bugs in the lath and sacking parts. We've no grievances—not a bit of them. I think workmen themselves might remedy some of their grievances. They should be united, and they shouldn't encourage low-priced shops of any kind by buying things there. I pay 12s. a pair for my shoes, and one of my sons tells me it's foolish to do so, but the shoemaker has as good a right to a good week's earnings as I have, and to encourage slop work is to help on our own trouble.". . .

From Letter LXIV, August 8th, 1850

The person from whom I received the following narrative was an elderly man, and a workman of great intelligence. He resided in a poor and crowded neighbourhood. His wife was a laundress, and there was a comfortable air of cleanliness in their rooms. I give this man's statement fully, as it contains much that has been repeated to me by others in different branches:

"I've known the London fancy cabinet trade," he said, "for forty-five years, as that's the time when I was apprenticed in London. My father was a button-maker in Birmingham, and gave a premium of fifty guineas with me. But he failed, and came to London, and was for some time a clerk with Rundell and Bridge, the great jewellers. My master was a tyrannical master; but he certainly made a workman of me and of all his apprentices. I don't recollect how many he had. I think that now even a little master treats his apprentices middling well; for if he don't they turn sulky, and he can hardly afford their being sulky, as he depends on them for work and profit, such as it is.

"I got work in a good shop immediately after I was out of my time. No good hand need, then, be a week out of work. Masters clamoured for a good man. I have made £3 3s. a week, and one week I made £3 15s. For twenty years after that I didn't know what it was to want a job. I once during that time had three letters altogether in my pocket from Mr. Middleton, the great fancy cabinet-maker—you may have heard of Middleton's pencils, for he was the first in that line too—pressing an engagement upon me. Then I prided myself (and so did my mates) that I was a fancy cabinet-maker. I felt myself a gentleman, and we all held up our heads like gentlemen. I was very fond at that time of reading all that Charles Lamb wrote, and all that Leigh Hunt wrote. As to reading now, why, if we have a quarter of cheese or butter, I get hold of the paper it's brought in, and read it every word. I can't afford a taste for reading if it's to be paid for. I got married twenty-five years ago, and could live very comfortably then without my wife having to work to help me. We had two houses towards the West-end, and let them out furnished. But twenty years ago, or less, I resisted reductions in our wages, and fought against them. I fought against them for $3\frac{3}{4}$ years, and things went wrong—uncommon wrong—and I had to sacrifice everything to meet arrears of rent and taxes, and I was seized at last; for it wanted a weekly lift through a man's earnings to keep all prosperous.

"I've done all sorts of work in my time, but I'm now making desks—'ladies' school,' or 'writing'—of mahogany, rosewood, and satin-wood. Those are the principal; though every now and then another fancy wood is used. Walnut sawn solid makes a beautiful desk or box. I think walnut's coming into fashion again for that work. Twenty years ago I made 35s. at the least a week the year through. My family then, and for five, six, or seven, or more years after that time, had the treat of smelling a real good tasty Sunday dinner of beef, or pork, or mutton, as it came hot from the baker's, steaming over the potatoes. And after smelling it we had the treat of eating it, with a drop of beer to wash it down. On week days, too, we had the same pretty regular. I've had six children. Now we have still the smell and the taste of a Sunday meat dinner, but there it stops. We have no such dinners for week days. I'm forced now-a-days to work on Sundays too, and almost every Sunday. People may talk as they like about Sunday labour; I know all about it; but an empty cupboard is stronger than everything.

"If I have the chance I may make 15s. a week at present prices. I work, as we mainly do, at my own bench, in my own place, and find my own tools, glue, glass-paper, candles, and et ceteras; so that my 15s. a week sometimes falls down to 12s. clear. I work for masters, but not always, that find their own materials; but a great many of us have to find material and all. When our work's taken in, if the key breaks, the foreman—and the foreman is often the master's very convenient tool—fines a man 2d., or he may take back the work, and make it good, if he's found the material—that's called 'stopping.' Locks for the low-priced works are paltry, infamous things. Good locks used to be put to good work; they cost 10d. and 1s. for inferior, and averaged 2s. for better and from 5s. to 7s. for desks and boxes, where security was wanted. Now locks cost 2d. and $2\frac{1}{2}$d.—slop things, that's no safeguard. What was reckoned, and indeed was, inferior box-locks, was 6d., and is now $1\frac{1}{2}$d. Work's huddled together any how.

"How it'll all end with me is a poser. I suppose in the workhouse. I almost always worked at piece-work, and don't object to it when wages are fair; indeed, piece-work is better for a good hand, and he's more independent. If a man was on by day he would be expected to do so much work a week, and that would come to about the same thing. In 1825 or 1826 I had 4s. for making a lady's workbox if it was ordered to be first-rate, as the customer was very particular; 3s. 6d. was the regular wages, and I could make ten or eleven, or, in long days, twelve, in a week. Candlelight isn't well adapted for our trade; and when a man works in his own room, as I've mostly done, and as has been and is the custom in our trade, he don't think of gas. Cheap provisions is a great blessing. No one knows what we suffered in '47, when bread was 11d. to 1s.; and when it was at the highest our wages were reduced.

"When I was first a journeyman I had 10s. for making a 20 inch desk, and it fell to 8s., and 7s., and 6s., and by littles and littles down to what it is now, 4s.; and it's pretty well two days' work to make it properly, but it ain't made properly nineteen times out of twenty. It can't be done at the money. Perhaps a scamping hand might make five such things in a week, or six if he worked on Sundays, and if he was kept regularly at it, but he never is, or very seldom. In my young days an inferior hand couldn't get work in London; now he has a better chance. I think that machinery has been a benefit to us: it increases the material for our work. If there wasn't so much veneering there wouldn't be so much fancy cabinet-work. To show how wages have fallen, I'll mention this. A month back I walked through the Lowther-arcade, and saw fancy boxes, made of different kinds of wood, marked 2s. 6d., and I've had twenty years ago—aye, and fifteen years ago, but not so often—3s. for the more making of them, and found nothing at all. The material couldn't cost less than 1s. or from that to 1s. 6d. altogether. Such boxes are plastered together by boys—or most likely by girls, if a man has sharpish girls in his family, and works at his own bench. Hawkers have sold such boxes so that they didn't get 1½d. a piece for making them. The French goods, in my opinion, don't harm us now; they did at one time. I fancy that little masters sprung up twenty years ago, and have gone on increasing. How many of them there are I don't know; Lord knows there's too many. I'm satisfied that a scamping hand will do his work in one quarter of the time that a good hand will. I can't scamp. A man must be brought up to it to do it.". . .

From Letter LXV, August 15th, 1850

[After a survey of the "honourable" branch of cabinet-making, Mayhew turned as usual to a survey of the "dishonourable" or slop trade. The two letters dealing with the slop cabinet-makers were partially reprinted in London Labour, *III, 221–231. A few interesting interviews omitted in* London Labour *are given below.]*

An elderly man, with a heavy careworn look, whom I found at work with his wife and family, gave me the following information concerning his occupations as *a little master.* He was then engaged in making tea-caddies, his wife and daughter being engaged in "lining" work-boxes for the husband's next employment. They resided in a large room, a few steps underground, in a poor part of Spitalfields. It was very light, from large windows both back and front, and was very clean. A large bed stood in the centre, and what few tables and chairs there were were old and mean, while the highly-polished rosewood tea-caddies, which were placed on a bare deal table, showed in startling contrast with all the worn furniture around. The wife was well-spoken and well-looking; and the daughter, who was also well-looking, had that almost painful look of precocity which characterises those whose childhood is one of toil:

"I have been upwards of 40 years a fancy cabinet-maker," the man said, "making tea-caddies and everything in the line. When I first worked on my own account I could earn £3 a week. I worked for the trade then, for men in the toy, or small furniture, or cabinet line only. There was no slaughter-shops in those days. And good times continued till about 21 years ago, or not so much. I can't tell exactly, but it was when the slaughter-houses came up. Before that, on a Saturday night, I could bring home, after getting my money, a new dress for my wife, for I was just married then, and something new for the children when they came, and a good joint for Sunday. Such a thing as a mechanic's wife doing needlework for any but her own family wasn't heard of then, as far as I know. There was no slop needlewomen in the wives of my trade. It's different now. They must work some way or other. Me and my father before me, for he brought me up to the business, used to supply honourable tradesmen at a fair price, finding our own material; all the family of us is in the trade, but there was good times then. This part didn't then swarm with slaughter-houses, as it does now. I think there's fifty at this end of the town.

"I have to work harder than ever. Sometimes I don't know how to lie down of a night to rest best, from tiredness. The slaughtermen give less and less. My wife and family help me, or I couldn't live. I have only one daughter now at home, and she and my wife line the work-boxes as you see. I have to carry out my goods now, and have for 15 years or more hawked to the slaughter-houses. I carried them out on a sort of certainty, or to order, before that. I carry them out complete, or I needn't carry them out at all. I've now been on tea-caddies, 12-inch, with raised tops. The materials—rosewood veneers, deal, locks, hinges, glue, and polish—cost me £1 for a dozen. I must work hard and very long hours, 13 or more a day, to make two dozen a week, and for them I only get at the warehouse 28s. a dozen, if I can sell them there. That's 16s. a week for labour. Sometimes I'm forced to take 25s.—that's 10s. a week for labour. Sometimes I bring them back unsold. Workboxes is no better pay, though my wife and daughter line them. If I get an order—and that's very seldom, not once a year—for a number of tea-caddies, I must take them in at a certain time, because they're mostly for shipping, and so I must have some help. But I can't get a journeyman to help me unless I can show him he'll make 15s. a week, because he knows I just want him for a turn, and can't do without him, and so the profit goes off.

"Old men can't work quick enough. They may be employed when there's no particular hurry. If I'm not to time with a shipping order, it's thrown on my hands. The slaughter-house men will often say to my asking 28s. for a dozen caddies, 'Oh, we don't want them; and we can get better at 25s.; but we don't mind giving you that.' Many a time, when trade's been very slack, I've had 20s. offered, or 19s., which is less than the stuff cost. They knew that, but say they must make their harvest. And they know well enough that we have no society, and no benefit fund, and nothing to look to but the workhouse. I have to buy my materials at the great cabinet-makers and at the pianoforte-makers, such as is over in their work—the odds and ends. If any of the veneer's flawed the slaughterer won't have it—it's flung on my hands, as many an article is, for pretended faults. No man on my earnings, which is 15s. some weeks, and 10s. others, and less sometimes, can bring up a family as a family ought to be brought up. Many a time I've had to pawn goods that I couldn't sell on a Saturday night to rise a Sunday's dinner."

"Yes, indeed," interposed the wife, "look you here, sir; here's forty or fifty duplicates (producing them) of goods in pawn. If ever we shall get them out, Lord above knows." "Yes, sir," said the man, taking up a ticket, "and look at this. Here you see the pawnbroker has lent me 2s. 6d. on this box. It's such as is sold in cheap shops at 5s. 6d. Well, after walking my feet off, I couldn't get more than 24s. a dozen offered at a slaughter-house. That's 2s. a piece, and I got 2s. 6d. at a pawn-shop. And here's another; it was the largest size, and the pawnbroker lent 5s. 6d. on it; more than I could get offered at a slaughter-house; though in Lowther Arcade, such an one will be marked 22s. 6d., just with the addition of a glass basin, which costs only 1s. wholesale. I haven't any apprentices; it wouldn't suit me, because I haven't any sure sale for my goods. The men that has apprentices is either slaughterers, or people they keep going."

This man sent his daughter to show me a house I had next to call at, but had not been able to ascertain the number. She was quick, but told me she could neither read nor write. She couldn't spare time to learn if she could be taught for nothing. She was eleven, and worked at the lining, and could work, she thought, as well as her mother. She had been thus working since she was six years old. . . .

From Letter LXVI, August 22nd, 1850

. . . The usual assistants of the small masters are their own children. Upon this subject I received the following extraordinary statement:

"The most on us has got large families. We put the children to work as soon as we can. My little girl began about six, but about eight or nine is the usual age." "Ah, poor little things," said the wife, "they are obliged to begin the very minute they can use their fingers at all. The most of the cabinet-makers of the East-end have from five to six in family, and they are generally all at work for them. The small masters mostly marry when they are turned of twenty. You see our trade's come to such a pass that unless a man has children to help him he can't live at all. I've worked more than a month together, and the longest night's rest I've had has been an hour and a quarter—aye, and I've been up three nights a week besides. I've had my children lying ill, and been obliged to wait on them into the bargain. You see, we couldn't live if it wasn't for the labour of our children, though it makes 'em, poor little things, old people long afore they're growed up."

"I leave you to judge how we're to live by our labour," said the man. "Just look here," he continued, producing a rosewood tea caddy. It was French polished, lined with tinfoil, and with lock and key. "Now, what do you think we get for that, materials, labour, and all? Why, 16d.; and out of that there's only 4d. for the labour. My wife and daughter polishes and lines them, and I make them, and all we get is fourpence, and we have to walk perhaps miles to sell them for that."

"Why I stood at this bench," said the wife, "with my child, only 10 years of age, from four o'clock on Friday morning till ten minutes past seven in the evening, without a bit to eat or drink. I never sat down a minute from the time I began till I finished my work, and then I went out to sell what I had done. I walked all the way from here (Shoreditch) down to the Lowther Arcade, to get rid of the articles." Here she burst out in a violent flood of tears, saying, "Oh, sir, it *is* hard to be obliged to labour from morning till night as we do—all of us, little ones and all—and yet not to be able to live by either."

"Why, there's Mr. ——, the warehouseman, in ——" the husband went on, "offered me £6 a gross for the making of these very caddies, as I showed just now, and that would have left me only 1½d. a dozen for my labour. Why, such men won't let poor people remain honest. And you see, the worst of it is here—children's labour is of such value now in our trade that there's more brought into the business every year, so that it's really for all the world like breeding slaves. Without my children I don't know how we should be able to get along. There's that little thing," said the man, pointing to the girl of ten years of age before alluded to, as she sat at the edge of the bed, "why, she works regularly every day from six in the morning till ten at night. She never goes to school; we can't spare her. There's schools enough about here for a penny a week, but we could not afford to keep her without working. If I'd ten more children I should be obligated to employ them all the same way. And there's hundreds and thousands of children now slaving at the business. There's the M——'s; they've a family of eight, and the youngest to the oldest of them all works at the bench; and the oldest ain't fourteen, I'm sure.

"Of the two thousand five hundred small masters in the cabinet line, you may safely say that two thousand of them, at the very least, has from five to six in family, and that's upwards of 12,000 children that's been put to the trade since the prices has come down. Twenty years ago I don't think there was a young child at work in our business, and I'm sure there isn't now a small master whose whole family doesn't assist him. But what I want to know is, what's to become of the 12,000 children when they're grow'd up, and come regular into the trade? Here are all my young ones growing up without being taught anything but a business that I know they must starve at."

In answer to my inquiry as to what dependence he had in case of sickness? "Oh, bless you," he said, "there's nothing but the parish for us. I did belong to a benefit society about four year ago, but I couldn't keep up my payments any longer. I was in the society above five-and-twenty year, and then was obliged to leave it after all. I don't know of one as belongs to any friendly society, and I don't think there is a man as can afford it in our trade now. They must all go to the workhouse when they're sick or old."...

To show the time consumed—or, as the men universally call it, "lost"—in the conveyance of the goods to the warehouses, I am able to give the following particulars. There can be no doubt, as I have stated, that more than one-half of the working cabinet-makers in London work for the supply of the warehouses; but that I may not over-estimate the number, I will say one-half. The least duration of time expended by these men in their commerce with the "slaughter-houses" is an average of eight hours weekly per man. But this is not all. At least one-fourth of their number expend 2s. 6d. each in the hire of carts and trucks for the conveyance of the heavier articles to the warehouses. Sometimes, when the bulk of the articles admits of it, trucks or barrows are used, the charge for which is 2d. an hour. But lighter articles of furniture are carried on the shoulder.

"Why, sir," said one man to me, "I have sometimes carried as much as three-quarters of a hundred weight on my shoulder, and have taken that weight as far as Knightsbridge and Pimlico and back again, and then not sold it. I have then been obliged to take it out again the next day in a different direction, as far as Woolwich, and have took what I could get for it, or else go without victuals. I find about Thursday to be the best day, and the most profitable, as I can generally get more on a Thursday for an article than on a Saturday or Monday, because if you call on Saturday they think you are hard up for Sunday's dinner, and if you take it on Monday they think you are hard up for rent, and so they play upon you, and, besides, they think you couldn't get rid of it on Saturday. The usual rounds we take for the sale of our articles are Moorfields, Tottenham-court-road, Oxford-street, Edgeware-road, Knightsbridge, Pimlico, and other parts of the West-end."

Another party informed me that he has had to call no less than seven or eight times for his money after he had "sold his goods to a butcher," and then only got about half of what was coming to him. At these slaughterhouses, I was informed, "the butchers occasionally pay part cash and part by check, due in two months. But when we get outside, their clerks meet us to know if we have only checks to cash, for which they charge 3d. in the pound."

Concerning the employment of a carter I had the following account from one of the body:

"I am a tradesman—a cornchandler—and having a horse and cart I am in the habit of doing little jobs for persons in this neighbourhood (Hoxton). I never let out to hire. I am often employed by the numerous small cabinet manufacturers in this locality, to take their work out with them, on what is call the 'buz,' (*i.e.* the hawk). The goods I am employed to carry out consist of loo tables, cheffoniers, pembroke tables, oak chairs, and other large articles of cabinet work, and for this I charge on the average 1s. per hour. Whether the goods are sold or not my charge is the same. Sometimes I am paid after the articles are sold, and sometimes I have to trust. There are no particular days in the week for the sale of the articles, but mostly Saturdays. There are dozens employed in the same line as myself.

"I generally start about nine or ten o'clock in the morning, calling first at several houses in Tottenham-court-road, then to Oxford-street, Wardour-street, Knightsbridge, and often back again with the whole lot to ——'s, where the articles are left and sold for what the slaughterer likes to give. In case of rain I cover the goods. Sometimes the articles are sold directly, and sometimes in five or six hours. The longest time I have known it to take to dispose of the goods is seven hours in one day and five the next. It is no uncommon occurrence for a poor working man to stand an hour, two, or three at a slaughter-house door before the master butcher will condescend to give him an answer." In answer to my inquiry where do they get their meals while out selling, the reply was, "Why they starve till the goods are sold."

TURNERS

From Letter LXVII, August 29th, 1850

I met a few intelligent men among the turners, but intelligence is not the characteristic of the great mass of them. The poverty of the little masters tempts them, as I have stated, to take numbers of apprentices, who in their turn become little masters, and boys reared as I have described cannot be expected to attain tastes beyond such as can be gratified in the tap-room or the skittle-ground. Their ordinary amusements are skittles, cards ("all fives" being their usual game), and dominoes, played in the tap-rooms for beer. Nor is there any distinction between the journeyman and the little master, except that the journeyman may be better off. Drunkenness is far less common among them than it used to be, but that I found to be mainly attributed to the scantiness of their means.

"Most turners in small wares," said a fringe turner to me, "amuse themselves in the public-houses near where they work. I amuse myself with reading the papers or anything when I have a little spare time; but the Spitalonians (Spitalfields men) are rare fellows for skittles, cards, and dominoes, and, badly as they're off, numbers of them don't work on a Monday. I like a game of knock-'em-downs (skittles) now and then myself. It's good exercise, and good for trade, as skittles is turners' work, but I hate cards without it be a hand at cribbage, and cribbage is a cut above the Spitalonians."

A highly intelligent man gave me an account of what he knew of the state of his calling:

"I have known the trade upwards of forty years; and as soon as I was out of my apprenticeship, I could make £2 to £2 10s. a week on the average the year through. Some made more. I know one man who made £2 in one day, in turning 'pateras' for billiard tables, but that was an exception. Pateras were 6s. a gross then; they're now 3s. 6d. Wages have been falling gradually these last twenty years. They fell long before provisions did. Now there's hardly a job we do, but there's a reduction or an attempt at it. "If you won't do it,' the masters say, 'there's plenty will.' 'Well, then,' I say, 'you'd better get them; I'll take no less;' for I know, you see, sir, that I'm a skilful hand, and that makes a man independent.

"I turn bed-posts, table and chair legs, and everything required in the furniture line, door knobs, and all those sort of things included. I average the year through 18s. a week, or hardly that; and them's the best earnings in the trade, excepting the turners employed by the best cabinet-makers, who have their own lathes and turners, and employ the men on their own premises. There may be seven cabinet-makers who do this, and their men may average from 32s. to 36s. a week. The reduction in the wages paid to us since I have known the trade, amounts to between one-third and two-thirds of what we formerly received, and there are still attempts to lower our wages further. We feel the want of a society, but it's no use to raise one, as the men won't stick to it, and on the whole, the main body of us turners are not so intelligent as other mechanics. Our works is noisy, too, and no talk can be carried on, as in a tailor's shop, by which men can pick up a little politics or knowledge. We are now like the bundle of sticks after it was opened, and masters know that, and know we have nothing to fall back upon, and they treat us accordingly.

"I am married, but have no family, and have the good fortune to have a careful wife, and a comfortable bit of home, but that can only be done by my being abstemious, for I often suffer from sickness, and that brings such a heavy expense that I can't save anything."

In connection with the general branch of the turning trade, there is engaged for the larger work a "turn-wheel" (or man to drive the lathe by means of "the big wheel"). This man is usually paid by time, 3d. per hour being the ordinary rate of remuneration. Those hired for this service are frequently old soldiers, but blind men are generally preferred to all others. The reason of this is, I am told, because men who are not deprived of their sight do not turn the wheel at one uniform speed. Their mind, to use the words of my informant, is wandering away from their labour, owing to their attention being taken off by surrounding objects. The blind man, however, like the blind horse in the mill, does his work without any alteration in his velocity. Formerly there used to be many blind men thus employed in the turning trade, and these were mostly soldiers who had lost their sight in Egypt. There were likewise many blind sailors gaining a livelihood in this manner. Now, owing to the use of steam power for the heavier work, there are no regular "turn-wheels" belonging to the business.

I am indebted for the following information concerning hard wood and ivory-turning, to a man to whom I was referred as a skilful and tasteful workman:

"I have known the London *hard wood and ivory turning* trade," he said, "upwards of twenty-one years. I believe that there are now about 200 working men in my business. We have no society, nor superannuation fund, nor any provision of the kind. In sickness or distress each man must shift for himself. We all work by piece. There is no printed or acknowledged list of prices. Masters and men understand, or agree, what should be paid for work, according to the character and scale of prices of the shop. I have worked at all branches of the business, and twelve years ago I could make, and did make, 12s. a day. Now-a-days an average workman can make 30s. a week in a good shop all the year through, for one season is about as good as another. The turning of chessmen in ivory is from £1 to £2 journeymen's wages, according to the size and quality. Wood chessmen, ebony and box, are, as a fair average price, 3s. 6d. the set, but they're not to compare, in form or work, with ivory.

"We turn—in ivory and hardwood, ebony, rosewood, satinwood, or any wood—pincushions, door handles, bell-pulls, small boxes, and a good deal of work for carriages, such as the door handles. All flat work in ivory is done by hand, not by the lathe. [My informant then showed and explained to me the mode of working, which I have already described.] I have had advantages besides regular work. I have given gentlemen lessons in turning. Many gentlemen, and some peers, are very good ivory turners. I gave lessons to a gentleman who had the lathe and all the turning tools and apparatus that old George III. used to work

with. It cost £500 at a sale. I have seen some of the old King's turning
and it was very fair. With industry he might have made 40s. or 50s. a week
as a hardwood and ivory turner. A first-rater at that time, when times and
wages were good, would earn twice as much or somewhere on to it. The King's
lathe and all connected with it was the best and the most beautiful I have seen.

"No women work at my trade. I ought to have told you before, that ivory
turners, when they have skill enough, are employed to carve the chessmen—though
that has nothing to do with the turning. Perhaps, to make a handsome knight,
or a good castle is the most difficult. Billiard balls are all made of ivory. We get 2s.
the set for turning them in good shops, 1s. in inferior shops, and they're done for
6d. by the 'master-men,' as we call the low-priced men, or what you call the slop-
workers. The billiard ball must of course be perfectly circular, and we form it
mainly by the eye, so that ours is really a nice art. Any little unevenness is regulated afterwards by 'papering,' that is by a rubbing it down with glasspaper; but
I can do it without papering. The ivory is first sawn, and by a very fine saw, to the
size wanted. It is then roughed with the gouge, towards the shape required. Then,
if it's for a good shop, it's laid by for nine months; for if it's worked wet—and
ivory's like wood that way—it will cast (warp) or crack. I have known billiard balls
made out of green stuff in ivory, go an eighth of an inch longer one way than another. But the 'master-men,' the cheap fellows, work it green, and so can do it
cheaper. They don't care whether their work stands true or not—not they. We
don't call the 'master-men's' work 'slop,' we call it 'bad' work. These men's work
is very inferior. It's hard to say to what degree they undersell a good master, for
every shop has, perhaps, a different scale of prices. Say they work for one half the
money, and with less than half the skill and pains. They hawk their goods to the
toy and fancy shops, and to private houses. They take lots of apprentices, who
grow as well into master-men. I know one man who has six, and another who has
fourteen of these apprentices, and the fourteen man has got most of them from
the workhouse. The Lord knows how they're treated. These master-men are very
poor. They live chiefly in Clerkenwell and Bethnal-green. I don't suppose they earn
more than 15s. a week, indeed not that the year through. These men expose the
better masters to a very unfair competition. The foreign trade doesn't affect us
much.

"One of our lathes costs from £4 to £5, and our tools may cost from £150 to
£200; perhaps there is more than 200 of them of all kinds and substances, of
firmers and the others. I'm speaking of the very best and handsomest sort of tools;
such as gentlemen have; and it was this as made George III.'s lathe and kit so
valuable. In our trade, however, the master finds tools (and they may generally
cost half what I've mentioned), and the journeyman, if he's not a master-man as
well, always works on the premises. The understanding is, that when new tools are
wanted the master finds the material, and the journeyman makes the tool. The
wear and tear of them isn't 6d. a week. We turn bones as well as hard woods and
ivory, but ivory's our main business. Leg-of-beef and shin bones are turned into
surgical instruments, such as syringes; calf shin-bones are turned into common
chessmen, but they have a scrubby look with them. When an article's turned, it's
polished off with putty-powder, or something of the kind. Some are dyed after
they're turned. There's two men in London who do nothing but dye our work, and
they must make £3 to £4 a week. They say they have secrets, but I dare say it's

just chemistry. The demand for chessmen has increased in my time. There is half as many more required now as when I first knew the trade. The ivory we work is African, Siam, and East Indian, or Ceylon. The Ceylon is the finest grain, but the Siam is the largest.''. . .

A pale but keen-looking man gave me the following account of *tassel and fringe mould turning*:

"I have known the London trade from my childhood, and my ancestors have been engaged in it 100 years back, though not all that time in London. When I first knew the trade, twenty-three years ago, it was very prosperous. A good hand would then earn 36s. a week by piece-work at fringe moulds; and now, for the same amount of work, he wouldn't earn a third of that, not more than 10s., if as much. We were paid by the piece then as now, for 'fringes' so much the gross. Tassel-mould turning is the best part of the trade. These moulds are used for upholsterers' hangings, either for the drapery of beds or windows, for bell pulls, blinds, pulpit cushions, and similar things. There's numbers made for what's known as 'pulpit cushions,' but only a small part of them's used for parson's pulpit cushions; they're used for sofa cushions and such like.

"Trade was better when tassels were the fashion for the hammer-cloths of gentlemen's carriages, and indeed almost all our work is still for 'the nobs,' and yet it's most badly paid. We turn the wooden moulds in the usual way, treading and standing on one leg all day long, and the upholsterers' work-women cover these moulds with silk, velvet, worsted, or whatever's wanted. They're very badly paid. The fringe moulds are made for the same purposes as the tassel. The tassel is a plain mould and the fringe is rounded. We generally do tassels—and tassels only—by day-work; a good shop gives 25s. a week day-work (30s. to a very extraordinary hand), and inferior shops 20s. An average workman will do four gross a day of the easiest style tassels, and short of a gross of the most difficult. It depends upon the pattern. The largest sizes are not the most difficult.

"It was all piece-work when first I knew the trade, but tassels hadn't come in then. I first worked on tassels ten years ago, and they'd come in a few years before that, perhaps. The wages haven't varied. We make about as many tassels as fringes; one tallies with the other. In turning fringes, we have, for 'short pipes' 9d. the gross; they are 9d. up to $3\frac{1}{2}$ inches, and they rise at the rate of a halfpenny and a penny a gross through the different sizes, the highest being 4s. a gross for twelve inches, and 6s. for fourteen inches. Work night and day—and the men do so nearly—and they make from 15s. to 20s. a week. These prices are a third of what they were twenty years ago, and they have kept falling gradually. I consider the fall is chiefly owing to so many small masters underselling each other, and eating one another up. When a lad's out of his apprenticeship, if he can only raise the expenses of a lathe (and you can get a second-hand one for £1—a good new lathe is worth £5), and can raise the tools required, which may be bought for another £1, these, with a bundle of wood, is all the stock in trade wanted for a start; and then the upholsterers and the cabinet-makers and the trade all know they have needy men to deal with, and make their bargains accordingly. The goods are hawked from shop to shop, and the customers put on the screw, and the little masters are left very little, hardly enough to pay just for their labour.

"I am a journeyman, but very few fringe turners employ journeymen, as their work is chiefly done by apprentices. I average 20s. a week. Among the apprentices a great many are parish boys, with whom a premium is given—I don't know what exactly. I know one who had several parish apprentices—it was for the sake of cheaper workpeople, not for the sake of the fees. The apprentices are bound for seven years generally, and must be kept all that time by the master. The little masters are drinking men frequently, and very poor. If anything happens to them there's nothing but the parish. Most of them have large families, and they live and work all in one room. The button-turners are amongst the worst off, but some button-turners are tassel-turners also, in which case they may take an apprentice. If they are only button-turners, I think an apprentice is almost beyond them. They live a good deal about Spitalfields. I can't say the turners I speak of are ever out of work, as they're little masters, and set themselves to work. But it's only raking up an existence, it's not a living; not to be called one.

"As for myself, I'm not very partial to the turning business, only I'm among friends who are in it. I may cut it soon, as I have before now. Altogether I think I have worked eight years at other things, for I'm an independent sort of a man. Nobody whatever shall put upon me; a word, and I'm off. I've worked at repairing guns, and at shoemaking. I picked up the skill somehow by seeing others, and being quick. [Another turner told me that he was his own tailor.] I did tidy that way. But my main employ when away from my own trade—and I was never apprenticed to it, but was taught by my relations—was in having the care of steam-engines in factories. I've made 27s. and 30s. a week that way. I've had the care of a steam-engine at a great brewer's, so you perceive I can make a shift many ways."

A man with a delicate look, and a stoop (not uncommon in his business, as the turners lean over their labour all day long), gave me the following statement concerning bobbin-turning:

"I am a *bobbin turner*, and may say I was born one, as I was born in Spitalfields, and have been in the trade all my life, and my father is 79, and has been in the trade since he was nine years of age. About 25 years ago my trade was good. I could live comfortably, and could have kept a wife and family comfortably. I wasn't married then, but I did marry 20 years ago, and at that time I had every prospect of keeping a wife and family well. It's a hard thing on working men like me, sir, that we marry when we find ourselves in a pretty good business, and of course we can't see why it should fall off, and then it does fall off, from no fault of ours, and so we are left to trouble and distress. It's a hard thing, sir; steam has taken away a great part of my labour, but how could I tell that? And yet I've often heard it said, that poor men shouldn't marry because trade was so bad. I have now a wife and seven children.

"I turn nothing but bobbins; that is a branch by itself. I turn cotton, lace, worsted, and silk bobbins. I work with the pole. The bobbins are made out of a solid piece of wood, always the trunk of the alder tree. The master supplies solid logs of wood, varying in length, which we cut into six or seven substances lengthways. We then cut these substances to the length required for the bobbins, and split them with a knife and mallet to the right thickness. The alder we use is grown chiefly in Kent and Berkshire. 'Reading staves' are the best in my trade. I am paid by the piece. 25 years ago I was paid 6s. a gross, journey-work, for silk bobbins, and could make five gross a week. I was paid 30s. a gross for large cotton bobbins, and could make a gross and a half a week; but for that work I had to find the material, which cost me from 12s. to 14s. Lace-bobbins were 8s. a gross, and

T

I could make 4 gross a week. At that time, sir, I averaged 30s. a week. 20 years ago I could make about the same, but 17 years ago the fall began. Steam first began it. Silk bobbins first fell 6d. a gross, and the others in proportion. Our wages have kept falling and falling ever since, until last year we had 3s. For silks and for cottons and laces there's no demand; they're all country work, made mostly at Leicester, where wood's cheap, and steam power 10d. a day. They make cotton and lace bobbins, and find their own material, at one quarter the price we used to get. When I last worked on cotton bobbins, about 18 months ago, I had 8s. for the gross, and it's horse's work; they're too heavy for the foot, and with slaving like a horse or a slave, I could only make 12s. a week; but that was for the labour. The fall was gradual, from 30s. a week to 8s.

"I am now occupied only on silk bobbins, and last year they were 3s. a gross, and we then said one to another, 'They can't be lower anyhow,' but this year they are lower, only 2s. 9d., and as my master knows I'm a poor man with a large family (seven children), he's on the look out to reduce me to 2s. 6d., and I haven't full work at 2s. 9d. I can make five gross a week, but don't average more than four, that's 11s. Out of that I have to keep a wife and six children; one of my girls is in service. My wife works for a slop tailor, and makes 2s. 6d. a week by very hard work, and finds her own thread, too. One of my sons earns 3s. a week at glass-blowing, he's grown up, but he's a cripple, and does it by night work; he can do nothing else. My other children are under nine years of age. My rent is 2s. 3d. a week for one room unfurnished. In that room I have to work, and in it my wife has to work, and we have to cook in it, but it's very little cooking does for us, though we have to keep a fire to heat the irons for pressing my wife's tailoring work. She works for a sweater, and is now making postmen's waistcoats at 6d. a piece.

"We have all to sleep in the same room, which is a goodish size. If I could afford it two rooms would be a great good to me. We live on bread and butter and tea, three times a day. That for breakfast at half-past seven, the same again between twelve and one, and the same again about seven at night. We may taste meat once in every four or five Sundays, mostly this time of the year" (this was said a few weeks ago), "for when the weather's so hot butchers are glad to get rid of meat at any price when they find it's a-going, and really it's not fit to eat. As for clothing, the children have oft enough to go without it, and so should I, if I hadn't an old thing given me by people my wife has nursed.

"I've never heard any particular reason for the reduction of our wages. Now the master weavers say that they can't afford the present wages, silk is so dear. The silk is wound ready for the weaver's use round the bobbins we turn. A great many in my trade have to live as I live. There's at least forty as badly off as I am in Spitalfields. I should have told you that I drink a great deal of water, and I really think that does me harm, for it's bad water, as one cock serves all the premises. I'm so weak in the evening I can hardly stand. My children play about in the court when it's fine, and when it's wet in the room. A girl of nine jobs and cleans about the house, or my wife could do no work at all. I have two children at a Ragged School. I can't afford to send them to any better place. They seem to like it very well. They are continually thinking of the loaf and bun they get at Christmas; last year they had a loaf and a twopenny pie; they often talk about that.

"All the families of the men situated as I am, live like mine. The little masters are a great cut-up to our business by underselling the better masters. I can't say that I know any drunkards among the journeymen in my trade. We've given over caring about politics since the time of the union, and then we didn't understand it. We are quiet men, and submit quietly to what we suffer. I can read and write, as I dare say most of us can. We have no fund, and no society, and never had. I see no prospect of better times, not at all; and if provisions were dearer, we might go to the parish, as we've done before, and in old age a man like me must come to the workhouse, and that's a sorrowful thought. A penny or a halfpenny a loaf makes a great difference to me; it does, indeed, sir—a very great difference, for bread's our great expense. It's dear eating, after all, is bread and butter for a family—there's no strength in it."

SHIP AND BOAT BUILDERS

From Letter LXVIII, September 5th, 1850

A *ship-joiner* whom I found in a very comfortable room with his wife and family, gave me the following account:

"My father was in the business, and I was brought up to it by a friend of his. That's often reckoned a better way, as fathers are too severe or too indulgent. I was regularly apprenticed, and have never worked anywhere but in London, except once. I have always worked under the contractors, and have made my 33s., 36s., and 38s. a week when at work, according to the piece work—it's all piece work—that I get through. There is no fixed price—so much for the job, whatever it may be—and I've done all parts, I think. There's an understanding as to the pay. We know that we can make our living out of it. I may work rather more than nine months in the year altogether. In a good yard, after a ship is finished, there may be a slack of two or three months before we are wanted on a new ship. We are not kept going regularly at any one yard—only as long as a ship's in hand. We look out at all the yards.

"I'm a society man, and wish everybody was. I earn as much now as I did twelve or thirteen years back, when I first worked as a journeyman, and as provisions are cheaper I'm better off, or I could not give my children—there's three of them—good schooling as I do. I don't know that I can do better than bring up my boy—the others are girls—to my own trade, if he grows up sharp and strong; it's no use without. I know of no grievances that we have. I worked, not long since, in the joinering of an iron ship. There's more joinering in them than in wood ships, as there's a lining of wood to back the iron work. I don't mix with the 'boiler-makers.' I seldom stir out of a night, as I'm generally well tired after my day's work. I live near my work, and take every meal at home, except my luncheon, and that's a draught of beer, and sometimes a crust with it and a crumb of cheese, that I now and then put in my pocket.". . .

A muscular, hearty, and hale-looking young man, whom I found at work in a shop *[where ships' figureheads were made]* . . . gave me the following information:

"I was apprenticed to Mr. ——, and have never left London. My father was connected with ship-building, and so put me to this branch. I'm unmarried, and live with my friends. I have nothing to complain of in the way of business, as I have pretty good employment. We all drink beer—some of us, perhaps, too much, but nothing compared to other trades. Ours is hard work, but we don't drink much at work. Look you here, sir, this log of ellum, with just the sides taken off by the sawyers, to make it square, has to be made into a 'head'—into a foreign nobleman or prince—I don't remember his name, but it's a queer one. To do that is heavy lifting and hard work. None of these fellows here (pointing to the figures), is the proper size, hardly big enough, or I could easily gouge this one now into a lord.

"We first axe the log into a rough shape, a sort of outline, and then finish it with chisels and gouges. I sometimes work from a drawing, but mostly out of my own head, and direct myself by my eye. We have nothing to do with painting or gilding the heads. They're sent home in their own woods just with a coat of paint over them, to save them from cracking. Yes, you're right, sir, that head will do for the Queen; but if a Queen isn't wanted, and it's the proper size, I can soon make her into any other female. Or she might do for a 'Mary Anne,' without altering; certainly she might. The way the hair's carved is the Queen's style, and has been in fashion these eight or ten years. Ringlets ain't easy; particularly cork-screw ringlets, as they're called. The watch-chain and seals to a gentleman ain't easy, as you have to bring out that part and cut away from it. The same with buttons and stars. Perhaps we aren't as good at legs as at other carving. We generally carve only to the knee. The shipwrights place our work on the ship's knee caps.

"We have no slop-workers among us; but there are two men who keeps a look out at the docks for broken heads, or heads damaged any way, and offer to repair them cheap. They're not workers themselves, but they get hold of any drunken carpenter, or any ship carver that happens to be hard up and out of work, and put them to the job at low prices. But the thing don't satisfy, and they do very little; still, it's a break in upon us. I make from 24s. to 30s. a week the year through, oftener nearer 30s. than 24s. I make 36s. at full work.". . .

COOPERS

From Letter LXIX, September 12th, 1850

A tall spare man, looking much older than he represented himself (a common case among coopers), whom I found in a comfortable home, gave me the following account of his earnings as a wet cooper:

"I have worked in London about seventeen years as apprentice and journeyman, and am now thirty-one. I lived at home during my apprenticeship, but my master was a relation of my father's, and they were very friendly, so my apprenticeship is not just a sample of what others may be. It was an understanding between the two. I have always worked for the best shops, and so I suppose I may reckon myself a good workman; but for all that I found great difficulty in learning the business when a boy. It was five years, or thereabouts, before I could 'joint' tolerably; and to know how to grind the tools well and quickly, is not an easy thing to learn, and many coopers who have mastered it don't like to let others see them grinding. Ours is hard and difficult work. There's no help with tools or colours for a cooper to regulate his work, or hide the faults of it. He must depend upon his eye. I have been always very fortunate in getting work, and that has allowed me to get a little on in the world. I think I have averaged from 30s. to 32s. a week for five years past, and rather more before that, though then I seldom worked on a Monday, as it was very little the custom of that shop. I consider it impossible to work without beer, but I very seldom care to taste it when I'm not at work; the heat and smoke causes such thirst when at work. There is still a good deal of drunkenness among the men certainly, but I think the journeymen have greatly improved of late in their habits. They are more temperate and more saving, perhaps more intelligent than was the case. They have become so gradually, I think, and within these eight or ten years.

"I am paid good wages, and work all the year through. My health is now pretty good, but many in my trade suffer greatly. When I first began I had bilious headaches, and flying pains about my back. We have so much stooping, you see, and perspire a good deal, some of us—it's not often you see a working cooper very fat— and go heated into cold air; and those things affect our health. I am a society man. I know of no grievances to complain of in the shops I have worked in. I can keep a wife comfortably, but I haven't been long married. I dare say my beer, when at work, doesn't cost me less than 3s. 6d. a week, and I'm one of the moderate ones. In many places a block cooper, or general hand, has a better chance of employment, than a man who wants to confine himself to one branch. In the great shops, especially for brewer's work, there's still a proper division of labour observed. I work by the piece, but I think if we were put on by day work, masters would be better served, for a man would take more time. To be sure a master might have *rather* less work done, but then a man not up to the average quantity of work in a day wouldn't often get regular employment, and so it might be all the same that way. I fancy, however, some men prefer piece work. It doesn't tie them so to time— they think they are more independent at it than at day work."

Concerning the dry-coopers, I had the subjoined statement from one of the most intelligent of the body. He was a society man:

"I am a dry-cooper," he said; "I have been twenty years in the trade. I served my time in the country, and ever since that I have been in London, in the 'dry' branch. I have always belonged to a society. The rate of wages was much better when I first came to London than it is now, but the quantity of work was much about the same. The men were paid by the piece, as at present.

"The decline in our wages has been in these ways. In the first place, we used to have what was called beer-money—that is a penny on every shilling that we earned was paid to us extra. This was termed 'beer money,' though it was part and parcel of our wages. Among the 'new (or brewers') coopers' there was always a cask on tap for the men to go to; but among 'the dry coopers' it was usual to pay in money only. At the time of the Income-tax Bill being brought in by Sir Robert Peel, the employers took off the beer money so as to meet the new tax. Since that time, cement casks have been reduced from 1s. to 10d., and bottle-porter casks have been lowered also, but I can't exactly state how much. Twenty years ago, I could earn five shillings a week more than I can now, working the same hours.

"After Christmas, my work is always very slack for three or four months. During that time I am employed on an average about four days a week, and so I think are most of the dry coopers. It was always the same as long as I can remember. About this time is, and always has been, our busiest time, in consequence of the ships going out to the West Indies, and the 'dry'—or, more properly speaking, 'the molasses—coopers' are busiest then. The main dependence of the dry coopers, however, is the sugar refiners' work. A large sugar house will keep eight men fully employed in the season, which lasts about six months in the year. There are about ten or twelve such large sugar houses in London. Altogether, I should say there are from 80 to 100 dry coopers in London employed in this way.

"I think a dry cooper's average earnings are about 24s. a week all the year round. Mine, perhaps, may be a little more than that; but then I am not a fair criterion, for I am considered a very quick hand. Most of our men would be glad to give up piece work, and take a constant situation at day work for 24s. a week. In the slack season we have nothing to depend upon but the sugar-house work, such as making puncheons for treacle, and casks for sugar. The small masters have already had a very injurious effect upon the dry branch of the trade, and I have no doubt they will injure us still more. To them only is to be attributed the decrease of our wages in the cement and bottle-porter cask work. The small masters cannot interfere with our sugar work, or our West India work. They have neither premises nor capital sufficient. They can only manage the small work—such as can be done in cellars and small premises."

The "slop" part of the coopering trade consists in what are called "cutting shops," and the "small trade-working masters." But these are confined solely to the "dry and white work." The cutting shops usually employ non-society men, with a number of apprentices, and are enabled to undersell the more honourable tradesmen by this cheaper labour. Many of these cutting masters are engaged in the manufacture of one article alone, and I was informed of one such master who had a number of hands continually engaged in converting old American flour barrels into bottled-porter casks, at 1d. a piece.

One of the small employers whom I visited, lived at the corner of a low, dirty street. His premises were entered by means of what was literally a hole in the wooden wall, on which swung a small door. In the interior of his shop were heaped hoops, staves, and all the requirements of the coopers' trade. In an inner room, four men were at work. "I make only colour kegs [dyes]," he said, "and have been in the trade many years. My men work by the piece, and the best and quickest hands make from 32s. to 33s. a week. Inferior hands get from 22s. to 25s. I used to employ fourteen hands, where I now employ half that number. Nearly all colour kegs, more than nineteen-twentieths of those made, are for exportation. For the home trade, a colourman will make the same casks go backwards and forwards fifty times. There used to be 800 hands employed in the wood keg trade for colourmen; now there is not half that quantity. The falling off is owing to the demand for sheet iron kegs, made under Brown's patent by steam machinery. They now make from 300,000 to 400,000 iron kegs every year, and have done so for five or six years past. They are much neater casks than the wooden to look at. I don't know about their durability, but that's little looked to in the export trade. I make every kind of style, kegs from two to twelve quarts; all those used for colours, white lead, &c. A two-quart sells at 6d., a twelve-quart at 14d. The iron are 20 to 30 per cent. higher. It's not the hawkers that have injured the trade masters like myself; it's only the introduction of iron kegs.". . .

The majority of the small masters are Irishmen, living in the neighbourhood of the docks; one of these, whom I saw, resided in a court at the back of Rosemary-lane. In the centre of this place stood clothes-props supporting lines laden with yellow-looking shirts and brown blankets, which swung backwards and forwards in the wind. Seated on the stones outside of each of the doors, were small groups of fuzzy-haired Irishwomen, all engaged in chopping wood and talking to one another across the court. The working cooper himself was a good-looking intelligent man, with the handsome grey eye and long sweeping lash peculiar to the natives of the Emerald Isle. He was very proud of the neatness of his sitting-room, and took me upstairs expressly to show it to me. It was decorated with portraits of Mitchell, Meagher, and Father Moore, together with a picture of the Siege of Limerick dedicated to the women of Ireland. Down stairs, amid the shavings, lay a copy of the *Nation* newspaper, in which my informant told me there was "some sublime poethry."

"I am a small master," he said, "though I don't know exactly that you can call me so rightly—I don't employ any one. You can put me down a manufacturer, if you please. I make up things on my own account. I have been a coopering now I dare say 26 years. I was about 14 when I first went to it. It was in Ireland I learnt the trade. I used to be engaged in my own unfortunate counthry making provision casks, but now that trade's entirely done away with.

"I came over here—let me see—fourteen years last May. Then I got my name on at the West India Dock as an extra cooper, and I have worked there in succession every year since. I got a number, and have kept at it all along. After working in the docks, if I don't feel too much fatigued, I do a bit of work for myself when I get home at night; or if I have an order for my customers that requires speed, then I stop here and work at it altogether. You see I am not obligated to go to work at the docks unless I please. I should say that, take it the year through, I am employed at the docks about three months out of the twelve. After October, the season is looked upon to be over, and it begins again about April. I don't always go to work after coming from the docks; but the most of the small masters works after their dock labour. When I work at home, I begin about seven and keep on till about nine at night, that's fourteen hours. One small master I know begins often at four or five in the morning. You see it all depends upon the industrial habits of men. If you're at work for an employer, you must leave off at a certain hour, but if you're your own master, you can work all night, if you've a fancy. I've often worked all night myself. I feel more pleasure doing a bit for myself here by candlelight than if I was wandering about the streets.

"I sell the goods I make to hawkers, and they make a living of it by hawking them to the public and to shops. I am in the habit of making oval tubs of different sizes—that's the principal branch that I'm employed in. Other small masters are engaged in making flour kegs, colour kegs, oyster barrels, mustard kegs—but that's all dry work. The small masters never do any large work. Some of the small masters will take round a sample of their work to a colour or mustard factory, or to a merchant, and so get an order; and many make up goods on speculation, and then take them round to sell. As simple a trade as oyster barrels is, still there's hundreds made up on speculation, and taken round to be sold. I've made them up myself. A man does this because he can't get other employment. May be there'll be a slackage at the docks, and a man will rather do that than be idle and starve. If he's out of work, he can make a dozen of oyster barrels for three shillings. The material will only cost him that much. It would take him a day to make them, and when he had done them, perhaps his wife, or may be his daughters, if he have any, will take them out to sell—to Billingsgate Market, may be. At oyster barrels the men frequently work all night, and some of them on the Sunday as well. Seventeen years ago, oyster barrels were nine shillings a dozen, and now they're four shillings and sixpence—that will show you how such work knocks up a trade. Many of the small masters lives about here, some in ground cellars, cobbling up old tubs and what not, to get a crust."

APPENDIX:
Chronological List of *Morning Chronicle* Letters by the Metropolitan Correspondent

[The following list gives the number, date, and general content of each of the eighty-two letters from the Metropolitan Correspondent which appeared in the Morning Chronicle *between October 1849 and December 1850. If a letter was reprinted in* London Labour and the London Poor, *a fourth column gives the volume number and notes whether the letter was reprinted completely or partially. However, this list is not intended to be complete; Mayhew sprinkled many separate paragraphs from the* Chronicle *letters throughout* London Labour. *Only the longer sections are noted here.]*

Number	Date	Subject	Reprinted in London Labour and the London Poor
I	Oct. 19, 1849	Description of London	
II	Oct. 23, 1849	Spitalfields Weavers	
III	Oct. 26, 1849	Dock Labourers	Complete, III
IV	Oct. 30, 1849	Dock Labourers	Partial, III
V	Nov. 2, 1849	Low Lodging Houses	Complete, III
VI	Nov. 6, 1849	Slop Workers	
VII	Nov. 9, 1849	Army Clothing Makers	
VIII	Nov. 13, 1849	Army Clothing Makers	
IX	Nov. 16, 1849	Needlewomen	
X	Nov. 20, 1849	Needlewomen	Partial, I
XI	Nov. 23, 1849	Needlewomen and Slopworkers	
XII	Nov. 27, 1849	Hucksters	Partial, I
XIII	Nov. 30, 1849	Hucksters	Partial, I
XIV	Dec. 4, 1849	Hucksters	Partial, I
XV	Dec. 7, 1849	Street Paper-sellers	Partial, I
XVI	Dec. 11, 1849	Honourable Tailor Trade	
XVII	Dec. 14, 1849	Slop Trade in East End	
XVIII	Dec. 18, 1849	Meeting of West-End Tailors	
XIX	Dec. 21, 1849	Coal Whippers and Porters	Complete, III
XX	Dec. 25, 1849	Coal Heavers and Meters	Complete, III
XXI	Dec. 28, 1849	Drunkenness in the Trades	Complete, III
XXII	Jan. 1, 1850	Ballast Men	Complete, III
XXIII	Jan. 4, 1850	Ballast Heavers and Drunkenness	Complete, III
XXIV	Jan. 8, 1850	Ballast Heavers' Wives; Lumpers	Partial, III
XXV	Jan. 11, 1850	Lumpers	
		Houses of Refuge for Poor	Complete, III
XXVI	Jan. 15, 1850	Asylum for the Houseless	Complete, III
XXVII	Jan. 18, 1850	Professional Vagrants	Complete, III
XXVIII	Jan. 22, 1850	History of Vagrancy	Partial, III
XXIX	Jan. 25, 1850	Conclusions on Vagrancy	Complete, III
XXX	Jan. 29, 1850	Vagrancy	
		Low Lodging Houses	Partial, I & III

Number	Date	Subject	Reprinted in London Labour and the London Poor.
XXXI	Jan. 31, 1850	Meeting of Vagrants	Partial, I
XXXII	Feb. 4, 1850	West End Boot and Shoe Trade	
XXXIII	Feb. 7, 1850	History of Duties on Shoes	
XXXIV	Feb. 11, 1850	"Women's Men" in Boot Trade	
XXXV	Feb. 14, 1850	Non-Society Boot Makers	
XXXVI	Feb. 18, 1850	Slop System in Boot Trade	
XXXVII	Feb. 21, 1850	Toy Makers for the Poor	Partial, III
XXXVIII	Feb. 25, 1850	Superior Toy Makers	
XXXIX	Feb. 28, 1850	Doll Makers	Partial, III
XL	Mar. 7, 1850	Merchant Seamen	
XLI	Mar. 11, 1850	Seamen Afloat	
XLII	Mar. 14, 1850	Seamen Afloat	
XLIII	Mar. 19, 1850	Ragged Schools	
XLIV	Mar. 25, 1850	Ragged Schools	
XLV	Mar. 29, 1850	Ragged Schools	
XLVI	Apr. 3, 1850	Seamen Afloat; Coasting Trade	
XLVII	Apr. 11, 1850	Seamen Ashore	
XLVIII	Apr. 19, 1850	Seamen's Homes and Boarding	
XLIX	Apr. 25, 1850	Reply to Sec. of R.S. Union	Partial, II
L	May 2, 1850	Merchant Seamen Ashore	
LI	May 9, 1850	Charitable Institutions	
LII	May 16, 1850	Classification	
		Street Showmen and Performers	Partial, III
LIII	May 25, 1850	Street Performers	
LIV	May 30, 1850	Clowns, etc.	Complete, III
LV	June 6, 1850	Street Musicians	Complete, III
LVI	June 13, 1850	Street Artists	Complete, III
LVII	June 20, 1850	Survey of Timber Trade	
LVIII	June 27, 1850	Imported Wood; Dock Workers	Complete, III
LIX	July 4, 1850	London Sawyers	
LX	July 11, 1850	Carpenters and Joiners	
LXI	July 18, 1850	Carpenter Slop Trade	
LXII	July 25, 1850	Mills	
LXIII	Aug. 1, 1850	Cabinet-Makers	
LXIV	Aug. 8, 1850	Fancy Cabinet-Making	
LXV	Aug. 15, 1850	Slop Cabinet-Makers	Partial, III
LXVI	Aug. 22, 1850	Garret Masters	Partial, III
LXVII	Aug. 29, 1850	Turners	
LXVIII	Sept. 5, 1850	Ship and Boat Builders	
LXIX	Sept. 12, 1850	Coopers	
LXX	Sept. 19, 1850	On the Transit System	Complete, III
LXXI	Sept. 26, 1850	Omnibuses	Complete, III
LXXII	Oct. 3, 1850	Hackney Coaches	Complete, III
LXXIII	Oct. 10, 1850	Carmen and Porters	Complete, III
LXXIV	Oct. 17, 1850	Watermen, etc.	Complete, III
LXXV	Oct. 24, 1850	Dressmakers, Honourable	
LXXVI	Oct. 31, 1850	Dressmakers, Slop	
LXXVII	Nov. 7, 1850	Journeymen Hatters	
LXXVIII	Nov. 15, 1850	London Tanners	
LXXIX	Nov. 21, 1850	"Live" Meat Markets	
LXXX	Nov. 28, 1850	"Dead" Meat Markets	
LXXXI	Dec. 5, 1850	Green Markets	
LXXXII	Dec. 12, 1850	Fish Markets	

The conditions in sweaters' dens
from the *Illustrated Police News*, July 21, 1888
(By courtesy of the Trustees of the British Museum)